African American Identity Development

Cobb & Henry Titles of Related Interest

Advances in African American Psychology. Reginald L. Jones (Editor)

African American Children, Youth and Parenting. Reginald L. Jones (Editor)

African American Mental Health. Reginald L. Jones (Editor)

Black Adolescents. Reginald L. Jones (Editor)

Black Adult Development and Aging. Reginald L. Jones (Editor)

Black Psychology, 3rd Edition. Reginald L. Jones (Editor)

Handbook of Tests and Measurements for Black Populations. (Volume 1)
    Reginald L. Jones (Editor)

Handbook of Tests and Measurements for Black Populations. (Volume 2)
    Reginald L. Jones (Editor)

Psychoeducational Assessment of Minority Group Children: A Casebook.
    Reginald L. Jones (Editor)

Forthcoming

Racial Socialization: Ecologies of Child and Adolescent Development.
    Deborah Johnson and Andrea G. Hunter (Editors)

Spirituality and Well-Being: African American Perspectives. John Rogers
    (Editor)

African American Identity Development

Reginald L. Jones, Editor
Hampton University

1998
Cobb & Henry Publishers, Hampton, VA

For information, contact:

Cobb & Henry Publishers
1 Sutton Place
Hampton, VA 23666
Telephone: (757) 827-7213
Fax: (757) 827-1060
E-mail: CobbHenry@aol.com

Manufactured in the United States of America

African American identity development / Reginald L. Jones, editor.
    p. cm.
Includes bibliographical references and index.
ISBN 0-943539-10-2
    1. Afro-Americans--Race identity. 2. Afro-Americans--Psychology.
I. Jones, Reginald Lanier, 1931- .
E185.625.A37 1998
155.8'496073--dc21   97-20397
                                      CIP

Contents

Part III. Other Perspectives and Models

Preface

The present volume, *African American Identity Development*, grew out of a response to my request of colleagues, more than a decade ago, for papers that described their innovative contributions to theory, research and intervention that might be included in a series of volumes that would be titled *Advances in Black Psychology*. In addition to issuing a general call for manuscripts, I personally invited a number of scholars to present their work. I was especially eager to include scholars who were associated with programmatic thinking, writing, and research programs. William Cross was one person I identified early on because of his pioneering, longstanding, and sustained research and writing on African American identity development. When the *Advances* series was conceptualized, I simply wanted him to synthesize his research and that of others on this topic and to point directions for future theorizing and research. The thought of a single volume devoted to this topic was not in mind when his manuscript arrived.

I continued to collect manuscripts for the *Advances* volumes and to consult with colleagues about the purpose and scope of the volumes. The consultation led me to conclude that interest would be greatest in topical volumes rather than in single volumes with a scattering of articles across diverse topics. As a result of their advice, I conceptualized and developed four volumes from the manuscripts that were received. The newly titled volumes were *African American Mental Health, African American Identity Development, African American Children, Youth and Parenting, and Advances in African American Psychology.*

The present volume, *African American Identity Development*, is the second book in the new series. Like the recently published *Mental Health* volume, I needed to expand scope and coverage in order to develop a work that was true to the topics. I therefore undertook a systematic search of individuals who were writing, developing theories, and conducting research on African American identity development. In the process of my research, I identified individuals who were strongly opposed to the stage theory of racial identity development. Some of these scholars had, themselves, developed alternative models, while others took issue with the notion of identity development itself, at least as presently conceptualized. The present volume has been developed to bring the various theories, identity models, and perspectives on African American identity development under a single cover.

I am pleased to acknowledge the many individuals who contributed to this volume. First and always are the chapter authors who have brought fresh insight and understanding, and new and provocative theories, research and opinion to the topic of *African American Identity Development*. Several individuals contributed to manuscript preparation: Katasha Harley and Elise Vestal played a significant role in word-processing and manuscript preparation. Proofreading was done by Carol Brooks and Pamela Reilly, cover design by Michelle Fleitz, and computer work by Wesley Kittling, Jr. I thank all of you for a job done competently, cheerfully, and timely.

My wife Michele has always been there for and with me in the marathon sessions associated with completion of a book. And on this occasion, as in the past, she has been unswerving in her love, support and understanding.

Reginald L. Jones
Hampton, Virginia

Contributors

Daudi Ajani ya Azibo, Ph.D.
Professor of Psychology and Distinguished Psychologist, Department of Psychology, Florida A & M University, Tallahassee, Florida

Sharon Boyd-Jackson, Ph.D.
Associate Professor, Department of Psychology, Kean College of New Jersey, Union, New Jersey

Robert T. Carter, Ph.D.
Associate Professor, Program in Counseling Psychology, Teachers College, Columbia University, New York, New York

David Chavez, Ph.D.
Associate Professor, Department of Psychology, California State University, San Bernardino, San Bernardino, California

Tabbye Chavous, Ph.D.
Department of Psychology, University of Virginia, Charlottesville, Virginia

Deanna Cooke, M.S.
Graduate Student, Department of Psychology, University of Michigan, Ann Arbor, Michigan

William E. Cross, Jr., Ph.D.
Professor and Chair, Department of Student Development and Pupil Personnel Services (SDPPS), School of Education, University of Massachusetts, Amherst, Massachusetts

Kristee L. Haggins, Ph.D.
Counseling Psychologist, University Counseling Center and Adjunct Assistant Professor, Department of African and African American Studies, University of California, Davis, Davis, California

Janet E. Helms, Ph.D.
Professor, Department of Psychology, Counseling Center and Department of Women's Studies, University of Maryland, College Park, Maryland

Carolyn Bennett Murray, Ph.D.
Associate Professor, Department of Psychology and Principal Investigator, African American Family Research Project, University of California, Riverside, Riverside, California

Linda James Myers, Ph.D.
Associate Professor of African American and African Studies and Psychology, The Ohio State University, Columbus, Ohio

Wade W. Nobles, Ph.D.
Professor, Department of Black Studies, San Francisco State University, and Executive Director, Institute for the Advanced Study of Black Family Life and Culture, Inc., Oakland, California

Thomas A. Parham, Ph.D.
Director, Career Planning and Placement and the Counseling Center, University of California, Irvine, Irvine, California

M. Jean Peacock, Ph.D.
Assistant Professor, Department of Psychology, California State University, San Bernardino, San Bernardino, California

Tina Q. Richardson, Ph.D.
Associate Professor, Counseling Psychology Program, Department of Education and Human Services, Lehigh University, Bethlehem, Pennsylvania

Stephanie Johnson Rowley, Ph.D.
Assistant Professor, Department of Psychology, University of North Carolina, Chapel Hill, North Carolina

Robert M. Sellers, Ph.D.
Associate Professor, Department of Psychology, University of Michigan, Ann Arbor, Michigan

Nicole Shelton, Ph.D.
Department of Psychology, University of Virginia, Charlotteville, Virginia

Mia Smith, Ph.D.
Department of Psychology, University of Virginia, Charlottesville, Virginia

Contributors

Howard C. Stevenson, Jr., Ph.D.
Associate Professor, School, Community, and Clinical Child Psychology Program, Graduate School of Education, University of Pennslyvania, Philadelphia, Pennslyvania

Julie E. Stokes, Ph.D.
Instructor, Department of Afro-Ethnic Studies and Department of Psychology, California State University, Fullerton, Fullerton, California

Jerome Taylor, Ph.D.
Executive Director, Center for Family Excellence, Pittsburgh, Pennslyvania

Introduction and Overview

African American Identity Development: Introduction and Overview

Reginald L. Jones

African American identity development has been a topic of great interest to social and behavioral scientists, professionals, and the lay public since the 1960's. In 1971 the late Charles Thomas published a seminal volume, *Boys No More*. One of the chapters he contributed to this volume included his ideas about identity development. In this chapter Thomas described stages in identity transformation that appeared to capture the essence of changes in behavior and self concept that were occurring among African American adults. At about the same time as Thomas, William Cross was developing his stage model of Black identity development. Like Thomas, Cross was interested in understanding reasons for the changes in level of activism in the civil rights struggle that seemed to be occurring among Black Americans.

Many studies were stimulated by Thomas and Cross' work and there has been a steady body of literature on identity development since their early conceptualizations. The prior work has been ably summarized by Cross (1991) in his book *Shades of Black: Diversity in African American Identity*, by Helms (1990) in her volume entitled *Black and White Racial Identity: Theory, Research and Practice*, and by Cross, Parham and Helms in a chapter in the present volume. Until recently, the many studies of identity were largely devoted to stage models. The present work includes not only the seminal stage model ideas, but also work that is critical of stage models, as well as alternative identity development models and perspectives. Several authors argue for rejection or reconceptualization of identity development as presently conceived.

The present volume consists of three parts: I. Stage Models and Perspectives; II. Symposium on Stage Models; and III. Other Perspectives and Models.

Part I. Stage Models and Perspectives

Four chapters are included in Part I. All chapters in this section describe a stage model or embrace a stage perspective as the authors explore implications of the models for research, understanding and intervention.

The first chapter by Cross, Parham and Helms ("Nigresence Revisited: Theory and Research") serves as a fitting introduction to the present volume in the sense that the authors place identity development research and studies in historical, social and political perspectives, highlight the writings of early important contributors to the identity development literature and conduct a comprehensive review of stage models—the progenitors of contemporary theories and perspectives.

In the chapter following, Richardson ("Continuity in the Identity Development Process for African Americans and Africans throughout the Diaspora") draws upon her observations and interactions in Ghana, West Africa as a basis for exploring the identity dilemma. Her thesis is that the dilemma of Africans is significantly influenced by the colonization of the continent and its people which has resulted in parallel struggles across the African continuum. Richardson elaborates upon the issues of parallel experiences of oppression, presents models of racial identity, and offers brief commentary on the applicability, strengths, and limitations of the models.

Taylor ("Cultural Conversion Experiences: Implications for Mental Health Research and Treatment") reviews support for a developmental theory of Black consciousness in relationship to theoretical and measurement approaches which affirm this point of view. A description of extant stage models of racial identity development is a noteworthy feature of the chapter. Using a cluster analytic strategy applied to Milliones' Developmental Inventory of Black Consciousness, Taylor identifies and describes five consciousness prototypes and relates these prototypes to personal, social and communal development and adjustment. Finally, Taylor draws implications from the studies for treatment and research.

The final chapter in this section shows how stage notions can be utilized in psychotherapeutic intervention. Carter and Boyd-Jackson ("Racial Identity and Psychotherapy: The Case of Black/African Americans") explore how racial socialization shapes the development of personality and in turn how one's racial identity ego status is expressed in the context of psychotherapy interactions. Utilizing Carter's Racially Inclusive Model of Psychotherapy as a framework, the authors illustrate the model by using Black cases. They note, however, that the dynamics can occur in any type of same or cross-race therapy dyad, group, family or organization.

Part II. Symposium on Cross' Stage Model

Initial theorizing and research on African American identity development was done within the stage framework. A comprehensive summary of this work has been presented by Cross, Parham and Helms (chapter one of the present volume) who address many of the debates, points of agreement and refinements, as well as points of disagreement about stages, their measurement and meaning.

Other areas of disagreement, remain, however, including questions about the efficacy and viability of stage models themselves. Some of these questions are raised in the first chapter in this section ("Cross's Stage Model Revisited: An Analysis of Theoretical Formulations and Empirical Evidence") in which Stokes, Murray, Chavez, and Peacock proffer a critical analysis of Cross' theory. Because of the substantive nature of the critique, several scholars, including William Cross, have been invited to respond to Stokes' et al.'s evaluation. In the final paper in this section, Stokes, et al., respond to authors who responded to their critique. The papers in this section are lively, pointed and highlight some of the diversity of opinion that abounds with respect to Cross' stage theory of identity development.

Noting the widespread use of Cross' model, Stokes et al. concluded that a critical review of it was again needed. Their review had three purposes: (1) to extend earlier efforts through a critical analysis of the model; (2) to suggest the heuristic use of the stage concept be abandoned; and (3) to suggest that researchers reconceptualize the Negro-to-Black Conversion model as experiential rather than developmental. Stokes et al. martial powerful arguments and considerable data in support of their positions.

Respondents support as well as take issue with some of Stokes et al.'s conclusions. In the first response, Rowley and Sellers ("Nigresence Theory: Critical Issues and Recommendations for Future Revisions") indicate agreement with Stokes et al.'s call for abandonment of the concept of a developmental stage model of racial identity development, but they disagree with them on several counts, including their belief that (1) there are areas where Stokes et al. overstate their case against nigresence theory by overlooking some of the revisions found in Cross's more recent work; (2) there are areas where Stokes et al. do not go far enough in their criticism of the nigresence literature; and (3) Stokes et al.'s fail to address important limitations in the conceptualization and measurement of nigresence. Rowley and Sellers conclude their critique with recommendations for modification of the nigresence model they believe will help to maximize its contribution to the understanding of African American racial identity.

Stevenson's response to Stokes et al. ("The Confluence of 'Both-And' in Black Racial Identity Theory: Response to Stokes, Murray, Chavez, and Peacock") focuses upon his belief in the importance of recognizing the changes Cross has made over the last decade, maintaining the model's intuitive accuracy, and proposing the adoption of multiple rather than singular perspectives on racial identity development research. In developing his theses, Stevenson focuses upon: the model's historical context; intuitive relevance, need for racial socialization; "both-and" dimensions of racial identity, and the imaging and stereotyping of blackness. Special attention is given to the need for exploring relationships between racial socialization and identity development.

In his response, Cross ("Commentary on the Stokes et al. Critique of Nigresence Theory") selectively addresses a number of issues raised by Stokes et al., including their summary of the stages, the generalizability of the nigresence paradigm to age groups other than Black adults, and the question of the place of nigresence in a lifespan perspective. Cross concludes by stating "Unlike the call by Stokes et al. to 'abandon nigresence theory', we show how the theory fills an important gap in the overall discourse on Black identity development" (p. 168).

In the final paper in this section, ("Stokes et al. respond to reactions to their critique of the Cross model that were made by Rowley and Sellers, by Stevenson and by Cross. The authors emphasize points of agreement, and their continued concerns about the and lack of empirical evidence for the validity of the model.

Part III. Other Perspectives and Models

The five papers in Part III present alternative perspectives on stage theories of African American Identity development and include philosophical and theoretical perspectives, as well as empirically based critiques. The papers in this section speak to the diversity of thought and opinion on this topic and clearly communicate that scholars are not of one mind on the nature, need and direction that theorizing and research should take in addressing African American identity development.

In the first paper, Nobles ("To Be African or Not to Be: The Question of Identity or Authenticity—Some Preliminary Thoughts") suggests that our "theoretical" understanding of what it means to be African (Black) in a non-African (White supremacist) society requires a radical theoretical departure from the orthodoxy in psychology. He argues that what is needed "is a theoretical and therapeutic practice that is centered in our own African essence and integrity." In attempting to "think deeply" about what it means to be African in America," Nobles proposes that the real understanding of Black identity and our resolute response to living in an Anti-African society will only be attainable when Black psychologists allow their theories to be guided by what it means to be a human being and, subsequently, how that meaning shapes our responses and reactions. In this regard, Nobles suggests that the African meaning of "authenticity" and its expression as the "person" are the constructs (and not Black identity) that could offer a new research agenda in which to explore the frontiers of "African psychological theory development."

In yet another critique and evaluation that represents strong displeasure with extant views on African American identity development, Azibo ("The Distinction Between African Personality Personologists and other African Personality Scholars: Implications and an Entreatment for Reconceptualization of Racial Identity Issues") makes a distinction between writers of "whole" (comprehensive) theories of African personality versus writers of more insular aspects of African personality versus writers of insular aspects of African identity development/formation, the latter orientation being part of only one aspect of the "whole" theories.

Azibo argues that all shortcomings and drawbacks of identity development models can be traced to the distinctions noted above. He indicates, for example, "that nonsensical nomenclature like nigresence and reference group orientation, and conceptual frames that are incompatible with African-centered thought like personal identity separated from African identity cannot constitute a legitimate conceptual platform; the voidableness of the 'racial identity attitudes' concept are direct outgrowths of encapsulation in the narrow developmental-process paradigm." Azibo believes identity development models must be rethought within the "whole" theories framework. "Otherwise, the identity development models—old and new—and contemporary reactions to them will continue to indirectly inject European-centered conceptualizing into African psychology discourse."

From yet another divergent perspective, Stevenson ("Theoretical Considerations in Measuring Racial Identity and Socialization: Extending the Self Further") reviews the theoretical underpinnings of and linkages between racial identity and racial socialization research, proposes an international perspective for measuring racial socialization attitudes, and provides a set of assumptions that undergird a theoretical framework for the development of racial socialization for adolescents and parents. Stevenson also contrasts dichotomous and diunital worldviews and their differing influences upon racial identity theory, and relates several person-environment perspectives—including cultural, ecological, symbolic interactionism, African psychology and family system concepts—to the development of the racial socialization construct.

Myers and Haggins ("Optimal Theory and Identity Development: Beyond the Cross Model") apply optimal theory to identity development. The authors present a model of identity development that provides an integrative framework for understanding dynamics that inform the aspects of beingness and functioning and influence self perception and self description. Finally, Myers and Haggins explore Cross' model "in the historical context of the evolution of human consciousness in contemporary times."

In the final chapter of Part III ("A Multidimensional Model of Racial Identity: Assumptions, Findings, and Future Directions") Sellers and his colleagues introduce a model of racial identity (The Multidimensional Model of Racial Identity [MMRI]) which attempts to more accurately represent the complexity of African American identity development than they believe has been the case heretofore. The MMRI reconceptualizes and organizes concepts already found in the identity research literature into four interrelated but independent dimensions: (1) racial salience—the extent to which one's race is a relevant part of one's self-concept during a particular moment or situation; (2) racial centrality—the extent to which a person normatively defines his or herself in terms of race; (3) racial regard—a person's affective and evaluative judgment of his or her race; and (4) racial ideology—a person's beliefs, opinions, and attitudes with respect to the way he or she feels that the members of the race should act. Research and data supporting the model and test instrument are presented as well as recommendations for future research to test the integrity of the model.

For additional information, contact:

Reginald L. Jones
Department of Psychology
Hampton University
Hampton, VA 23668
Telephone: (757) 727-5104 (w)
         (757) 838-1980 (h)
Fax: (757) 727-5131 (w)
         (757) 827-1060 (h)
E-mail: CobbHenry@aol.com

Part 1

Stage Models And Perspectives

Nigrescence Revisited: Theory and Research

William E. Cross Jr., Thomas A. Parham, and Janet E. Helms

"...And on the 12th of May, 1828, I heard a loud noise in the heavens, and the Spirit instantly appeared to me and said the Serpent was loosened, and Christ had laid down the yoke he had borne for the sins of men, and that I should take it on and fight against the Serpent, for the time was fast approaching when the first should be last and the last should be first." *Confession of Nat Turner*, 1831

"It is a peculiar sensation, this double-consciousness. . . , one ever feels his twoness—An American, a Negro; two souls, two thoughts, two unreconciled strivings, two warring ideals in one dark body, whose dogged strength alone keeps it from being torn asunder." *Souls of Black Folk*, by W.E.B. DuBois, 1903

"In the last decade something beyond the watch and guard of statistics has happened in the life of the American Negro and the three norns who have traditionally presided over the Negro problem have a changeling in their laps. The Sociologist, the Philanthropist, the Race-leader are not unaware of the New Negro, but they are at a loss to account for him. He simply cannot be swathed in their formulae. For the younger generation is vibrant with a new psychology; the new spirit is awake in the masses, and under the very eyes of the professional observers is transforming what has been a perennial problem into the progressive phases of contemporary Negro life." *The New Negro*, by Alain Locke, 1925

"I still marvel at how swiftly my previous life's thinking pattern slid away from me, like snow off a roof. It is as though someone else I knew of had lived by hustling and crime. I would be startled to catch myself thinking in a remote way of my earlier self as another person." *The Autobiography of Malcolm X*, 1964

"Black as a physical fact has little significance. Color, as a cultural, social, and political fact, is the most significant fact of our era. Black is important because it gives us ground from which to fight—a way to feel and think about ourselves and our own reality—a way to define." *Black Arts Notebook*, by John O'Neal, 1971

Introduction

Psychologically speaking, the social history of African-Americans has been dominated by two competing processes: *deracination,* or the attempt to erase Black consciousness, and *nigrescence,* or the struggle for Black self-awareness. Throughout Black history, the exploitation of Black labor has been an important dimension of American commerce. In anticipation that African Americans would attempt to counter the forces of oppression through collective actions, racist Whites sought to control the political and cultural socialization of Blacks in order to, (a) increase the probability of deracination and false consciousness, which in turn would, (b) decrease the probability of the development of individual, and, more importantly, collective awareness around issues of culture and class. Thus, whether it be the "breaking in process" during slavery, or the miseducation of Blacks in the 20th century, adult African-Americans have repeatedly commented that, to varying degrees, their experiences as children and youth in formal educational institutions seemed deliberately designed to promote confusion and a self-blame perspective, regarding the problems Black people confront, and a diminished appreciation, if not out right ignorance, about the evolution and existence of African-American culture.

Given the ubiquity of the White emphasis on deracination, it comes as no surprise that within African-American history are accounts of Blacks, who, having first been successfully deculturalized, experienced revitalization through the process of nigrescence. Nigrescence is derived from French and means "to become Black," and as the five quotes in the epigraph attest, Black figures out of the distant past through the present have traversed a Negro-to-Black identity conversion. Sometimes it was recorded as a singular metamorphosis in isolation from the community, as was the transformation of Nat Turner in 1831, and other times as the parallel experience of hundreds of cohorts involved in various Black social movements, such as the Garvey Movement and Harlem Renaissance of the twenties, or in the case of the more recent epochal period of nigrescence, the contemporary Black Consciousness Movement of the 1960s and 1970s.

While the search for an authentic (cultural) self-image is an omnipresent theme in Black social history, the appearance of dedicated psychologically oriented nigrescence models, for application in the analysis of the psychology of Black identity change, is a fairly recent phenomenon—dating back no further than 1968 or 1969. Shortly thereafter, a modest number of theoretical and empirical articles on nigrescence began to accumulate, and in 1978 these were the subject of the first review article on the topic (Cross, 1978). The field has continued to engage the time and interest of a large cluster of scholars, and since the earlier review, well over 65 nigrescence essays and empirical studies have been completed, suggesting, of course, that the time is ripe for another comprehensive review. That is the focus of the current effort. What follows is (a) a summary of the stages depicted by nigrescence theorists as well as a summary of recent theoretical advances; (b) a review of the unpublished and published empirical studies on nigrescence; and (c) a concluding note on directions for future research. The summary of the stages borrows greatly from another work by the senior author (Cross, 1991), whereas the literature review and final commentary are published here for the first time.

Evolution of Nigrescence Models

The contemporary African-American social movement lasted from about 1954 to 1975 and had two phases: a civil rights phase (1954-1967); and a Black power or Black consciousness period (1968-1975). While today the concept of Black identity is generally taken for granted, and is sometimes associated with the Movement as a whole, in point of fact, notions of Blackness, Black identity and nigrescence stem from the dynamics and ideological emphasis of the second, not the first phase. The earliest attempts to analyze the Blackness phenomena led many researchers to construct psychological profiles which differentiated "Black militants" from "traditional" Negroes (Caplan, 1970; Cross, 1991; McCord, et al., 1969), but this approach more often than not led to a pejorative and stereotypical vision of Black identity, a perspective which, amazingly enough, still finds favor in some circles, as evidenced by the pathetic and pseudo-scientific diatribe against any and all forms of Black identity recently offered by Wortham (1981). Almost from the onset, the profile approach came under considerable criticism. For example, in 1971 Cedrick Clark commented that "...the language of contemporary psychology, particularly dealing with Black Americans, is basically monodic: phenomena are described in terms of entities and characteristics which a person possesses instead of the processes in which he/she is engaged (Clark, 1971, page 33)." Comments like Clark's, calling for a developmental perspective, struck a strong chord amongst Black psychologists trained in the more process oriented fields of psychology (developmental, personality, psychotherapy, sensitivity training, etc.), and in the aftermath of the assassination of Martin L. King, Jr., nigrescence models came into prominence:

> "...models on the psychology of nigrescence depict the stages of the Negro-to-Black identity transformation experienced by many Black adults within the context of the Black Power Period of the Black Social Movement. With the murder of Martin Luther King, Jr., the Black community became enchanted

with Black power, and the dynamics of the Black power period seemed relatively similar whether one lived in the Northern, Southern, Eastern or Western quarter of the United States. Consequently, observers of Black life from every region of the country penned nigrescence models during the late 1960's and early 1970's. Amongst Blacks themselves, perhaps it is not surprising that the most significant efforts at nigrescence model-building were attempted by Blacks whose previous training and work was in some dimension of process psychology. For example, Charles Thomas received his doctorate in counseling psychology, and he wrote his nigrescence model based on experiences as a clinical and community psychologist in the Watts community of Los Angeles. While he would eventually complete an academic research doctorate, Cross' experiences as a clinician in Jacksonville, Illinois, and his participant observation of Black life in Evanston and Chicago, Illinois, provided the foundation for his analysis. The late Jake Milliones refined his model as a graduate student in clinical psychology at the University of Pittsburgh and as a final case in point, Bailey Jackson formulated his model while working as a trainer and process consultant in Albany, New York. Although they were not clinical psychologists, most of the White scholars who contributed to the nigrescence orientation, such as Sherif and Sherif, Luther Gerlach or Herbert Kelman, were quite familiar with the application of a developmental and process perspective to problems of social change. (Cross, 1991).

Between 1968 and 1976, the literature exploded with nigrescence models in the works of Cross (1971); Crawford and Naditch (1970); Downton (1973); Gerlach and Hine (1971); Jackson (1976); Kelman (1970); Milliones (1973); Napper (1973), Pinderhughes (1968); Sherif and Sherif (1970); Thomas (1971); and Toldson and Pasteur (1975). The simultaneous publication of the different models has been met with a certain degree of egotism and destructive competition, as some have sought the status of "founder" of the Black identity change paradigm. Besides being counterproductive, i.e., few of the theorists have co-authored publications or conducted collaborative research, such a vacuous title could only be awarded from an ahistorical perspective. Anyone who takes the time to interview some of the key actors will readily discover each was working independently of the other, and the similarity in their writings is not the product of a "copy-cat" phenomena, but the reflection of the fact that whether observed in Watts (Charles Thomas), Chicago (William Cross), Albany, New York (Bailey Jackson), New Orleans (I. Toldson and A. Pasteur) or Pittsburgh (Jake Milliones), the dynamics of Black identity change during the sixties was, and remains, basically the same all across America. The similarity, then, is not so much with the models, but in the *phenomena being observed*, although the date of the publication of each model differs from a few months to a few years. Consequently, other than perhaps to mention Frantz Fanon, the origin of the field of nigrescence is a shared discovery, as much the product of the Black community itself, as it is one intellect. More recently, this element of competition has greatly diminished as Bailey Jackson, Jake Milliones, Janet Helms, Raymond Weston, Gerald Jackson, Rita Hardiman, Thomas Parham, William Cross, Robert Carter, and Robert Williams, to mention a few, have been making a concerted effort to share information and research, and to cross reference their respective work.

Summary of Stages

We will not attempt a microscopic analysis of the eleven or so process models. However, in the section to follow, a summary of the stages common to most nigrescence models will be presented, with highlights drawn from the works of Cross (1971); Jackson (1976); and Thomas (1971).

Nigrescence models tend to have four or five stages (we will stress a four stage summary), and the common point of departure is not the change process per se, but an analysis of the identity to be changed. The person is first described as functioning in an ongoing steady-state (Stage 1), with a deracinated or "Negro identity"; following this, some event or series of events compel the person to seek and be a part of change (Stage 2); this is followed by psychological metamorphosis (Stage 3); and finally, the person is described as having internalized the new Black identity and enters another steady-state (Stage 4). The period of metamorphosis or transition is depicted as an intense struggle between the "old" and emerging "new" self; consequently, *the process writers depict the change process as being informed by, rather than divorced from, the character of the identity to be transformed.*

Stage 1: Setting the Conditions for Change

This stage describes the nature of the old identity or frame of reference to be changed. The process writers seem to understand the Negro community reflects a great deal of psychological diversity, in that Negroes differ in their personalities, lifestyles and behavior. Nevertheless, they have attempted to isolate a modal pattern Negroes employ, when dealing with the issue of race. Thus, Stage 1 focuses on the central ideas, basic attitudes, value systems, frames of reference and worldviews linked to Negroism:

"It (Negroism) is an American concept not based on economic deprivation or lack of education or cultural sterility, but on White America's idea of the African type of (Black person) and that person's place in American society. It is an American concept that is socially derived, politically sanctioned, and economically abused" (Onwauchi, 1967).

At the core of the Stage 1 description is an aggressive assimilation-integration agenda, an agenda linked not only to the search for a secure place in the socio-economic mainstream, but motivated as well by a desperate attempt to escape from the implications of being a "Negro." In this light, the Stage 1 Negro is depicted as a *deracinated* person who views being Black as an obstacle, problem or *stigma,* and seldom a symbol of culture, tradition or struggle. The Negro is thus preoccupied with thoughts of how to overcome his stigma, or how he can assist Whites in discovering that he is "just another human being" who wants to assimilate.

The process writers depict the Negro as someone who sees himself as having nothing to offer Whites in exchange for social acceptance. Since Whites might question Negro humanity, given their Eurocentric interpretation of African History, the slavery experience, and the nature of contemporary Black life— a perspective no doubt shared by the Negro — the Stage 1 person is said to be *very* defensive about race issues, and burdened with a sense of shame about his/her African roots, slave heritage, and the lowly condition of rural and urban Negro communities. *In a sense, the Negro is depicted as one who views herself or himself, and her or his group, from the perspective of Whites, and will do almost anything to overcome the stigma of race, in order to obtain White approval.*

More often than not, the Stage 1 person rejects the notion that he or she is personally inferior, and sees the problem as the stigma attached to his/her *group identity*. Consequently, since identifying with the group might well impinge upon his/her search for *personal approval*, the Stage 1 person is often described as an uncompromising *individualist* who marks progress by how far he/she (or other individuals) progress in a system rather than how the system treats "his" group.

In his model, Cross stressed that the Negro identity is in evidence across social class, but that its manner of expression varies by class. For instance, middle class and lower class Stage 1 Negroes share a common distaste for the quality of their hair texture. Lower class Blacks might "straighten" their "bad" hair to make it "better" whereas middle class Blacks might prefer a "very short" style in which the "bad" hair is cut away. Either class-based style is traceable to the same theme: discontent with one's body features.

The extent to which the Stage 1 identity is also linked to behavioral problems differs from writer to writer. The late Charles Thomas associated conformity, compliance, subservience, repressed rage and unproductive lifestyles to the Stage 1 identity, while in their respective models, Jackson and Cross spend more time describing the peculiar features of the Negro value system and worldview than on the possible correlation of this worldview with general personality variables. In any case, implicit in all of the models is the notion that the Stage 1 identity reflects some level of impaired mental health. What seems necessary for this review, however, is the recognition that a deracinated personality influences cognitions, affect, *and* behaviors, all of which are interrelated. That each model may have a different focus (i.e., behaviors versus values or worldview) is less important than highlighting the degree of thematic congruence each seems to share.

Stage 2: "Pulling the Rug From Under One's Feet"

The "Negro" or Stage 1 identity, the identity to be changed, is the product of traditional macro-temporal developmental experiences, and as is the case for any steady-state identity, it performs its functions in a habitual and unconscious manner, a point stressed in the Jackson model. Furthermore, while people may gradually change modest dimensions of their identity, they tend to resist wholesale identity change. In fact, the *stability* and *predictability* functions of identity converge to form a barrier against major change. Such a notion is analogous to the development of psychological defense mechanisms which help to fortify one's ego against any threat of anxiety.

The second stage focuses on an event or series of events that manage to work around this resistance or even *shatter* the person's current feeling about herself/ himself and his or her interpretation of the condition of Blacks in America. In brief, the Stage 2 "encounter" has the effect of "pulling the rug" from under the feet of the person operating with the Negro identity. The change event or encounter involves two steps: first, experiencing and personalizing the event and, secondly, beginning to reinterpret the world as a consequence of the encounter. The second part is depicted by Cross as a testing phase, during which the individual cautiously tries to validate his/her new perceptions. When the person absorbs enough information and receives enough social support to conclude that (a) the old identity seems inappropriate; and (b) the proposed new identity is highly attractive, the person throws caution to the wind and begins a frantic, determined, obsessive and extremely motivated search for Black identity. At the end of the second stage the person is not depicted as having obtained the new identity, *but as having made the decision to start the journey toward the new identity.*

Stage 3: The Agony, Comedy, Tragedy and Romance of Metamorphosis

This stage encompasses the most sensational aspects of Black identity development, as it is the vortex of psychological metamorphosis. The nigrescence writers see this as the period of transition in which the struggle to destroy all vestiges of the "old" perspective occurs simultaneously with an equally intense concern to clarify the personal implications of the "new" frame of reference.

There is nothing subtle about this stage, and for good reason. Although the new recruit has just affirmed a desire for change, in point of fact, he or she is more familiar with the identity to be destroyed than the one to be embraced. Having lost patience with the past, the boundaries and essence of the old self are truncated, collapsed, and codified in *very* pejorative terms, images, and emotions. On the other hand, he/she is *unfamiliar* with the new self, for that is exactly what he/she hopes to *become*; thus, the person is forced to erect simplistic, glorified, highly romantic and speculative images of what he or she assumes the new self will be like. Under the spell of this dynamic, the person can be vicious in attacks on aspects of the old self that appear in others or her/himself, and he or she may even appear bizarre in his or her affirmation of the new self. It is one of the ironies of social change that the most demonstrative displays of a new (Black) identity are generally performed by people who are the least at ease with the new identity.

The potential personal chaos of this stage is generally tempered by the social support a person gains through group activities. The groups joined during this period are "counterculture institutions" (i.e., counter to the "Negro" culture) which have rituals, obligations, and reward systems that nurture and reward the developing identity, while inhibiting the efficacy of the decaying "old identity." In fact, in the midst of rebellion against the larger society, the Stage 3 person is described as being quite *conforming* within Black consciousness groups. Since the new Black identity is something yet to be achieved, the Stage 3 person is generally anxious about how to demonstrate to others that he/she is becoming the right kind of Black person. Demonstrating and "proving" one's level of Blackness, of course, requires an audience before which to perform, and a set of group standards toward which to conform. A great deal of comedy and tragedy related to "new" Blackness or "new found" Afrocentricity can be traced to those acts and activities of commitment and conformity designed to "prove one's Blackness."

Although the initial part of Stage 3 involves total immersion and personal withdrawal into Blackness, the latter segment of this stage represents emergence from the reactionary, "either-or" and racist aspects of the immersion experience. The nigrescence writers claim that the person's emotions begin to level off, and psychological defensiveness is replaced by affective and cognitive openness. This allows the person to begin to be more critical in his or her analysis of what it means to be Black. The strengths, weaknesses and oversimplifications of Blackness can now be sorted out, as the person's degree of ego-involvement diminishes, and her or his sense of "perspective" expands. The person begins to feel in greater control of himself/herself, and the most difficult period of nigrescence comes to an end.

Stage 4: Internalizing the New Identity

Following the depiction of the transition period, all nigrescence models present a fourth or fifth stage describing the habituation and internalization of the new identity. The fourth stage signals the resolution of conflicts between the "old" and "new" worldview, thus tension, emotionality, and defensiveness are replaced by a calm, secure demeanor. Ideological flexibility, psychological openness, and self-confidence about one's Blackness are evident in interpersonal transactions. Anti-White feelings decline to the point that friendships with White associates can be renegotiated. While still using Blacks as a primary reference group, the person moves toward a pluralistic and nonracist perspective, although relationships are negotiated from a position of strength rather than weakness.

In the Thomas model, persons who have incorporated the new sense of self are said to have a clearer understanding of where they want to go in life, on the basis of resources that are actually available; evidence an increased capacity to respond and act effectively across a variety of situations, and are capable of more extensive self-criticism and self-evaluation. Thomas argued, however, that Blackness involves more than a positive feeling of self, it also includes *assertive behavior* within a social context. Upon gaining a stable sense of self; the (new) Afro-American assaults oppressive institutions that brought about the necessity for a search for Black identity in the first place, with an eye on affecting change for the benefit of one's people, rather than just oneself. Certainly, Thomas' position reflects a more collective view of self, which is philosophically consistent with an African American frame of reference.

For Bailey Jackson, the nigrescence process at first involved the isolation and the reformulation of a single dimension of a person's self-concept, followed by the reconstitution of the total self-system through the syntheses of the new Black self component, during Stage 4:

> "For the person who sees him/herself as a Black only or to view his/her Blackness completely separate from the other aspects of the person is seen as a dysfunctional fragmentation of self. While recognizing the necessity for the separation of the person's Blackness from other parts of him/herself in earlier stages as a strategy for making sense of that aspect of self, the person now needs to complete the developmental process by internalizing and synthesizing this new sense of Blackness" (Jackson, 1976a, p. 42).

Being Black is placed into perspective and balanced with the other demands of one's personhood (gender identity, spiritual identity, various role identities, etc.), aspects of which some are quite race neutral.

Stage 4 is also a point at which the person re-examines the bi-cultural nature of Black existence, a factor which requires explication. The nigrescence writers note that in a generic sense, any identity reflects, and is a product of, the physical and metaphysical realities that frame the childhood and adolescent socialization process. Then, as the person develops and becomes more and more an actor in his/ her own right, one's identity enables the person, given adequate ego structures and interpersonal skills, to exploit and conduct social and material exchanges with one's reality. Blacks tend to live in *two* material and cultural realities, realities which at times are quite distinctive, and at other moments are so interwoven as to give the appearance of a common fabric. From this perspective, Cross and Jackson stress that all Blacks, to one degree or another, have a *bi-cultural identity structure*. It is this notion of a bi-cultural identity structure that helps to connect the struggles of the contemporary Black American with the legacy of Negro America captured in the writing of W.E.B. DuBois (1903). As Americans, Blacks have as part of their overall identity, components of self *commonplace to the identity of most Americans*, and as Blacks, there is a sphere of self which is ethnically and psychologically unique. Part of the work of Stage 4 is coming to accept the enigmatic, conflictual as well as advantageous and supportive aspects of being an "American," but most of all, Stage 4 is coming to grips with the incontestability of one's Americanness. This fact, along with being Black, is the ubiquitous "twoness" found in all Black psyches. Recall that during the earlier transition stage, Blackness was romanticized and played off against the "evils" of Whiteness. Not only did the new convert denigrate all that was White, he or she frequently proclaimed that in becoming Black, one ceased to be an American, and at best, the convert saw no value in such a predicament (i.e., being American). Just as Stage 4 represents movement away from a "blind faith" analysis of Blackness, likewise this period of resolution and internalization leads to a rapprochement with one's Americanness. To paraphrase Bailey Jackson, in Stage 4, the bi-cultural basis of Black existence ceases to be disarming, psychologically speaking, and instead comes to be viewed as a multifaceted reality which, depending on one's circumstances, can be personally advantageous, supportive, as well as at times perturbing and problematic. In a more recent publication he elaborates in the following way:

> "The individual (in Stage 4) also has a new sense of the American culture. The person is able to identify and own those aspects of the American culture that are acceptable (e.g., materials possessions, financial security, independence, etc.) and stand against those aspects which are toxic (racism, sexism, war, imperialism, and other forms of oppression). The ownership of the acceptable aspects of the American culture does not preclude or override the ownership of Black culture" (Jackson, 1976a, p. 62).

This notion of the factual acceptance and selective ownership of one's Americanness is not to be confused with assimilation, for we are seeking more of an anthropologically derived concept of acceptance. Perhaps the following hypothetical situation will help clarify the point. Two people of African descent meet at a conference, one from Brazil, the other from the United States. Both agree that historically and metaphysically speaking, each is an African person, but neither wastes time trying to deny the non-African elements of their respective worldviews and cultural frames of reference. Thus, they compare notes not only on their shared Africanity, but on the manner in which that Africanity has been reformulated through either the North American or South American experience. It is from this same type of vantage point that the Stage 4 person has learned to accept the reality that she or he is neither solely Black nor American, he or she is very much an African American.

It has already been noted that one's identity is a cognitive map which functions to guide intercourse with society and the physical environment. As a way of bringing to a close our brief summary of the nigrescence paradigm, let us focus on the functions of Black identity as revealed in the discussion of internalization by Jackson, Thomas, and particularly, Cross (1991). For the person who has reached Stage 4 and beyond, the internalized Black identity tends to perform three dynamic functions: (1) to defend and protect a person from psychological insults and, where possible, to warn of impending psychological attacks that stem from having to live in a racist society; (2) to provide social anchorage and meaning to one's existence by establishing Black people as a primary reference group; (3) to serve as a conduit or point of departure for gaining awareness about, and completing transactions with, the broader world of which Blackness is but a part.

1. Defensive Mode. An easily perceived but nonetheless essential function of the stabilized Black identity which the nigrescence writers address is the protection of the individual from psychological harm that may result from daily existence in a racist society. A person with a well developed defensive modality is aware that racism exists, anticipates encounters with racism, has developed reactive strategies for use in racist situations, and has a keen sense of personal efficacy. Black identity helps the person to be aware that oppressive and racist factors are realities in everyday life in America, and that personal encounters with racism should come as no surprise. This sense of awareness combined with the "anticipatory set," function to buffer or blunt the impact of racist encounters. Through experience and maturity, the person develops and learns to apply strategies of withdrawal, avoidance, and assertiveness, when confronted by racist circumstances. In the past, withdrawal, avoidance and passive-aggression were the hallmark of Black survival, but the new Black identity stresses effective counterattacks and personal aggressiveness. Finally, one of the primary consequences of racism is that many Blacks are forced to live in poverty and degradation, and some Blacks may blame such circumstances on themselves. However, in a properly functioning defensive mode, self-blame, depression and despair are less likely, because the person combines a high level of personal efficacy with a system blame orientation. The lowly state of one's material conditions are linked to oppression and racism, rather than being viewed as an extension of one's self-concept.

There are two extremes to this modality: in one, the person may deny the significance of racism in which case the defensive function will be inadequately developed and the person's self-protection abilities will be nil. In the other, the person may be overly-sensitive or even paranoid, "seeing" racism where it does not exist.

2. Reference Group Functions. It is generally the case that each Black person has a number of options from which to satisfy one's group affiliation needs. However, in the case of an individual with a Black identity, social anchorage and a sense of being, existence, or purpose in life, derive from making Black people a primary, although not necessarily the only, reference group. While religion, occupational status, political affiliation, gender, etc., will all constitute some component of the self, having a Black identity means that one's personal interpretation of the meaning of Blackness will frame one's value system, aesthetics, personal social network, daily interactions, and personal conduct. In one of two ways, and perhaps a mixture of both, "race" becomes highly salient to the person. When viewed as a socio-historical variable, "race" refers to an *experientially derived perspective* or worldview; from the vantage point of a reactionary ideology, one's perspective flows "naturally" from one's racial or biogenetic characteristics. At its best, the reference group functions of Black identity lead to the celebration of Blackness, the press to solve Black problems, and a desire to promulgate Black culture and history. At its worst, it provides the basis for inhibiting, if not destructive, social conformity, ethnic chauvinism, reactionary cultural ideologies (biogenetically based ideologies), and a tendency to view as less than human, to one degree or another, those who are "not Black" (such negative and positive potential goes along with any and all forms of nationalism, ethnicity or group affiliation and is thus not unique to the Black experience; one can embrace a cultural perspective without being reactionary, but all biogenetically defined notions of culture are inherently reactionary).

3. Proactive and Transcendental Functions. When Malcolm X returned from Mecca, he was no less committed to Black people; however, his "tunnel" vision had been expanded, enabling him to see Blackness and Black people as but *one* cultural and historical expression of the human condition. His new vision did not question the basic integrity of the Black experience, rather it made Blackness his point of departure for discovering the universe of ideas, cultures, and experiences beyond Blackness, in place of mistaking Blackness as the universe itself. It is often assumed that ethnicity acts as a barrier to humanism, but in its highest expression Black identity functions as a window on the world. The humanism, ever present in the life of Martin Luther King, and increasingly apparent in the final period of Malcolm X's life, did not represent a contradiction to their Blackness; on the contrary, it was a product of Blackness. In coming to know Black people, both Malcolm and King had to explain Black diversity. In tracing this diversity to the various cultural, economic, linguistic, social and political *systems* under which Blacks lived throughout the diaspora, it was only natural that each should eventually try to make sense of the behavior of non-Black people and nations through a similar analysis. Thus, the more deeply Blacks explore themselves and the lives of those around them, the more likely they are to understand people as reflections of systems and personal experiences, and less so as clusters of ever distinct "racial groups."

The development of the capacity to proactively perceive and transcend one's Blackness is the primary function of the third and final functional mode of the Stage 4 Black identity. The nigrescence theorists see it is a mediating or *bridging mode* which links the person to other spheres such as the world of work, politics, gender, social class, international affairs and religion. Some critics have suggested that in the transcendence of Stage 4, the nigrescence writers are depicting a person who ceases to be anchored in a Black world, but this is a gross distortion of their use of the term. Transcendence depicts a person who *is Black—oriented,* but has the capacity to interact with and comprehend non-Black social systems, cultures and individuals, which, in effect, is all of the world beyond Blackness. It is through mediation, proactivity, and transcendence that the stage is set for future identity growth. Finally, this last mode helps people to feel reasonably comfortable with unanswered questions, life's contradictions, and the rapid change in American society. In today's ever-changing world, learning to live with ambiguity, in juxtaposition with a firm sense of self (Blackness), are at the vortex of modern mental health for Black people, as it is for most Americans.

As in the case of the other two functional modes, there are extremes to which the third mode can descend: (a) For some, having the "correct" ideology and a rigid sense of self precludes "learning to live the questions" and facing ambiguity; consequently, transcendence is seldom experienced; (b) either because they are overwhelmed by the need to compromise or are tempted by opportunism, another group makes so many compromises that eventually having a sense of Blackness ceases to have meaning; (c) finally, others become enveloped in the world of Eurocentric or pseudo-humanism and forsake any commitment to Blackness, seeing Blackness as a contradiction to humanism rather than its expression within a particular social-historical context.

Recent Theoretical Advances

Parham's Lifespan Nigrescence Model and the Concept of Recycling

In the opinion of the two senior authors of this review, perhaps the most important theoretical advance in the field of nigrescence is Parham's application of a lifespan perspective to the study of nigrescence. In an article titled "Cycles of Psychological Nigrescence," Parham presents a life cycle nigrescence model based on a modification of the Cross Model:

> "...within the context of normal development, racial identity is a phenomenon which is subject to continuous change during the life cycle. While the psychological nigrescence research certainly documents how a person's racial identity can change from one stage to another (i.e., Pre-encounter to Encounter to Immersion-Emersion to internalization), previous research has failed to detail how the various stages of racial identity will be accentuated at different phases of life. My model seeks to describe how the stages of racial identity are manifested at three phases of life, (late adolescence/early adulthood, midlife, and late adulthood) and how each phase of life is characterized by a central underlying theme" (Parham, 1992).

The first object of Parham's concern is pinpointing the earliest phase of the life cycle at which one is capable of experiencing nigrescence. He presupposes that the manifestation of identity during childhood are "more the reflection of parental attitudes or societal stereotypes which a youngster has incorporated," than the integrated, cognitively complex, identity structures found in adults. Consequently, Parham hypothesizes it is during adolescence and early adulthood that one might first experience nigrescence, and thereafter, the potential is present for the remainder of one's life. Parham then notes there is probably a qualitative difference between the nigrescence experience at adolescence or early adulthood, than say nigrescence at middle or late adulthood, because a Black person's concept of Blackness will be influenced by the distinctive developmental tasks associated with each phase of the adult life span. A major portion of the remainder of his article is then devoted to walking the reader through nigrescence, first as might be experienced by an adolescent or young adult, then by a middle aged adult, and finally by an elderly Black person.

Perhaps the most profound issue Parham raises is not so much that aspects of the *initial* nigrescence episode varies with age, but having completed nigrescence, he sees the demand characteristics of each phase of adult development, making more likely a person's recycling through the stages.

> "*Recycling* is defined as the reinitiation into the racial identity struggle and resolution process after having gone through the identity process at an earlier stage in one's life. In essence, a person could theoretically achieve identity resolution by completing one cycle through the nigrescence process (internalization), and as a result of identity confusion, recycle through the stages again" (Parham, 1989).

Parham's use of the term, "identity confusion" is misleading, for recycling may have less to do with confusion, disintegration, or regression, and more to do with a mid-life challenge for which one's initial nigrescence cycle, experienced during an earlier period of development, provides few answers. For example, having experienced nigrescence as a single person, marriage and/or the challenge of raising one's progeny, especially during *their* adolescence, is enough to drive any otherwise normal person to "rethink" attitudes about Blackness. From Parham's perspective, recycling does not mean the person reverts to the old (Pre-encounter) identity and then traverses all the stages. Rather he is inclined to believe that the challenge or trauma acts as a new *Encounter episode,* which exposes small or giant gaps in the person's thinking about Blackness, and the person recycles in order to fill such gaps. Thus depending upon the nature of the challenge or new encounter, recycling may mean anything from a mild "refocusing experience" to one involving full fledge Immersion-Emersion and Internalization episodes.

Another important advancement in Parham's model is his recognition that a person's initial identity state is not restricted to Pre-encounter attitudes. This assertion represents a significant departure from the traditional nigrescence models (i.e., Cross, Jackson, Thomas), which implicitly and explicitly suggest that everyone's racial identity development begins with a pro-White/anti-Black frame of reference or worldview. Parham speculates, for example, that if a young adolescent is exposed to, and indoctrinated with, parental and social messages which are very pro-Black in orientation, the reference group orientation initially developed by that youngster might be pro-Black as well.

A third point of interest in Parham's model is his articulation that identity resolution can occur in at least three ways: (1) stagnation (failure to move beyond one's initial identity state); (2) stage-wise linear progression (movement from one identity state to another in a sequential, linear fashion); (3) and recycling. The Cross (1971), B. Jackson (1975), and Thomas (1971) models imply that nigrescence occurs in a linear fashion, with no other alternatives being proposed.

Helms' Concept of Worldview

Recall that the origin of the field of nigrescence was in part a reaction against the tendency to apply typological profiles to people who, because they were in the midst of identity change, were likely to have a *continuously changing profile.* The typology or non-process approach was said to obscure process:

"...the non-process studies relied on a "single snap-shot" of the (new) Black person, generally at the height of militancy. The process writers....noted that militancy was less an identity and more a trait of identity during metamorphosis. In place of a single snapshot, they would require a series of pictures, if not a motion picture. We should note, however, that the process writers were not rejecting the non-process research strategies. They generally understood that once large numbers of Black people had internalized the new Black identity, a non-process or steady state profile of the new identity would be extremely important. They did object to the application of research techniques which assumed steady state conditions when all the evidence seemed to point to a condition of identity in transition" (Cross, 1991).

History has now made clear, however, that a process orientation is subject to the reverse error, in that the attributes associated with anything other than the Internalization stage are treated as diaphanous and evanescent, and thus the identity implication of each earlier stage is underestimated, if not overlooked all together. Recent research, which we will review shortly, has led to the perception that in steady-state or non-change conditions (periods in history in which there are no ongoing large scale social movements which induce nigrescence), the stage related profiles constitute identities in their own right, and not necessarily transition points toward nigrescence. Perhaps the only stage for which there is an inherent change component is the Encounter Stage, which describes the event or events that cause a person to be conscious of the need to change. Otherwise, each stage related profile may reflect a complete identity.

Helms (1986a, 1986b), in synthesizing the work of Cross (1971) and Sue (1978), has taken this a step further and asked that we consider each stage profile as a distinctive *worldview*.

"In explicating his model of racial identity development, Cross...used the concept of 'stages of identity' to describe the different ways in which Black people may resolve the identity issues caused by their need to function in a racist society. If one reads Cross' descriptions of the stages carefully, one comes to realize that in each of the stages, he is describing a complex interaction between feelings, cognitions, attitudes, and behaviors. In my opinion, Cross uses stages as a synonym for what Sue...called 'worldviews'..." (Helms, 1986, p. 62).

Quoting Sue, Helms (1986) defines worldview as "the way in which people perceive their relationship to nature, institutions, other people and things. Worldview constitutes our psychological orientation in life and can determine how we think, behave, make decisions, and define events" (Sue, 1978, p. 458). The racial identity stages refer to that portion of the person's worldview that is designed to organize and interpret one's personal (internal) and society's (external) definition of the worth and salience of the group to which one is ascribed. Thus, Helms attempts to provide a broader cognitive definition of the stages and to suggest the ways in which identity might function, even in the absence of an ongoing large scale social movement.

In recent discussions between the first author and Bailey Jackson of the University of Massachusetts, one of the most active of the nigrescence theorists, Jackson stated that the Pre-encounter, Immersion-Emersion and (new) Black identities are *not* period specific, in the sense that each can only be found in the dynamics of contemporary Black life. Instead, Jackson sees the three identities as ever present throughout the social history of Black America. At any particular historical period, one identity may be normative for reasons unique to that period, while the other identity profiles, though in evidence, may take on less significance. As time progresses, the ancillary identity may become normative, and the previously normative identity, less popular. Together, Helms' notions of worldview and Jackson's historical perspective bring the field of nigrescence ever closer to the capacity to articulate a comprehensive psychohistory of Black America. While such a venture is beyond the purview of the current effort, an outline of the psychohistory will likely be based on the following four points:

1. Slavery in the Americas Begins: Africans are introduced to the Americas as slaves, and various deracination schemes are devised to mute and disable their Afrocentric perspective. Also, in the course of simply learning to adopt to their new circumstances, a degree of acculturation occurs and Africans, at least over several generations of slavery, become African Americans.

2. Effects of the Institutionalization of Slavery: In an anthropological sense, slavery fails to dehumanize Blacks, and it fails in its attempt to destroy all vestiges of Africanity, although deracination and acculturation result in Blacks themselves no longer being able to *consciously* identify the Africanity in their daily life. It is in the realm of identity and worldview that slavery is *most* successful in a destructive sense, for early on, the historical record shows many Black slaves with a Pre-encounter oriented worldview, as the dialectics of oppression (deracination) and liberation (nigrescence) are etched in stone. In the aftermath of slavery's destruction of a conscious African worldview, slaves forge new ways of codifying their vision of themselves and the world around them. Some like Phillis Wheatley, Benjamin North, Booker T. Washington, and the African Americans who "colonize" Liberia, exhibit a Pre-encounter perspective, unique not so much by themes of self-hatred (the notion of self-hatred has been exaggerated in depictions of Pre-encounter) , but in the tendency to view the world from a Euro-American perspective. Others, from a very early age, are socialized into pro-Black orientations, and their identity never seems to necessitate conversion. In fact, Sojourner Truth and Frederick Douglas even exhibit the qualities of transcendence. But Douglas and Truth seem more the exception than the rule, and the successes of deracination makes slavery the initial theater for nigrescence, with the life of Nat Turner being one of its most demonstrative performances.

3. The Post-Slavery Experience, 1865-1975: After slavery, the three worldviews are easily spotted in autobiographies written by Blacks between 1870 and 1900, but in the formation of Black urban America at the turn of the century, a new phenomena is revealed in the Black response to oppression. In place of singular conversions experienced in isolation from the community, the dynamics of Black social movements show thousands of Blacks moving through the stages of nigrescence together. This first epoch of collective nigrescence is the Garvey Movement and the

Harlem Renaissance. However, the forces of deracination, in conjunction with the effects of the Depression, dilute the gains made toward nigrescence in the 1920s and 30s. Furthermore, the McCarthy era destroys the lives of many Blacks who might otherwise act to bridge the generations of the sixties with the earlier nigrescence period. In their place, the McCarthy debacle helps evolve a moderate (mainstream) Black leadership that is assimilationist to the extreme. As the limitations of the deracinated assimilationists unfold, the stage is set for the most recent epoch of nigrescence, the Black Consciousness Movement of the sixties.

4. Nigrescence in the Present and Future: Although the actual date can be debated, the Movement of the sixties and seventies seems to lose its mass movement dynamics by the mid-nineteen-seventies. In accordance with anyone's standards, the Movement is only partially successful in creating sustained and meaningful opportunities for *some* Blacks. On the other hand the accumulated victories of historical racism give birth to the Black underclass. Ironically, the *success* of the Movement has meant a socialization period (1975-1985) in which race, for some Blacks, has taken on less significance, and merit more importance. Thus, while yesterday's Pre-encounter Negro displayed a strategy of *seeking* approval and acceptance, today's Pre-encounter Negro is more the product of perceptions that she/he has *gained* acceptance and approval. The new Negro, in effect, rejects Blackness from both a cultural and class position. In any case, it takes no magician to predict that the forces are building toward another period of nigrescence, one in which social class issues may be as dominant as cultural factors. Should it come soon enough, the Black community will likely be prepared, for the personalities and organizations which might bridge such a movement with the events of the sixties continue to have status in the Black community.

In explicating our psychohistorical scenario of nigrescence, we have not done justice to another important factor, that being Parham's notion of recycling. This would become evident were we to examine in comprehensive detail the individual lives of Blacks for any of the periods (slavery, 1865-1900, 1900-1920, etc.) to which we made reference. It probably has not escaped the attention of some readers; however, that perhaps recycling can also be applied to the Black community as a whole, in that periodically our communities, and not simply individuals, seem in need of recycling.

Review of Empirical Research on Nigrescence

Empirical research on nigrescence clusters into five sub-topics: (a) works that have sought to confirm the validity of the models as a whole; (b) the development of appropriate tasks or instruments for measuring the stages phenomena; (c) isolation of the correlates of nigrescence; (d) laboratory replications of the models; (e) the relationship between counselor preferences and stage related identities.

Confirmation of Process

Much of the early research focused on the process as a gestalt i.e., the process as an integrated phenomenon, and less so on the amplification of the details for any one stage. The aim appeared to be the confirmation of the existence of the process. Two tactics were employed in these earliest of nigrescence studies, both of which exploited the fact that the research was conducted during a period when the Black Movement was an ongoing event (circa 1969 to 1974). In one approach, researchers took advantage of the perceptions of college students, who were likely to have recently observed Black identity change in others. In another approach, researchers analyzed, for stages content, the retrospective stories of Black persons situated in the final stage of development, who had recently completed nigrescence. In either instance, the descriptive categories and images used to depict observed (Cross, 1976; Hall, Cross & Freedle, 1972) or personally experienced metamorphosis (Cross, 1979; Krate, Leventhal & Silverstein, 1974; Williams, 1975;) were found to resemble the stages of nigrescence.

Each of these early confirmation studies were limited by sample size and representativeness. Consequently, it was difficult to attribute the dynamics of nigrescence to the entire Black Movement. However, a recent study of survey data collected between 1968 and 1976 in a large urban community tends to show the connection between nigrescence and the Movement. Working out of the Institute for Survey Research at the University of Michigan, Hatchett (1982) studied racial attitude change in Blacks living in Detroit, Michigan, from large scale surveys conducted in 1968, 1971 and 1976. Items reflective of Immersion-Emersion attitudes and activities showed an increase between 1968 and 1971, and a decrease in 1976. On the other hand, items demonstrative of a pro-Black perspective in conjunction with an increasing pluralistic attitude about the world, and a decrease in a sense of alienation from Whites, were more characteristic of Blacks in 1976, than 1971 or 1968. Through a series of sub-analyses, Hatchett concluded such trends were not artifactual, and that the Detroit data were probably reflective of the experiences of Black communities across the nation from 1968 to 1976. Thus, the combination of the consensus, retrospective, and survey studies seemed to show nigrescence as a reality of Black life for the period from 1968 to 1976.

Developing Objective Measures of Nigrescence

A central and early concern in the literature has been the need to develop techniques for measuring nigrescence. When the movement was ongoing, Jackson and Kirschner (1973) found ethnic or nationalistic self-designation was a sensitive measure of stage progressions, but in short order such an approach proved too transparent and grossly subject to social desirability factors (Parham & Helms,

1981; Weston, 1975, 1977). Type of membership and organizational affiliation (Davidson, 1974) has also been used to define one's stage placement, as well as performance on racially or culturally related forced-choice preference tasks (Weston, 1975, 1977). Given that each stage can be linked to various characteristics and tendencies, another approach has been to administer a battery of personality and attitudinal tests for the purpose of constructing stage specific psychological profiles (Brown, 1979; Denton, 1985; Williams, 1975, Parham & Helms, 1985). Studies by Hall, Cross, and Freedle (1972) and Krate, Leventhal, and Silverstein (1974) employed an individually administered Q-sort task which allowed a subject considerable flexibility in depicting the number of stages present in either observed or self-perceived identity change. Williams (1975) used the items from the Hall, Cross and Freedle Q-sort to construct a nigrescence interview schedule. The interviews he eventually conducted were taped, and judges rated the stage place-ment for each subject. Furthermore, Williams administered a battery of tests and explored the correlation between the stages and various personality traits.

The Q-sort task or Williams' multimethod procedure can be very time consuming, and, not surprisingly, students of nigrescence have struggled to develop a paper-pencil inventory capable of isolating the stage placement for any subject (Cross, 1976; Davidson, 1974; Harrison, 1974). Two inventories have come to dominate the field, and our focus now shifts to a detailed examination of each.

Racial Identity Attitude Scale (RIAS). The most widely referenced measure of the stages construct is the Racial Identity Attitude Scale (RIAS). Developed jointly by Parham and Helms (1981), it has three versions. The first version, called the RIAS-Short Form A, was developed by transforming the Hall, Cross and Freedle (1972) Q-sort into attitude items, by requiring respondents to use a 5-point scale (ranging from 1 = strongly disagree to 5 = strongly agree) to indicate their amount of agreement with each of the 30 items. This response format has been maintained throughout the subsequent revisions of the scale. In developing the second version (Short Form B), factor analysis was employed, and those Pre-encounter, Encounter, Immersion-Emersion and Internalization items were maintained which loaded significantly on a single stage related factor. As a further refinement aimed at increasing the reliability of the various scales, additional items have been generated, resulting in the RIAS-Long form, an exploratory version which has been used in two studies (Carter, 1987; Carter & Helms, 1984). At present, RIAS-Short Form B is the most commonly used version.

Originally, Parham and Helms (1981) experimented with assigning a stage identity to subjects based on the identity subscale on which he or she achieved the highest value, but they came to realize that classification of people into a single stage presumes a model of discrete rather than continuous stages:

"However, a discrete attitudinal model is likely to provide misleading infor-mation about racial identity attitudes because only the people who are at the peak of a particular stage can be classified under such a model, even though people with lower levels of measured attitudes actually might be further along the developmental continuum, if they have already experienced the stage or are in the process of entering a new stage. Furthermore, because, according to theory, certain of the racial identity attitudes (e.g., Immersion and Internalization) appear to be additive to some extent, then placing people in single categories causes one to ignore variance associated with the different types of attitudes that an individual might hold simultaneously and that could be important for predictive purposes" (Parham & Helms, 1985, p. 432).

With the above in mind, Parham and Helms (1985) recommend that the nigrescence stages be considered as different types of *attitudes* that one might possess, with the strength of each type of attitude varying across individuals. Thus, while Parham and Helms (1981) once attempted to use RIAS data to fit subjects into particular stages, they have since tended to stress the application of linear regression models in which each type of stage related attitudes is taken into account for each individual.

The decision by Parham and Helms to include items for the Encounter Stage has become the subject of debate. With few exceptions, nigrescence theorists are in agreement that an "encounter" type stage must be included in any serious *theoretical* discussion of nigrescence. However, the evanescent nature of the stage has led some researchers to forgo any attempt to measure it (Milliones, 1973; Cross, 1979, 1976). Parham and Helms (1981) have felt otherwise, and in every version of the RIAS, an Encounter subscale has been included. Several studies on the psychometric properties of the RIAS have reached contradictory conclusions, with arguments for and against maintenance of the Encounter subscale being advocated.

The main empirical support for dropping the Encounter scale of the RIAS are of two kinds: (a) sometimes the Encounter scale correlates positively and significantly with the Immersion/ Emersion scale and (b) factor analyses of the items do not always yield the same factor structure. Providing evidence for the first point, Grace's (1984) examination of the intercorrelations between RIAS scales showed that three of the subscales are relatively distinctive, but as predicted by Cross in his communications with Parham, the Encounter and Immersion/Emersion subscale are significantly positively correlated (r. = .62). Ponterotto and Wise (1987) found a similar pattern of intercorrelations between subscales: Pre-encounter - Encounter, -.01, Pre-encounter - Immersion, .03, Pre-encounter - Internalization, .03; Encounter - Immersion/Emersion, .49; Encounter-Internalization, -.15; Immersion/Emersion - Internalization, .10. Some people might interpret the correlations of .62 and .49 as evidence that the two scales are redundant. One observation which argues against this conclusion is that though the scales are correlated, in fact, these correlations suggest that the shared or common variance is only somewhere in the range of 24 to 38%. In other words, from 62 to 76% of the Encounter scale variance is *not*

Immersion/Emersion oriented. Thus, the two scales clearly are measuring much that is different. One might also note that an absence of correlation between the two scales is not necessary nor is it particularly desirable. Representing as they do different kinds of Black identities, it would not be surprising to find correlations among the Encounter, Immersion/Emersion, and/or Internalization scales. Thus, such correlations would only present a problem to the theorist if they were, in fact, redundant and/or were negative rather than positive.

Concerning the factor structure of the items, Ponterotto and Wise (1987) conducted a factor analysis the results of which led to their recommendation that the Encounter scale be eliminated. These scholars found a different factor structure than had Helms and Parham (1996). Though Ponterotto and Wise, in fact, found a four factor solution could be applied to their results, they chose a three-factor solution because they could explain it more easily. There are at least two explanations why Helms and Parham and Ponterotto and Wise may have found different factor structures. The first is that the two studies used different procedures for rotating factors. Ponterotto and Wise used oblique rotation, which makes the a priori assumption that factors are correlated; Helms and Parham used varimax rotation, which assumes that they are not. Tinsley and Tinsley (1987) have advised that interpreting factors resulting from oblique rotations is often difficult, and they recommend against its general use. Be that as it may, even if Helms and Parham and Ponterotto and Wise had used the same statistical procedures, different factor structures might have resulted. Such differences are to be expected, because characteristics of subjects, which may differ across research settings, interact with item content. Stated another way, factor structures are supposed to differ when samples differ on important constructs. Consequently, recommendations for scale revisions should not be based on single analyses, unless one can show that one's sample is markedly similar to (or different from) the samples on which the scales were developed.

Issues of the factorial structure of the RIAS aside, the fact of the matter is, a growing body of literature is demonstrating that subjects in the Encounter Stage have enhanced general personality characteristics (Parham & Helms, 1985, Pomales, Claiborn, & LaFromboise, 1986; Richardson, 1987). For example, Parham and Helms (1985) found Encounter Stage attitudes, relative to the other stages, were associated with the highest levels of self-esteem and the lowest levels of anxiety. The overall pattern showed low self-esteem for Pre-encounter, enhanced levels at Encounter, a fall in esteem at Immersion-Emersion, and a mildly elevated pattern for Internalization that did not approach the peak reached at Encounter. If one views the first (Pre-encounter) and the fourth (Internalization) stages as the "before and after" points of identity change, and Encounter, along with Immersion-Emersion, as the stages of "transition," then perhaps Parham and Helms have isolated *bi-modal trends within transition*, wherein identity change begins with an emotional high, followed by a dip, if not emotional crash, ending with the recovery and leveling of affect at Internalization. As we shall see shortly, such an interpretation is supported by similar findings in other studies (Williams, 1975; Denton, 1985). On the other hand, Helms and Parham have produced little evidence which suggests a difference in worldview and racial preference between Encounter and Immersion-Emersion subjects, though they do find differences with respect to personal identity variables. In other words depending upon the correlates being studied, the RIAS may appear to have a three or four stage structure. If the above patterns are confirmed in future research, then the RIAS, in conjunction with personal identity or general personality variables, may reveal differential involvement during all four stages, while group identity factors may provide a three point analysis involving the first and last stages, and a common or undifferentiated profile for the middle or "transition" stages (i.e., Encounter and Immersion-Emersion). *Nevertheless, since abandonment of the Encounter Stage of the RIAS would diminish one's capacity to uncover such complex possibilities, we strongly advise that the RIAS be maintained as a four stage inventory.*

Developmental Inventory of Black Consciousness (DIBC). A lesser known but equally promising nigrescence measure is the Developmental Inventory of Black Consciousness, (DIBC) developed by Jake Milliones and his associates at the University of Pittsburgh (Milliones, 1980). Although designed and constructed six to seven years before the RIAS (Milliones, 1974), and although it has been the object of as many, if not more, empirical studies as the RIAS, including one based on a sample of over 1000 students, the DIBC has received less attention. This can be explained, in part, because fewer of the DIBC related studies have been published, as most are unpublished dissertations from the University of Pittsburgh. In many ways, the DIBC, Jake Milliones, Jerome Taylor and the "Pittsburgh Project" (Taylor, 1976a) are, taken as a whole, one of the best kept secrets in Black Psychology today.

Milliones' (1974) doctoral dissertation, published in 1980, depicts the making of the DIBC. Using the Thomas and Cross Models as frames of reference, construction began with a 160-item pool. Assignment of items to stages was based upon consensus among three judges, with items being judged, eliminated, or rewritten until 40 items were agreed upon for each of four stages (Preconscious; Confrontation; Internalization; Integration). As previously mentioned, Milliones' justification for eliminating an Encounter Stage was that the length of time one experiences the encounter phenomena is likely to be minimal, and hence, its measurement may be unreliable. The subjects consisted of 160 Black freshmen and sophomore males from a southern Black college. Along with the DIBC, each subject was administered a 20-item social desirability scale and a 60-item "Nadanolization Scale" (Taylor, Wilson, & Dobbins, 1972). The latter is designed to measure the degree of incorporation, by Blacks, of stereotypic attitudes traditionally assumed, by racist Whites, in reference to Blacks. Thus, the higher Blacks score on this test, the higher is their presumed incorporation of negative stereotypic attitudes toward other Blacks. Milliones used the Nadanolization Scale in a construct validity study to explore the expected probability that the relationship between Nadanolization scores and the progressive transformation of DIBC scores would be inversely related. Four operations were used to evaluate the DIBC item pool, and 66 of the original 160 items survived the process: 22 Preconscious items, 26 Confrontation items, 9 Internalization items, and 9 items for Integration. The results of the construct validation study were consistent with the view that as Black identity progressively unfolds, there is a corresponding relinquishment of internalized White stereotypes of the (Black) self.

The DIBC has since been incorporated in one of the most important data sets for the contemporary study of Black Identity in general, and nigrescence in particular. In 1976, Jerome Taylor, a professor of psychology at the University of Pittsburgh and an unheralded giant of empirical research in Black Psychology, received a grant from the Public Health Service of HEW (SR-01MH-1675402) to conduct a large scale study of Blackness and its psychological correlates. The study was titled: "Mental Health Consequences of Black Awareness," and co-investigators for the grant were Joyce Allen, Jake Milliones, and Francis Terrell. When completed in the Spring of 1976, data were collected on 1,023 Black female and male college students from nine predominantly Black colleges and universities, and two predominantly White universities. The resulting data set (henceforth referred to as the Pittsburgh Project or Pittsburgh Data Set) included assessments, for almost all subjects, on a variety of measures (the other measures will be identified and discussed in sections to follow), including the DIBC. Two dissertations aimed at validating and refining the psychometric properties of the DIBC, and employing the Pittsburgh Data Set, have been conducted (Brown, 1979; Denton, 1986). Each study relied heavily on cluster analysis. In the first study by Brown (1979), seven clusters were identified. One cluster included a large number of subjects who were undifferentiated with regards to their stage placement, while the remaining six showed a definite connection to the stages of nigrescence. Subsequent to Brown's analysis, Denton (1986) conducted a re-analysis, employing a more powerful cluster procedure, such as the one incorporated by Helms in her analysis of the RIAS. Denton's analysis resulted in only five clusters, and thus a better "fit" with the nigrescence stages, but more importantly, a larger percentage of the subjects were accounted for than was the case in Brown's analysis, with very few falling in an undifferentiated category. The first four clusters showed the DIBC differentiating subjects, along the lines of the Preconscious, Confrontation, Internalization and Integration Stages. A fifth cluster, reflecting a group of subjects who had Preconscious and Integration characteristics, was said to be an example of people with a bi-culturally oriented internalized identity.

The late Jake Milliones, originator of the DIBC, and William Cross, a nigrescence theorist, maintained a close personal and professional relationship, and Milliones encouraged the students and scholars working with the Pittsburgh Data

Set to show the parallels, where evident, between Milliones' conceptualization of nigrescence and Cross' work. Milliones, Brown and Denton tended to equate the Pre-conscious, Confrontation, Internalization and Integration sub-scales of the DIBC, with Cross' conceptualizations of the Pre-encounter, Immersion-Emersion, Internalization and Internalization/Commitment Stages, respectively. However, an examination of the *items* incorporated in the DIBC suggests that Milliones and Cross are using the term "internalization" in two different fashions. Milliones uses the term "internalization" to describe the incorporation of a highly charged Black nationalist perspective. A person in Milliones third stage *is not* open to other ideological perspectives and has not achieved transcendence, a rapprochement with Whites, or a bi-cultural frame. Instead, what the Internalization sub-scale of the DIBC is attempting to measure is more akin to what Cross would call Immersion/ Emersion attitudes and behaviors, *not those of internalization*. The items selected for the Confrontation sub-scale of the DIBC were explicitly designed to capture Immersion/Emersion behavior, but when compared, the distinction between DIBC-Confrontation and DIBC-Internalization is minimal. For example:

DIBC Confrontation Items	*DIBC-Internalization Items*
"Uncle Toms" should be punished severely for holding back the "Black cause."	There is no place in the Black Struggle for those Blacks who associate with Whites.
It is now evident that the Black culture is superior to White culture.	Black art is more superior than White art.
Blacks and Whites can never live in true harmony because of racial differences.	Black people are more human than Whites.

If there is a difference between the two sets, Confrontation depicts a more fanatical definition of Blackness, and Internalization, somewhat less so, but each sub-scale depicts the embracement of an exclusively Black frame of reference in which Whites are of little value. Taken together, the DIBC-Confrontation and-Internalization sub-scales are both measuring what Cross and other nigrescence theorists (Bailey Jackson and Charles Thomas, for example) would call stages of *transition* or Immersion/Emersion. Interestingly enough, both Brown (1979) and Denton (1985) reported a correlation of .77 or 59% of shared variance between the two sub-scales in question. Recalling our discussion of the RIAS, we have already seen that although the variance shared by the transition stages may be extremely high, this does not preclude the possibility that the respective stages are still capable of differentiating subjects. Consequently, as with the RIAS, we do not recommend that any of the scales of the DIBC be fused or withdrawn until additional research has been completed.

Finally, a word is required about the items in the last sub-scale of the DIBC, "Integration." Here Milliones is trying to capture the person who has a Black identity and believes in Black culture, but who also exhibits considerable flexibility and openness in relationships with *some* Whites. However, the sub-scale takes the issues of *identity and culture as givens*. Thus, most of the items focus on the openness and flexibility dimensions of the final stage, but not the measurement of one's commitment to Black culture and identity. This should lead to problems in differentiating someone who is Black oriented and flexible versus someone who is White-oriented and flexible. To make our point, let's take an example from another group identity experience and then return to the issue of nigrescence and Milliones' notion of Stage 4. Suppose we have two women, one a traditionalist and the other a feminist. On the issue of identity, they are miles apart. But let's suppose both advocate flexibility in relationships with men, that is, both are willing to work and associate with men. If the primary focus of one's *measure of feminist identity* was simply, willingness to work with men, the two women would appear the same. One really cannot take issues of identity and culture for granted, because the differentiating factors between the traditional and feminist identity is not in a sense of flexibility on which they overlap, but in their distinctive frames of reference. On the flexibility factor, they look the same, but the Stage 4 feminist is someone who is flexible within the context of a feminist identity; consequently, the ideological terms on which she will negotiate exchanges with men differ from those of the traditional woman. The same may well be true of the DIBC-Integration sub-scale. A person achieving a high score on this scale is thought to exhibit flexibility in relationships with Blacks and especially White people. The scale does *not* include items that anchor the person's identity and cultural orientation. In other words, it appears that a person with a Pre-encounter identity, who advocates Black and White relationships, can score as high on Milliones' last scale as someone with a Black identity who advocates flexibility when dealing with Whites. In both the Brown and Denton analysis of the Pittsburgh Data Set, a group of people with a "1-4" identity split (high scores on first and last stages) were isolated. In some ways the two dissertations constitute a debate of sorts, with Brown arguing that the "1-4 split" cluster cannot be differentiated by the stages concept, while Denton tries to garner support that the cluster represents a special case of advanced Black identity. At another point we will return to what Weston (1974) calls the "1-4 split" profile, but for the present we note that in using the DIBC, the absence of identity and culture items on the last subscale (Integration-DIBC) makes a high score on this sub-scale difficult to interpret. We are of the opinion that those continuing the work on the DIBC should give strong consideration to adding some Black identity items to the DIBC-Integration sub-scale, resulting in a measure of both cultural orientation and flexibility. This will likely result in a slight increase in the correlation between the

Integration subscale and the two transition subscales (Confrontation and Internalization), but this is as it should be. The Black identity of the transition stages is carried over and mellowed in the final stages, not discarded; consequently, any measure of the final stage should be expected to correlate to some degree with measures of the transition period.

Correlates of Nigrescence and Stage Prototypes

In times of societal and individual change, nigrescence theory and research help us comprehend how a person may evolve from one stage to another. Under steady-state conditions, the focus shifts toward isolating the correlates of each stage related worldview or identity. In this section we describe and then summarize the small but important cluster of studies which have attempted to identify the correlates of nigrescence such as social class, value orientations, cognitive styles, affective states and self-actualization trends, and mental health characteristics. As will become evident, these correlational studies have invariably led to attempts at the construction of stage specific profiles, typologies or prototypes.

1. Socio-economic status. In the introduction to their study on the relationship between stage-anchored identities and socio-economic status, Carter and Helms (1984) point out there is a long standing debate in the personality literature on whether socio-economic characteristics or adaptations to Black culture best explain the personality development of Blacks. On one side of the debate are proponents of the social class or culture of poverty models who believe that social class status is the most crucial variable for explaining Black personality characteristics (Lewis, 1966; Wilson, 1978). On the other hand are proponents of cultural integrity models, such as Boykin (1981) or Nobles (1972), who hold that the socialization experiences of Blacks, rather than their social class standing per se, are the most salient features influencing Black culture and personality development. Adherents of the cultural integrity model see racial frame of reference varying not so much by social class, as by one's stage related racial identity (Pre-encounter, Immersion/Emersion, Internalization, etc.). To test the hypothesis that social class and racial identity vary independently of one another, Carter and Helms (1984) ran a series of multiple regressions on socio-economic and racial identity data obtained from 174 Black community college students. The dependent variables in the regression analyses were racial identity attitudes (Pre-encounter, Encounter, Immersion/Emersion, and Internalization), as measured by the RIAS, while the independent variables were reference group socio-economic status, mothers' and fathers' educational levels, mothers' and fathers' occupational status, mothers' and fathers' years on a job, students' own educational level, and sex of subject. None of the multiple regression

analyses was significant. F-ratios for all models ranged from .37 to 1.08. The results suggested that none of the stage-anchored identities could be predicted by socio-economic status variables, a finding replicated in a study by Parham and Helms (1985). In explicating their findings, Carter and Helms stated:

"Racial Identity attitudes and socio-economic status appear to represent separate constructs. Thus, it seems that it may be important to consider the subjects' or clients' attitudes toward themselves and their ascribed racial group. Researchers can not assume automatically that if one is Black, that one identifies with Blacks or Black culture, or that if one is middle class or upper class, that one does not identify with Blacks or Black culture.Socio-economic status may be an important demographic variable indicating social position and economic resources, both of which are based on external criterion, however, racial identity attitudes appear to be related more to internal functioning then to external forces. It seems that this developmental psychosocial process is more a result of an individuals' interpretation of his or her socialization experiences and personal development than it is a reflection of actual external conditions imposed by social class" (Carter & Helms, 1984, pp. 10-11).

2. The Personal Identity and Reference Group Correlates of Nigrescence. A plethora of attributes are embedded in nigrescence theory, however, recently Cross (1986, 1987) has shown, in an extension of the work of Clark (1955); Lewin (1948); McAdoo (1970), Porter (1971); and Storm (1970), that nigrescence research tends to focus on the isolation of attributes or traits from but two psychological domains: a general personality or personal identity (PI) domain, and a group identity or reference group orientation (RGO) sector. In the study of personal identity or PI, the focus is on generic or universal, unidimensional personality correlates, such as high versus low anxiety, field versus ground dependence, aggression-nurturance, externality-internality, high or low self-esteem, intrapersonal competence-incompetence, dependence-independence, happiness-depression, wellness-neuroticism, etc. It is a multidimensional domain each measure of which is thought to anchor a person somewhere on *the continuum of psychological well being to symptomatology, neuroticism or pathology*. Thus, when a self-esteem or level of anxiety scale is administered, the researcher often interprets the results not simply in terms of the single trait in question (i.e., anxiety or self-esteem), but as insight into the total domain of personal identity (i.e., self-esteem level as a reflection of general well being).

The second type of variables frequently explored, according to Cross, falls under the reference group orientation or RGO domain. Here the focus is on ideologies, value systems, worldviews, cultural (racial) preferences in the arts and music, organizational memberships, religious affiliations, aesthetics, etc. Measures of RGO are generally designed to show that a person taking the test (or task) falls somewhere on a continuum of an "in-group" orientation, at one extreme, and an "out-group" orientation, at the other, where "in-group" is defined as the group to which one is generally ascribed. To confuse matters, studies employing RGO measures, such as a racial preference task, have often injected the phrase "self-hatred," a PI variable, in explicating their results. This is because in studies of Negro or Black identity, researchers typically presume the PI and RGO domains, though distinctive in nature, are highly correlated. That is to say, people who score average to above average on some PI measure of psychological well being are predicted to show an "in-group" orientation on some measure of RGO. In effect, PI and RGO are hypothesized to follow a positive, linear, correlation, and it has also been presumed that this correlation accounts for a significant amount of variance in studies of Black identity. More often than not, this relationship has typically been taken for granted, so much so that from 1936 to the present, most studies of Negro or Black identity have involved a single measure from only one domain; however, the results were discussed "as if" the researcher had tested both domains. For example, all of the famous identity studies conducted by Kenneth and Mamie Clark involved only one type of measure, a racial preference or RGO task. The Clarks *never* administered a PI test to any of their subjects, yet they interpreted their results not simply in terms of evidence of an out-group orientation, but as evidence of neuroticism and psychopathology, both of which are PI variables. Obviously their "leap of faith" was based on the presumed relationship between measures of RGO and the concept of psychological well being.

Nigrescence theory is very much wedded to the same psychological assumptions that guided the Clarks. The correlates of Pre-encounter (Negro identity) have been hypothesized as low scores on measures of psychological well being (PI domain), paralleled by a demonstrable out-group perspective on measures of RGO. On the other hand, the latter stages of nigrescence are presumed to be reflective of average to high scores on measures of mental health (PI domain) accompanied by clear cut evidence of the incorporation of an in-group cultural and political orientation (RGO domain). The transition stages, such as Immersion/Emersion, have been hypothesized as a period of flux and intrapsyche volatility (PI pattern) in association with ideological purity (an RGO pattern showing extreme Blackness and a "blind faith" analysis).

Now let us turn to the empirical literature to see if the hypothesized correlates and prototypes of the nigrescence stages have been confirmed. As the reader is probably well aware, not every study of the new Black identity has employed a nigrescence inventory such as the DIBC or RIAS. Thus, technically we have two types of Black identity correlational studies: (1) those explicitly guided by nigrescence theory and employing a direct measure of nigrescence, frequently either the DIBC or RIAS; (2) those which while interested in Black identity or Black identity change, have not operationalized Blackness via a nigrescence task or instrument. Since there have been far more of the latter than the former, we shall refer to the first type as the "nigrescence guided" empirical studies of Black identity, and the second as the "general literature on Black identity." Recently, Cross (1991) conducted a comprehensive review of the "general literature on the new Black identity," and now with the current review, we can compare the two types of studies. Consequently, our review will highlight empirical studies of PI and RGO that have been driven by nigrescence theory and methodology, and where appropriate, we will compare the results with Cross' findings based on the more voluminous general Black identity literature.

RGO Correlates of Nigrescence. Both the general (Cross, 1991) and nigrescence related empirical literature on Black identity provide almost categoric evidence of profound change in traits or tendencies clearly related to the RGO domain. Up until the mid-1970s, even the simple act of self-identification differentiated one's stage of development, as Pre-encounter subjects used the labels "Negro," "colored," or "human being" while persons in the other stages used Black, Black American, African or African American (Jackson & Kirschner, 1973; Weston, 1975). However, more recent studies suggest that self-designation is no longer a differentiating factor, since both Pre-encounter and Internalization types are as likely as the other to use the label Black to self-identity, although a significant number of the former still uses the term Negro, a label almost never used by people who have reached Internalization. Weston (1975) offered the following explanation on why self-designation no longer distinguishes Pre-encounter from advanced identity development:

> "...It is important to note that the majority of (low awareness) individuals responded to the nationality variable as Black, etc., although a significant number responded as Americans. How can this be explained in the face of the theoretical expectations? We can look at the environment for an answer to this question. We can...speculate that this choice is an effect of the "Black is Beautiful" model on all stratas of the Black society. In light of the constant reminders of this "new" emphasis on Blackness, it is highly unlikely that any strata of the Black population would remain unchanged in their attitudes. Although these people retain many of their Stage 1 type attitudes, we can imagine the entire Black population moving upward in level of Black awareness. Therefore, the Stage 1 person is a "notch" up in his Blackness, reflected by the many self-designations of "Black," on the variable. This is a relative rather than an absolute gain, since the entire strata can be said to have moved up a notch" (Weston, 1975, p. 27).

At a deeper and more lasting level, nigrescence has changed the way Black people perceive Blacks as a group. In one of the earliest (Milliones, 1974) and most recent studies (Denton, 1986), the first involving 160 subjects, and the second over one thousand, the DIBC along with Jerome Taylor's Nadanolitization Scale were administered. The Nadanolitization Scale is a 60-item instrument designed to measure the degree of internalization, by Blacks, of stereotypic attitudes tradition-ally assumed, by Whites, in reference to Blacks. In both studies, Pre-encounter subjects scored high on the Nadanolitization Scale, while high awareness subjects registered low. Likewise, Williams' (1975) study of 57 Black adults showed Pre-encounter, as compared to Internalization subjects, had a strong anti-Black bias, and they perceived Blacks as not trustworthy. In his analysis of the Pittsburgh data set, Denton (1986) also examined the results of another scale developed by Taylor (1976) designed to measure the quality of Black social relationships. This "Black affiliation scale" had two sub-scales. In one cluster the focus was on how the respondent saw him/herself affiliating with other Blacks ("I look forward to being in the company of other Blacks," "I give consistent support to other Blacks"), while in the other the focus shifted to how the respondent saw other Blacks affiliating with him/her ("other Blacks are consistently supportive of me"). The results showed Pre-encounter subjects were more closed and distant to other Blacks, while persons in the other stages showed a more open and engaging attitude toward Black affiliation, and felt more supported by Blacks.

The social distance and mistrust Pre-encounter Negroes have of other Blacks means that Pre-encounter Negroes do not perceive Blacks as a resource for collective action. In his study, Williams found that not one Pre-encounter Negro was a member of a "Black" (as opposed to Negro oriented) organization, and Pre-encounter people tended to blame Black people themselves for the "Black situa-tion." The development of Black consciousness resulted in an increase in a system blame orientation, and a propensity to join with other Blacks in various cultural and political collective efforts. Weston (1975) found that Pre-encounter and Internaliza-tion subjects both belonged to all-Black organizations, but the former tended to be religious and "apolitical," while the latter were more politically and culturally oriented. *In other words, Blackness may not differentiate actives from non-actives per se, but it may determine the kind of organization in which one is active.* This was certainly the finding in a study by Davidson (1974). Black college students who scored low on her measure of Black identity were no less active in college as a group than others; however, the organizations they joined were frequently White oriented or showed a low salience to Blackness. At the other end of her scale, high Black identity scores predicted membership in groups for which being Black was highly salient. McCaine (1986) used the RIAS attitudes to predict general need for affiliation. He found that for Black women, Encounter attitudes were related to weak motivation to initiate contact with others (disregarding race), whereas Internalization attitudes were related to strong motivation to initiate affiliative contact. Perhaps these differences reflect the greater concern with social issues characteristic of the Internalization Stage.

The salutary effects of nigrescence have not been limited to the organizational behavior of Black college students or the Black middle class. Terrell, Taylor, and Terrell (1980) found young incarcerated Black males convicted of serious Black-on-Black crime were rated more Pre-encounter oriented than those charged with less serious Black-on-Black crime. Glasgow's (1980) study of the Black underclass of Los Angeles before, during, and after the 1965 Watts Riot, clearly showed the young men of the underclass experienced nigrescence following the riot, as they moved from commonplace street activities to the establishment of positive and proactive Black cultural and social organizations. In a study of low income Black high school students, Weston (1977) found students with low awareness were more apt to model their behavior after a White model, while high awareness reflective of the Internalization Stage, seemed to induce Black-on-Black modeling behavior. As in his earlier study (Weston, 1975), Weston found the distinction between Pre-encounter and Internalization subjects was not always apparent, since the effect of the Movement has been to make the salience of race more socially desirable. For example, when the high school students observed Black and White models in a positive situation, both low and high awareness Black students concurred with the decision of the Black model. However, when Weston introduced a mildly *negative* dimension to the task, the high awareness students persisted in their attachment to the Black model, while the low awareness group shifted to the White model.

The change in how Blacks view other Blacks and the shift in their group affiliation tendencies all point to a change in ideology, racial and cultural frame of reference, value system, reference group orientation and worldview (Williams, 1975). Both the general and nigrescence specific Black identity studies confirm this, although the pattern of change reveals considerable complexity. The Pittsburgh Project employed a Black ideology measure, and in an over all sense Pre-encounter Negroes scored lower on this measure than did Internalizers. However, the sub-scale patterns revealed a great deal of texture. Both groups *endorsed* independent Black economic activities, but on issues of culture and identity, Pre-encounter types were strongly assimilationist and displayed an anti-Black perspective with regard to Black culture and Black identity, whereas Internalizers showed a strong commit-ment to the integrity of Black culture, Black education, and Black identity. On the matter of separatism or extreme nationalism, at one level the two groups could not be distinguished, as both were non-separatist in orientation; however, the pattern for Pre-encounter showed a non-separatist stance derived from their assimilationists and anti-Black cultural attitudes, in contrast to the Internalizers whose non-separatist frame was based on a commitment to a pluralistic society, inclusive of a belief in the legitimacy of Black identity, and the need to explore and protect Black culture. The complex pattern of these results are supported by the general literature on Black identity. For example, Maish (1978) studied the political, identity and cultural correlates of persons of high and low Black awareness. As in the Pittsburgh study, low awareness was linked to lower scores on identity, culture and ideology. Furthermore, he found that while Black identity, Black cultural orientation, and a nationalists ideology are correlated, they are not one in the same. His results showed that a belief in Black nationalism requires commitment to issues of Black identity

Table 1
Kluckhohn and Strodtbeck (1961) Value-Orientations Model with Alternative Solutions.*

Orientation	Alternatives		
Human nature	Evil: People are born with evil inclinations. Little can be done to change this state. Control of evil behavior is the only hope.	Mixed: People are both good and bad at birth. The differences among people are shaped by one's experiences.	Good: People are basically good. They have innate inclinations toward good behavior.
Person to nature	Subjugation to nature: People have little control over natural forces and therefore are subject to nature. Nature guides one's life.	Harmony with nature: One's sense of wholeness is grounded in a continual interaction with nature and natural forces. People are one with nature. Nature is one's partner in life.	Mastery over nature: One is expected to overcome natural forces and use them for one's own purpose. Nature is to be ruled.
Time sense	Past: Tradition is of central importance. Therefore, the temporal focus is the past.	Present: The past and future are of little importance. The present situation is paramount.	Future: The temporal focus is on planning for events that are to occur, for places in time beyond the present.
Activity	Being: Emphasis is on activity that expresses what is natural in people' and part of human personality. Expression of emotions, desires,and impulses is spontaneous.	Being in becoming: Emphasis is on activity that expresses integration of the personality. The goal is to develop an integrated personality through containment, control, mediation, and detachment.	Doing: Emphasis is on action-oriented activity, which is measurable by external criteria to the acting person (e.g., achievement).
Social relations	Lineal: Lines of authority are clearly established and hierarchical relationships dominate subordinate relationships. Respect for andobedience to elders and those of higher rank guide individual behavior.	Collateral: People are independent and members of groups as well. Individual goals are subordinate to group goals (collective decision making).	Individual: People are autonomous of the group. Individual goals are not subordinate to group goals.

*From Carter and Helms (1987). The relationship of Black Value-Orientations to Racial Identity Attitudes, p. 187.

and Black culture, but all persons who score high on identity and culture did not necessarily endorse Black nationalism. Maish's analysis also differentiated Black separatism as it pertains to life in America versus Pan-Africanism. He found evidence of persons scoring high on Black identity and culture who rejected Black separatism but endorsed Pan-Africanism. The pattern seemed to suggest; (1) an acceptance of Black culture and identity; (2) a rejection of separatist notions within the United States; and (3) a belief in Pan-Africanism, whereby Pan-Africanism is defined as a unified and strong Africa, but not a segregated and separatist Africa (Africa as a unified participant in world affairs rather than one which is strong but secluded).

Findings for another RGO factor, one's value system, also suggest complexity and texture. In a study by Carter and Helms (1987), the relationship between the stages in the Cross Model and the values incorporated in the value-orientation model of Kluckhohn and Strodtbeck (1961) was explored. The Racial Identity Attitude Scale (RIAS), along with the Intercultural Values Inventory, a measure based on the Kluckhohn and Strodtbeck Value System, were administered to 174 Black students, 66 men and 108 women. In interpreting their results, Carter and Helms configured the Kluckhohn and Strodtbeck Model in two ways, one to reflect an Afrocentric value orientation, and another to depict a Eurocentric perspective. Referring to Table 1, the Afrocentric was defined as good (human nature), at harmony with nature (person to nature), present oriented (time sense), "doing" or action-oriented (activity) and collaterally anchored (social relations). The Eurocentric value system was said to stress the evil in human nature, mastery over natural forces, a future time orientation, being in becoming activities, and individualism in social relations. With this scheme in mind, Carter and Helms found that racial identity attitudes predicted three of the Afrocentric (Harmony with Nature; Doing Activity; and Collateral Social Relations) but none of the Eurocentric alternatives. Immersion/Emersion and Internalization significantly predicted belief in group oriented or collateral social relations, with the former hypothesized to be more ethnocentrically defined (blind faith in all that is Black), while the latter was thought to be more realistic, broader in scope, and capable of seeing value in pluralistic as well as all Black group activities. Internalization attitudes were also shown to be significantly related to a belief in Harmony with Nature and the Doing Activity orientations. The relationship between Doing Activity and Internalization is consistent with Cross' (1971) emphasis on commitment and Thomas' (1971) concern for social action in the final stages of their respective nigrescence models. Additional analyses, which disregarded the stages categories and looked at the value pattern for the sample as a whole, showed Blacks exhibiting a dualistic value frame, indicating that Black American-culture contains elements of both Black and White society:

> "...Such an interpretation would make sense given the essentially joint participation (in many ways) of Blacks and Whites in the development of the country. Just as Future Time and Individual Social Relations may reflect American cultural influences, the Harmony with Nature and Collateral Social Relations preferences may, as noted above, reflect African cultural elements in Black Afro-American culture" (Carter & Helms, 1987, p. 193).

Carter and Helms concluded that the value orientation of Black Americans is probably more complex and bi-culturally oriented than theorists and researchers have anticipated.

If the only thing nigrescence research produced was a comparison between the old (Pre-encounter) and new (Internalization) identities, then it would offer nothing beyond what can already be found in the general literature on Blackness. However, in its emphasis on process, nigrescence research generates RGO information on the all important *transition stages*. In many cases, the inclusion of information on the middle stages shows that the evolution of correlates of nigrescence follows a curvilinear, rather than linear path, with some traits peaking in intensity during transition, and then leveling off or disappearing altogether at Internalization. This is dramatically demonstrated in the relationship between nigrescence and Black attitudes toward Whites. Practically every study of nigrescence has included at least one item or a separate scale to measure anti-White attitudes and the results have always been the same. Pre-encounter Negroes score low on anti-Whiteness, Immersion/Emersion types show an intensely elevated high score, while the level of anti-Whiteness in Internalizers is lower than that found during the middle stages, and sometimes as low as that associated with the first stage. Williams (1975), who found both Immersion/Emersion and Internalization types were critical of Whites, noted the qualitative differences between people in the two stages. Persons in the transition stage were more emotional and quick to generalize or stereotype, and Internalizers more rational and differential, when discussing Whites:

> "The critical dimension separating Stage III respondents from the other stages was anti-White sentiment. Stage III subjects demonstrated significantly more general anti-White sentiments, were more angry at Whites for the discrimination experienced by Blacks and had more fantasies about killing Whites, than subjects from any other Stage. On one measure of attitude toward Whites, Stage IV subjects were slightly more negative than were Stage III subjects. However, the responses given by the 55% of Stage IV subjects who expressed negative attitudes towards Whites in general, differed qualitatively from the responses given by the 50% of Stage III subjects who had negative attitudes toward Whites in general. Stage IV responses to the question "What do you think of Whites in general?" reflected more negative attitudes toward racist behaviors of Whites as a group" (Williams, 1975, pp. 79-80).

Closely related to the hostility toward Whites, is the attempt by persons in identity transition to exorcise from their self-image, qualities they associate with the White world. Simultaneously, the person makes a dramatic presentation of the new self through changes in personal appearance (hairstyle, clothing), speech pattern (sometimes an African language will be mastered), value system, and self-designation (it is not uncommon for the person to "add" an African nickname or to change it entirely to an African name). This complex pattern of disassociation from the White world, and embracement of a world and self-image perceived as being exclusively Black, was demonstrated in the Pittsburgh Project (Brown, 1976; Denton, 1985; Taylor, 1986). Persons in transition were shown to be rejecting of White culture and institutions but accepting of Black culture and institutions. Furthermore, they were more likely to embrace the goal of separatism, and not simply, independence and shared power:

"...the Confrontation cluster displayed significantly higher Black nationalist orientations on each of the categories than either the Preconscious or Integration clusters. On the (Black separatism) sub-scale, for example, the Confrontation cluster obtained a mean of 165.35 in comparison to a combined mean of only 103.03 for the Preconscious and Integration clusters—a difference of more than two standard deviations. This suggests that Confrontation individuals strongly advocate a policy of racial polarization in the social, educational, and religious infrastructures of American society" (Denton, 1985, p. 57).

In the midst of this struggle to tear down the old, while erecting the new, Napper (1973) found people in transition developed a "Blacker than thou" syndrome in which one tried to demonstrate that his/her level of Blackness was more "pure" and "correct" than that of another person. This notion of "self-purity" is linked to a romantic perception of a faultless and "ever beautiful" Black community. Williams (1975) found people in Immersion/Emersion had the lowest score on an anti-Black measure, while for persons in Internalization, the anti-Black score showed a mild increase, thus reflective of the former's *uncritical* acceptance of Blacks during the earlier stage, and the emergence in the latter of a more critical and realistic appraisal. Likewise, in the analysis of Black attitudes toward relationships with other Blacks (i.e., an interpersonal relationship measure), Denton (1986) found persons at the earliest point of identity transition peaked on this measure, as they felt extremely accepting of and coveted by other Blacks, so much so as to suggest a euphoric and even occult like attachment to Blacks. In terms of the flaws of Black people, transition types are less likely to be concerned with flaws per se than the origin of such blemishes, and, not surprisingly, Williams (1975) found Immersion/Emersion types peaked on a measure of system blame, compared to the more muted and balanced system blame orientation of Internalizers.

In an article by Cross (1979), based on a study of Black college students conducted in 1972, when the Movement was still ongoing, he found that for RGO related attitudes and perceptions, persons who achieved Stage 4 (Internalization) status admitted having first traversed a period of transition characterized by..." perturbation, effrontery, cultural chauvinism, a high degree of risk taking, and a destructive mood in constant tension with dreams of revitalization" (Cross, 1979, p. 124). When the convert *emerged* from his or her *immersion* into Blackness, a new synthesis was achieved that allowed for the orchestration of RGO elements linked to previous (Pre-encounter) as well as more recent (Immersion/Emersion) experiences:

"The mellowing of Black students appears to have been a highly complex phenomenon, one that challenged them to isolate substantive from diaphanous Immersion/Emersion traits and to develop enough personal insight, interlaced with a touch of humility, to be able to recognize and carry over strengths of the old self-image for construction of the new. The interface of the old with the new was demonstrated by the students' response to item 43 on the Stages Scale, an item classified as a Pre-encounter attribute: "I feel it is important for me to speak good English." Students associated this statement with the old identity because it reminded them of their attempts to develop qualities that would increase their chances of being accepted by White society, as well as of the shame they once felt toward "Black English" (read "bad English"). During the Immersion/Emersion Stage the students sought to affirm their relationship with the masses and Black culture; consequently, trying to be White, to act White, or to talk White was an anathema at this stage. But as the mesmeric dimensions of the militancy stage declined, the maturing converts came to understand language as an important system of communication rather than as a negative or positive symbol of social status; thus explaining the use of the item to define the self in the present. Wallace...has reminded us that innovation usually involves the ability to perceive, analyze, synthesize, and act upon pre-existing elements in a unique manner. Likewise, the new Black self-image is probably composed not of entirely new attributes but of old and new attributes that are synthesized within a different perspective" (Cross, 1979, p. 124).

In summary, then, empirical research on the RGO correlates of nigrescence has isolated three RGO attributional and attitudinal clusters, each of which depicts the old, transition and internalized new idenies, respectively. In some studies (Brown, 1979; Denton, 1986; Helms & Parham in press) these over arching clusters have been further sub-divided, but, with one exception to which we will turn shortly, the so-called "1-4" split, the sub-level clusters have added little or no new RGO information about the three dominant clusters (old, transition and new).

PI Correlates of Nigrescence. While a great deal of consensus exists about the RGO correlates of nigrescence, the same is not true for personal identity or PI correlates. Initially, most expected research to show Stage 1 subjects would suffer from diminished mental health, perhaps even a "self-hatred" profile, while higher levels of self-esteem, self-actualization and improved mental health were the anticipated correlates of advanced development. As we shall see, there is evidence supportive of this total change perspective. More recently (Cross, 1991; Barnes, 1980; Gordon, 1980; Weston, 1975), theorists have begun to reject the notion that the self-hating and psychologically incapacitated person is prototypical of the Negro, and improved or normal mental health the unique consequences of Internalization. They suggest that more often than not, the differences between the initial and latter stage persons are philosophical (i.e., RGO related), not psychological (i.e., PI related), in that people with a Eurocentric or Pro-American worldview are frequently no less psychologically vulnerable or healthy than are those who are Afrocentric. From this vantage point, nigrescence is thought to be highly correlated with RGO variables, but no such association is predicted for PI variables such as self-esteem, level of anxiety, or level of general happiness etc. As we shall see, there is evidence in support of this perspective as well as its alternative. Since in the absolute, the "total change" and "no change" perspectives cannot both be correct, we conclude this section with an interpretive scheme that points to a synthesis of sorts.

Perhaps the easiest place to start is where there is consensus: the PI correlates of Immersion-Emersion or the "transition PI profile." Though more studies need to be completed, those studies that have been conducted point to a period of emotional and intellectual revitalization and turmoil. In both the Brown (1979) and Denton (1985) analysis of the Pittsburgh Data Set, persons in transition showed an exaggerated self-esteem level, and this finding was replicated in a study by Parham and Helms (1985). In addition Denton (1985), Parham and Helms (1985), and Williams (1975) noted that level of self-esteem seems to "shoot through the ceiling" during entrance into the transition period, only to be followed by a precipitous *drop* in level of self-esteem during deeper involvement in transition. This shift in self-esteem may help explain why some transition types seem egotistical and self-involved, on the one hand, and self-sacrificing, submissive and devoid of ego in other instances. Furthermore, both profiles can lead to high-risk taking ventures, one out of an exaggerated sense of personal efficacy, the other as martyrdom for the greater cause or will. Of course, the fluctuations in self-esteem could mean no more or less than emotional flux. In an unpublished master's thesis, Brown (1976) reported transition types were impulsive and emotionally unstable. Cross (1979) reported people in Immersion-Emersion saw themselves as more aroused, angry, and less calm than they recalled being before nigrescence or after Internalization. Williams (1975) also recorded people in transition as being at an apex of emotional arousal, anger, hatred (toward Whites) and impulsivity. Given that people in transition are subject to extremes on both PI and RGO measures, it is no wonder that the stereotype of the angry Black Militant has often been associated with the transition profile (Cross, 1976).

We now shift our attention to the similarities and differences between the total change and continuity models for the other stages. The total change perspective predicts that for PI correlates of nigrescence, scores will be below average at Pre-encounter, reach an apex during the transition period, and at Internalization of the new identity, average to above average scores are anticipated. In the total change model, people at Internalization, as compared to Pre-encounter, should register significantly higher PI scores, signaling positive mental health changes with nigrescence. In this sense, the total change model presumes most people in Stage 1 experience psychological deficits, and that nigrescence is both a political (RGO) and psychological (PI) corrective. The continuity model, on the other hand, represents the more revisionist trend in nigrescence theory. Rather than view Kenneth Clark's self-hating (PI) and out-group oriented (RGO) person as the prototype of Pre-encounter, the revisionists believe the deficit orientation for PI variables was exaggerated in the original nigrescence models. Thus, while they agree that nigrescence has probably radically changed the RGO component of Black identity, they predict little or no change in the PI sector, since Negroes frequently brought many PI strengths to the nigrescence experience. Furthermore, the revisionists view the PI and RGO sectors as independent, and thus change in one sector is thought to be able to take place independent of change in the other:

> "...evidence points to the possibility that the conversion experience radically transformed the values, ideologies, reference group orientation or worldview of Black people, but left intact, or only moderately modified, their self-concept or personality...(T)his suggests that people who began the conversion as "neurotic Negroes" emerged from the experience as "neurotic Blacks"; likewise fairly well adjusted non-neurotic Negroes were well adjusted non-neurotic people with a new Black worldview at the completion of their conversion. In a more general sense, if we could demonstrate that people can be depicted by x number of personality types, the point being expressed here is that the distribution of personality types for persons with either a "Negro" or "Black" worldview would be practically the same" (Cross, 1978, p. 29).

Let us commence with the evidence which supports the total change hypothesis. On June 20th, 1986, Jerome Taylor presented a paper at the Menninger Foundation (Taylor, 1986) in celebration of the 40th Anniversary of the Menninger School of Psychiatry on the correlates and mental health implications of nigrescence. His remarks summarized the findings of at least eight unpublished studies, including the Brown and Denton analysis of the Pittsburgh Data Set. Taylor noted that Stage 1 types had been shown to suffer from low self-esteem, depression, low levels of self-actualization, aggressive as opposed to nurturing social attitudes, and a greater propensity, when involved in asocial behavior, to commit violent crimes. Taylor concluded that Stage 1 "persons may be more vulnerable to psychological maladjustment of the neurotic range" than persons with the new identity, and that nigrescence seemed to improve one's cultural and psychological adjustment since internalization of Blackness was marked by high levels of self-esteem and self-actualization, more nurturing than hostile social attitudes, and fewer instances of depression.

In a study previously mentioned, Williams (1974) explored the PI and RGO traits of working adults (professionals and working class) who were classified as Pre-encounter, Encounter, Immersion-Emersion or Internalization prototypes. For PI measures of internal-external control and level of self-esteem, Pre-encounter, as compared to Internalization, was linked to a defeatist, individual-blame orientation and low self-esteem.

Helms (1984) reviewed a half-dozen studies employing the RIAS and various PI measures, and reported finding evidence of PI deficits in Pre-encounter but not Internalization types. For example, in one study involving 65 male and 101 female Black college students, Parham and Helms (1985) administered the RIAS, along with several paper pencil inventories, and found Pre-encounter attitudes were related to low levels of self-actualization as well as feelings of inferiority, inadequacy, hypersensitivity, anxiety and lack of self-acceptance. Thus, for studies conducted with the Black underclass and Black college populations, and which employed both the RIAS and DIBC, PI deficits have been found in Stage 1 types, and more healthy and normal trends with internalized Blackness.

Arguing a continuity or "no change" perspective, Cross (1991, 1978) has pointed to evidence that Pre-encounter persons have average to normal PI characteristics, and except for evanescent peaking at Immersion/Emersion stage, the PI profile for Pre-encounter and Internalization appears to be the same. Such a pattern can be found in a recent study of nigrescence and cognitive styles carried out by Helms and Parham (1990). Black male and female college students (N = 142), ages 17 to 25, with backgrounds reflective of a broad range of socio-economic status, were administered the RIAS and a test designed to assess three decision making styles derived from the work of Harren (1979). According to Harren, *the rational style* reflects a logical, systematic and objective approach to decision-making; *intuitive decision making* is characterized by a reliance on the use of fantasy, attention to present feelings, and self-awareness; *the dependent style* is characterized by conformity to other people's opinions and expectations. In the exploration of linear trends, only one relationship between stages scores and cognitive style was found. Increased levels of Internalization were related to increased usage of the rational mode. However, when cluster analysis was employed, the results showed both the Pre-encounter and Internalization subjects applied the rational mode more frequently, while subjects located in the transition stages showed no dominant decision making style. The dominant style for the entire sample was rational, consequently, the results suggest that (1) Pre-encounter Negroes are basically rational in their cognitive styles; (2) people in identity transition stages show a mixed cognitive profile in conjunction with a great deal of impulsivity and emotionality; and (3) people located in or who have progressed to Internalization are more rational and less emotional than people in transition, but are no more rationally oriented than are people who have the Pre-encounter worldview. These results are consistent with Cross' (1978) contention that Immersion-Emersion only temporarily changes the person's basic personality and cognitive style, and that with re-integration (Internalization), the changed worldview is incorporated in the personality and cognitive orientation that characterized the person before nigrescence.

However, outside of the Helms and Parham (1990) study of nigrescence and cognitive style, almost all of Cross' evidence in support of the continuity thesis comes from indirect sources. That is to say, the majority of studies driven by nigrescence theory and incorporating direct measures of nigrescence, such as the DIBC and RIAS, have found deficit PI traits to be characteristic of Pre-encounter. Cross' evidence stems from an analysis of over 45 PI/RGO correlational studies of Black identity, for which the relationship with nigrescence is inferred, and is thus indirect. These studies generally employed the same types of PI measures found in nigrescence studies (self-esteem measures, various personality inventories, etc.), but the identity or racial attitude measures usually assessed Blackness in terms of a high or low score on Black consciousness, in the case of adult studies, or racial preference choices, in the case of children. Cross reasoned that if it is true that nigrescence or "becoming Black" is paralleled by improved mental health, then this relationship should reveal itself in the general Black identity literature as well as in nigrescence specific research. What Cross found was quite surprising to many, but quite consistent with revisionist thinking: almost 80% of the correlational studies failed to find a significant overall relationship between level of Black identity and one's level of mental health. This pattern was observed whether the subjects were children, adolescents or adults. A small but critical number of studies did report highly significant interactions. In other words, while very little evidence was found to support an overall relationship between PI and RGO in studies of the correlates of Blackness, there was clearly evidence that, under special circumstances, the two variables may be related. However, more relevant to the debate here, Cross could find no evidence that the interactions were traceable solely to Pre-encounter factors. To pursue the matter still further, Cross examined three additional types of studies which should be sensitive to the existence of any overall relationship between PI and RGO in Black identity. In studies of the relationship between Black studies and Black self-concept, the RGO component (values, racial perspective, philosophical orientation) seemed subject to change after taking Black studies, but PI components (level of self-esteem, personality) remained unchanged. Studies of transracially adopted Black children, as compared to Black children adopted or raised in Black homes, show no differences between children on PI variables, but in some instances, clear differences on RGO measures. Finally, in the few instances in which researchers have attempted to replicate the stages of nigrescence in laboratory settings (i.e., sensitivity training sessions or human relations courses designed around a nigrescence curriculum), Cross found few, if any, which could substantiate PI effects from the training, while RGO changes were more readily demonstrated.

Clearly, then, there is a great deal of evidence which calls into question any presumed overall relationship between PI and RGO in the dynamics of Black identity. However, even in these indirect studies of nigrescence, a small percentage did find an overall relationship, and a critical number reported highly significant interactions. This would suggest that though the hypothesis of an overall relationship is unlikely, under certain circumstances PI and RGO can be expected to show a great deal of interdependency. Unfortunately, as we noted earlier, the indirect studies of nigrescence shed practically no light on the special circumstances of this interdependency, probably because the RGO measures employed in general studies of Black identity are not sensitive to the process and stage related nuances of Blackness, as are the DIBC or the RIAS. But here's the rub. When the more sensitive and direct measures have been employed, not only have the dynamics between PI and RGO for each particular stage been recorded, revelations very much consistent with the "interactions" noted in the indirect studies, revealed as well has been a significant trend *across all the stages*. The pattern revealed seemed to be one of a global, persistent, positive, linear relationship between PI and RGO. That is to say, psychological damage seemed to mark the origin of nigrescence, and increased mental health, its evolution.

As it turns out, it is possible to reconcile the differences between the two types of studies, although the synthesis of the findings from the indirect studies and the results of the Pittsburgh Data Set present a challenge of no small magnitude. Let us briefly state what we think is happening here, and then through a re-analysis of a select number of the direct studies, we will attempt to show how empirical findings give credence to our speculations. To begin with, we believe that one of the more crucial flaws in the original nigrescence models was the tendency to exaggerate the psychological consequences of holding Pre-encounter ideas. This leads us to predict that in most instances, there is very little in the way of PI characteristics which differentiate Pre-encounter from Internalization profiles. On the other hand, we also believe that Cross in his attempt to rewrite the Pre-encounter Stage, has not given enough recognition to what happens, psychologically speaking, when, for whatever reason, a large number of Pre-encounter attributes are concentrated in one person. In such instances we believe the self-hating, out-group oriented person is real, not a myth. However, related to our first point, we do not believe the "self-hating Negro" is the *prototype* of Pre-encounter. That is to say, being Pro-American or holding some other Pre-encounter frame of reference, in which "race" is not made a highly salient factor in one's life, probably does not lead to personal denial or self-hatred, and likewise, being Pro-Black does not guarantee personal happiness and emotional stability. But are we trying to bake our cake and eat it too? No, such speculations lead us to believe that (1) there is no overall relationship between PI and RGO in studies of Black identity; (2) in most instances Pre-encounter attitudes are not related to PI deficits; and (3) a small but critical and recognizable number of persons with Pre-encounter attitudes do suffer from self or personal rejection. In order for the above to be confirmed, one would have to produce evidence of a bi-model trend for Pre-encounter in which the percentage of people with psychological deficits is small, and those with average PI profiles is large. Furthermore, it must be shown that for the large group of healthy Pre-encounter types, their PI levels are no different from that found in Internalization subjects.

A re-examination of three of the most important of the studies in which nigrescence was measured directly offer support for our perspective (Denton, 1986, Parham & Helms, 1985; Williams, 1975). Let us begin with Irvin Williams' dissertation. Recall that after categorizing subjects into either the Pre-encounter, Encounter, Immersion/Emersion and Internalization stages, Williams collected data on a variety of PI and RGO characteristics and found differences between the first and last stages on both types of measures. The differences on RGO were dramatic and robust, and while the PI differences followed the predicted trend, a closer examination reveals ambiguity. Pre-encounter subjects were said to have low self-esteem and a defeatist attitude, while Internalization was marked by high self-esteem and a system blame and activist orientation. Williams employed two self-concept measures: the 10 item *Rosenberg Self-Esteem Scale* and the 100 item, standardized, and multi-dimensional *Tennessee Self-Concept Scale*. A significant difference between the Pre-encounter and Internalization subjects was registered on the Rosenberg, but not the TSCS, although the trend from low to high esteem was clearly evident on the TSCS as well. However, the mean self-esteem score for Pre-encounter on the TSCS was 330.47 (S.D. = 32.24), well within the average or normal range for the TSCS. In other words, the difference between Pre-encounter and Internalization seemed to be one of movement from a normal to above normal score and not a change from below normal to normal. While Williams' results support the notion that nigrescence may enhance self-esteem, his results do not underscore a link between Pre-encounter and self-esteem deficits, since the baseline for self-esteem for Pre-encounter fell well within the normal range for the TSCS. Finally, from his interview data, Williams coded as high, medium and low, each subject's self-evaluation made in response to the following inquiry: "how do you feel about the kind of person you are at this point in your life?" The percentage of Pre-encounter and Internalization with low self-evaluations was practically the same i.e., 6.25% and 5.0% respectively.

This pattern is all the more evident on the results of his administration of the *Gurin Internal-External Locus of Control Scale*. This scale has both PI and RGO oriented subscales in that it measures whether or not the person is personally efficacious (person control ideology sub-scale), in addition to measuring one's perception about the social forces that shape, enhance or inhibit one's life chances (Racial Militancy, Individual System Blame and Individual-Collective sub-scales). The overall differences between Pre-encounter and Internalization subjects showed that as expected, Internalizers were more racially militant, more likely to blame the system for Black problems, and were more favorably disposed toward collective or group actions against racism. But in order to show that a person's ideological stance enhances or depletes one's sense of personal efficacy, differences must also be recorded on the "personal control subscale." However, with regard to personal efficacy, there was no difference between Pre-encounter and Internalization subjects, not even a trend toward significance, since the Personal Control score for Pre-encounter (M = 1.89) was actually higher than for Internalization (M = 1.43). Thus, rather than associate a generalized defeatist attitude with Pre-encounter, Williams' results showed no differences on the PI dimensions of his I-E measure, along with highly significant differences for the two groups' social and ideological I-E attitudes, the latter to the favor of the Internalization types. Thus, a closer look at the

Williams study hardly reveals a grossly deficit Pre-encounter profile in so far as PI characteristics are concerned. To the extent that the overall results suggest some degree of pathology with Pre-encounter, one could infer such a trend accounted for very little of the variance, a point demonstrated in the study by Parham and Helms (1985).

A fine-tooth-comb is not necessary in the re-examination of the Parham and Helms (1985) study. Here we need simply note that certain points which Parham and Helms (1985) stressed can easily be overlooked. Recall that their study involved the administration of the RIAS and various paper-and-pencil PI measures to a large group of Black college students. To test the hypothesis that racial identity attitudes were differentially related to one's mental health profile, seven independent multiple regression analyses were conducted, and the mean stage scores for Pre-encounter, Encounter, Immersion/Emersion and Internalization were used as predictor variables in each of the regression analyses. Their results showed a significant relationship between the stages and mental health to the favor of Internalization. However, Parham and Helms (1985) cautioned against over generalizing their results:

> "In interpreting the results of the present study, it is important to take several methodological issues into consideration. First of all, only one aspect of a person's identity - his or her adaptations to race and racism - was investigated. Thus, even when the regression analyses were significant, only 8% to 18% of the variance was explained by linear combinations of racial identity attitudes." (p. 439)

Focusing more specifically on the Pre-encounter Stage attitudes, their results seemed to suggest that while Pre-encounter attitudes were related to personal inadequacies, these attitudes could not be defined in neurotic, let alone pathological terms.

Standing in the way of this interpretation is Denton's (1985) cluster analysis of the Pittsburgh Data Set. Recall that Denton isolated five different clusters:

Cluster 1: Subjects scored high on Stage 1 identity attributes and their mental health profile was negative.

Clusters 2 & 3: These two clusters fit the RGO and PI pattern of a person in identity transition.

Cluster 4: Subjects exhibited an advanced stage of identity development and relative to subjects in the first cluster, their mental health profile seemed more normal if not enhanced.

Cluster 5: Subjects in this category were said to show a split or dualistic identity pattern along with a very positive mental health profile. The identity pattern was interpreted as "bi-culturalism" and another form of advanced identity development.

The assignment of subjects to the first four clusters was statistically derived and the identity for each was unambiguous. Furthermore, the PI trend associated with these four robust RGO clusters was equally unambiguous, as poor mental health was strongly linked to the first cluster, and enhanced mental health with cluster four. This neurotic to enhanced mental health trend was reinforced when Denton decided to assign the fifth cluster to the "advanced identity" side of the identity development spectrum, since people in the fifth cluster had very positive PI characteristics. However, the racial identity of this last cluster was *ambiguous*, given that subjects scored high on both Stage 1 and 4, forming what Weston (1975, 1977) has called a 1-4 split profile. Had Denton found reason to assign this fifth cluster to the Pre-encounter or Stage 1 side of the equation, then the overall effect would have been a bi-model Stage 1 pattern, indicating that in some instances Pre-encounter can lead to diminished mental health, while in others it does not. Such a finding would be more in line with the authors' interpretation and would compliment the findings of the indirect studies of nigrescence. Thus, whether one accepts or reverses Denton's placement of the fifth cluster is somewhat crucial to any attempt to synthesize the trends of the direct and indirect studies of the PI correlates of nigrescence.

It is our contention that the fifth cluster could just as well be viewed from the perspective of Pre-encounter as Internalization, if not moreso. Denton used three types of measures to inform his decision: (1) two primary measures of Black identity (2) two secondary Black identity variables; and (3) three personal identity variables. On his first primary measure of RGO, Milliones' DIBC Inventory, a 1-4 split was registered. Although it was a split profile, the actual level of the fifth cluster's Pre-encounter score was the *highest* received for any group. On his second primary identity measure, the fifth cluster received the *lowest* score on Black identity than any other group. Thus on his two primary measures, the fifth cluster looked Pre-encounter, not advanced identity oriented. Weston (1975, 1979), who was the first to discover the 1-4 split, faced the same predicament in both his master's thesis (1975) and doctoral dissertation (1977). Weston believes that when a subject receives a 1-4 split on a nigrescence measure, his stage placement should be determined by a second identity measure. Thus, in both his studies, he classified as Pre-encounter anyone with a 1-4 split plus a low Black identity score on a second measure, or Internalizer when the 1-4 split was accompanied by a high identity score on a second measure. Denton's fifth cluster clearly falls into what Weston would call the Pre-encounter pattern, with a 1-4 split on the DIBC and an extremely low Black identity score on a second identity measure. Keeping in mind what we said earlier about the Integration Sub-Scale of the DIBC, i.e., it tends to be a weak measure of Black identity and a strong measure of flexibility in relationships with Whites, then one could argue that the fifth cluster includes Pre-encounter oriented subjects who are flexible in their relationships with Whites (i.e., the 1-4 split) and display a *weak* Black identity (i.e., low score on second Black identity measure). In any case, it should be clear that Denton did *not* classify the fifth cluster as "advanced identity" based on the DIBC or the Black identity scores.

On the two secondary identity measures, people in the fifth cluster displayed very little propensity to view Black people in the negative stereotypes often promoted by White racists, and they showed strong and positive Black affiliation tendencies. While it is certainly true that both tendencies have been shown to increase with advanced stages of identity, it would be risky to pass judgment on the nature of one's Black identity based on such inferential measures, since it is easy to conceive of someone being classified as Pre-encounter on evidence other than their having displayed anti-Black attitudes or a limited sense of connection to other Black people.

Finally, as to the use of any PI measure to infer Black identity or RGO, the work of Spencer (1984); McAdoo (1970); and Cross (1986, 1991); to mention a few, have made it emphatically clear that PI and RGO are extremely poor predictors of each other. In order to show an interrelationship, a study must have an unambiguous racial identity measure and a valid and reliable PI measure. In Denton's first four clusters, a stable measure of identity for each was etched, and then the PI correlates were examined, but for the fifth cluster, this procedure was reversed. On page 68 of his thesis, Denton practically admits that the 1-4 split cluster seems Pre-encounter oriented in so far as the pattern of his two primary identity measures are considered. However, he discounts the primary evidence and concludes that the fifth cluster must be a form of advanced identity, since it was difficult for him to imagine Pre-encounter types with normal PI patterns. We believe the fifth cluster should be approached in the same manner as the previous four. Taking evidence from the primary identity measures, as a point of departure, the fifth cluster should be classified, along with the first, as Pre-encounter oriented. In so doing, this would not contradict the deficit PI trend found in Cluster One. The two together would simply show the Pre-encounter Stage to be more complicated than has been imagined, with some constellations of Pre-encounter attitudes leading to psychological deficits and others not. When this adjustment is made (i.e., interpreting clusters one and five as Stage 1 oriented), the beauty of Denton's data is that it helps to clarify under what circumstances Pre-encounter attitudes *do* predict self-hatred. In Cluster Five, the mature and mentally healthy Pre-encounter types were devoid of anti-Black sentiment and they seemed to relish affiliations with Blacks, but in the first cluster, the Pre-encounter subjects, who held negative stereotypes about Blacks in general, and had negative feelings about affiliating with Blacks, were found to suffer from self-hatred and diminished mental health. Denton's finding, as we have reinterpreted them, are supported by a related study from the general literature. Cole (1978) studied the relationship between race esteem and self-esteem in 200 Blacks stratified by class, age and sex. Although she found little relationship between self and race esteem, and although she concluded that most Blacks have average self-esteem, Cole also found that for the small number of "Blacks who used Whites as their significant others instead of Blacks, a larger percentage displayed low self-esteem (Cole, 1978, p. 40)."

In conclusion, we believe the most plausible interpretation of the findings of direct and indirect studies of the effects of nigrescence on general mental health variables is that for those who have experienced nigrescence, an overwhelming majority have shown very little evidence of change in their PI characteristics, including level of self-esteem. However, while seldom revealed in the indirect studies of Blackness, other than as vague interactions or infrequent main effects, the more sensitive nigrescence measures, such as the DIBC and RIAS, have uncovered evidence that a still undetermined and likely modest number of Pre-encounter types did enter the nigrescence process with PI deficits directly linked to the dynamics of their negative racial identity. More specifically, when characterized by (1) a Eurocentric perspective, (2) a tendency to feel distant, unsupported and unaffiliated with other Blacks, and (3) a tendency to hold negative stereotypes about other Blacks, the Pre-encounter profile has been linked to problems of low self-esteem, hypersensitivity, hostility, increased anxiety, tension, a defeatist attitude and a diminished level of self-actualization. Since such a pattern accounts for very little variance, it appears that although oppression has in far too many cases succeeded in promoting a Eurocentric orientation and identity in Pre-encounter Negroes, it is equally true that most Pre-encounter types have not internalized racist thinking about other Blacks, they nurture and relish the support of Black friends and associates, and they feel good about themselves, personally. Perhaps Beverly Cole said it best:

"...Black Americans have done rather well in preserving their self-esteem in spite of the many hardships, humiliations, and discriminatory obstacles. They have succeeded in resisting the dominant society's definition of themselves more effectively than they usually are credited with. This ego-strength and unyielding determination is the reason for the race's survival" (Cole, 1978, p. 81).

In spirit with but going beyond Cole's insight, Cross has suggested that:

"...any plausible theory on minority identity development should be capable of distinguishing between the psychological consequences of oppression and the psychological triumphs of an oppressed group. Furthermore, we must come to understand that the exploitation of a minority group does not presuppose the dehumanization of the minority group. If and when an oppressor can control the reference group orientation of a minority, it really does not matter that the exploited group has members who, individually speaking, present extremely attractive profiles on various measures of personal identity (PI). In the early 1950's the Negro community turned its back on Paul Robeson and W.E.B. DuBois not out of a sense of personal self-hatred but rather because their White-oriented worldview dictated that certain kinds of Negroes should be condemned while others, like Booker T. Washington, deified. That today such figures as DuBois, Robeson, Garvey, Malcolm X as well as Washington are held in considerable esteem is hardly a symptom of personality change, but it most certainly reflects a dramatic reorganization of the reference groups to which the worldview of many Blacks is anchored" (Cross, 1987, p. 129).

To paraphrase Cross, the price of the Stage 1 identity or assimilation is not necessarily "poor mental health" but rather the development of a worldview and value system which can inhibit one's knowledge about, and capacity to advocate, the political and cultural interests that flow from the frame of reference of the non-assimilated members on one's ascriptive-group. "With the rising influence of minority group members who are assimilated and right-wing oriented but otherwise "normal" in their behavior, it is important that we make ourselves keenly aware of the PI and RGO distinctions. One of the ultimate values of differentiating PI from RGO is that change in RGO, whether toward assimilation or increased ethnicity, can be comprehended without resorting to either pejorative psychological models which inevitably fail to predict the healthy behavior of the assimilated, or romantic "ethnicity" models which imply that through an increase in one's ethnic awareness, all of one's problems can be solved (Cross, 1987, p. 133).

Nigrescence theory, when fused with the notion of the independence of PI and RGO, provides an extremely powerful theoretical framework from which to approach issues and controversies surrounding the structure and dynamics of Black identity and Black personality development. It allows us to avoid oversimplification, while introducing a complex and textured analysis of all the stage related identities, be they Pre-encounter or Internalization oriented. We are released from "either/or" thinking that imply nigrescence is about "one way change" (i.e., "bad to good" or "mental illness to mental health"), and become free to explore the issues of continuity and change in the effects of nigrescence. From these reformulations we can speculate that the Negro who entered upon the path toward nigrescence had neither a pathogenic or extraordinarily positive general personality, rather he/she was probably quite average across a variety of PI measures related to general mental health:

"The positive and relatively stable nature of the PI sector of the Negro self-concept helps us to understand better, psychologically speaking, the multitude of accomplishments and heroics that dot the Black experience throughout Black history, a task never seriously approached by the traditional-pejorative theorists. At the group identity level, however, the storyline has been different. The sense of heritage and race consciousness which embraced the Black community during the Garvey Movement and the Harlem Renaissance, began to fade through the Depression, was suppressed during McCarthyism, and was considered antithetical to the assimilationist-integration themes of the Civil Rights Movement. Thus, the "Negro" was a deracinated person concerned with the stigma, not the heritage, associated with his ascriptive-identity and preoccupied with the development of a reference group orientation and worldview that would make him acceptable to Whites on terms dictated by Whites. Such a person was probably not in need of change at the level of general personality, but under the circumstances of the nigrescence thrust, may have felt compelled to make more nationalistic, his group identity" (Cross, 1987, p. 127-128).

Laboratory Replications of Nigrescence

A small number of studies have attempted to replicate the identity transformation process within the context of human relations workshops, T-group experiences, human relations courses, Black identity group counseling interventions, etc. Generally, such ventures have engaged groups of 10 to 15 students in workshops or courses lasting anywhere from one weekend to a full semester. Regardless of the length of the experience, the training or course curriculum typically tried to replicate the phrases and activities suggested by a particular nigrescence model that had caught the fancy of the facilitator. Effects of the training have often been determined by the difference between pre- and post-test scores on either an objective measure of self-esteem or self-concept and/or some measure of Black identity. The particular outcome measure selected has been crucial to the demonstration of training effects. For the three studies which relied solely on PI measures of identity (self-esteem or self-concept scales), no training effects were found (Livingston, 1971; Lunceford, 1973; Suggs, 1980), while for the three studies in which an RGO measure was employed, effects were more readily demonstrated (Carter, 1974; Griffin, 1975; Jefferson, 1981).

Livingston (1971) divided 22 Black male college students into control (N = 11) and experimental (N = 11) groups. The experimental group experienced an intense weekend long Black awareness encounter workshop which Livingston hypothesized would have a positive effect on self-concept, as measured by the Tennessee Self-Concept Scale. Pre and post-test administration of the TSCS failed to note any difference between controls and experimentals. An examination of the pre-test means showed that for the control and experimental groups, both commenced the project with normal range scores, consequently, had the training had any effect, it would have been to enhance self-esteem, not change it from low to high. Although the focus of the workshop was Blackness, Livingston did not include a measure of Blackness, but on the basis of his clinical notes, he believed the workshop did have an effect on the participants' Black identity.

In an experiment almost identical to Livingston's, only this time involving all Black female groups, Lunceford (1973) divided 30 Black female college students into an experimental and control group. The experimentals were then given a weekend long "Black experience encounter workshop," and as in the Livingston study, no effects were recorded on the basis of differences in pre-test and post-test performance on the TSCS for controls and experimentals. Suggs (1979) also employed the TSCS to measure the effects of his ten session (1-1/2 hours each) "Black identity" group experience, but again, controls could not be differentiated from experimentals, after the treatment. Like Lunceford and Livingston, Suggs did not think to include a measure of Black identity, even though Blackness was the object of manipulation in the treatment.

Why would three researchers, who set out to directly manipulate the Blackness or the RGO domain of Black self-concept, select as their outcome measure a PI scale which is at best an indirect or inferential measure of RGO? Because each believed that, in the dynamics of Black self-concept, PI and RGO are highly correlated. Ironically, then, these researchers employed a measure which, given one understands that PI and RGO are not one in the same, is otherwise fine for assessing PI effects, but predictably insensitive to RGO change. The clinical notes from each study suggested that the Black identity or RGO manipulations did effect the RGO components of self-concept, and had each employed a direct measure of RGO, RGO effects would likely have been demonstrated. Certainly this is the pattern in three other studies.

Griffin (1975) developed a 12 week group experience (based on Milliones' nigrescence model) for increasing Black consciousness in African Americans. Black college students (N = 40) were divided into three groups (N = 15, 13 and 12) and all received the same treatment (i.e., no control group was used). Clinical notes, an evaluation form completed by each participant, and the results of pre and post-testing on the DIBC provided the evaluation data. While no statistical data were presented, Griffin claimed that subjects showed significant signs of increased identity development on the DIBC, the evaluation forms, and the clinical notes systematically kept by the three facilitators. Less impressionistic and more robust evidence of RGO change following nigrescence-related training was reported by Jefferson (1981). Black volunteers (N = 46) were recruited from a two-year college, and a treatment group of 20 students was randomly selected from the 46, with the remaining volunteers constituting the control group. The control group received no treatment while the experimental group took part in a three-day workshop on "Black Identity Development" based on the nigrescence ideas of Bailey Jackson. The title of the workshop was somewhat misleading, since the workshop, while primarily aimed at changing RGO, also incorporated activities and group experiences designed to enhance self-esteem (PI). Thus, Jefferson set out to directly manipulate both the PI (self-esteem) and RGO (Black identity) components of the students' self-concepts, with most of the activities geared toward RGO change. Self-esteem was measured with the Tennessee Self-Concept Scale, and the Bailey Jackson Black Identity Development Scale was used to measure change in Black identity. Overall, there was no significant difference between treatment and controls for the total score of the TSCS, although a significant difference was recorded on the "social self" subscale of the TSCS. Thus, little if any PI effects were recorded. Furthermore, the self-esteem scores for control and treatment groups were well within the normal range for the TSCS. A highly significant degree of change between treatment and controls was recorded on the Black identity measure, as the treatment seemed to advance the identity development of the experimental subjects.

Probably the best demonstration to date that nigrescence workshops and encounter groups are more likely to effect RGO and not PI has come from a study by A. Carter (1974). A sample of 30 Black college students, almost evenly divided by sex, were randomly assigned to either an Experimental, Attention Placebo or Control Group. In the Experimental Treatment, participants were exposed to a curriculum of Black musical, literary and historical information, in conjunction with Black identity oriented group counseling discussions, the sum of which was designed to take the participants through the stages of nigrescence. The experimenter functioned as an active facilitator, making certain that all stage material and discussions progressed as planned. In the Attention Placebo, the experimenter held non-directive rapping sessions stimulated by listening to Black music. The Control Group received no treatment and did not meet together. Carter tried to measure change through the use of a rather odd self-esteem scale, and the importance of Carter's effort lies not with her confused self-concept scale (which showed no effects), but in the analysis of daily diaries. Each participant kept a daily diary which was checked weekly. One randomly selected entry was taken from each diary per week, and over the course of the experiment, which lasted 10 weeks, each student had 10 entries that were analyzed. With 30 subjects, the total number of entries analyzed was 300. Three judges classified all entries according to the following PI and RGO self-reference (SR) categories (Carter used different letters to label her categories, but to save time and to facilitate discussion, the PI and RGO labels will be used instead):

PI+   Positive or approving SR. Response indicates subject approves of him/herself or approves of an action or characteristic mentioned in the SR. Adjectives which describe positive PI's are good, admirable, respectable, superior, happy, glad, improving, etc. *Positive personal identity self-referent.*

RGO+   The same as PI+ except the SR refers specifically to positive concepts and activities related to Blackness. *Positive referent group self referent.*

PI-   Negative or Disapproving SR. The student indicates that he/she disapproves of
               himself/herself or of some action or characteristic of himself/herself mentioned
               in the SR. Adjectives which describe Negative PI's include: unattractive,
               unadmirable, disagreeable, bad, hindered, hampered, etc. Symptoms such as fear,
               worry, sadness, anxiety, etc. are negative PI's. *Negative personal identity self-*
               referent.

RGO-   The same as PI- except it refers to negative concepts and activities
               related to Blackness. *Negative reference group self-reference.*

API   Ambiguous/Ambivalent Personal Identity SR. The entry, while PI oriented,
               does not include enough information to determine whether it is a
               positive or negative PI, or the entries clearly indicate a conflict between
               positive and negative personal identity attitudes toward the self.

ARGO   Same as API except it refers to ambiguous/ambivalent concepts and activities
               related to Blackness.

After collapsing categories 5 and 6 (the ambiguous PI and RGO self-referents), Chi Square analysis was applied to the categorical data resulting from the 900 classifications made by the three judges (300 entries x three judges = 900 classifications). Table 2 shows the final frequencies for the three groups across the five categories.

The overall Chi Square was significant, with differences between groups traceable to the RGO+ cell, and unexpectedly, the collapsed ambiguous cell. No other differences were recorded. Starting to the left of Table 2, we see that for all three groups the fewest entries were made for the negative perceptions about one's Blackness (RGO- cell), suggesting a critical but not unduly negative attitude about being Black. Note that the treatment did not diminish the Treatment Group's capacity to be critical about Blackness, as they were no more or less critical than the Attention Placebo or Control Groups. The ambiguous cell showed a clear and statistically significant difference between the three groups, with the Treatment Group having far fewer ambiguous entries than the other two groups. Next we see the three groups cannot be distinguished for positive PI entries (PI+ cell). Thus, one overall finding becomes clear—the intervention had little if any effect on the PI domain, as no differences between groups were recorded, for either the PI+ or PI- cells. It is the last cell dealing with the RGO+ entries which accounted for most of the treatment effect. Carter's Black identity or RGO oriented intervention, practically incapable of effecting the PI domain, greatly enhanced the RGO(+) component of the RGO domain, left the RGO(-) cell practically untouched, and made the treatment subjects less ambiguous. Given the overall trend of Carter's data, the decrease in ambiguity for the Treatment Group probably pertained to the RGO and *not* PI sector (i.e., fewer RGO but not PI related ambiguous entries) in which case

Table 2
Frequencies Showing How Daily Diary Entries of Participants in Three Groups were Classified by Independent Judges for a Study by Carter (1974).

Groups	Self-Referent Categories					
	PI-	RGO-	A	PI+	RGO+	N
Experimental Group	7	27	166	34	66	300
Attention Placebo Group	7	32	211	32	18	300
Control Group	6	26	216	28	24	300
Totals	20	85	593	94	108	900

the treatment may have helped the participants to be more self-assured about their Blackness, while leaving untouched, the personal identity conflicts, strengths, flaws and uncertainties with which they entered training.

In summary, all six of these training experiments were greatly flawed, methodologically speaking. Nevertheless, like the studies reviewed in the last section, the trend of the results suggest that nigrescence has a greater capacity to change the RGO than PI domain of a person's self-concept.

Nigrescence and Counselor Preference

A number of theoretical papers on the counseling implications of nigrescence have been written (Butler, 1975; Helms, 1984; Jackson, 1977; Jefferson, 1981; Milliones, 1980, Parham & Helms, 1981). However, in the field of counseling psychology, empirical studies of nigrescence have focused on the questions of whether or not one's stage of Black identity determines the extent of same-race counselor preference, or influences one's perceptions of opposite race counseling interactions. In most instances, it has been hypothesized that Pre-encounter types prefer White therapists, people in transition prefer Black counselors, and Internalizers have no preference or an openness to both White and Black counselors who appear competent to handle problems unique to Blacks. While not the first study of counselor preference, the first such effort to be driven by nigrescence theory was published by Jackson and Kirschner (1973). In an earlier unpublished work for which Kirschner was the lead author (Kirschner & Jackson, 1972), it was found that the majority of both Black and White subjects did not show a same-race counselor preference, but within the sample of Black subjects, students who referred to themselves as Afro-American did prefer a same-race counselor to a greater degree than did those who called themselves Negro or colored. As a follow-up to their initial unpublished finding, a second study was conducted with 391 Black students, randomly selected from the entering Black freshmen at a predominantly Black and urban county college (144 males and 247 females). Each subject completed a counselor preference questionnaire that focused on various counselor characteristics such as sex, age, socio-economic background and race. Students also checked whether they were Black, colored, Afro-American or Negro, although in the data analysis, the category colored was dropped due to the limited number of subjects who used this label for self-designation. The results showed that students who self-designated as Black or Afro-American had a stronger same-race counselor preference than those who label themselves Negro. Both of the studies by Jackson and Kirschner were conducted when the Black Movement was ongoing, and the stage of a person's identity could readily be assessed by such straight forward procedures, as self-designation, choice of hairstyle and even choice of clothing (Enty, 1979). However, as Weston (1977) has pointed out, the general success of the Movement caused people in all stages, including Pre-encounter, to take a more favorable attitude toward some labels, rituals and habits that were once the exclusive markers of radical Blackness. This has pretty much been confirmed by replications of the Jackson and Kirschner study in the late 1970's by Gordon and Grantham (1979), Parham and Helms (1981) and Morten (1984). In all three studies, no relationship between racial self-designation and same-race counselor preference was found, indicating, of course, that simple self-designation is no longer useful as a measure of nigrescence, and that the relationship between nigrescence and counselor preference must be explored with more sophisticated measures.

Parham and Helms (1981) were the first to employ an in-depth measure of nigrescence in the study of counselor preference. In their study, 92 Black college students (52 females and 40 males) were administered the RIAS, a 30-item counselor preference scale, and a demographic information sheet which included a racial self designation section, (this allowed a comparison between the RIAS and self-designations as measures of identity development). The results showed that possession of racial identity attitudes as measured by the RIAS, but not self-designation, influenced counselor selection:

> "...Pre-encounter attitudes tended to be associated with pro-White, anti-Black counselor preferences; encounter and immersion-emersion attitudes were associated with pro-Black, anti-White counselor preferences. However, internalization attitudes were not strongly related to preferences for a counselor of either race. These results suggest that, as the Black person becomes more comfortable with her or his racial identity, race of the counselor per se becomes a less crucial variable, perhaps personal characteristics of the counselor such

as her or his racial attitudes and skill level, become more important" (Parham & Helms, 1981, p. 255).

In a similar study, Morten and Atkinson (1983) administered a nigrescence-like measure (Minority Identity Development Scale) along with a counselor preference questionnaire to 160 Black college students (98 males and 62 females). For their sample, students clustered into the transition and Internalization stages, but too few were found in the first stage for analysis. It was hypothesized that subjects in identity transition would show a strong same-race preference, while persons with advanced identity development would not. Statistically significant trends supported these predictions.

One study employing the RIAS did not find a relationship between nigrescence and counselor preference. Ponterotto, Anderson and Grieger (1986) administered the RIAS, a measure of one's attitudes about seeking help from mental health professionals, and a counselor preference inventory to 107 Black college students (69 female and 38 males). The students clustered into only two of the four RIAS stages. Consequently, comparisons were made only between Encounter and Internalization Stages. No significant relationship was found between either the Encounter or Internalization Stages and counselor preference. This was predicted for Internalization, since no racial preference was anticipated. However, the failure to find a link between same-race counselor preference and Encounter was surprising. In contrast, Helms and Carter (1987) recently replicated Parham and Helms' (1981) counselor preference study, except that they were interested in what combination of counselor race *and* gender Black female and male participants preferred. They found that Internalization attitudes predicted preferences for every Black/White counselor race/gender combination, except White females. The lack of a significant relationship for this group is likely due to their finding that Black males and females did not tend to share similar feelings about White female counselors. Nevertheless, in general, higher Internalization attitudes were related to stronger preferences for counselors, regardless of their race and gender combinations. Since the mean level of the Internalization attitudes of Helms and Carter's sample placed it beyond the 90th percentile, using Helms and Parham's (1996) preliminary norms, then their results possibly indicate that when Internalization attitudes are high enough (i.e., crystallized), then they encourage involvement with others, regardless of their physical characteristics.

Another recent study in this area appears to offer little evidence in support of a link between nigrescence and counselor preference; however, upon closer inspection, the method employed to operationalize Blackness was predictably unreliable and invalid. Atkinson, Furlong and Poston (1986) studied counselor preference trends in a sample of 128 Black college students using a very sensitive, multi-dimensional, counselor preference measurement scheme, and a one-item measure of identity. For the counselor preference measure, each subject completed a 120 item questionnaire in which each item involved a comparison between any two of 16 counselor preference traits: education (more/similar), attitudes and values (similar/dissimilar), personality (similar/dissimilar), ethnicity (similar/dissimilar), sex (same/opposite), socio-economic status (similar/dissimilar), age (similar/older), and religion (similar/dissimilar). To control for various order effects, the 16 characteristics were presented in computer generated booklets which incorporated a forced choice, paired comparison format. Juxtaposed to this highly creative and complex measure of one domain (counselor preference), the authors resorted to a single item "measure" of nigrescence and Black identity. Subjects were asked to indicate their commitment to Anglo-American and African-American cultures (strong for both, strong Anglo-American and weak Afro-American, weak Anglo-American and strong Afro-American, or weak for both). This type of question is not far removed from the self-designation measure of nigrescence which, in a study published seven years ago, was shown to have practically no ability to predict counselor preference in Blacks (Parham & Helms, 1981). Thus, although one can summarize from their literature review that Atkinson, et al. (1986) were attempting to extend the debate about the relationship between nigrescence and counselor preference, and though their review makes it equally clear that they were well aware of the value of using multidimensional nigrescence scales and the problems associated with simplistic measures of nigrescence, nevertheless, the single-item measure described above constituted the definition of identity development for their study.

Not surprisingly, the single item nigrescence measure showed no relationship to same-race counselor preference; however, for the sample as a whole, same-race counselor preference was clearly in evidence. When asked whether they preferred a counselor who was ethnically similar or dissimilar, 69.5% of the Black subjects made the ethnically similar choice. Thus while demonstrating in a global sense that ethnicity is a significant counselor preference factor for many Blacks but not for others, the study did not advance our knowledge about the stages of Black identity development for which a same-race counselor preference is a distinguishing characteristic.

The results of their counselor preference paired comparisons were much more productive. The resulting rank order of preferences showed same-race counselor preference ranked fifth behind the concern that the preferred counselor be: (a) more educated; (b) have similar attitudes; (c) be older; and (d) have a personality similar to that of the respondent. Atkinson et al. (1986) concluded that (1) race per se is not of concern to Afro-American college students in the selection of a counselor; and (2) in contradistinction to those who advocate that Black (college) students are better served by Black paraprofessionals than Black (or White) professionals, their results show Blacks place first priority on professionalism. Let us examine both of these conclusions beginning with the second.

It comes as a surprise to the reader to discover in the "discussion" section of their article that Atkinson et al. (1986) were not testing the hypothesis "do Blacks prefer a Black or White professional counselor," but were addressing instead the hypothesis "do Blacks prefer an untrained Black person per se over any other possible choice, including a trained Black or White professional counselor." To imply that this has been the thrust of the nigrescence and counselor preference research represents a unique reading of the literature. No where in the research by Gordon and Grantham (1979), Jackson and Kirscher (1973), Morten and Atkinson (1983) or Parham and Helms (1981) is there mention of such a hypothesis. In almost every instance researchers have taken as "a given" the issue of professionalism, and from there explored the relationship between nigrescence and counselor preference. But how do Atkinson et al. (1986) make the "link" between previous counselor preference research and the "race is everything " proposition? They do it by citing an article published in 1970 by E. J. Ward. One would think that Ward's article was a pivotal work in the counselor preference literature, but the fact of the matter is that other than Atkinson, et al. (1986), not one of the articles reviewed here even references, let alone gives credence to, the "race is everything" hypothesis. The Ward article is not even referenced by Donald Atkinson himself in his excellent review articles on cross-cultural counseling (Atkinson, 1983, 1985). We think it a disservice, whether intended or not, to link the previous counselor preference research to the simple-minded "race is everything" hypothesis. Other than a half crazed Immersion/Emersion type, no Black person with any ounce of sanity would prefer an incompetent Black counselor to a Black or White competent counselor.

Moving back to the other conclusion reached by Atkinson et al. (1986), having to do with the context of Black preferences, we want to differ somewhat with their interpretation of the findings. In the results section (p. 328), Atkinson et al, state that Black students "did not express a strong preference for an ethnically [sic] similar counselor". Yet in the discussion section, they conclude, "[It] seems obvious from these data, however, that a Black, [sic] professionally trained counselor would best meet the preferences of most Black clients." The two statements seem to be at odds. Did or did not the students prefer a counselor of similar ethnicity? In order for the "no preference" conclusion to be true, the students would have had to show no preference on comparisons between ethnicity and generic or non-race related counselor traits, as well as no preference when asked to choose between a Black and White counselor. To rank generic factors above ethnicity, and to show no racial preference, when asked directly to choose between a Black and White counselor, would mean Black students could best be serviced by *any* well trained counselor. But this is not the pattern observed. Of the 16 factors ranked, ethnicity did rank high (5th), with only four generic counselor traits ranked above ethnicity. But when asked directly to choose between a Black and White counselor, practically 70% of the Black students opted for an ethnically similar counselor. The evidence can be viewed as conflictual or the following interpretation is possible: when asked directly, the students did show a very strong same-race counselor preference, and for less direct comparisons (ethnicity vs. generic factors), the importance of similar ethnicity remained in focus (ranked 5th out of 16). The pattern of the ethnic vs. generic traits suggests that what a Black student means by ethnically similar counselor is someone who is educated, mature and shares similar attitudes and personality traits. We can think of no Pre-encounter or Internalization type who would not consider ethnicity in conjunction with certain generic factors. The Pre-encounter person who prefers White does not prefer an incompetent White. Nor does the Internalization person relish treatment by an incompetent Black person. From our vantage point, the value of the counselor preference measure incorporated in the Atkinson et al. (1986) study is that not only does it allow one to directly measure same-race counselor preference, it also reveals the generic attributes (non-race related characteristics) that Black students look for in an idealized Black counselor. As previously noted, however, the study did not clarify for which Black students the same or opposite race match is important.

A small group of studies (Bradby & Helms, 1987; Carter, 1987, Pomales, Claiborn, & LaFromboise, 1987; Richardson, 1987) have examined the effects of racial identity attitudes, as measured by some version of the RIAS, on participants' reactions to counseling stimulations or interactions. Bradby and Helms (1987) asked Black clients involved in brief therapy (maximum of 12 sessions possible) with White counselors to complete the RIAS prior to counseling and a satisfaction measure after five potential sessions. In addition, they also collected information about the total number of sessions clients desired. Their results indicated that Pre-encounter and Internalization attitudes were related to client satisfaction such that the higher these attitudes, the more satisfied they were with therapy after five sessions; Encounter attitudes were negatively related to the number of sessions desired such that the higher these attitudes, the fewer were the number of sessions desired with the White counselors.

Pomales et al. (1986) and Richardson (1987) used vicarious participation analogues to examine Black male participants' reactions to interactions involving White female and male counselors, respectively. Pomales et al. (1986), who used only participants whose highest attitudes were either Encounter or Internalization, found that White female counselors were evaluated more positively by the participants, when they did, rather than did not, discuss racial issues with the Black male client in a counseling simulation. For Internalization participants, the topic of discussion did not differentially influence their perceptions.

Richardson (1987) used all four RIAS attitudes to predict Black male college students' reactions to two White-male-counselor/Black-male-client counseling stimulations in which racial issues were discussed. She found that Encounter attitudes predicted anticipated self-disclosure to the portrayed counselors as well as more general reactions to the stimulations. The higher respondents' Encounter attitudes, the less likely they were to anticipate that they would disclose to the counselor and the more negative were their general reactions to the simulation.

In a rather complex study of "counseling-like" interviews concerning "racial problems" and involving therapists of a variety of experience levels, Carter (1987) found that interviewees' racial identity attitudes were related to their reactions to the interviewers' counseling interventions. For instance, interviewees' Pre-encounter and Immersion/Emersion attitudes were positively related to the perception that interviewers understood them; interviewees with high Encounter and Immersion/Emersion attitudes felt little relief due to the interviewers' interventions; high Encounter, Immersion/Emersion, and Internalization attitudes resulted in few negative thoughts and behaviors.

Taken together, the interaction studies seem to reveal some consistencies. For instance, Encounter attitudes appear to be significantly related to some of the participants' reactions, regardless of the methodology used. In general, the direction of the relationships suggest that when Encounter attitudes predominate, participants respond positively to counselors/interviewers, who discuss racial issues, if the manner of discussing such issues is not beyond the client/interviewee's level of development, regardless of the counselor's physical characteristics.

Summary and Recommendations

Summary

In this article we have attempted to discuss numerous models of nigrescence, highlighting those authors whose work has been the most compelling in terms of stage-related models and related measures. Works by Cross (1971); Jackson (1976); and Thomas (1971); in particular, were a major focus of attention. Studies which have sought to correlate various psychological constructs with identity development models were also reviewed.

Our repeated emphasis on "process" is not accidental, for we believe that the development of racial identity attitudes is a phenomenon which occurs over time. In attempting to isolate the correlates of nigrescence, however, our discussion does allow the reader to construct a profile of the "typical" Black person whose racial attitudes correspond to one of the four identity stages. While the typology approach we adopted was necessary to facilitate our outline and discussion of the material, it in no way was it intended to imply that we believe "typing" or classifying people by stage is the most appropriate use of the models. On the contrary, classifying according to a single stage may lead to less appropriate interpretations, because such a procedure connotes rigidity and stagnation, and clouds the potential for change and growth which more accurately characterize the nigrescence process. Indeed,

Parham and Helms (1985) and Helms (1986) have consistently argued for the treatment of racial identity attitudes as continuous rather than discrete variables.

In some respects, this review has helped the present authors to better crystallize (through mutual exchange and debate) our own attitudes on the identity change process. No doubt, our efforts have been aided by the fact that the second and third authors (Parham & Helms) have used the senior author's model (Cross) as a foundation for their writings. In other respects, this review represents a historical collaboration in that this is the first attempt to bring together different generations of nigrescence researchers in a single forum to discuss and debate issues central to identity development and identity change in Black people. It is our sincere hope that other nigrescence writers (past, present, and future) will engage in more collaborative efforts as well.

Recommendations

What is clear from this review is that nigrescence, as an area of research, has a much more substantial foundation than is generally recognized. Yet, much more research is necessary. It seems to us that future needs for research fall roughly into two categories: those studies designed to advance the theory and those designed to apply the theory. Studies which correspond to the first category are as follows:

1. In line with Helms' (1987) recommendation, construct validity studies of all existing measures are needed. Ideally, such a study would involve administering all of the attitudinal and behavioral measures discussed in this paper to a large, well-described Black sample. Scales representing similar stages of identity should correlate highly and positively with one another, whereas scales measuring different stages should not. Furthermore, such a study should include some measures of constructs not thought to be related to racial identity (e.g., reading comprehension, social class, etc.). By examining the correlations between the identity measures and the "non-related" variables, one should be able to establish the differential discriminant validity of each of the measures. The reader is referred to Campbell and Fiske (1959), for further guidance as to how such a study might be conducted.

2. In addition to the construct validity studies using *established measures* related and unrelated to racial identity, more work needs to be done on exploring different theoretical constructs and their relationship to nigrescence theory. For example, the significance of the construct of African self-consciousness in understanding Black personality has been the focus of recent research efforts (Akbar, 1981; Azibo, 1983). As a natural consequence, the question of racial identity attitudes and operational definitions of mental health, which emerge from an African psychological context, must also be addressed. Similarly, instruments designed to measure newly created constructs must be developed (e.g. Baldwin,

1984), and ultimately validated against other existing measures which have their basis in nigrescence theory (e.g. Parham & Helms, 1981).

3. Since the theories propose a change in identity over time, longitudinal studies of identity development are sorely needed, as are cross-sectional studies in which age of respondents is "manipulated." Undoubtedly, the initiative, innovation, and effort required to produce such research will be enormous. However, collaborative research efforts (similar to the one used by the present authors) in which individuals engaged in identity research, with different populations (childhood, adolescents, young adults, older adults), would pool their collective talents, energies, and perspectives might be a way to accomplish such a task. In some sense, any study of these types over any period of time would be useful because it would provide empirical information about the stability and/or the direction of progression of the identity stages. Even so, many interesting designs from developmental psychology could be readily adapted to study theoretical questions which have not been empirically addressed so far. Wohlwill (1970), for instance, described a cohort-longitudinal design in which groups of cohorts or age-mates are sampled over several occasions. An advantage of use of this type of design in identity research is that by comparing identities within as well as across cohorts, the effects of common historical experiences on identity development could be separated from other time-linked influences. Similarly, N of 1 case studies which document changes in personal identity (PI) and reference group orientation (RGO) over time might yield some interesting data as well.

4. Although there have been several fairly recent attempts to discuss generic lifespan issues as they relate to Blacks (Gooden, 1989), apparently no one has explored, either through case studies or objective methods, the interface of nigrescence and lifespan development. In Parham's (1987) article on the relationship between nigrescence theory and adult development stages, we now have a potential framework from which research can be conceptualized. What is urgently needed is for such research to commence.

In the category of applications, the kinds of research questions still in need of answers are numerous. Some questions pertaining to the counseling process are as follows:

1. In the area of assessment and diagnosis, researchers have only touched the surface. Various measures of personality (e.g., Tennessee Self-Concept Scale) and psychopathology (e.g., MMPI) are frequently used to assess and/or describe the mental health status of Black people. In the current review we have argued that such measures explore the mental health or personal identity (PI) dimension of Black personality, while the RIAS or DIBC tap the RGO factor. Furthermore, we attempted to show that the relationship between racial identity (RGO) and personal identity (PI) is much more complicated than had originally been articulated in nigrescence theory. In particular we attempted to show that the self-hatred syndrome tied to Pre-encounter fails to explain the behavior of other Pre-encounter

types who do not experience self-hatred. Much of our analysis was ad-hoc and speculative in nature. Thus, research is now needed which explores PI and RGO trends within and across the stages. Such research should bring us closer to a more substantive understanding of the relationship between mental health and racial identity development.

2. With regard to the counseling and psychotherapy process, previous studies of how these interventions affect and/or are affected by racial identity have been sporadic and often are unrelated to theory. Here are some basic client-focused questions which could be addressed within he context of mental health agencies: (a) How are the stages of identity differentially related to clients' premature attrition? (b) What types of identities characterize individuals who seek services from the various kinds of mental facilities (e.g., outpatient vs inpatient facilities)? (c) How does identity following therapy compare to identity prior to therapy? (d) Which diagnoses or symptoms are characterized by which stages of identity? (e) How is client behavior during therapy related to racial identity? One could examine issues related to the therapist/interveners' quality of functioning. Some such questions might include: (a) How are therapists orientations related to their racial identity? (b) How is therapists' racial identity differentially related to their success (e.g., attrition, symptom elimination) with Black versus White clients? (c) How is what the therapist does during therapy related to his/her racial identity (cf., Carter, 1987)? Any of these questions could be addressed via relatively simple naturalistic designs in which identity measures are correlated with scales or behaviors representing the other constructs.

Finally, this manuscript can serve as a compendium of sorts. It catalogs and inventories the various models of nigrescence, the instruments designed to measure the nigrescence construct, the research which has been stimulated by the models, and offers suggestions for future research directions. Understandably, this review was unable to include those studies which are currently in progress. If, as we expect, the number of published articles on nigrescence theory and applications increases, then undoubtedly, another "Nigrescence Revisited" update will be necessary in five years.

References

Akbar, N. (1981). Mental disorders among African-Americans. *Black Books Bulletin, 7(2)*, 18-25.

Atkinson, D. R. (1985). A meta-review of research on cross-cultural counseling and psychotherapy. *Journal of Multicultural Counseling and Development, 13(4)*, 138-153.

Atkinson, D. R. (1983). Ethnic similarity in counseling: A review of research. *The Counseling Psychologist, 11(3)*, 79-92.

Atkinson, D. R., Furlong, M. J., & Poston, W. C. (1986). Afro-American preferences for counselor characteristics. *Journal of Counseling Psychology, 33(3)*, 326-330.

Azibo, D. (1983). Perceived attractiveness and the Black personality. *Western Journal of Black Studies, 7(4)*, 229-238.

Baldwin, J. A. (1984). African self-sonciousness and the mental health of African Americans. *Journal of Black Studies, 5(3)*, 172-179.

Barnes, E. J. (1980). The Black community as the source of positive self-concept for Black children: A theoretical perspective. In R. Jones (Ed.), *Black Psychology* (2nd ed., pp. 106-130). New York: Harper & Row.

Boykin, A. W. (1981, April). *Research directions of Black psychologists.* Paper presented at the University of Maryland, College Park, MD.

Bradby, D., & Helms, J. E. (in press). Black racial identity attitudes in cross-racial therapy dyads. In J. E. Helms (Ed.), *Black and White racial identity: Theory, research, and practice.* Greenwood Press.

Brown, A. (1976). *Personality correlates of the developmental inventory of Black consciousness.* Unpublished master's thesis, University of Pittsburgh, PA.

Brown, A. (1979). *Black consciousness prototypes: A profile analysis of the developmental stages of Black consciousness.* Unpublished doctoral dissertation, University of Pittsburgh, PA.

Butler, R. O. (1975). Psychotherapy: implications of a Black-consciousness process model. *Psychotherapy: Theory, research and practice, 12*, 407-411.

Campbell, D. T., & Fiske, D. W. (1959). Convergent and discriminant validity by the multitrait-multimethod matrix. *Psychological Bulletin, 56*, 81-105.

Caplan, N. (1970). The new ghetto man: A review of recent empirical studies. *Journal of Social Issues, 26*, 57-73.

Carter, A. L. (1974). *An analysis of the use of contemporary Black literature and music and its effects upon self-concept in group counseling procedures.* Unpublished doctoral dissertation, Purdue University, West Lafayette, IN.

Carter, R. T. (1987). *An empirical test of a theory on the influence of racial identity attitudes on the counseling process within a workshop setting.* Unpublished doctoral dissertation, University of Maryland, College Park, MD.

Carter, R. T., & Helms, J. E. (1984, August). *The relationship between racial identity attitudes and socioeconomic status.* Paper presented at the American Psychological Association Convention. Toronto, Canada.

Carter, R. T., & Helms, J. E. (1987). The relationship of Black value-orientations to racial attitudes. *Measurement and Evaluation in Counseling and Development, 17*, 185-195.

Clark, C. C. (1971). General systems theory and Black studies: Some points of convergence. In C.W. Thomas (Ed.), *Boys no more* (pp. 28-47). Beverly Hills: Glencoe Press.

Clark, K. (1955). *Prejudice and your children.* Boston: Beacon Press.

Cole, B. P. (1978). *Race and self-esteem: A comparative study of Black and White adults.* Unpublished doctoral dissertation, University of California, Los Angeles.

Crawford, T. J., & Naditch, M. (1970). Relative deprivation, powerlessness and militancy. *Journal of Psychiatry, 33(2),* 208-223.

Cross, W. E., Jr. (1971). Negro-to-Black conversion experience. *Black World, 20,* 13-26.

Cross, W. E., Jr. (1976). *Stereotypic and non-stereotypic images associated with the Negro-to-Black conversion experience: An empirical analysis.* Unpublished doctoral dissertation, Princeton University, Princeton, NJ.

Cross, W. E., Jr. (1978). The Thomas and Cross models of psychological nigrescence: A review. *Journal of Black Psychology, 5(1),* 13-31.

Cross, W. E., Jr. (1979). The Negro-to-Black conversion experience: An empirical analysis. In A. W. Boykin, A. J. Anderson, & J. F. Yates (Eds.), *Research Directions of Black Psychologists* (pp.107-125). New York: Russell Sage.

Cross, W. E., Jr. (1981). Black families and Black identity development: Rediscovering the distinction between self-esteem and reference group orientation. *Journal of Comparative Family Studies, 12(1),* i-ii & 19-49.

Cross, W. E., Jr. (1986). Black identity: Rediscovering the distinction between personal identity and reference group orientation. In M. Spencer, G. Brookins, & W. Allen (Eds.), *Beginnings: The social and affective development of Black children* (pp.155-171). Hillside: Erlbaum.

Cross, W. E., Jr. (1987). Two factor theory of Black identity: Implications for the study of identity development in minority children. In J. S. Phinney & M. J. Rotheram (Eds.), *Children's ethnic socialization* (117-133). Newbury Park, CA.: Sage.

Cross, W. E., Jr. (1991). *Shades of Black: Diversity in African American identity.* Temple University Press.

Davidson, J. P. (1974). *Empirical development of a measure of Black student identity.* Unpublished doctoral dissertation, University of Maryland, College Park, MD.

Denton, S. E. (1985). *A methodological refinement and validation analysis of the developmental inventory of Black consciousness.* Unpublished doctoral dissertation, University of Pittsburgh, PA.

Downton, J. V. (1973). *Rebel leadership: Commitment and charisma in the revolutionary process.* New York: The Free Press.

Dubois, W. E. B. (1903). *Souls of Black folk.* Chicago: A. C. McClurg.

Enty, J. E. (1979). *Clothing symbolism: A study of Afro fashions and their relation to Black identity and self-concepts of Black university students.* Unpublished doctoral dissertation, Penn State University, University Park, PA.

Erikson, E. (1950). *Childhood and society.* New York: Norton.

Gerlach, L. P., & Hine, V. H. (1970). *People power and change: Movements of social transformation*. New York: Bobbs-Merrill.

Glasgow, D. (1980). *The Black underclass*. New York: Jossey-Bass.

Gooden, W. E. Development of Black men in early adulthood. In R.L. Jones (Ed.), *Black adult development and aging* (pp. 63-89). Berkeley, CA: Cobb & Henry Publishers.

Gordon, M., & Grantham, R. J. (1979). Helper preference in disadvantaged students. *Journal of Counseling Psychology, 26(4),* 337-343.

Gordon, V. V. (1980). *The self-concept of Black Americans*. Lanham: University Press of America.

Grace, C. A. (1984). *The relationship between racial identity attitudes and choice of typical and atypical occupations among Black college students.* Doctoral dissertation, Columbia Teachers College, New York.

Griffin, J. D. (1975). *The design, implementation, and evaluation of a group experience for increasing Black consciousness of Afro-Americans.* Unpublished doctoral dissertation, University of Pittsburgh, PA.

Hall, W. S., Cross, W. E., Jr., & Freedle, R. (1972). *Stages in the development of Black awareness: An exploratory investigation.* In R. L. Jones (Ed.), *Black psychology* (1st ed., pp.156-165). New York: Harper & Row.

Hall, W. S., Freedle, R., & Cross, W. E., Jr. (1972). *Stages in the development of a Black identity.* (ACT research report No. 50). Iowa City: The American Testing Program, Research and Development Division.

Harren, V. A. (1979). A model of career decision-making for college students. *Journal of Vocational Behavior, 14,* 113-119.

Harrison, A. M. (1974). *Construction of a contemporary Cross identity scale.* Unpublished master's thesis, Livingston College, Rutgers University, New Brunswick, NJ.

Hatchett, S. J. (1976). *Black racial attitude change in Detroit, 1968-1976.* Unpublished doctoral dissertation, University of Michigan, Ann Arbor.

Helms, J. E. (1984). Toward a theoretical explanation of the effects of race on counseling: A Black and White model. *The Counseling Psychologist, 12(4),* 153-165.

Helms, J. E. (1986a). Expanding racial identity theory to cover counseling process. *Journal of Counseling Psychology, 33(1),* 62-64.

Helms, J. E. (1986b, November). *Black psychology: Stages of nigrescence.* Paper presented at the University of Pennsylvania Conference on Leadership, Afro-American Studies Department, Philadelphia, PA.

Helms, J. E. (1990).The measurement of Black racial identity. In J. E. Helms (Ed.), *Black and White racial identity: Theory, research, and practice.* Greenwood Press.

Helms, J. E. (1987). *Considering some methodological issues in racial identity research* . Manuscript submitted for publication.

Helms, J. E., & Carter, R. T. (1987). *Effects of racial identity attitudes and demographic similarity on counselor preferences.* Manuscript submitted for publication.

Helms, J. E., & Parham, T. A. (1996). The racial identity attitude scale (RIAS). In R. L. Jones (Ed.), *Handbook of Black tests and measurements for Black Populations, (Vol. 2).* New York: Harper & Row.

Helms, J. E., & Parham, T. A. (1990). The relationship between Black racial identity attitudes and cognitive styles. In J. E. Helms (Ed.), *Black and White racial identity: Theory, research and practice.* Greenwood Press.

Jackson, B. W. (1976a). *The functions of Black identity development theory in achieving relevance in education.* Unpublished doctoral dissertation, University of Massachusetts.

Jackson, B. W. (1976b). Black identity development. In L. Golubschick & B. Persky (Eds.), *Urban Social and Educational Issues* (pp. 158-164). Dubuque: Kendall-Hall.

Jackson, G. G. (1977). The emergence of a Black perspective in counseling. *Journal of Negro Education, 46 (Summer),* 230-253.

Jackson, G. G., & Kirschner, S. A. (1973). Racial self-designation and preference for a counselor. *Journal of Counseling Psychology, 20(6),* 560-564.

Jefferson, F. C. (1981). *A learning procedure that increases self-esteem and Black identity development in Black college students.* Unpublished doctoral dissertation, University of Massachusetts at Amherst.

Kelman, H. C. (1970). A socio-psychological model of political legitimacy and its relevance to Black and White student protest movements. *Psychiatry, 33 (2),* 224-246.

Kirschner, S., & Jackson, G. G. (1972). *Race and preference for counselor.* Unpublished manuscript, Essex County College, Baltimore, MD.

Kluckhohn, F. R., & Strodtbeck, F. L. (1961). *Variations in value orientations.* Evanston: Row, Peterson.

Krate, R. Leventhal, G., & Silverstein, B. (1974). Self-perceived transformation of Negro-to-Black identity. *Psychological Reports, 35,* 1071-1075.

Lewin, K. (1948). Self-hatred in Jews. In K. Lewin (Ed.), *Resolving social conflicts.* New York: Harper & Row.

Lewis, O. (1966). *La Vida.* New York: Random House.

Livingston, L. B. (1971). *Self-concept change of Black college males as a result of a weekend Black experience encounter workshop.* Unpublished doctoral dissertation, Arizona State University, Tempe.

Looney, J. (1984). *The relationship of ego development and identity formation in Black males and females.* Unpublished doctoral dissertation, Vanderbilt University, Nashville, TN.

Lunceford, R. D. (1973). *Self-concept change of Black college females as a result of a weekend Black experience encounter workshop.* Unpublished doctoral dissertation, United States International University, San Diego, CA.

Maish, K. (1978). *Black political orientation, political activism and positive mental health.* Unpublished doctoral dissertation, University of Maryland at College Park, MD.

McAdoo, H. P. (1970). *An exploratory study of racial attitude change in Black pre-school children.* Unpublished doctoral dissertation, University of Michigan, Ann Arbor, MI.

McCaine, J. (1986). *The relationship of conceptual systems to racial and gender identity and the impact of reference group identity development on interpersonal styles of behavior and level of anxiety.* Unpublished doctoral dissertation, University of Maryland, College Park, MD.

McCord, W., Howard, J., Friedberg, B., & Harwood, E. (1969). *Life styles in the Black ghetto.* New York: W. W. Norton.

Milliones, J. (1973). *Construction of the developmental inventory of Black consciousness.* Unpublished doctoral dissertation, University of Pittsburgh, PA.

Milliones, J. (1980). Construction of a Black consciousness measure: Psychotherapeutic implications. *Psychotherapy: Theory, Research, and Practice, 17(2)* 175-182.

Morten, G. H. (1984). Racial self-labeling and preference for counselor race. *Journal of Non-White Concerns, 12,* 105-109.

Morten, G., & Atkinson, D. R. (1983). Minority identity development and preference for counselor race. *Journal of Negro Education, 52(2)* 156-161.

Napper, G. (1973). *Blacker than thou.* Michigan: W. B. Eerdmans.

Nobles, W. W. (1972). African philosophy: foundations for Black psychology. In R. L. Jones (Ed.), *Black psychology* (1st ed., pp.18-32). New York: Harper & Row.

Onwuachi, P. C. (1967). Identity and Black power: an African viewpoint. *Negro Digest,* (March), 31-37.

Parham, T. A. (1992). Cycles of psychological nigrescence. *The Counseling Psychologist, 17(2),* 187-226.

Parham, T. A., & Helms, J. E. (1981). The influence of Black students' racial identity attitudes on preferences for counselor's race. *Journal of Counseling Psychology, 28(3),* 250-257.

Parham, T. A., & Helms, J. E. (1985). Relation of racial identity attitudes to self-actualization and affective states of Black students. *Journal of Counseling Psychology, 32(2),* 431-440.

Parham, T. A., & Helms, J. E. (1985a). Attitudes of racial identity and self-esteem: an exploratory investigation. *Journal of College Student Personnel, 26,* 143-146.

Pinderhughes, C. A. (1968). The psychodynamics of dissent. In J. H. Masserman (Ed.), *The dynamics of dissent* (pp. 56-79). New York: Grune and Stranon.

Pomales, J., Claiborn, C.D., & LaFromboise, T.D. (1986). Effects of Black students' racial identity on perceptions of White counselors varying in cultural sensitivity. *Journal of Counseling Psychology, 33,* 57-61.

Ponterotto, J. G., Anderson, W. H., Jr., & Grieger, I. Z. (1986). Black student attitudes toward counseling as a function of racial identity. *Journal of Multicultural Counseling and Development, 14(2),* 50-59.

Ponterotto, J. G., & Wise, S. L. (1992). A construct validity study of the racial identity attitude scale. Journal of Counseling Psychology, 34*(2)*, 218-223.

Porter, J. D. R. (1971). *Black children and self-esteem: The development of racial attitudes.* Cambridge: Harvard University.

Richardson, T. (1987). *The relationship of racial identity attitudes to Black males' perceptions of counseling dyads.* Unpublished masters thesis, University of Maryland, College Park.

Sherif, M., & Sherif, C. (1970). Black unrest as a social movement toward an emerging self-identity. *Journal of Social and Behavioral Sciences, 15(3),* 41-52.

Spencer, M. (1984). Black children's race awareness, racial attitudes and self-concept: A reinterpretation. *Journal of Child Psychology and Psychiatry, 25,* 433-441.

Storm, P. (1970). *An investigation of self-concept, race image, and race preference in racial minority and majority children.* Unpublished doctoral dissertation, University of Maryland, College Park.

Sue, D. W. (1978). Worldviews and counseling. *Personnel and Guidance Journal, 56,* 458-462.

Suggs, R. C. (1975). An identity group experience: Changing priorities. *Journal of Non-White Concerns in Personnel and Guidance, 3(2),* 75-81.

Suggs, R. H. (1979). *The effects of an identity group experience on Black college students.* Unpublished doctoral dissertation, State University of New York at Albany.

Taylor, J. (1976). *Affiliation Inventory.* Pittsburgh, PA: Institute for the Black Family, University of Pittsburgh.

Taylor, J. (1976a). The Pittsburgh project - part one: Toward community growth and survival. In W. E. Cross, Jr., (Ed.), *The Third Conference on Empirical Research in Black Psychology.* Washington, D.C.: National Institute of Education, 34-46.

Taylor, J. (1986, June). *Cultural conversion experiences: Implications for mental health research and treatment.* Paper presented at Menninger Foundation for the 40th Anniversary of the Menninger School of Psychiatry, Topeka, KS.

Taylor, J., Wilson, M., & Dobbins, J. E. (1972). *Nadanolitization scale.* Pittsburgh, PA: University of Pittsburgh.

Terrell, F., Taylor, J., & Terrell, S. (1980). Self-concept of juveniles who commit Black-on-Black crimes. *Corrective and Social Psychiatry, 26,* 107-109.

Thomas, C. W. (1971). *Boys no more.* Beverly Hills: Glencoe Press.

Tinsley, H. E. A., & Tinsley, D. J. (1987). Uses of factor analysis in counseling psychology research. *Journal of Counseling Psychology, 34,* 414-424.

Toldson, I., & Pasteur, A. (1975). Developmental stages of Black self-discovery: implications for using Black art forms in group interaction. *Journal of Negro Education, 44,* 130-138.

Vontress, C. E. (1971). Racial differences: impediments to rapport. *Journal of Counseling Psychology, 18,* 7-13.

Ward, E.J. (1970). A gift from the ghetto. *Personnel & Guidance Journal, 48,* 753-756.

Weston, R. (1977). *Level of Black awareness, race of experimenter, race of model, and modeling task as factors in vicarious learning.* Unpublished doctoral dissertation, Rutgers University.

Weston, R. (1975). *Commitment and awareness.* Unpublished master's thesis, Rutgers University.

Williams, I. J. (1975). *An investigation of the developmental stages of Black consciousness.* Unpublished doctoral dissertation, University of Cincinnati.

Wilson, W. J. (1978). *The declining significance of race.* Chicago: University of Chicago.

Wohlwill, J.F. (1970). Methodology and research strategy in the study of developmental change. In L. R. Goulet & P. B. Baltes (Eds.), *Life-span developmental psychology* (pp. 150-191), New York: Academic Press.

Wortham, A. (1981). *The other side of racism: A philosophical study of Black race consciousness.* Ohio: Ohio State University Press.

Author

William E. Cross, Jr. Professor
Chair, Dept. of Student Development
and Pupil Personnel Services
(SDPPS)
School of Education
University of Massachusetts
366 Hills South
Amherst, MA 01003-4160
Telephone: (413) 545-0543
Fax (413) 545-1523

Continuity in the Identity Development Process for African Americans and Africans Throughout the Diaspora

Tina Richardson

As an African American and a Psychologist, I have spent much of my life and my career working to understanding the identity development process for African Americans. During my training to become a counseling psychologist, I became involved in research that addressed the racial identity development process for African American people. This research has involved integrating the psychological literature with real life experiences of my own, my friends, my clients and my students who were identified as being at various stages in the process of developing a healthy African American identity. This is no small task in a race-conscious society which places White people of European descent as the 'idealized' norm and Eurocentric values as the worldview system from which the dominant political group governs the masses.

I discuss two issues in this paper: (1) issues of continuity and differences in the identity development process due to context (geographic) and (2) the appropriateness of using racial and/or Black consciousness models to describe the identity formation of African people in the diaspora. The author's teaching, research, and ethnographic experiences in the United States and Ghana will provide the basis for the paper.

Origins of Parallel Process

One very important concept is at the core of any discussion of identity development for people of African descent. The concept is colonialism, the process by which European countries invaded foreign territories in order to expand their social, political and economic control world wide. The Congress of Berlin in 1885 subdivided Africa among various European countries including Great Britain, France, Portugal, Holland, Belgium, et al. This system of domination by its very nature was designed to rob the African continent of its natural resources (i.e., its people, language, land, and the associated values) and thereby destroy the tribal identities of African people. For European (White) people, the privileges associated with this system of oppression were obviously economic in nature, but equally salient was the privilege which solidified a dominant identity status for Whites as well. Consequently, colonialism intended to establish a subjugated identity status for Africans. Tribal traditions and identities were dislodged and replaced through the use of military presence, human anihalation, imposed values, European education systems (i.e., a miseducation process) (Woodson, 1933), and Christian religions (Delavignette, 1964, p. 53) and replaced with national or racial identities which served the European agenda. Few if any aspects of the lives of colonized people went untouched by colonialism (Memmi, 1965). To date, for the masses of Africans on the continent and throughout the diaspora, many Africans continue to see themselves and identify their place in society through the lens of colonialism.

The thesis of this chapter is that the net effect of colonialism on African people has resulted in an identity dilemma which has striking parallels for all people of African origins. I do not argue that Africans are a monolithic group nor that colonialism on the African continent is identical to the type of domination that took place on the American continents. What I do suggest is that colonialism as applied to Africans transplanted to the Americas is a continuation of the colonialism that was initially applied to Africans in their homelands. Therefore, parallels may exist with respect to the identity development process for most if not all African descendants who were victim to this oppression. It is not my intention to discuss whose victimization (diasporic Africans or continental Africans) was more horrific for that would be a wasted endeavor based on the Eurocentric axiomatic assumptions of dichotomous or oppositional identities without respect for the collect experience of African peoples. What I argue is that the shared experience of being violently raped of ones' land, language, people, values, history, etc., has resulted in parallel processes of overidentifying with the colonizer and trying to reconnect and/ or maintain connections with the essence of one's African origins. For the vast majority of diasporic Africans, the challenges one faces in attempting to remain connected may seem insurmountable at times, but as one comes to understand the nature of life from an African philosophical perspective the continuity is illuminating.

Colonialism in the United States is more commonly discussed in terms of slavery and labeled in terms of racism. In 1860, three years before President Lincoln signed the emancipation proclamation, the population of African people enslaved in the United States numbered 4 million. Comparatively, this was a small proportion of the total number of Africans who were enslaved, because approximately 95% of Africans who survived the Atlantic passage went to the Caribbean and Latin America (Palmer, 1992). The institution of racism was a means by which much of the social, political, and economic separation of races which was established in slavery could be maintained post—emancipation. One of the more comprehensive definitions of racism was provide by Jones (1981) in that he addresses three levels on which racism can occur: individual, cultural, and institutional. Thus racism is the transformation of race prejudice and/or ethnocentrism through the exercise of power against a racial group defined as inferior, by individuals and institutions with the intentional or unintentional support of the entire culture. At the core of the concept of racism is the characteristic of systematic unequal outcomes for different races based on a superiority-inferiority paradigm.

What is important to note is that both slavery and racism are direct outgrowths of colonialism that was initially forced on Africans. It is because of colonialism in Africa that scholars report that countless millions died on the African coast waiting shipment or perished during the Atlantic passage. An estimated 10-12 million Africans were shipped off to the Americas where they were enslaved (Palmer, 1992). For Africans who were continentally transplanted, the process of destroying the groups' tribal identities was an 'easier' and more thorough task. That is, when African people were removed from their land, origins and resources, survival was fundamentally of a dependent nature. The institution of slavery led to and legitimized a dichotomous system of superiority and inferiority based on race.

Race classifications became increasingly relevant for Africans in the new world because status and access to resources were based on physiognomy (skin color, hair texture, and facial features). Slavery and its associated physical and psychological abuse was a comprehensive method of erasing an African consciousness and replacing it with a racial consciousness—deracination. In fact, the internalization of an identity based on race (e.g., Negro, Colored, Black) symbolizes the epitome of the totality of the deracination process, at least on the surface.

In an attempt to highlight aspects of the process of identity development for Black people, African American psychologists proposed models of Nigrescence or Racial Identity Development (NRID) (Cross, 1971; Helms, 1984, 1990) and Black consciousness (Baldwin, 1976, 1980, 1984, 1987; Kambon, 1992). These two major theoretical approaches attempted to define the direction of healthy Black identity development and proposed that overidentification with White culture is psychologically unhealthy. While these models were initially developed in order to address the deracination process for African Americans, there is compelling evidence that Africans who have experienced colonization on the African continent can also relate to aspects of both conceptual identity frameworks.

Racial Consciousness

The NRID models are stage models in which theorists proposed that individuals could potentially move from least healthy, White-defined stages of identity, to most healthy, self-defined racial transcendence. Nigrescence refers to the psychology of becoming Black (Cross, 1995). Although there is variability in labeling the stages, the content of the models are relatively consistent. For example, Thomas (1971) proposed a five stage process by which Blacks shed a devalued self-worth and dependence on White society for self-definition. Thus, the first stage in this model, Withdrawal, is manifested when one takes the first steps away from White definition toward a new Black identity. The next stage, Testifying, is characterized by confronting the anxiety about becoming a self-defined African American person. The Information Processing stage refers to the process of acquiring knowledge about Black heritage and the Black experience. The fourth stage, Activity, is characterized by involvement in a host of endeavors to find communion within the Black experience. The final stage, Transcendental, is characterized by individuals being relatively free of conflict regarding issues of race, age, sex, and social class.

One of the nigrescence models that has received a great deal of attention in the literature was developed by Cross (1971). He proposed a stage model wherein each stage was characterized by self-concept issues which had implication for a person's feelings, thoughts, and behaviors. The first stage, Pre-Encounter, is characterized by the belief that Blacks are basically inferior and need to internalize Eurocentric values, definitions and concepts. The next stage, Encounter, is marked by a shift from the anti-Black sentiments of the first stage toward a posture that is pro-Black. This shift is believed to be brought about as a result of some type of external event which challenges the Eurocentric perspective previously expressed. Immersion, the third stage, reflects an all consuming engagement in the Black experience with a corresponding denigration of Whiteness and Eurocentricity. Individuals in this stage generally involve themselves in activities or organizations which endeavor to improve the present conditions of African American people. The next stage, Internalization, characterizes individuals who have achieved a positive and person- ally relevant identity. The last stage in Cross' (1971) model was Internalization/ Commitment. This stage reflected a behavioral style that was grounded in social activism which sought to challenge and eliminate systems of oppression.

Several significant innovations have occurred in the evolution of NRID perspectives. Helms (1986, 1990) amended Cross' model in several respects. First, she suggests that each stage be considered a distinct 'worldview' or cognitive template that people use to organize information (particularly racial) about them- selves, other people, and institutions. Second, she suggests that it might be useful to think of each of the stages as bimodal, that is, as having two potentially distinguishable forms of expression (see Helms, 1990 for detailed description). In addition, subsequent theorists have combined the Internalization and Internaliza- tion/Commitment phases of Cross' model thereby creating a four stage model of racial identity (Helm, 1989, 1990). (A comprehensive review of stage models is presented by Cross, Parham and Helms in Chapter 1 of the present volume.)

Issues of Parallel Process

Many of my experiences traveling in Ghana have helped me to recognize aspects of the continuity in the identity process. However, it is necessary to reiterate that continuity does not mean identical experience. In many respects, I naively expected to discover profound differences without supportive evidence of parallel experience.

Many of the parallels I will discuss became crystallized as I traveled between the urban cities and traditional villages. However, it was not until I gave a lecture in the Department of Psychology at the University of Ghana, Legon that a profoundly meaningful dialogue took place regarding identity issues for African Americans and Ghanians. The lecture I gave was entitled 'The Search For An African Identity For Black Americans.' In the lecture, the concepts of deracination and nigrescence as a function of colonialism were presented. This was followed by an overview of Cross' (Helms, 1971, 1985, 1990, 1991) NRID model. The questions that followed the lecture proved very interesting in that students were able to inquire about African Americans in ways they had not been able to in the past.

One of the first questions posed was an inquiry regarding why it seems that so many African Americans continue to denigrate Africans—in particular, those who come to the United States for further study. They raise an issue of how inhospitable African Americans are to their African brothers and sisters who travel to America. Students acknowledge their disappointment and anger with African Americans who look like them but do not acknowledge that we are the same people. From the lecture we were able to begin to address each of these issues in some relevant detail.

After we had developed a significant level of comfort and trust, students began to share issues of parallel experience with respect to the model regarding their own lives. Several issues I had observed independently became more clearly expressed from the students. Deracination, according to the students, was relevant for them as well. While race was not the system of categorization, national identity (British) was sometime preferred to tribal identity. Christianity replaced indigenous religions and access to education for many of the students and/or their parents was directly related to their Christian faith. Living in urban cities versus their hometowns (i.e., villages) further removed them from some of the traditional values which was the source of some intergenerational conflict. Students could identify with the Pre-Encounter stage as they discussed various ways in which denigration of Africaness was present within themselves and the people they knew. For example, students were able to discuss the reality that for more than a hundred years Ghanians have been pressing and chemically processing their hair and bleaching their skin, all in an endeavor to look like the master (i.e., colonizer)(Morrow, 1973). One student even discussed a current media issue with respect to skin color. Several stories in local newspaper criticized President Rawling's leadership; derogatory references were made to his light complexion, and him being a half-breed.

They talked about past and present ways they were losing their traditions and gradually becoming more Westernized. Although Ghana has been an independent country since 1957 (Woronoff, 1972), the formal education system continued to be structured after the British colonizer and failed to educate them about their own history. One of the students even commented on how it is a status symbol to wear western attire versus Ghanian textiles. They likened their struggle between Western and African ideology to aspects of the Encounter stage. Comparisons were drawn between elders who were entrenched in traditional ways to the Immersion-Emersion stage. And lastly, their desire to integrate and balance their respect for Western technology and values without having to give up their traditions was likened to the goals of the Internalization stage. We discussed the value of defining one's identity on one's own terms—African terms.

As they shared their experiences, it became increasingly clear that what was being shared was a continuation of their own story. They expressed what the British, Dutch, and Portuguese had done to colonize them and the lecture outlined what the British, Dutch, and Portuguese, etc., had done to colonize Africans in the Americas. The Ghanian and American experiences shared were not identical experiences, but were intimately parallel. Some of the drastic differences related to the impact of being transplanted Africans versus being continent-based Africans. The Ghanians in the lecture still have direct access to their tribal origins, whereas African Americans usually do not. Nevertheless, the parallel experiences solidified the reality that we are all of the same people and connections between us are historically and spiritually strong.

Black Consciousness Models

Although my lecture did not discuss Black consciousness models, this perspective on identity development has a great deal to offer any attempt to understand issues of continuity for Africans throughout the diaspora. As one alternative to the NRID models, it describes the Black personality in radically different terms. Baldwin's (Baldwin, 1976, 1980, 1984, 1987; Kambon, 1992) model proposes that the Black personality comprises a complex biopsychical structure consisting of two core components: the African self-extension orientation and African self-consciousness. The African self-extension orientation represents the fundamental organizing principle of the Black personality system. It is a deep-seated, innate, and unconscious process that is operationally defined by the concept of spirituality. Spirituality provides the interconnecting energy which allows the self to extend into the total communal phenomenal experience. This spirituality, or Africanity is the key ingredient that allows for "self-extension" to occur in the African American psychological experience. This component gives coherence, continuity, and

Africanity to the basic behaviors and psychological functioning of African American people.

The second major component of the African personality system is African self-consciousness which refers to the conscious level expression of the African self-extension orientation, and it represents the conscious collective survival thrust of African people (Baldwin, Brown, & Rackley, 1990). According to Baldwin (1984), under natural conditions, these two components of the Black personality operate as one unified or undifferentiated process. Baldwin proposes that African self-consciousness plays a vital role in defining the normal psychological function of the Black personality.

The four basic characteristics or indices of African self-consciousness are as follows: (1) The person possesses an awareness of his/her African identity and cultural heritage, and sees value in the pursuit of self-knowledge; (2) The person recognizes African survival priorities and the true necessity for Africentric institutions to affirm Black life; (3) The person actively participates in the survival, liberation, and proactive development of African people, and defends their dignity, worth, and integrity; (4) The person recognizes the opposition and detrimental nature of racial oppression to Black survival and actively resists it. Thus, when these basic indices of African self-consciousness are fully operational in the functioning of the Black personality, they generate self-affirming behaviors among African people (Baldwin, Brown, & Rackley, 1990).

Parallel Process

It is difficult to elaborate on whether Ghanians resonate to the concepts of African self-extension orientation and African self-consciousness. However, the terms do have face validity in the discussion of parallel identity issues due to the impact of colonialism and the deracination process. In many respects the identity process for Africans, regardless of their geographic context, can be discussed in terms of the basic indices.

With respect to an awareness of African heritage and culture, unlike many African Americans, Ghanians have a strong sense of African identity and cultural heritage and self knowledge evolves out of this awareness. Their familial, tribal and traditional foundation has remained sufficiently stable to withstand the attacks of colonialism. Nevertheless, as indicated by the comments of students at the University of Ghana, European influence has resulted in identity conflicts for many if not all Ghanians who came in contact with it or were educated in British and/or Christian institutions. Particularly, the presence of European based Christian religions have played a most salient role in enticing Africans away from their traditional spiritual existence. In addition, exposure to and a desire for Western technology has also been successful in challenging peoples' desire to remain

African centered. Likewise, Christianity and technology also played a significant role in the identity struggles for African Americans as well.

Kambon's (1992) second index, African survival priorities and the true necessity for Africentric institutions, is also relevant in the discussion of parallel identity struggles. In 1992, the Secretary of Education, Esi Sutherland, was leading a revolutionary effort to revise the educational curriculum in primary and secondary school. At the core of this reform was the reality that British history, literature, and language continued to be the primary content in the curriculum while the Ghanian content was missing. Ultimately, educational reform meant throwing out the British texts and replacing them with content, pictures and texts that were more affirming of Ghanians. This is not unlike the call for multicultural curriculum and the necessity of Afrocentric schools in the United States. It seems that in both Ghanians and African Americans are actively working to liberate and proactively develop African people who possess dignity, self-worth, and integrity (index 3). The psychology students did an excellent job of recognizing the detrimental nature of oppression (i.e., colonialism and racism) as it was imposed on African people (index 4). Their desire to resist it was also imbedded in the discussion, but one of the first steps was to recognize its many faces.

Conclusion

Both models of identity have a great deal to offer anyone who wants to understand the impact of oppression on people of African descent. The most comprehensive understanding seems to come from applying both models to the process identity development. For example, there is nothing explicitly imbedded in the African NRID process which suggests African Americans know Africa. The process seems to be finished once an individual comes to terms with race in America and transcends ascribed societal limitations based on race. This leaves an important aspect of the identity development process undone. Undoubtedly it will be an almost insurmountable task to truly reevaluate Eurocentricity (the Encounter stage) if there is a lack of knowledge or awareness that other worldview frameworks exist as alternatives (e.g., Afrocentricity, African axiology). Colonized Africans need to know that their origins predated racism, the African slave trade, and the nature of African history and axiology.

One of the primary contributions that the Black consciousness model (Kambon, 1992) makes to the complexity of issues related to Black consciousness is that it provides direction for reconnection with African origins but it intentionally lacks a discussion of race. Implicit in the model for African Americans is the necessity of learning about the component of one's African heritage in order to undo the effects of deracination. For African people (e.g., Americans, Ghanians), it is essential that they understand the impact of colonialism on Africans throughout the diaspora.

Reconnection for African Americans means understanding their African origins and the significance of their presence in the Americas and how it relates to Africans on the continent. Connection for Africans in the motherland means understanding the nature and impact of colonialism on their own context and how it relates to their brothers and sisters throughout the diaspora. The lack of knowledge that exists on both ends of the African continuum is striking. Clearly, African Americans have not overcome the deleterious impact of the American education system and the erroneous propaganda they have learned about Africa and subsequently about themselves. This has allowed the masses to internalize racism and limited their potential accordingly. The British style education that indoctrinated Ghanians did not include exposure to the Ghanian experience that did not serve the colonizer. Thus, undoubtedly, for the majority of educated Ghanians there may be a dearth of exposure to the significant role their countrymen and women played in shaping world history. In fact, numerous African college students studying in the United States have indicated that they learn more about Africa from a historical context after being enrolling in American or European institutions of higher education than in their own country. In large part, this was due to the multiplicity of resources available once they leave their countries of origin. African Americans need to use the same resources to fill similar gaps in their knowledge base which negatively influence their identity development. Collectively Africans throughout the diaspora need each other in order to fully understand the continuity in our shared existence. According to the west African tradition of collective unity (Mbiti, 1970), the individual owed his very existence to other members of the "tribe," not only those who conceived and nourished him but also those long dead and still unborn. In the spirit of this value, I submit that Africans in the diaspora and those who are in Africa still have a communal connection which needs to be acknowledged and honored in order to resolve our collective identity dilemma. One aspect of Afrocentric ontology is the belief that self knowledge is the basis of all knowledge (Myers, 1991). Thus self knowledge in the identity process must include a thorough understanding of African epistemology, axiology, and history; the permutations that have taken place due to social context and present realities. Africans throughout the diaspora must know the significant collective role and responsibility they have in the restoration of Africa/Africans.

References

Anyidoho, K. (1989). *The pan African ideal in literatures of the Black world.* Accra: Ghana Universities Press.

Baldwin, J.A., & Bell, Y. (1985). The African self-consciousness scale: An africentric personality questionnaire. *The Western Journal of Black Studies, 9(2),* 61-68.

Baldwin, J.A., Duncan, J.A., & Bell, Y.R. (1987, February). Assessment of African self-consciousness among Black students from two college environments. *Journal of Black Psychology, 13(2)*, 27-41.

Cross, W.E. (1995). The psychology of nigrescence. In J. G. Ponterotto, J. M. Casas, L.A. Suzuki, & C.M. Alexander (Ed.), *Handbook of multicultural counseling*. Thousand Oaks, CA: Sage.

Cross, W.E. (1991). *Shades of Black*. Philadelphia, PA: Temple University Press.

Cross, W.E. (1985). Black identity: Rediscovering the distinction between personal identity and reference group orientation. In M.B. Spencer, G.K. Brookins, & W.R. Allen (Eds.), *Beginnings: The social and affective development of Black children* (pp. 155-171). Hillsdale, NJ: Lawrence Erlbaum.

Cross, W.E. Jr. (1971, July). The Negro-to-Black conversion experience. *Black World,* 13-27.

Delavignette, R. (1964). *Christianity and colonialism*. New York: Hawthorn Books.

Freire, P. (1993). *Pedagogy of the oppressed*. New York: Continuum Publishing Co.

Helms, J. E. (1992). *Black and White racial identity: Theory, research, and practice*. Conneticut: Greenwood Press.

Jones, R.M. (1981). The concept of racism and its changing reality. In B.P. Bowser & R.G. Hunt (Eds.), *Impact of racism on White Americans* (pp. 27-49). Beverly Hills, CA: Sage.

Kambon, K.K. (1992). *The African personality in America*: *An African-centered framework*. Tallahassee, FL: Nubian Nations Publications.

Martin, P.M., & O'Meara, P. (1986). *Africa*. Bloomington: Indiana University Press.

Memmi, A. (1965). *The colonizer and the colonized*. Boston, MA: Beacon Press.

Mbiti, J.S. (1970). *African religions and philosophy*. New York: Doubleday.

Morrow, W.L. (1973). *Four hundred years without a comb*. San Diego, CA: Black Publishers of San Diego.

Myers, L.J. (1991). Expanding the psychology of knowledge optimally: The importance of worldview revisited. In R.L. Jones (Ed.), *Black psychology* (3rd ed.). Hampton, VA: Cobb & Henry Publishers.

Palmer, C. (1992). African slave trade: The cruelest commerce. *National Geographic*, 64-91.

Richardson, T.Q. (1992). The search for an African identity among Africans in America. *Alternatives & Solutions, 2*, 28-29.

Sertima, I.V. (1989). *Nile valley civilizations*. Atlanta, GA: Morehouse College Editing.

Woodson, C. G. (1933). *Miseducation of the Negro*. Washington, DC: Associated Publishers.

Woronoff, J. (1972). *West African wager*. Metuchen, NJ: Scarecrow Press.

Author

Tina Q. Richardson
College of Education
Lehigh University
111 Research Drive
Bethlehem, PA 18015
Fax: (610) 758-6223
E-mail: TQRO@lehigh.edu

Cultural Conversion Experiences: Implications for Mental Health Research and Treatment

Jerome Taylor

Conversion in general refers to the giving over of one system of beliefs for another, one system of values for another, one worldview for another, one set of behavioral dispositions for another. Conversion, then, is more sweeping than a change of opinion, a change of belief, or a change in attitude. In a fundamental sense, it reflects a change of heart. Black cultural conversion will be used as a case study for understanding conversion processes generally.

Theories of Black Cultural Conversion

Essentially all theorists in the field speak of Black cultural conversion as an identity-seeking itinerary anchored at one end by disavowal or suppression and at the other by affirmation and integration of one's culture of origin. Becoming Black is seen, then, as an ontogenetic journey with definable markers.

The starting point for Thomas (1971) is Negromachy, a stage characterized by devaluation of things Black and glorification of things White, by a sense of alienation and marginalization, and by an uncritical and unselfconscious reliance on White values for evaluating Black worth. This stage of active disavowal of or antipathy toward one's cultural origins is referred to as Preconsciousness by Milliones (1973), Pre-Encounter by Cross (1971, 1980), and Ethnic Captivity by Banks (1982) and Banks and Grambs (1972).

Withdrawal, a period of painful awakening, is the second developmental marker identified by Thomas (1971). Something happens which challenges and finally overthrows the validity of assumptions, preferences, values, and ideologies of the first period. The dethroning or decathexis of cherished cognitive and affective structures along with the objects to which they are attached is the leading charac-

---

Dedicated to the memory of Jake Milliones, 1940-1993.

85

teristic of this phase which also is called Encounter by Cross (1971, 1980) and Emergence by Denton (1986).

Following on the heels of Withdrawal, Thomas (1971) identifies two closely related stages—Testifying and Information Processing. In the first, witness is given to the personal and collective pain Blacks have suffered and endured in America, and in the second to disciplined study and discussion of political and cultural history of Blacks in Africa, America, and elsewhere. Thomas' Testifying stage is called Immersion-Emersion by Cross (1971, 1980), Confrontation by Milliones (1973), and Encapsulation by Banks (1981). In these same investigations, Thomas' Information Processing phase corresponds to stages identified by Banks as Ethnic Identity Clarification and by Cross and Milliones as Internalization.

A sense of mission and personal commitment and evidence of involvement in collective action characterize the fifth stage, Activity, described by Thomas (1971). Active citizenship— political involvement, joining activities, and individual effort—characterizes this phase which is called Internalization-Commitment by Cross (1971, 1980) and Integration by Milliones (1973). Many of the attributes of Banks' Ethnic Identity Clarification stage apply here as well.

Thomas offers a sixth and final stage, Transcendental, wherein the individual is liberated from conflicts by race, sex, age, or social class, becoming an effective local and world citizen. This stage corresponds roughly to Banks' (1981) Biethnicity phase and possibly to Brown (1979) or Denton's (1986) Longhorn or Double Consciousness phase.

Table 1 provides a summary of the four major theories of cultural transformation just introduced. From the Table, it is clear that there is good agreement on four of six stages: 1) (Negromachy, Pre-Encounter, Preconsciousness, and Ethnic Captivity); 3) (Testifying, Immersion-Emersion, Confrontation, Encapsulation); 4) (Information Processing, Internalization, Identity, Clarification); and 5) (Activity, Internalization-Commitment, Integration, Identity Clarification). There is less concensus on stages 2) (Withdrawal, Encounter) and 6) (Transcendental, Biethnicity) although some support exists for both. Altogether, these theoretical models of cultural conversion are more similar than different. They provide a heuristic basis for both clinical and empirical research.

Measurement of Cultural Conversion

In a program of research extending over the last fifteen years, the writer and his students have investigated the structure and meaning of cultural conversion processes in close to 1,500 Black college students attending public and private institutions located in the North and South, East and Midwest. In all these studies, Milliones' (1973) Developmental Inventory of Black Consciousness (DIB-C) was used to index progress on the four stages of conversion identified by him:

Table 1
A Comparison of Theoretical Models of Black Cultural Conversion

Stage	Thomas/Cross	Milliones	Banks
1. Negromachy	Pre-Encounter	Preconsciousness	Ethnic Captivity
2. Withdrawal	Encounter	—	—
3. Testifying	Immersion-Emmersion	Confrontation	Encapsulation
4. Information Processing	Internalization	Internalization	Identity Clarification
5. Activity	Internalization/Commitment	Integration	Identity Clarification
6. Transcendental	—	—	Biethnic

1. **Preconsciousness**. Blacks of this stage uncritically adapt the system of beliefs and values of the host culture. *Examples*: "Blacks should be loyal to this country in every respect," "A few militant Black power advocates can make it bad for other Blacks," "Blacks should be proud of being Americans," "There has been enough talk and debate by Blacks about what direction the Black struggle should go," "The democratic process is now working for Blacks as well as Whites," or "I prefer being called Negro rather than Black." In all, there are 18 items, 12 positively keyed and 6 negatively keyed.

2. **Confrontation**. A phase of strident militancy during which time things Black are seen as good and things White as bad. *Examples:* "White people can never be trusted where Blacks are concerned," "It is now evident that the Black culture is superior to White culture," "As a rule, Whites are ethnically corrupt," "White people are incapable of loving anyone Black," "Blacks have shown themselves to be more humane than Whites," or "White values are destructive for Black people." There are 26 items, 16 positively keyed and 10 negatively keyed.

3. **Internalization**. Here there is a quickening of interest in Black history, Black art, Black politics, Black philosophy, all things Black. There is a continuing romantization of things Black and animosity toward things White. *Examples*: "Blacks cannot afford to waste time educating Whites who are ignorant about Black people," "Wearing African clothes indicates race pride," "Black art is superior to White art," or "White culture can provide no benefits to Blacks." There are 17 items, 10 positively keyed and 7 negatively keyed.

4. **Integration**. A phase of synthesis and resolution where persons are committed to working in the best interest of Blacks but also are able to work with Whites toward this end. Integration persons are comfortable in pointing out the

weaknesses as well as strengths of Black people and are quite sympathetic to those who have not fully negotiated the conversion process. *Examples*: "Coalitions between Blacks and Whites may sometimes serve the interests of both groups," "Strong disagreement among Black people may at times be quite productive," "Blacks should be tolerant of other Blacks who have middle-class attitudes," or "Blacks can no longer afford to reject Whites because of color alone." There are 19 items, 10 positively and 9 negatively keyed.

Each of the 80 DIB-C items is rated on a 9-point differential scale. Psychometric strategies designed to enhance the discriminability and reliability of the DIB-C are reported in Milliones (1973); and Brown (1976, 1979) and Denton (1986) have reported additional reliability and validational information on this measure. The immediate objective of this section, however, is to identify five prototypes of Black cultural conversion based on the DIB-C instrument.

Denton (1986) analyzed DIB-C scores obtained from 924 Black students enrolled in seven public and private institutions of higher learning located in the North, South, and East. Based upon a non-hierarchical cluster analysis of DIB-C scores, Denton found that the five clusters or conversion prototypes summarized in Table 2 provided the most theory-consistent fit with the data.

The four stages identified in the Milliones model, Preconsciousness through Integration, are represented as rows in Table 2. The remaining columns identify how the five conversion prototypes score on each of Milliones' stages. The values posted are z-score transformations of raw scores such that the mean is 0 and standard deviation 1. To aid interpretation, the letters L, M, and H are used to represent relatively Low, Moderate, and High standard (z) scores on Milliones' stages in relation to each conversion prototype.

In Column I, the Preconsciousness Prototype is characterized by a moderately high score on the Preconsciousness stage and relatively low scores on Confrontation, Internalization, and Integration. This prototype corresponds closely to Thomas' Negromachy, to Cross' Pre-Encounter, and to Banks' Ethnic Captivity stages.

In Column II, the Emergence Prototype is characterized by relatively low scores on all stage components. In comparing Preconsciousness Prototype I to Emergence Prototype II, however, the remarkable difference is on the Preconsciousness stage score which shifts from a positive 0.79 under Preconsciousness to a negative 0.58 under Emergence. The magnitude of this oppositely directed shift corresponds to more than one standard deviation (1.37 to be exact). There is here, then, evidence of questioning basic assumptions and values of the host culture. The correlated increase in Confrontation from I to II and decrease in Integration is suggestive of an awakening process which does not yet include studied involvement of the culture of origin (Internalization score decreases from I to II). This pattern characterizing the Emergence Prototype is consistent with the low negative score associated with the Preconsciousness stage. This Emergence

Table 2
Identification of Five Conversion Prototypes Adapted from Denton (1986)
Based on N=924 Black College Students

Stage	I n=314 34%	II n=221 24%	III n=88 10%	IV n=178 19%	V n=123 13%
Precon.	+0.79M	-0.58L	-1.46L	-0.54L	+0.85M
Confron.	+0.15L	+0.30L	+1.88H	-0.56L	-1.44L
Internaliz.	+0.32L	+0.25L	+1.61H	-0.67L	-1.46L
Integration	- 0.30L	-0.45L	-1.14L	+0.58M	+1.39H

Table Note = Cultural Conversion Prototypes are defined as follows: I (Preconscious); II (Emergence): III (Confrontation); IV (Integration); and V (Double Consciousness). All tabled values are z-score transformations used to identify and interpret conversion prototypes.

Prototype seems related conceptually to Thomas' Withdrawal and to Cross' Encounter stages.

In Column III, the Confrontation Prototype features relatively high scores on Confrontation and Internalization and relatively low scores on Preconsciousness and Integration. The militant stridency, antipathy toward Whites, and distrust of White symbols and values characterizing this prototype is similar to Thomas' Testifying and Information Processing, to Cross' Immersion-Emersion and Internalization, and to Banks' Ethnic Encapsulation and Identity Clarification.

In Column IV, the Integration Prototype is characterized by a relatively moderate positive score on Integration and relatively low negative scores on Preconsciousness, Confrontation, and Internalization. Integration Prototypes, tolerant of other Blacks who have not completed their cultural journey and open to Whites with whom they are now able to form coalitions, may be most similar to Thomas' Activity and to Cross' Internalization-Commitment stages.

In final Column V, the Double Consciousness Prototype features a moderately positive score on Preconsciousness, a relatively high positive score on Integration, and relatively low scores on Confrontation and Internalization. Simultaneously, persons of this prototype identify with elements of the host culture (Preconsciousness) and display relatively tolerant attitudes toward Blacks and Whites who also are subjects of critical appraisal (Integration). Such persons may be similar to those characterizing Banks' Biethnicity and Thomas' Transcendental stages.

Five conversion prototypes, then, have been identified empirically. Are there variations in personal, social, and cultural adjustment across these prototypes?

Correlates of Conversion Prototypes

Table 3, which summarizes relationships between conversion prototypes and indicators of personal, social, and cultural adjustment, is adapted from Denton's (1986) study of 924 Black college students. Results will be discussed in terms of an ecosystemic continuum of adjustment—from cultural to social to person—in relation to which other studies of cultural conversion will be introduced and summarized as well.

In all instances, analysis of variance indicates that mean differences across prototypes are significant at p <.001. Unfortunately the clustering program utilized produced means only, not standard deviations as well, and we were unable to recover case identities to calculate standard deviations independently.

Cultural Adjustment

How are cognitions about Blacks transformed over conversion prototypes? Answers to this question clarify how sense of Black culture is similar or different across the five conversion prototypes. Two contrasting indicators were used, Terrell's (1975) Black Ideology Scale and Taylor, Wilson, and Dobbins' (1972) Nadanolitization Scale. The Nationalist Philosophy Subscale of Terrell's inventory is designed to evaluate the extent to which respondents identify with a Black nationalist orientation: "Blacks should work toward full separation from this American society," "Black children should be taught only by Black teachers," "Christianity works against Blacks because it encourages peace," and so on. The Nadanolitization Scale was developed to evaluate the extent to which Blacks have internalized White racist stereotypes about Blacks: "Blacks are born with greater sexual lust than White people," "Whites are better in abstract thinking than Blacks," "Racial differences explain why Blacks don't live as long as Whites," and so on. Table 3 indicates that there is a progressive reduction in level of internalized racism from the Preconsciousness Prototype, where it is highest, through the Double Consciousness Prototype, where it is lowest. Indeed, the mean level of internalized racism in Double Consciousness is almost half of what it is in Preconsciousness, the drop in internalized racism being particularly precipitous from Preconsciousness to Emergence. From Table 3 it is clear also that nationalistic fervor peaks during Emergence, declining thereafter through Double Consciousness where surprisingly the mean level is considerably less than it is in Preconsciousness. The diminution of racist stereotypes over the cycle of conversion suggests a progressive liberation of mind, a dethroning of oppressor images and cognitions of the Fifth Column that previously had ruled home territory (cf. Milliones, 1973; Brown, 1979). As this implied decathexis occurs during Emergence, cresting interest in nationalism may well provide new opportunities for recathexis. Through recathexis of a new order,

Table 3
Relationships Between Conversion Prototypes and Indicators of Cultural,
Social, and Personal Adjustment Adapted from Denton (1986)
Based on N=924

Measure	Conversion Prototype				
	I n=314	II n=221	III n=83	IV n=178	V n=123
Nationalist Philosophy	103.60	165.35	117.84	102.46	72.95
Internalized Racism	66.31	44.04	44.01	35.25	34.03
Aggression	8.86	7.59	8.22	7.59	7.08
Nurturance	11.73	15.34	13.45	14.46	15.03
Self to Other Blacks	68.15	82.87	72.00	73.16	73.32
Other Blacks to Self	68.05	81.88	74.23	75.92	74.42
Self Esteem	67.22	75.85	69.40	72.49	72.98
Identity: Future	110.65	139.69	127.47	139.38	147.80
Identity: Present	78.77	101.81	86.58	98.66	106.34

Table Note= All tabled values are means associated with each conversion prototype: I (Preconsciousness); II (Emergence); III (Confrontation); IV (Integration); and V (Double Consciousness).

a degree of stability is provided for this dramatic period of awakening and uncertitude. While nationalism should and must have a political basis, it appears to have a psychological one as well. In overview, negative cognitions about Blacks decrease over the course of conversion while negative cognitions about Whites increase transitorily but not permanently. Full conversion through Integration or Double Consciousness, then, is associated with significant reductions in mistrust and hatred of Blacks and Whites, thus preparing such persons to live in two worlds, Black and White, one mark of cultural adjustment.

Social Adjustment

Social adjustment is inferred here from quality of relations to others in general and to Blacks in particular. The Aggression and Nurturance subscales from Jackson's (1973) Personality Research Form were used to estimate quality of relations to others in general, and Taylor's (1976) Affiliation Inventory was adapted to estimate relational quality of the respondent to other Blacks and relational quality of other Blacks to the respondent. The Aggression Subscale contained true-false items such as "I get a kick out of seeing someone I dislike appear foolish in front of others," "I become angry more easily than most people," and "I often find it necessary to criticize a person sharply if he annoys me," and the Nurturance Subscale items such as "I am usually the first to offer a helping hand when it is needed," "When I see someone who looks confused, I usually ask if I can be of any assistance," and "I believe in giving friends lots of help and advice." Affiliative relation to other Blacks was evaluated from 0-9 point ratings of such items as "I look forward to being in the company of other Blacks," "I am quick to brag about other Blacks," and "I give consistent support to other Blacks." Affiliation from other Blacks was estimated from simple rearrangement of item stems, for example, "Other Blacks are consistently supportive of me." Table 3 suggests that Preconscious Prototypes tend to have a higher level of aggression and lower level of nurturance than the remaining conversion prototypes, a pattern confirmed statistically by Denton (1986). Relatedly, Preconscious Prototypes seem to enjoy the least affiliative relationships with other Blacks. Altogether, these patterns suggest that the period of Emergence ushers in more adaptive relations to people in general and to Blacks in particular. Beyond Emergence, these positive differences are maintained above Preconsciousness levels but not consistently above Emergence levels. These patterns affirm a stepwise function: Once the threshold of Emergence has been reached, salutary social effects are observed over the range of conversion prototypes. In an earlier study, Terrell, Taylor, and Terrell (1980) found that young incarcerated Black males committing more serious Black-on-Black crimes were more preconscious than those committing less serious Black-on-Black crimes. Evolving sense of culture, then, seems to have generally positive effects on a relatively broad range of social behaviors.

Personal Adjustment

In this sample of college-aged subjects, level of self-esteem and adaptability of adolescent identity were used to provide a very rough estimate of quality of personal adjustment. Taylor's 16-item Self-Esteem measure contains statements such as "I enjoy being who I am," "I have persistent confidence in my opinions," and "I tackle new problems with optimism," each rated on a 0-10 point scale. The Identity Measure, developed and validated by Smith (1973) and Murdock (1974), is structured around Erikson's (1950) conception of identity during the adolescent years. Level of performance on seven phases of identity hypothesized by Erikson—Time Perspective, Self-Certainty, Role Experimentation, Anticipation of Achievement, Sexual Identity, Leadership Polarization, and Ideological Polarization—can be estimated from the Identity Measure. Underlying these seven phases are two independent dimensions which have been identified through factor analytic studies: I. Future Orientation ("I see emptiness in my future," [-], "I feel few ties to future generations," [-], "I doubt my ability to be a leader" [-]) and II. Present Orientation ("I feel good about the different things I do," [+], "I like how my body looks since I have grown" [+], "My choice of life work will satisfy my family" [+]). From Table 3, it appears that Self-Esteem and adaptive Future and Present orientation are lowest for Preconscious Prototypes. This pattern is confirmed statistically by Denton (1986). There is a sharp increase in self-esteem and adaptive identity during the period of Emergence and a slight dip in these values during Confrontation. From Confrontation through Double Consciousness, mean levels of self-esteem and adaptive identity increase without exception, more so for the latter than former. Altogether, these results suggest, in relation to measures used here, that level of personal adjustment is enhanced over conversion prototypes, from Preconsciousness to Double Consciousness. This conclusion is consistent with investigations by Franklin (1986) who found that single Black mothers reporting relatively high levels of preconsciousness were at higher risk of depression than mothers reporting relatively low levels of preconsciousness, by Tomes and Brown (1986) who found that Black mothers relatively high in depression were correspondingly high in preconsciousness, by Williams (1973) who reported that Preconscious Black college students have low self-esteem, and by Brown (1976) who found using the Holzman Inkblot Technique that Black female college students with high Preconscious scores are more emotionally constricted than those with low Preconscious scores. Using the Jackson Personality Research Form, Brown (1976) also found that persons with relatively high Preconscious scores tend to be more trusting, ingratiating, and dependent and to feel more helpless and insecure than persons with relatively low Preconscious scores. Together, these studies suggest that Preconscious persons may be more vulnerable to psychological maladjustment (in the neurotic range) than persons of other conversion prototypes. The fact that Preconscious types also commit more serious Black-on-Black crimes than Conscious types (Terrell, Taylor, & Terrell, 1980) would suggest that cultural conversion may have implications for sociopathy as well.

Implications for Treatment and Research

Based upon the evidence reviewed, cultural conversion is not simply a repositioning of ideological commitments. It brings with it health promotive consequences over a wide domain—cultural, social, and personal. Simultaneously, cultural conversion may have ameliorative and preventive implications with respect to variables of persisting interest to mental health professionals.

Since higher level conversion processes have such positive implications for cultural, social, and personal adjustment, it is rather disquieting to report that the modal conversion prototype is Preconsciousness. From Table 2, 34% of the sample falls in the Preconscious Prototype, 24% in the Emergence Prototype, 10% in the Confrontation Prototype, 19% in the Integration Prototype, and 13% in the Double Consciousness Prototype. For the most mature conversion prototypes, Integration and Double Consciousness, the combined percentage is 32, slightly less than the percentage associated with Preconsciousness alone. All the more alarming is the fact that these estimates are obtained on samples of tomorrow's middle and upper income elites—Black college students. Certainly it is possible that patterns reported for the college years could shift in the direction of cultural maturity in later years, but this would not undo concern over intervening effects associated with the relatively large numbers falling into Preconsciousness during earlier years.

If the conversion experience has implications for the cultural, social, and personal health of Blacks as has been argued, who are the principal guardians or facilitators of the conversion process? Principal guardians must be the institutional gatekeepers of the Black community—churches and fraternal, masonic, cultural, social, and service organizations. Regretfully, no standardized system of enculturation is being implemented presently in the Black community. It is the author's view that patterns of conversion reflected in Table 2 represent earlier failures in enculturation, an absence of well conceptualized and implemented plans to implant a sense of culture during the earlier years. Culturally enriched full-day, after-school, or occasional programs are scarce to nonexistent in urban and rural areas of Black America. Such programs systematically implemented over the nursery, elementary, and secondary school years could possibly reduce the number of students falling into Preconsciousness, enhancing levels of cultural, social, and personal health as a result.

While gatekeepers of the Black community must serve as guardians, mental health professionals can serve as facilitators of the conversion process. First, however, there must be a recognition that such a process exists. Second, there must be an openness to understanding the contribution of conversion processes to transference as well as countertransference in treatment. Patients in Preconsciousness, based upon the results of studies reviewed, may tend to be ingratiating and compliant, anxious to please, and careful not to offend the therapist whose race and insight may be critical in understanding and interpreting the intrapsychic and social dimension of the transference. As the patient enters Emergence or Confrontation, managing the distrustful and hostile outpourings of the patient creates transference and countertransference problems of a different order, requiring here as in Preconsciousness special attention to both the intrapsychic and social dimensions. Even in Integration and Double Consciousness, special attention to both dimensions is required to facilitate healing and restoration.

It is expected that better understanding and sensitive management of Black conversion processes will have implications for other conversion processes as well—feminist conversion, political conversion, and religious conversion. Popular accounts of feminist conversion closely parallel prototypes described for Black cultural conversion Preconsciousness; Emergence; Confrontation; Integration; Double Consciousness. Analysis of autobiographies of political radicals reveals a similar process, as do conversion accounts of persons entering the spiritual realm. If these correspondences can be established empirically, and if there are wide-ranging value, attitudinal, and behavioral changes accompanying these transformations, then would it not be appropriate to encourage multidiciplinary studies of conversion processes?

At least seven issues should occupy the initial research agenda of multidisciplinary inquiry. First, there is the conceptual problem of characterizing conversion processes in different domains, identifying continuities as well as discontinuities and articulating discovered patterns with existing ego theory. Second, the problem of assessment requires resolution. Quite possibly, inventory and interview approaches could be combined with observational approaches in identifying conversion phases. Third, the directionality of effects must be clarified through longitudinal research. Is it the case as has been argued here that conversion affects quality of cultural, social, and personal adjustment? Or is it the case that cultural, social, and personal adjustment affect level of conversion? At the moment, data do not exist to settle this issue one way or another. Fourth, the convergence or independence of various conversion processes requires investigation. Does cultural conversion have implications for feminist conversion? Does one conversion type suppress conversion potential in other domains? Fifth, it is theoretically important to determine if conversion prototypes are the result primarily of developmental or socialization processes. If conversion is strictly developmental, then it is possible to arrive at Double Consciousness only through Emergence, Confrontation, and Integration. If conversion prototypes are primarily the products of socialization, then it should be possible to bring up children and youth in ways that carry them directly to Integration or Double Consciousness without passage through Emergence or Confrontation. Or is it the case that conversion prototypes are under the control of developmental processes in some instances and socialization processes in others? Sixth, research needs to clarify whether conversion processes are linear, cyclical, or random in nature. Is it possible that phases in the process may be skipped? Are there risks of regression? And seventh, therapeutic and institutional methods for gaining control of conversion processes need to be developed, implemented, and evaluated. Just as we now have behavioral therapies, psychodynamic therapies, and cognitive therapies, so may we need to consider cultural and other conversion therapies as preventive and ameliorative options. To what range of persons or nosological groups would conversion therapies apply? Could they be used as supplementary or primary instruments of change? How would conversion therapies compare with conventional therapies in terms of depth and scope of change?

Quite possibly, through serious dialogue involving religionists, psychologists, and political and other social scientists, innovative programs of development and research could be implemented to advance general and particular knowledge of how to change hearts, the fundamental passion of conversion research.

Notes

1.The research summarized was funded by NIMH Grant MH 26754 administered by the Center for Minority Groups Mental Health. An earlier version of this paper was presented at the 40th Anniversary of the Menninger School of Psychiatry, June, 1986.

References

Banks, J. (1981). *Multiethnic education: Theory and practice*. Boston, Mass: Allyn and Bacon.

Banks, J., & Grambs, J. (1972). *Black self-concept*. New York: McGraw-Hill.

Brown, A. (1976). *Personality correlates of the developmental inventory of consciousness*. Master's Thesis, University of Pittsburgh.

Brown, A. (1979). *Consciousness prototypes: A profile analysis of the developmental stages of consciousness*. Doctoral Dissertation, University of Pittsburgh.

Crawford, T., & Naditch, M. (1970). Relative deprivation, powerlessness, and militancy. *Journal of Psychiatry, 33*, 208-233.

Cross, W. E. (1971). The Negro-to-Black conversion experience: Toward a psychology of liberation. *Black World, 20,* 13-26

Cross, W. E. (1980). Modes of psychological nigrescence: A literature review. In R.L. Jones (Ed.), *Black Psychology*. NewYork:Harper & Row.

Denton, S. E. (1986). *A methodological refinement and validational analysis of the developmental inventory of consciousness* (DIB-C). Unpublished doctoral dissertation, University of Pittsburgh.

Erikson, E. (1950). *Childhood and society*. New York: W W. Norton.

Franklin, A. (1986). *The role of social, cultural, and religious factors on depression among single mothers with male.* Unpublished doctoral. dissertation, University of Pittsburgh.

Jackson, D. (1973). *Personality research form manual.* New York: Research Psychologists Press.

Milliones, J. (1973). *Construction of the developmental inventory of consciousness.* Unpublished doctoral dissertation, University of Pittsburgh.

Murdock, L. I. (1974). *Utilizing Smith's inventory to investigate male and female differences in identity structure.* Unpublished doctoral dissertation, University of Pittsburgh.

Smith, P. M. (1973). *Construction of an identity measure.* Unpublished doctoral dissertation, University of Pittsburgh.

Taylor, J., Wilson, M., & Dobbins, J. (1972). *Nadanolitization Scale.* Pittsburgh: Center for Family Excellence.

Taylor, J. (1976). *Affiliation Inventory.* Pittsburgh: Center for Family Excellence.

Terrell, F. (1975). *The development of an inventory to measure certain aspects of nationalist ideology.* Unpublished doctoral dissertation, University of Pittsburgh.

Terrell, F., Taylor, J., & Terrell, S. (1980). Self-concept of juveniles who commit on crimes. *Corrective and Social Psychiatry, 26,* 107-109.

Thomas, C. S. (1971). *Boys no more.* Beverly Hills: Glencoe Press.

Tomes, E., & Brown, A. (1986). *Psychological factors and depression among women of low socioeonomic status.* Unpublished manuscript, University of Pittsburgh.

Williams, I. (1975). *An investigation of the developmental stages of consciousness.* Unpublished doctoral dissertation, University of Cincinnati.

Author

Jerome Taylor
Center For Family Excellence
1835 Centre Avenue
Pittsburgh, PA 15219
Telephone: (412) 392-4422

Racial Identity and Psychotherapy

Robert T. Carter and Sharon Boyd-Jackson

Race and racial issues are vital forces that affect group and individual identity in the United States (Carter, 1995; Cyrus, 1993; Rothenberg, 1995; Sue & Sue, 1990; Thompson & Carter, 1997). Smedley (1993) views race as a powerful barrier that comes between groups and serves as a permanent marker of individual or group behavior and status. The effects of race on individual functioning is far more complex than most social scientists have been able to describe. Race, as a variable, impacts an individual in a variety of ways. Furthermore, there is a need for a more comprehensive approach to understanding the interaction between racial issues and mental health.

Racial barriers exist in psychotherapy and counseling largely because traditional theories have not considered race in human and personality development. Neither have the personal meaning and significance of race been extended to White Americans. For the most part and in the minds of many, some people of color are not actively included in the racial categories. When race is used to describe people Black people are often the referent group. Thus, a model is needed that includes all groups in the description and analysis of race. There also has been no theory to guide our understanding about how race influences psychotheraputic interactions and personal development. Race as a variable has not been studied directly and is often implied when other concepts are used such as culture and ethnicity (Betancourt & Lopez, 1993). The above circumstances exist primarily because race has been thought to be a social descriptor rather than a psychological variable with wide variation and forms of expression. However, before we discuss these matters further we would like to define our terms. In particular, we want to distinguish race from ethnicity and culture.

Defining Terms

Culture

During the past two decades, clinicians and mental health professionals have increasingly acknowledged the salience of ethnic and cultural differences (McGoldrick et al, 1982; Sue & Sue, 1990; Vargas & Ross-Chioino, 1992). More

99

often than not race is used interchangeably with other terms such as ethnicity and culture (Betancourt & Lopez, 1993). We believe that each term has a distinct but related meaning. Johnson (1990) uses the notion of context to distinguish race, ethnicity, and culture. He argues that the larger sociocultural system determines the superordinate cultural framework that gives meaning to people's behavior, language, communication style, and thinking pattern. Brislin (1990) argues that culture best describes recurring behavioral patterns that vary from location to location (usually, from country to country) and are observable in many generations. Furthermore, he notes that adults have the primary responsibility for socializing children such that the behaviors indicative of the group are learned. In this way, the child becomes a well-accepted socialized adult. Similarly, Smedley (1993) points out that culture is learned, not inherited, and that one learns how to behave and think during the process of development in a particular society. Thus, the term culture, in this chapter, is defined as the transmission of knowledge, skills, attitudes, behaviors, and language from one generation to the next, usually within the confines of a physical environment. According to this view, culture is a learned behavior. Therefore, within a country, it is possible, as a result of group separation and isolation, for several (i.e., racial) groups to have some distinct cultural patterns while at the same time sharing some cultural forms with the dominant cultural group, particularly those cultural forms and roles needed to function in the larger society.

Ethnicity and Race

There are many definitions for the term ethnic or ethnicity which can cause some confusion. Like culture, the term ethnicity or ethnic refers to a group and a social-physical context based on common experiences that come, in time, to distinguish one group from another. The basis for group commonness may vary widely, depending on many considerations. Smedley (1993) suggests that ethnic or ethnicity be used as an analytic term to refer to a group of people seen by others and themselves as having distinct cultural features and a clearly defined sociocultural history. Thus, the term ethnic group can denote national origin, religious affiliation, or other types of socially or geographically defined groups. However, in the United States, ethnicity has been used as a euphemism for race when referring to people of color and as a non-racial designation for Whites (Betancourt & Lopez, 1993). Nevertheless, ethnic group will be defined here as a group with a specific national or religious identity.

Race has a long history in intellectual thinking and writing. In its original use, race referred to a presumed biological taxonomy that was applied to humans and represented the assumption that a group's shared genetic heritage was evident from physical characteristics (i.e., skin-color) (Guthrie, 1976; Johnson, 1990). The

Racial Identity and Psychotherapy

validity of race as a purely biological variable has been hotly debated and rejected and race has come to have a social and political meaning that, in part, is related to its original biological roots (Yee et al., 1993). Cyrus, (1993) describes race as a social construct—"a classification based on social values" (p. 11). Thus in the United States, race is primarily determined by skin color, physical features, and for some, language, and is associated with powerful social and psychological meaning. Race also has been used to make psychological and cultural inferences about one's ascribed membership in a designated group. Because groups were thought to have particular characteristics due to their race, this notion has lead directly to ranking and evaluating human groups on physical and behavioral characteristics. Pinderhughes (1989) notes that: "[r]ace constitutes a different level of cultural meaning than ethnicity. Originally carrying a meaning that referred to biological origin and physical appearance, the concept of race was always more inclusive, embracing a number of ethnic groups within a given racial category. Overtime, race has acquired a social meaning in which these biological differences, via the mechanism of stereotyping, have become markers for status assignment within the social system. The status assignment based on skin color identity has evolved into complex social structures that promote a power differential between Whites and various people of color" (p. 71).

Race, then, is defined as a construct that refers to a presumed classification of humans into groups on the basis of visible physical traits. Following such a grouping is the idea that one group, typically Whites (the creators of the concept of races), is better than all others (Allen, 1994). When race, in North America, is used as a social classification system, physical characteristics of different human groups are believed to reflect emotional, cognitive, psychological, intellectual, and moral qualities (Fredrickson, 1989; Gould, 1981; Smedley, 1993).

The idea and construct of race is distinct from culture and ethnicity because for many people racial traits are considered static or permanent, whereas culture and ethnicity are thought to be more fluid. It is this notion of permanence that makes the idea and construct so powerful and one of the major reasons why we must understand race within the context of it's own complexity. Race should not be subsumed under culture or ethnicity, but rather confronted directly. It is a complex socially constructed idea that deserves further study in order to determine its psychological implications.

Race and Socialization

Race as a sociopolitical designation has associated with it the idea that certain characteristics belong to various racial groups. Omi and Winant, (1995) state that:

"Racial categories and the meaning of race are given concrete expression by the specific social relations and historical context in which they are embedded.

Racial formation refers to the process by which social, economic and political forces determine the content and importance of racial categories, and by which they are in turn shaped by racial meanings (p.13).

This sociopolitical process of defining the characteristics of race has had far reaching effects when trying to comprehend how race may impact the psychological functioning of an individual.

We contend that there is a socialization process that affects how a person becomes aware of their own race and the race of others, as well as the understanding and value of race in the social structure. This socialization process either consciously or unconsciously affects our understanding of our racial role (i.e., the role appropriate for some one in your racial group) in society. That is, we are socialized to obtain appropriate race role behavior in much the same way we develop gender roles, and the appropiate behaviors and attitudes associated with them. Race appropriate behaviors and beliefs are socially constructed notions that are forced upon us whether we are aware of their impact or not. Even those who choose to consciously suppress or unconsciously deny the salience of race are compelled to acknowledge its existence repeatedly in life by simply filling out a census form, applying for a job, forming relationships, choosing a loved one, or attempting to get into school, etc. Race, among other variables, may determine whether or not two people are attracted to one another. It can determine where and how one lives, the type of opportunities one is able to take advantage of and how valued and accepted one is as a person. We are often socialized not to mix interpersonally with other races and interracial marriages are often not condoned in many families. People in visible racial/ethnic groups (Black, Hispanic, Native and Asian American) are constantly reminded of their race and the legacy of their race via racial stereotypes and the social burdens they endure as a consequence of racism and discrimination. In American society where racial groups remain relatively segregated, race retains its central role in the socialization process, most racial groups are isolated and evolve distinct world views about life and death in the United States.

In order to create a more comprehensive understanding of how race impacts individual behavior, we need to further study and investigate the socialization process with respect to race and the developmental processes that affect our racial identity ego statuses.

Race and Mental Health

Race is often discussed and dismissed (in the clinical literature) as irrelevant because many Whites do not think of themselves in racial terms. Thinking of oneself in racial terms seems to be reserved for visible racial/ethnic group members, particularly Black people (Wilkerson, 1992). However, to assume that race does not have meaning for all American people, including Whites, reflects an ahistorical understanding of being an American, and ignores assumptions about race in the mental health literature. Race, primarily determined by skin color, has and continues to divide American society. This social division also exists in the mental health profession. The assumptions about race that pervade the mental health literature reflect a profound denial of the reality of race by conceptualizing personality in decontextualized and ahistorical terms.

Race and the ideological framework erected to support and justify its use has lead to the formation of individual, institutional, and cultural racism. Institutional and cultural racism have permeated all aspects of life in North America and it's effects can be found in disciplines such as history, economics, politics, education, anthropology, sociology, law, language, and communication patterns. Race and racism, operate as complex and dynamic systems that have come to characterize the structure and institutional functions of American society. As a consequence, race affects the social and psychological life of all its citizens. Kovel (1984) states that:

> "Racism is the activity within history and culture through which races are created, oppressed, and fantasized about without the aid of bigots. It evades the history of our culture at the deepest of levels at which the primary fantasies are generated. The problem of racism is part of the problem of Western culture, (p. 95)."

Although some scholars and clinicians acknowledge that race and racism are integral aspects of American society and culture, human development and personality theorists seldom, if ever, include race as an important personality or psychological variable. This is unfortunate because human development and personality theories constitute the fundamental perspectives on which psychotherapy is constructed, it follows that the mental health literature also rarely conceives of race as a central factor. However, because of the sociopolitical nature of race, early writings concerning the racial make-up of individuals described visibly racial/ethnic group members as inferior, deprived, or inhumane regarding their behavior and mental functioning (Carter, 1995).

Jackson (1990), summarizing how race has been addressed in the mental health literature, presents five conceptual and clinical approaches to psychotheraputic treatment: (a) Differential; (b) Parallel; (c) Collaborative; (d) Culture-free; and (e) Culture-specific. According to Jackson,

> "Differential treatment ignores race, Parallel treatment models simply use interpreters or presume only people who are the same race are capable of understanding. Collaborative treatment models which are rare involve cooperative efforts between traditional and indigenous health care providers (p. 428)."

Culture-free models are similar to the Differential model, the difference being that they believe that psychological principles are universal and thus are applicable to all individuals regardless of race or culture. Culture-specific models of treatment are believed to incorporate the norms and values of the client's particular culture in identifying abnormal behavior and treatment approaches. Culture-specific models that presume to be guided by a group's particular racial patterns are the only treatment approaches that do not rely solely on traditional theories and approaches.

Jackson argues that when politically conservative ideas are dominant, racism becomes more overt and explicit, and traditional models of treatment (i.e., Differential, Partial, Collaborative) become more popular. In this climate, Jackson (1990) notes,

> "Stereotypes are likely to be unquestioned and racist practices are thoroughly enmeshed in institutional practices" (p. 428).

In contrast, she suggests that Culture-specific models are likely to be endorsed when culturally diverse groups increase in size, economic conditions are stable, and political and racial issues are less evident in social systems and interactions. Jackson's analysis of treatment models highlights the influence and role of race, racism, and the sociopolitical climate, in psychotherapy. Implicit in each model are the ideas and concepts about race that are communicated in the mental health literature and produced by its adherents.

All clinical scholars acknowledge that Blacks and other people of color were and continue to be subjected to racially based discrimination and social oppression. Nevertheless, the psychological and behavioral patterns they experienced were, and to some degree continue to be, attributed to poor or aberrant ego functioning, uncontrollable id impulses, or a restrained superego, rather than to the racial oppression that created their poor and complicated life conditions. In the traditional clinical literature the dysfunctional personality organization attributed to racial group membership of Blacks is thought to produce particularly distinct and difficult transference phenomena. Also, countertransference is thought to be stimulated by the unique problems posed by a patient of color. For the most part, therapists have been instructed to guard against such influences, with little or no instruction as to how to develop these needed gaurds. Often ignored is the therapists own racial group membership and the attributes associated with it—not to mention the lack of existing psychological theory to explain psychological variation regarding race and its impact.

Schachter and Butts (1968) reported on several effects associated with interracial analysis. They suggested that race may have no effect or influence, or it may be central in the therapy. Racial differences and stereotypes can impede both a therapist and a client in the psychotherapeutic process (e.g., accepted race-specific cultural behaviors may be misinterpreted, and important racial material, like racial stereotypes, may be overlooked by the clinician).

Benard (1953) pointed out that significance of race may vary for Black patients, depending on their conscious awareness of its role in their lives. She felt that both the patient and the White therapist can deny race, and suggested that White therapists who think they are free of racial prejudice are particularly prone to denial.

"While some White analysts seem compelled to over sympathize the effects of being a Negro...others have an apparent need to deny and sidestep any such effects altogether "(p. 262).

The therapist or patient may use racial resistance in the course of treatment. That is the patient or the therapist may avoid discussing pathological issues for fear of reinforcing racial stereotypes. In interracial therapy, a White therapist may misread the Black client's pathological character traits as defenses, particularly when they coincide with the therapist's racial stereotypes. Thus, a therapist's lack of racial and cultural knowledge can cause countertransference reactions that hamper and prolong treatment.

More recently Comas-Diaz and Jacobsen (1991) have described ethnocultural transference and countertransference phenomena from inter-ethnic and intra-ethnic perspectives. These authors acknowledge that in the past racial and ethnic issues have been interpreted as underlying conflicts, defenses, and resistance (p. 392). They offer and describe a list of reactions that they contend arise from ethno-cultural sources. These are basically updated versions of the same issues described by other authors in the past. For instance, ethnocultural issues that occur between groups may be overcompliant, mistrusted, or ambivalent. These were alluded to by previous authors. An important contribution that Comas-Diaz and Jacobsen make however, is the recognition of within ethnic group issues. They describe several types of transference issues that clients may engage in such as seeing the therapists as the all knowing therapist or the traitor, and so forth. Similarly with countertransference they list possible reactions that are consistent with previous writers. However, these authors do not distinguish race from ethnicity and culture.

Comas-Diaz and Jacobsen (1991) and many clinical scholars can be considered cultural difference adherents- they tend to argue for cultural and ethnic consideration in clinical treatment, however they continue to use racial categories to characterize ethnocultural issues among visible racial/ethnic group people (i.e. Indians, Asians, Blacks, and Hispanics).

The cultural difference approach, currently the most widely endorsed perspective, represents an important advance in our thinking about racial difference. Cultural diversity proponents have highlighted the importance of class, culture, and language differences as having profound impact on cross-racial interaction (Sue & Sue, 1990). In terms of mental health practice, advocates of the cultural difference paradigm have slowly begun to develop interventions and instructional guidelines that reflect the cultural experiences of visible racial/ethnic group people. Nevertheless, this approach leaves the burden of change on those who are racially or culturally different, rather than on the individuals or systems that provide mental health services. The manner in which people of color should adapt themselves to traditional counseling approaches has been less a question of how racial and cultural issues influence the psychotherapy process and more a matter of how visible racial/ethnic people can be taught and prepared to benefit from traditional treatment approaches (Garfield, 1978).

Although much has been written about the therapeutic needs of the members of various racial/ethnic groups, less is known about how race, as a psychological construct, influences these groups as well as Whites. Because race is such a salient variable in the therapeutic process, Carter (1995) thoughtfully argues for a Racially Inclusive Model of psychotherapy that takes race as a group and individual characteristics, via racial identity theory, into consideration. Such a model can address the many dimensions of the therapeutic process that are affected by race for members of all racial groups, not just people of color. The model presented by Carter (1995) includes a discussion of White racial identity as an aspect of personality for Whites as well as people of color.

Racial Identity and the Psychotherapeutic Process

Racial identity theories have been constructed to help understand how White and visible racial group members identify with their racial group membership. The need for a racial theory that examines intrapsychic dynamics and interpersonal relationships is long overdue and supported by clinical research (Carter, 1995). Typically, racial issues in the therapeutic process have been seen only from the therapists perspective: clinicians are taught what they do not know or understand about cross-racial interactions and visible racial/ethnic group members' cultures (Helms, 1990). There are a few different racial identity theories, and, to our knowledge, only one theory (i.e., Helms 1984, 1990) delineates intrapsychic and interactional process issues in the development of racial identity.

Overview of Racial Identity Theory

Theories of the psychological development of racial identity for visible racial/ethnic people have existed in the psychological literature for some time (Cross 1980, 1991; Helms, 1984, 1990, 1994; Thomas, 1971). An individual's sense of connection to a particular racial group varies with respect to his or her psychological identification with that group. These models offer a way to comprehend the psychosocial complexity associated with racial identity issues.

Racial identity theories were first introduced in the 1970's. The first models of racial identity were proposed to explain Black American metamorphoses from a people referred to as colored to a people who insisted on being called Black Americans. Some of these initial models proposed that there were different types of

Blacks whose personalities varied according to how they understood who they were racially. Vontress (1971), suggested that three invariant types of Black people existed: (a) Colored; (b) Negro; and (c) Black. In addition, each type displayed a distinct form of race identity. Some scholars who proposed typologies similar to this, often believed it was not possible to alter ones type. Stage theorists believed one could progress from one stage of racial identity to an advanced one. Thomas (1971), for instance, proposed a stage model that stands as a precursor for later models. In the typical stage model of racial identity, a person would move in a linear progression from the least developed stage to the most advanced stage (Cross, 1980). Each stage had associated with it emotional, psychological, and behavioral elements.

Scholars began to extend Black racial identity theories to other groups in the late 1970's and 1980's. Atkinson, Morten, and Sue (1979) introduced a minority identity development model that was supposed to be applicable to all people of color. In the mid 1980's, Helms (1984) first introduced a White racial identity model and, in subsequent writing, extended and expanded Black racial identity theory and has recently presented a People of color model (Helms, 1995: Thompson & Carter, 1997). More recently, racial identity theory has been expanded further (e.g., Carter, 1995, 1996; Helms, 1995; Helms & Piper, 1994; Thompson & Carter, 1997) and now contends that:

1. Racial identity development is applicable to all racial groups, even though separate models are presented for Blacks, Whites, and members of other racial groups. The different models reflect the distinct sociopolitical histories of the groups, because each group's history and sociopolitical interaction in the society has had some impact on how racial issues are understood and dealt with. One might think of race and racial groups on a continuum, with Whites at one pole, Asians, Indians, and Hispanics in the middle, and Blacks at the other pole.

2. Racial identity involves two sets of perspectives, one about self which influences how one views and understands members of the dominant and non-dominant groups and the second involving one's view of his or her own group and personality.

3. Racial identity represents ego differentiation of the personality or statuses, where one's racial worldview is more or less mature. Less mature ego statuses derive definition from external sources (peers, media, family, institutions, and so on), and more mature and differentiated racial identity ego statuses are internally derived through a personal process of exploration, discovery, integration, and maturation. Race at more mature levels of racial identity is seen in complex and dynamic ways based on accurate information and examined personal and group experience. Less mature racial identity statuses are simplistic, inaccurate, and contain unexamined personal and group notions about race and race relations.

Thus, progressive thinking about racial identity theory and changes in these models reflect a gradual shift from initially referring to a racial typology, to a linear stage model and presently to an ego statuses or levels. Racial identity statuses are comprised of attitudes, thoughts, feelings and behaviors toward oneself, as a member of a racial group, and toward members of the dominant and non-dominant racial group(s). The manner in which one's own racial identity is integrated into his or her personality depends on one's family composition and experience, the composition and attitudes of one's neighborhood or community, one's personal and unique interpretive style, and the ways in which peers validate or ignore race as an aspect of one's identity. The following sections will discuss racial identity development for Black Americans and how the psychological concepts of race impact the psychotherapy process.

Black Racial Identity

Cross (1980, 1991) building on the work of Thomas (1971), suggests that Black racial identity is a developmental process that consists of five stages: (a) Pre-encounter; (b) Encounter; (c) Immersion-Emersion; (d) Internalization; and (e) Internalization-Commitment. Helms (1984, 1990, 1995) and Helms and Piper (1994), using the same names for identity stages as Cross, expanded Black racial identity theory. As noted in the previous section, Helms suggests that racial identity is best understood in terms of statuses rather than developmental stages. At any one point in time an individual has many levels of racial identity but only one dominant level. According to Helms, the predominant racial identity level operates psychologically as a worldview or ego state, and each level has its own constellation of emotions, beliefs, motives, and behaviors, which influences its expression. Helms also proposes in each level of racial identity, a two phase process that is present.

The Pre-encounter level, according to Helms (1990) may be expressed in two distinct ways, passively or actively. Pre-encounter is characterized by a psychological or ego identity status where race issues are intrapsychically isolated. At this level race is given no personal or social meaning and one's personal and social status is determined by other aspects of personality, ability, and effort. An individual in passive Pre-encounter has fairly rigid individualistic views that are characteristic of American cultural beliefs.

The following is a case example of a person who may be functioning at the Pre-encounter level of racial identity: Roger is a 23-year-old Black male college student who has been raised in the a small rural neighborhood in the Southwest. He was raised by both parents in a working class neighborhood with his older brother and sister. He really looks up to his older brother who obtained a scholarship to attend college and presently works as an electrical engineer. His parents are both factory workers and his sister is a school teacher. Roger does not remember being given any messages about race issues or racism as a child. During his childhood when he ran into uncomfortable or negative incidences that may have been race related he usually blamed himself for the encounter. He applauds himself for his ability to use his experiences as something he can learn from in order to better himself. Roger feels race issues are non-existent and he believes that people are treated negatively when they do something to deserve it or if they run into a person who is unfair. In other words, because individuals can be unfair, anybody can encounter an unfair act. As a college student Roger is beginning to experience some anxiety connected to his interpersonal relationships as he meets other Black students with different worldviews about race. Roger, who is operating at the passive Pre-encounter level, may choose a White therapist, reflecting a subconscious internalization of White American cultural values. However, if Roger was in active Pre-encounter, he may more deliberately and consciously choose a White therapist because of his idealization of White culture and belief in White superiority. Nevertheless, a person functioning at the Pre-encounter level may seek therapy and never bring up or address race issues in the course of treatment. Although Roger may enter therapy, he may not divulge any feelings about race.

The Encounter level of racial identity is the most tumultuous and disconcerting for a Black person. At this level, an individual has an experience or a series of experiences that challenge his or her previously held beliefs and often leads to a search for a new Black/African identity. Encounter ego identity status reflects a state of psychological confusion and emotional turmoil, thus, the cognitive dissonance encountered may lead to the beginning the process of restructuring racial identity. The first phase of the Encounter level is operating as the individual experiences situations that shake or even shatter views of themselves regarding race and the interpretation of the condition of Blacks in America. Phase two of the Encounter level occurs when an energized decision is made to discover the meaning and significance of one's Blackness.

The following is a case example: Janet is a 25-year-old Black female nursing student who recently graduated nursing school and has landed her first job as a registered nurse. Her families ideology is that although racism may exist, it is not a major problem. She remembers clearly hearing her father exclaim racism is the problem of the racist and it should never be used as an obstacle to achievement. When Janet begins to encounter racist behavior on the job she tries to ignore it, but only after she gets past the disbelief that it is actually happening her. She enters therapy after a period of six months with mild depression and anxiety symptoms. Janet consciously chooses a Black therapist this may be an attempt to gain support and encouragement for the movement toward understanding a new African identity. However, if a White therapist is consciously chosen, this may be an attempt to gain clarity and gather support for the old identity being questioned (White cultural worldview). A person at this level may choose therapy more often than those at other levels due to the emotional upheaval that is often experienced. The race of the therapist may not matter at this point and the person may address race either directly or indirectly in the therapeutic process. However, the person will be strongly affected by the racial identity ego status of the clinician regardless of race.

Immersion-Emersion has two distinct phases in which an individual becomes deeply involved in discovering his or her Black or African American cultural heritage. The first phase, Immersion, is characterized by an all-consuming and obsessive involvement in Black life and culture. This person may idealize everything Black, have an abundance of Black pride and devalue Whites which may lead to rejection of a White therapist. Emersion, the second phase, is entered when the person begins to integrate this new identity into his or her personality. The person at the second level of Emersion can begin to integrate the perceived strengths and weakness of their new Black/African American identity.

A case example for this status is as follows: Kenya, a 29 year-old Black female who comes from a middle class background is actively seeking a Black therapist. She decided to go into therapy to gain clarity regarding her relationship with her husband, Toby. They began having problems when Kenya, a financial analyst returned from her trip to Africa. This trip was a combination of vacationing and educational adventure that Kenya had been looking forward to for a long time. For the past two years, she had been educating herself about African history and culture which she found fascinating and intriguing. Toby has been complaining to her that her new found interest in African history is overdone. He feels she has less time for him, however, Kenya feels her husband should participate in new activities.

A person who is at the Immersion/Emersion level of racial identity may consciously look for a therapist who has a well integrated racially identity, although this therapist can be a Black or White. However, it is more likely that there will be a preference for a Black therapist, as in Renya's case.

Helms (1984, 1986, 1990, 1994, 1995), combines the last phases of racial identity described by Cross, into a two phase process of ego status. This level is described as Internalization, which is a complete integration of the new Black/African American identity. The first phase of Internalization leads to an achievement of inner pride. A person at this phase is proud of his or her Black identity and develops a sense of security with respect to cultural heritage. During the second phase of Internalization, an individual adopts a behavioral style that is characterized by social and political activism and is consistent with their new personality and Black/African american identity.

The following case illustrates this: James is 40-year-old Black male who recently returned to school in order to obtain his law degree. He has been married since his late twenties when he first finished graduate school with a degree in social work. He and his wife Jeri live comfortably in a lower middle class residential neighborhood with their two boys ages five and seven. James works for a state agency that recently developed a new program that provides opportunities for employees to increase their education. He has always wanted to go to law school and although he doesn't totally regret getting a degree in social work, he does feel he made the wrong career choice.

James has endured many struggles in his life, including the difficulty he faced while trying to get through college, maintaining finances, and keeping his marriage together. There was always tension in the household when money got low and he sometimes had to take on more than one job. James always enjoyed school, especially taking classes that helped him to understand African culture and history. He viewed this as the most important part of his education.

James had been in and out of therapy at the local clinic, seeking help when he felt overwhelmed throughout his adult life. As a teenager, James was not very interested in doing much with his life. He felt defeated by society and did not think there were many opportunities for Black men. However, he also had a very supportive family who was proud of their heritage and tried to instill this pride in James. Although, he grew up in a depressed neighborhood and sometimes felt despair, their was enough support and encouragement from his family and surrounding community to help him keep focused. James is presently involved in community organizations developed to help give kids hope and opportunities for a progressive future. He is well aware of race issues and how racism affects people of color. His goal is to obtain a law degree and become more politically active in his community.

The individual operating at this last level of racial identity may consciously search for a therapist that has a well integrated sense of racial identity. In the case of James, he was able to get assistance from at least two of the three therapists he had seen intermittently, who all maintained at least one higher identity level than he was at the time.

The reader should keep in mind that each ego identity status can be expressed by the same person at any given time or in any given situation. What will matter most is the prevailing theme in one's racial identity expressions. The last section of this chapter will discuss case examples and clinical implications of how racial identity may impact interactional work in psychotherapy.

A Process Model of Race and Psychotherapy

The influence of race in the therapeutic process can occur a number of different ways. Clients may present racial issues cloaked in life situations such as work settings, deciding on a career path, interpersonal relations, family relations or self concerns (i.e., motivation, esteem, etc.). As discussed throughout this chapter, race is a psychological construct that affects thoughts, feelings and behavior depending on how one views themselves racially. Racial identity theory provides an understanding of the complexity surrounding race and racial issues for an individual. It is our belief that to understand how race influences psychotherapy, one must have an understanding of racial identity ego statuses. Knowing a patients racial identity level provides an initial step toward understanding how race-related issues may affect him or her and how race may be manifested in his or her intrapsychic and interpersonal relations (Carter, 1995).

Carter further suggests that focusing solely on the patients racial identity level is insufficient when trying to fully grasp the process of psychotherapy; the therapist's level of racial identity must also be considered. The racial identity interactions that influence the process and outcome of the therapeutic encounter, demonstrate a critical element in Carter's Racially Inclusive Model of Psychotherapy.

Helms (1984) describes four types of relationships that emerge when a clients and therapists levels of racial identity are assessed and used to characterize the psychotherapeutic process. The four relationship types are categorized as either: (a) parallel; (b) crossed; (c) progressive; or (d) regressive. Each type of relationship, regardless of racial composition, is associated with particular process dimensions and psychotherapeutic outcomes.

The parallel relationship exists when a therapist and client share similar racial identity attitudes. For example, in a parallel relationship with a Black therapist and a Black patient, when both participants have low levels of racial identity, a client may leave treatment with minimal therapeutic gain, and a counselor may encourage a client to terminate or to seek treatment with another therapist. Higher and more mature racial identity ego statuses would result in positive therapeutic gains.

A crossed relationship, may involve participants of the same race or of different races, and is characterized by opposition of racial identity status in the dyad. A therapist may have a worldview of race that either contradicts or opposes the worldview of the patient. For example, in an all-Black crossed relationship, a patient may have a predominantly Pre-encounter status, and a therapist may have a predominantly Immersion status. Regardless of the participant's race, in crossed dyads, neither the therapist nor the patient empathizes with the others attitudes; however, both may engage in educative strategies.

A progressive relationship exists when the therapist's racial identity status is at least one level above the patient's. For example, in a Black dyad consisting of a patient who has a predominance of Encounter status attitudes and a therapist who has a predominance of Immersion/Emersion status attitudes, the therapist may be supportive and helpful in encouraging clarity for the patient. In this type of relationship, the therapist can encourage the patient to explore racial issues in a broader sense, move beyond individual acts and include an understanding of how race has societal and institutional components as well as explore with the patient how his or her racial identity ego status effect her or his functioning. Lastly, a regressive relationship exists when the patient's racial identity status is at least one level more advanced than the therapist's. In this type of relationship, the process may resemble a power struggle; both participants may have strong affective reactions to each other, and conflict may characterize the therapeutic process. For example, if a patient has predominately Internalized status attitudes while the therapist has predominately Pre-encounter status attitudes, the therapist's worldview may prevent any genuine understanding of the patients' pain and hurt as described in their encounters with racism or experiences that have racial components. In this type of relationship, the therapist often totally misinterprets or misdiagnoses the situation and little real gain is experienced by the patient.

The process dimensions believed to be salient in these psychotherapeutic relationship types are: (a) affective reactions and responses; (b) the therapists and patients' perceptions and experiences of the therapy sessions, overall processes, and outcomes; and (c) the counselors and clients verbal and nonverbal strategies. The following section will provide clinical examples to help illustrate the possible outcomes of some of these interactions. The case examples described below will focus on Black racial identity and employ racial identity statuses, as presented in this chapter.

Case Examples

The following case illustrates some of the process dimensions prevalent in regressive therapeutic relationships. The therapist, Karen, is a 35-year-old, dark-skinned African American woman who was raised in a middle class neighborhood in the Northeast with mostly White neighbors. She was raised in a small family that consisted of her parents and two younger sisters, and she occassionally had contact with extended family members who lived in the area. Her family emphasized the importance of achievement and taught Karen that only lack of self-confidence could hold a person back from achieving their goals. Race issues were often minimized or denied importance when discussed or brought up in her family. Karen excelled academically and attended a prestigious university close to home, obtaining her undergraduate and doctoral degree in psychology. She was taught psychodynamic psychotherapy and throughout her training, never took courses focusing on treatment issues related to service delivery and people of color. There was an elective course available in her graduate program but Karen thought it was unnecessary to take this course.

She felt that she could be effective in treating anyone and that race issues should be treated as an obstacle to therapy. Karen never encountered a patient who presented a race related issue during her academic training or internship. However, as a newly licensed psychologist in private practice, she recently encountered a patient who is experiencing problems with racial discrimination.

The patient, John, is a 30-year-old, middle class Black male who moved to the United States from Jamaica, West Indies as a young adult. He is married with two children and works as a computer analyst in a prestigious company. John has been successful academically and vocationally and has always considered himself a hard worker. He was raised by his grandparents who he describes as hard workers, and fairly strict disciplinarians. He felt his grandparents were supportive, encouraging and proud maintaining strong cultural values. They encouraged John to achieve beyond their accomplishments and supported his desire to move to America. After graduating High School he came to live with his brothers in the United States.

John has been working at the same company for two and a half years and has received outstanding evaluations with the exception of this past year. He sought therapy to address symptoms of anxiety due to job stress. John was promoted last year and under his new supervisor, who happens to be a White male, he began to get poor evaluations and was warned to improve his work or inevitably face termination.

John believes he is being unfairly treated because he is a Black male. He has seen other Blacks leave the company after achieving a certain level. He feels he now understands why so many Blacks have left the company. Karen believes that John's anxiety is due to conflictual feelings that he may harbor regarding his success and achievement. She is spending time trying to understand the relationship between John and his grandfather and his biological father. John is willing to discuss this family constellation but, he is getting little satisfaction from the discovery of his feelings and his symptoms seemed to worsen. He often becomes more anxious and angry after therapy because he feels his feelings about race issues are often dismissed or reframed as achievement issues. Karen recommends a psychiatric consult due to the resistance she feels from John and his increased anxiety. John drops out of therapy and seeks another therapist who he feels may be more knowledgeable about race issues.

In this case, Karen appears to be functioning at the Pre-encounter level of racial identity. Her patient, John is at least operating at the Encounter level. He was experiencing mixed feelings of anger and anxiety that were at first generated by the racist encounters, then exacerbated by a therapist who was unable to comprehend his situation and misinterpreted the roots of his conflicts. Karen summarized John's reactions as resistance to therapy.

The next case will illustrate process dimensions of a progressive relationship in a therapeutic dyad. The therapist, Monica is a light-skinned, 40-year-old Black female who received her doctoral degree in clinical psychology from a prestigious East Coast school. She was raised by both parents in a large family of eight children. Monica was the oldest girl in the family and learned responsibility early in life. She grew up in a Black neighborhood and learned the values of her culture not only from her family but also from structured community programs. Monica seemed to always hold the position of caretaker in various roles in her life, especially with her family, peers, and friends.

When she graduated from school she came back to her community to volunteer her time at the local church and other community agencies. Monica is well aware of racism which was learned through her own experiences and her college education. She is active in her community in fighting against racism on individual and institutional levels.

The patient, Iman is a brown-skinned, 29-year-old Black female who entered therapy due to feelings of depression. She reports a history of depression which has spanned of her life, but she believes that she is only now recognizing it. Iman is a financial analyst and also reports feeling discontent with her career and relationships, especially with men. Her goal for therapy is to become more focused and develop clear career goals.

Iman is an only child who was raised primarily by her mother and extended family maternal aunts, uncles and grandparents. Her family overindulged her and often put her on a pedestal, showering her with undue attention. Iman loved her family who she felt always supported and encouraged her, often having undoubtedly high expectations of her. Nevertheless, Iman was bothered by one thing regarding her family, and that was the lack of contact she had with her father, Louis. She only knew that her father was born in Haiti and still lived there. Iman's parents divorced when she was a young child and she had no contact with the paternal side of her family until only a few years ago.

During the course of therapy, Iman gained insight about her depression and discovered it was partly due to a need to become more psychologically independent from her family. Although she began to take steps toward independence, she realized under the guidance of Monica that she was still uncomfortable with some aspects of her life. Her depression improved, however, she still experienced career indecisiveness.

Throughout the course of treatment Iman expressed the discomfort she experience working in a corporate situation. As Iman gradually realized that she was not comfortable in the corporate environment, due the lack of freedom fully express herself, race issues began to be discussed.

Monica provided an understanding environment for Iman to explore these feelings, Monica was not confused about race nor did she think her patient's life issues that she had been harboring for some time now were disconnected from race. Iman discussed the need to present herself in a certain way at work and the relief of returning to her own space where she could be herself. She discussed not wanting to seem too pretentious with her friends and being careful not to bring what she called her work attitude home with her. She struggled with how to integrate her White middle class values and her African identity. Iman worked hard throughout this process as she questioned which values actually belonged to her. She became closer to her father and his family as she worked through this identity issue. Iman became more educated about her culture and race identity and even took a trip to Africa. She changed her hair style to African braids and was surprised at the reception she received by her co-workers to the outward declaration of her changed attitudes about race. They were not all accepting, however, the people closest to her made no ill remarks as she had once feared. The change was acknowledged in a positive way.

In this case, Monica is at the level of Internalization in racial identity development, while Iman began at the Pre-encounter level and evolved to the Immersion/Emersion level in the process of therapy. Monica was able to help Iman develop the skills she needed to become more independent which lead to an enhanced ego development. As Iman became more mature, she was able to confront the issues about race and racism that she had struggled with for a long time.

Conclusion

The determination of race as an important psychological construct that impacts the therapeutic process is pertinent to developing further understanding of the psychotherapeutic process in working with all patients' or client's. We have tried to show that race is salient in the society we live in. In the formation of all its institutions and integral to an understanding of our core cultural values. We have also argued that race is an integral aspect of each person's personality. And as such, each person who is raised and immigrates to this country is taught through socialization or acculturation appropriate race role attitudes, feelings and behaviors. It is essential that race, through the use of racial identity and the Racially Inclusive Model of Psychotherapy, be actively incorporated in the work of mental health professionals.

Currently, most mental health professionals are ill-equipped personally and/or professionally to help their clients learn about, cope with, and grow from an understanding of race in their personal and interpersonal lives (Carter, 1995). We must effectively combat the effects of race and racism on all people (See Jones & Carter, 1996). But such battles will be waged in vain unless we accept the role and effects of psychological race and the types of interactions in treatment that arise from the combinations of racial identity ego statuses. All mental health professionals should be versed in the ideas and models presented in this chapter. The ideas allow for new directions, deeper analyses, and complex characterizations of the psychology of race and it's manifestations, both at the individual and group levels. The models presented in this chapter allow clinicians and scholars to take into account both levels in their efforts to understand the relationship of individuals to social and group level phenomena like institutional and cultural racism (Jones & Carter, 1996). We need to break down the barriers due to race in our work as mental health professionals. Now we have the ammunition to succeed.

References

Adams, W.A. (1950). The Negro patient in psychiatric treatment. *American Journal of Orthopsychiatry, 20*, 305-310.

Allen, T.W. (1994). *The invention of the White race: Racial oppression and social control.* London, England: Verso.

Atkinson, D.R., Morten, G. & Sue, D.W. (1979). *Counseling American minorities: A cross-cultural perspective.* Dubuque, IA: W.C. Brown.

Benard V.W. (1953). Psychoanalysis and members of minority groups. *Journal of the American Psychoanalytic Association, 1,* 256- 267.

Betancourt, H., & Lopez, S.R. (1993). The study of culture, ethnicity, and race in American psychology. *American Psychologist, 48(6)*, 629-637.

Brislin, R.W. (Ed.), (1990). *Applied cross-cultural psychology.* Newbury Park, CA: Sage.

Carter, R.T. (1995). The *influence of race and racial identity in psychotherapy: Toward a racially inclusive model.* New York: John Wiley.

Carter, R.T. (1996). Exploring the complexity of racial identity measures. In G. R. Sodowsky & J. Impara (Eds.), *Multicultural assessment.* Lincoln, NB: Buros Institute of Mental Measurement.

Comas-Diaz, L., & Jacobsen, F. M. (1991). Ethnocultural transference and countertransference in the therapeutic dyad. *American Journal of Orthopsychiatry, 6(3)*, 392-402.

Cook, D.A., & Helms, J. (1988). Visible racial/ethnic group supervisees satifaction with cross-cultural supervision as predict by relationship characterics. *Journal of Counseling Psychology, 33*, 168-174.

Cross, W.E. (1978). The Cross and Thomas models of psychological Nigrescence. *Journal of Black Psychology, 5*, 13-19.

Cross, W.E. (1980). Models of psychological Nigrescence: A literature review. In R.L. Jones (Ed.), *Black psychology* (2nd ed., pp. 81-89). New York: Harper & Row.

Cross, W.E. (1991). *Shades of Black.* Philadelphia: Temple University Press.

Cyrus, V. (1993). *Experiencing race, class, and gender in the United States.* Mountain View, CA: Mayfield Publishing Company.

Fredrickson, G.M. (1989). *The arrogance of race.* Middletown, CT: Wesleyan University Press.

Garfield, S.L. (1978). Research on client variables in psychotherapy. In S.L. Garfield & A.E. Bergin (Eds.), *Handbook of psychotherapy and behavior change* (2nd ed., pp. 191-232). New York: John Wiley.

Gould, S.J. (1981). *The mismeasure of man.* New York: Norton.

Guthrie, R.V. (1976). *Even the rat was White: A historical view of psychology.* New York: Bantam.

Heine, R.W. (1950). The Negro patient in psychotherapy. *Journal of Clinical Psychology, 16,* 373-376.

Helms, J.E. (1984). Toward an explanation of the influence of in the counseling process: A Black-White model. *The Counseling Psychologist, 12,* 153-165.

Helms, J.E. (Ed.), (1990). *Black and White racial identity: Theory, research, and practice.* Westport, CT. Greenwood Press.

Helms, J.E. (1994). Racial identity and racial constructs. In E.J. Trickett, R. Watts, & D. Birman (Eds.), *Human diversity* (pp. 285-311). San Francisco, CA: Jossey-Bass.

Helms, J.E., & Carter, R.T. (1990). The development of the White Racial Identity Inventory. In J.E. Helms (Ed.), *Black and White racial identity* (pp. 145-164). Westport, CT: Greenwood Press.

Helms, J.E., & Piper, R.E. (1994). Implications of racial identity theory for vocational psychology. *Journal of Vocational Behavior, 44,* 124-138.

Highlen, P.S., & Hill, C. E. (1984). Factors affecting client change in Jackson, A.M. (1990). Evolution of ethnocultural psychotherapy. *Psychotherapy, 27(3),* 428-435.

Johnson, S.D. (1990). Toward clarifying culture, race and ethnicity in the context of multicultural counseling. *Journal of Multicultural Counseling and Development, 18(1),* 41, 50.

Jones, J.M., & Carter, R.T. (1996) Racism and White racial identity: Merging realities. In B. P. Bowser & R. G. Hunt (Eds.) *Impacts of racism on White Americans* (2nd ed., pp. 1-23). Thousand Oaks, CA.; Sage Publications.

Kennedy, J. (1952). Problems posed in the analysis of black patients. *Psychiatry, 15,* 313-327.

Kovel, J. (1984). *White racism.* New York: Columbia University Press.

McGoldrick, M., Pearce, J.K., & Giordano, J. (Eds.), (1982). *Ethnicity and family therapy.* New York: Guilford Press.

Omi, M., & Winant, H. (1995). In P. Rothenberg (Ed.), *Race, class, and gender in the United States* (3rd ed., pp. 13-22). New York: St. Martin Press.

Orlinsky, D.E., & Howard, K.I. (1978). The relations of process to outcome in psychotherapy. In S. L. Garfield & A.E. Bergin (Eds.), *Handbook of psychotherapy and behavior change* (2nd ed, pp. 283-330). New York: John Wiley.

Parloff, M.B. Waskow, I., & Wolfe, B.E. (1978). Research on therapist variables in relation to process and outcome. In L. Garfield & A. E. Bergin (Eds.), *Handbook of psychotherapy and behavior change* (2nd ed., pp. 233-282). New York: John Wiley.

Pinderhughes, E. (1989). *Understanding race, ethnicity and power: The key to efficacy in clinical practice.* New York: Free Press.

Rothenberg, P. (Ed.), (1995). *Race, class, and gender in the United States* (3rd ed.). New York: St. Martin Press.

Rotheram, M.J., & Phinney, J.S. (1987). Ethnic behavior patterns as an aspect of identity. In J.S. Phinney & M.J. Rotheram (Eds.), *Children's ethnic socialization: Pluralism and development.* Newbury Park, CA: Sage.

Schachter, J.S., & Butts, H.F. (1950). Transference and countertransference in interracial analysis. *Journal of the American Psychoanalytic Association, 16,* 792-808.

St. Clair, H. (1951). Psychiatric interview experience withNegroes. *American Journal of Psychiatry, 108,* 113-119.

Smedley, A. (1993). *Race in North America: Origin and evolution of a world view.* Boulder, CO: Westview Press.

Sue, D.W., & Sue, D. (1990). *Counseling the culturally different: Theory and practice* (2nd ed.). New York: John Wiley.

Thomas, C. (1971). *Boys no more.* Beverly Hills, CA: Glencoe Press.

Thomas, A., & Sillen, S. (1972). *Racism and psychiatry.* New York: Carol Publishing Group.

Thompson, C., & Carter, R.T. (1997) *Applications of racial identity theory to individuals, groups, and organizations.* Mawhaw, New Jersey: Lawrence Earlbaum.

Vargas, L., & Ross-Chioino, J.D. (Eds.), (1992). *Working with the culture: Psychotherapeutic interventions with ethnic minority children and adolescents.* San Francisco, CA: Jossey Bass.

Vontress, C.E. (1971). *Counseling Negroes.* Boston: Houghton Mifflin.

Wilkerson, I. (1992, June 21). Two neighborhoods and a wall called race. *New York Times,* (p. 1.)

Yee, A.H., Fairchild, H.H., Weizmann, F., & Wyatt, G.E. (1993). Addressing psychology's problem with race. *American Psychologist, 48(11),* 1132-1140.

Authors

Robert T. Carter
Teachers College
Columbia University
525 W. 120th St., Box 32
New York, N.Y. 10027
Telephone: (212) 678-3346
Fax: (212) 678-3275
E-mail: rtcro@columbia.educ

Sharon Boyd-Jackson
Department of Psychology
Kean College
Union, N.J., 07083

Part 2

Symposium on Cross' Stage Model

Cross' Stage Model Revisited: An Analysis of Theoretical Formulations and Empirical Evidence

Julie E. Stokes, Carolyn B. Murray, David Chavez, and M. Jean Peacock

Introduction

Twenty-seven years after its introduction, Cross' adult identity development model remains ubiquitously cited in studies attempting to explain the process of developing a sense of racial identity in African American populations (Looney, 1988; Parham, 1989; Parham & Helms, 1985; Ponterotto & Wise, 1987; Sue & Sue, 1990). Cross' theoretical framework is also used when describing how "racial identity" development proceeds in other groups (Helms, 1990; Sue & Sue, 1990). Likewise, much of the recent content of other racial identity attitude measures stem from theoretical formulations found in Cross' work (Munford, 1994; Parham & Helms, 1981; Ponterotto & Wise, 1987). The wide-spread application of Cross' Negro-to-Black conversion experience model (Brookins, Anyabwile, & Nacoste, 1992; Claiborn, & LaFromboise, 1986; Helms, 1984b; Pomales, Lewis & Adams, 1990; Walter & Simoni, 1993; Watts, 1992) led researchers to describe it as representing "one of the most highly developed of those proposed" (Sue & Sue, 1990, p. 94). Thus, when one considers how widely the Negro-to-Black conversion experience model has been used, the necessity of critical reviews of the model is clear.

The present review has three purposes: (a) to extend earlier efforts through a critical analysis of Cross' racial identity development model (see *The Counseling Psychologist*, Special Issue, 1989); (b) to suggest the heuristic use of the stage concept be abandoned; and (c) to suggest researchers reconceptualize the Negro-to-Black Conversion model as experiential rather than developmental.

The Negro-to Black Identity Model

Smith (1989) asked "What is nigrescence?" (p. 278). The concept of "nigrescence," coined by Cross (1971), provided a phenomenologically descriptive interpretation of the Cross model. The Negro-to-Black conversion experience model described "the process of developing a Black identity," by describing "movement from one level of racial awareness to another" (Parham & Helms, 1985, p. 143). The Negro-to-Black conversion is currently a five stage model characterized by interactions Blacks have with members of their own and other racial groups, particularly Whites. The five stages are (1) Pre-encounter, (2) Encounter, (3) Immersion/Emersion, (4) Internalization, and (5) Internalization-Commitment.

Stage 1

Initially, Black social interactions reflect an unexamined ideation of White ideas and beliefs. Cross proposed that the attitudes of Blacks at the Pre-encounter stage manifested a bias toward positive views of Whites and negative views of other Blacks.

Stage 2

In the Encounter stage, the individual experiences a profound crisis or event, vis-a-vis White society, thus challenging his/her previously unexamined beliefs. Following this racially salient Encounter, a temporary dislodging of worldview and identity occurs (Sue & Sue, 1990). Blacks in the Encounter stage have experienced a breakdown in beliefs about race relations in general and their social reality in particular. Thus, they begin to question their relationship with White America and examine issues related to race.

Stage 3

Immersion/Emersion is the stage characterized as an intense search for a sense of identity related to the emerging awareness that one is Black in a White world. The person withdraws from the dominant culture. Black pride develops but is minimally Internalization. Blacks in the early Immersion stage have either/or thinking (e.g., positive attitudes towards Blacks/negative attitudes toward Whites). They describe their victimization and the victimization of other Black people at the hands of Whites. Blacks at the end of the stage, Emersion, have replaced psychological defensiveness with affective and cognitive openness, allowing a critical analysis of racial issues, according to Cross. Eventually, the individual expresses primarily positive attitudes toward other Blacks. Further, a preference for primarily interacting with one's own racial group is indicative of a move toward an Internalization Black identity.

Stage 4

Internalization is the fourth stage in Cross' current model. It is characterized by a feeling of inner security, more flexibility, more tolerance of others, and more openness in attitudes and behaviors (Sue, 1991). Thus, Internalization of a racial identity moves one toward an ingroup acceptance of both negative and positive aspects or characteristics of other Blacks and/or an absence of racial bias toward Whites.

Stage 5

The Internalization-Commitment stage first appeared in Cross' original theoretical work (Cross, 1971), but following empirical research Stage 5 was dropped from the theory. Recently however, Stage 5 has been reinstated into Cross' most current model (Cross, 1991). But, Cross states that current theory suggests few differences between "the fourth and fifth stages" (p. 220). He further adds that empirical investigation of Stage 5 is an endeavor to be undertaken in future research. Therefore, the reminder of this paper will focus on Cross' four stage model. Cross concluded that one of the results of an identity transformation was an increased ability to consider a variety of social perspectives operating in a given setting. This occurs because racial dichotomies (i.e., Black/White) "no longer have meaning" (Helms, 1984b, p. 157). One's life issues reflect concerns with simply becoming the best person possible (irrespective of race). The result is others are primarily judged on character rather than skin color. The shift in Blacks' attitudes and behaviors occurs as a consequence of one's increased search for self- understanding and search for unbiased knowledge of their racial group.

The Problem

There are a number of weaknesses in Cross' work. They include the following: (1) a lack of conceptual clarity in the definition of nigrescence (Smith, 1989); (2) the heuristic application or misapplication of the stage concept (Akbar, 1989); (3) an intrinsic bias in descriptions of identifiable attitudes and behaviors considered as appropriate at the various stages. First, with regard to the term nigrescence, "the author never really defines the concept" (Smith, 1989, p. 278). Furthermore, the concept as used in the model reflects a helplessness in the victims (i.e., Blacks).

Smith asserts that Cross' projection of a sense of helplessness in Blacks is a position which does not consider that many Blacks (1) adopt survival strategies by not revealing their true selves to Whites, (2) have developed techniques which allow them to "stand outside and reflect upon" (Jones, 1980, p. 23) White society, and (3) simply engage in role play with White America. These points should be seen as an important limitation to the applicability of the model (Nobles, 1989). Social adaptation within the context of a hostile environment in no way suggests helplessness. Therefore, psychological and behavioral adaptations to one's environment, as well as, psychological adaptations to the situations one finds oneself in when interacting with Whites are not considered.

The appropriate usage of the stage concept also seems problematic, given that stages are described as sequential levels of adapting (Miller, 1989) that result from, (a) invariant sequencing (stages must occur in a particular order, by everyone, and no stage can be skipped); (b) hierarchical transformations (each stage integrates the previous stage in preparation for the next stage); (c) universal expression (the structures and concepts are acquired by all humans); and (d) determine one's levels of cognition functioning apart from a specific content. Whites would need to experience racial identity development in the same manner as African Americans. Early research findings suggests that is not the case (Phinney, 1992). Beyond that, the resolution of stages reflect a qualitatively adaptable, not necessarily more socially effective, way of thinking, as Cross suggests. Cross' model is also filled with prescriptions for the way an individual should think, feel, and behave, with regard to race, in order to be perceived as being at a particular stage.

The primary theme of the model is racial awareness and identity development through social interactions related to race. The metamorphosis of identity is context specific (Nobles, 1989), occurring as a result of some interpersonal experience. There is no accounting for positive, goal-directed thoughts or behaviors. Nobles (1989) points out that these limitations arise because Cross' original and current theoretical assumptions remain rooted in the biases of "traditional Western psychology" (p. 254). Aside from the intrinsic bias in Cross' model, critics object to applications of the model for other reasons (Smith, 1989; Whittler, Calantone, Young, 1991). Their objections address the fact that: (a) there is no consensus among researchers regarding exactly what the definition of an African American ethnic identity should be nor what role racial identity should play in healthy psychological adjustment (Smith, 1989); (b) researchers have not agreed on how to measure racial or ethnic identity and/or expressions of exhibited behaviors (Stokes, Murray, Peacock, & Kaiser, 1994); and (c) there is no consensus among researchers regarding exactly what constitutes appropriate levels of racial or ethnic identity and/or expressions of exhibited behaviors. Yet, Cross' stage theory initially postulated one starting place and only one possible destination, from degradation—to a secure acceptance of self as African American (Parham & Helms, 1985) and acceptance of members of other racial groups, as well.

Racial Identity

A race is defined as "any people who are distinguished, or consider themselves distinguished, in social relations with other people, by their physical characteristics" (Feagin & Feagin, 1993, p. 6). Consequently, a racial identity would primarily reflect one's perception of similarity with others contingent upon: (a) real or alleged physical characteristics (e.g., skin color, hair, nose, lips); and (b) behaviors (e.g., treatment of other Blacks and/or of Whites). Cross illustrated the point by referring to hair styles and interracial contact when providing the early framework for his theory. Cross stated that "Blackness is a state of mind, that is explained by dynamic rather than static paradigms" (Cross, 1971, p. 15). Blackness can be conceptualized as the psychological understanding one has of socially ascribed racial characteristics. Still, Cross does not explicitly state what is meant by Blackness, a key concept, which is used considerably throughout his theoretical discourse. Furthermore, he does not explore the social ascriptions generated within African American groups. Nor does Cross consider how variability in the racial features of other African Americans is perceived.

Ethnic Identification

Ethnic identification, a broader concept (Smith, 1989) often mistakenly used synonymously with racial identification, results from both one's personal "understanding of shared definitions employed by the group" (White & Burke, 1987, p. 313) and the social categorization practices of other non-group members (Stokes, 1994). These shared definitions are created by identification with (1) physical similarities; (2) African/African American history; (3) African/African American Culture (e.g., dress, music, art); (4) similar social experiences (i.e., prejudice and discrimination); and (5) concern for social conditions experienced by many African Americans (political, educational, economic). These are separate, probably related issues influenced by (a) age (Helms, 1989); (b) socioeconomic class (Smith, 1989); and (c) life experiences (Stokes, 1994). Therefore, "Race is but one outward sign of a shared identity" (Smith, 1989, p. 282). There are possibly other, potentially more salient (e.g., gender), issues and/or concerns related to ones racial or ethnic identity. Cross (1991) suggested other identity concerns become salient only after one resolves issues related to race identity. Summarizing these points, the question still remains, "What is a sound racial identity?" (Smith, 1989, p. 280).

Other Influences

Many parts of the model "perpetuate a view of racial conflict that is relevant but perhaps a little outdated," (Smith, 1989, p. 279). Direct conflict, such as lynching and/or fire bombing rarely take place today. Furthermore, many of the symbols of racism have also changed (Smith, 1989) and neither the influence of more contemporary historical events (e.g., Rodney King), nor current zeitgeist (increased racial tension) have been incorporated into the theoretical formulations. Furthermore, antecedents affecting racial identity orientations are not discussed (e.g., media, parent influences, and peers).

Race socialization strategies utilized by parents and significant others differ in form (i.e., proactive, reactive, passive). Many socialization agents have adopted a proactive strategy with regard to promoting their children's racial/ethnic identity development. Therefore, even young children think about race and racial identity. The prevailing contemporary research literature suggests that by age nine young children move toward an ingroup preference with regard to their ethnic group (McAdoo, 1985). On the other hand, some parents never address or respond to racial issues (Thornton, Chatters, Taylor, & Allen, 1990). Race socialization strategies vary, and consequently, race orientations vary. One of the most salient problems evident in Cross' approach is Cross' failure to address the impact of race socialization factors (e.g. the race orientation of immediate family) on an individual's reference group orientation. Consequently, Cross only recently (1991) considers the fact that there are many prominent African Americans who do not view Whites as either important or as a predominantly defining influences in regard to their behaviors. Moreover, discussion of the impact of other defining influence which affect one's race orientation are still minimally considered (e.g., community, media, peers, etc.).

The point is clearly articulated by Boykin and Toms (1985), who theorized that ethnic members proximal or distal relationship to White society should determine the race socialization agendas to which individuals are exposed. For example, the individual's survival in White society would not necessarily be beneficial to the child or the parent if they live in a segregated urban center. They further point out that with a White orientation the child may not survive to interact with any community outside of its own. Thus, it appears that establishing individual relationships with other African Americans may be a more pressing concern for some. Other factors, such as one's gender, physical features, (e.g., weight), behaviors, geographic region, and/or exposure to social stereotypes (held by either African Americans and/or Whites) also potentially affect one's reference group orientation. Furthermore, sociocultural (e.g., family, peers), psychological (e.g., self-concept, personal coping style, and personality) may also systematically influence one's racial identity attitudes, along with or parallel to exposure to prejudice and racial discrimination. Some studies examining these influences will be described later. The evidence is still sparse, however. There are also other potential influences such as (1) maturational influences; (2) social influences related to the timing of one's exploration; (3) activities defined as important in one's exploration of ethnic identity issues; and (4) how one resolves complex issues pertaining to perceived social and/or cultural differences that remain unexplored. In sum, Cross (1971; 1978) did not address many possible influences such as personality, social structure, and social class (Jones, 1980, p. 18). He described adult racial awareness issues as if they occur in relationship to only one event, racial Encounters. Therefore, this theory can best be described as restrictive and limiting when exploring issues related to identity development in African Americans (Akbar, 1989; Nobles, 1989; Smith, 1989). There is little discussion acknowledging that the issues are a complex interaction of behaviors, attitudes, feelings, and cognitions that occur in a real and often hostile social world. Moreover, the level of cognitive understanding or the emotional intensity of responses felt by African Americans experiencing identity reformulations may reflect differences that were brought about by just the circumstances or events that Cross does not explore. Thus, it appears time to once again revisit Cross' model.

Review of Key Assumptions in the Cross Model

The following represents some of the key assumptions in the model:

1. Motivational catalysts prompting developmental progression are related to racially salient social experiences.
2. At the Internalization stage of racial identity there is no relationship between one's racial group identity and positive self-esteem.
3. There is a positive linear relationship between acceptance of self, as a member of an ethnic group, and acceptance of racially different others.
4. Stages are related to levels of cognition and are apart from specific content reasoning.
5. Preference for similar others based upon sex and socioeconomic status should not be systematically related to racial attitudes.
6. An ideological metamorphosis resulting in moving toward a positive expression of one's racial identity is liberating, and psychologically healthy (Helms, 1990).
7. Higher stages of racial identification are better stages with regard to psychological functioning and result in greater interpersonal adjustment.
8. Whites are always the comparative reference group against which racial attitudes are explored.

Each stage carries with it an attitude toward Whites, as well as Blacks (Helms, 1984b). But there is still little evidence to support Cross' theoretical assumptions. Therefore, Parham (1989) now suggests that the model be expanded to a "multistage and multidimensional structure" (Smith, 1989, p. 275). Then "cycling," the reexperiencing of a stage contingent upon new developmentally sanctioned social demands, can be incorporated. For example, when an individual moves from home into the broader social setting (i.e., White society) an Encounter may be experienced, sending the individual backwards into an earlier stage of racial attitudes. Beyond that, Parham (1989) indicates that "the process of racial identity for many Black Americans deviates from general principles of universal experience" (Smith, 1989, p. 283). Thus, the idea of only one starting point and one end point loses its tenability, so much so, that Cross (1991) now posits two possible developmental trajectories: (1) Black Nationalism; or (2) Biculturalism/Multiculturalism with varying dynamic functions, which include; (a) defending oneself against racism; (b) providing oneself with a sense of belonging; and (c) providing oneself with a foundation for social interactions. Beyond the issue of where one starts or ends in the racial identity development process, the model does not consider African Americans who realize they are a member of the group, but through a conscious choice, prefer not to interact with the group. Their race preference choices may be due to negative experiences with other African Americans, not Whites. It could also be the case that self-interests are more salient (e.g., status) and thus, interacting with the group might hinder one's efforts. There are clear social rewards for African Americans who behave in socially prescribed ways (Akbar, 1989). An examination of the empirical research offers a way of assessing the utility of the Racial Identity Model when seeking to understand African American psychological functioning.

Research Using The Cross Model

In exploring the plausibility of the identity transformation hypothesis advanced by Cross (1971), a study was conducted by Hall, Cross and Freedle (1972). Using a Q-methodology, Black and White Princeton college students performed person perception Q-sorts to delineate consensual validation pertaining to Black identity transformation stages as theorized by Cross (1971). Due to the fact that "all correlations between groups were significant well beyond the .01 level" (Hall, Cross, Freedle, 1972, p. 162) the tenability of the Cross (1971) theory was supported. Yet, it is the high intercorrelations among Q-sort items that call the validity of the results into question. Q-sort methodology seriously over estimates correlation coefficients when investigating monotrait items, especially "when only one trait (i.e. Black identity) is being considered" (Sunland, 1962, p. 62). Following from this, researchers dismissal of items not reflecting "any systematic patterns across comparisons" (Hall, Cross, & Freedle, 1972, p. 163) of the stages, after only one empirical test, suggests a further possible bias in results. Other potential factors biasing results include the use of Princeton students as subjects. They (the subjects), more than likely, were atypical African Americans (Krate, Leventhal, & Silverstein, 1974). Therefore, the study of identity transformation issues within the African American population required the involvement of more representative subjects.

Krate, Leventhal, and Silverstein (1974) assessed identity change with 50 urban low-income Black college students. Each student performed four separate Q-sort tasks. They sorted in accordance with how they viewed themselves: (1) 4 years ago; (2) 2 years ago; (3) now; and (4) in the future. The authors concluded that the self-perceived, retrospect, present, and future oriented responses were congruent with the direction of change indicated in the Cross (1971) model. Statistically however, Q-sort correlations are overestimates of pre-post data or in this case multiple accounts of emerging attributes (Sunland, 1962), as well. Consequently, one could conclude that Q-sort methodology provides weak and biased supporting evidence relating to the Black Identity transformation model. Still, the results of these two studies offered empirical support demonstrating the existence of several stages that suggested a developmental progression toward Black awareness. Therefore, Cross' (1971) Q-sort items were reworded, removing, (1) items with a negative social desirability component (e.g., "I believe to be Black is to be low down and dirty") (Parham & Helms, 1981, p. 252); (2) items containing more than one issue; and (3) items with incomprehensible language (for college undergraduates). The Q-sort items were then converted to a 5-point attitude measure scale and administered to 20 college students. The scale was item analyzed with data from the first sample of college students. After final revisions of the scale, the same 20 plus an additional 72 (N=92) college students completed the instrument.

The revised scale was titled the Racial Identity Attitude Scale (RIAS) (Parham & Helm, 1981). The RIAS was used as an independent variable to predict African American college students' preference for race, gender and socioeconomic status of counselors. Subscale Alpha reliabilities ranged from .66 to .71. Interscale correlation ranged from -.17 to .64. Based upon Cross' theory, Pre-encounter individuals should show a preference for a White counselor. Encounter individuals should have a preference for Black counselors. The 92 subjects' mean scores on the four attitude scales were entered into two multiple regression analyses. Preference for a Black or White counselor was the criterion variable. Close inspection of the results reveal there was a negative relationship between Pre-encounter and preference for a Black counselor and a positive relationship for a White counselor. Encounter attitudes were related to preference for a Black counselor. Immersion-Emersion relationships were in the expected direction, but there was no relationship between the Internalization stage and preference for a Black counselor. Furthermore, there was a positive relationship between the Internalization stage and preference for a White counselor. This last finding directly contradicts Cross' theoretical prediction. When examining between stage mean differences, there was no statistically significant difference between Encounter and Internalized preferences for same race counselor. Consequently, the Cross construct Internalization did not completely predict student preferences. Parham and Helms (1981) concluded that the Cross (1971) identity model was possibly useful for race-related research. This is despite the fact that not all students, in their study, could be placed into separate racial attitude categories. They indicated that one weakness in the results related to the fact that stages are continuous. Thus, students may have been in a transition between stages. The reliability of the measure was then questioned. Parham and Helms suggested that the measure probably required modifications. One other possible problem with the study (Parham & Helms, 1981) is that 25% of the sample was completing the measure for the second time. Thus, subjects were already familiar with the content of the questions and possibly recognized the more positive response options and may have responded accordingly.

In 1980, Milliones investigated the influence of ones Black consciousness orientation upon African American response to a scale designed to measure Whites attitudes toward Blacks. He reported that the results of his study did not validate the Cross model. He pointed out, as a weakness in his study, that since phenomena-stages evolve in an invariant sequential order, the study probably should have been longitudinal and age focused. In a study using 166 Black college students, Parham and Helms (1985) reported that correlations between the four racial identity subscales were .07 Internalization-Immersion to -.37 Pre-encounter and Encounter. There was no relationship between early movement toward racial identification and one's later Internalization racial identity. They then performed a regression analysis. The four racial identity attitude subscales were predictors. Subscales of a symptoms checklist were criteria. Parham and Helms were predicting interpersonal moods and psychological symptoms on the symptom-90 checklist (SCL-90) (Derogatis, Rickels, & Rock, 1976) from racial identity attitudes. The multiple r squared accounted for only 8% of the variance on the subscales, sensitivity and anxiety, and only 3% on hostility, and on obsessive-compulsive. These findings only partially supported Cross' model. Pomales, Claiborn, & LaFromboise (1986) studied the effects of student's racial identity on perceptions of White counselors varying in cultural sensitivity. They concluded after conducting analysis of variance statistics, that the findings were partially consistent with predictions from Cross' (1971) model, at the Encounter stage. They further reported that Internalization students were harder to interpret. Ponterotto and Wise (1987) investigated the construct validity of the Racial Identity Attitude Scale. They reported the following Alpha coefficients, .63 for Pre-encounter, .37 for Encounter, .72 for Immersion-Emersion, and .37 for Internalization. Subscale intercorrelations were - .01 for Pre-encounter and Encounter, -.03 for Pre-encounter and Immersion-Emersion, .03 for Pre-encounter and Internalization, .49 for Encounter and Immersion-Emersion, -.15 for Encounter and Internalization and .10 for Immersion-Emersion and Internalization. They then factor analyzed the scale using principal axes factor analysis, followed by an Oblique rotation. The purpose was to examine the structure of the RIAS. Results indicated that the common variance accounted for before rotation was, 36.1% and after rotation, 26.7%. Three of Cross' subscales as represented by RIAS were identified. The researchers pointed out that the results pertaining to the Encounter subscale rendered confidence in RIAS as a measure of Cross' stages questionable (Ponterotto & Wise, 1987). They further suggested that a three factor solution provided a "more concise and parsimonious solution" (Ponterotto & Wise, 1987, p. 220). They also concluded that construct validity for the Internalization stage was demonstrated by both the 3 and the 4 factor solutions. Still, the three-factor solution (a) appeared to be at odds with Cross' (1971) original theoretical model (Ponterotto & Wise, 1987, p. 221) and (b) only partially supported the constructs as given. Little evidence was found to validate the Encounter stage. Therefore only limited support for the theoretical constructs in the original Cross model and Parham & Helms' (1981) attitudes scale resulted. Further, some have suggested that due to conflicting evidence regarding internal consistency of RIAS subscales and fairly high intercorrelations among subscales, a lack of distinctiveness and independence may exist (Ponterotto & Wise, 1987).

Carter (1991) in an attempt to describe racial identity in psychologically relevant terms suggested that (1) Pre-encounter attitudes are associated with impaired psychological functioning; (2) Encounter attitudes reflect a state of psychological confusion and emotional disturbance; (3) Immersion-Emersion individuals feel anxious about their racial identity and negative attitudes towards Whites, and (4) Internalization attitudes are associated with an awareness and acceptance of a bicultural identity structure. Thus Internalization racial identity attitudes are probably psychologically healthier. These hypotheses were then tested with 95 college students who completed the Racial Identity Attitude Scale (Cross stages operationalized) and the Bell Global Psychopathology Scale, assessing phobia, compulsiveness, memory impairment, paranoia, hallucinations, and alcohol and drug concerns. The results revealed Pre-encounter attitudes were related to anxiety and memory impairment, paranoia and more self-reported psychological stress. Internalization attitudes were also related to paranoia. Thus, Carter suggested that paranoia may serve psychologically different purposes, depending upon the level of one's racial awareness, as a way to account for the findings. In fact, the author suggested that it may reflect psychological sensitivity to a hostile environment or a price one pays for their bicultural identity. Still, researchers have pointed out that research findings are difficult to interpret because there is difficulty with (a) the definition of Cross' concepts (Akbar, 1989) and (b) the way attitudinal scales attempt to measure a stable personality trait.

Watts (1992) used the Racial Identity Attitude Scale to assess preferences for social change among African Americans in a population of 142 Black civil service employees. They reported that Pre-encounter attitudes tended to reject education for Whites, r= -.29 and for lobbying, r= -.30 as effective social change strategies. None of the RIAS subscale predicted strategies used for social change. Watts called for a revision of the Immersion subscale. Racial identity attitudes and psychological feelings of closeness were investigated by Brookins, Anyabwile, and Nacoste (1992), in a population of 171 African American college students. A regression analyses was conducted. They reported that Internalization attitudes were strongly and positively related to African American students feelings of psychological closeness. They also concluded, however, that their study provided only limited support for Cross' (1971) model.

Parham and Williams (1993) examined the relationship of Demographic Background Factors (e.g., age, racial designation, socioeconomic status, region of the country born) to Racial Identity Attitudes. They found Racial Identity Attitudes (1) to be significantly related to where a person was born; those born in the West had lower Pre-encounter scores than those born in the South or East; (2) had no relationship to messages received from parents when growing up; and (3) had a significant relationship to racial designations. Those who identify as Black or African American disagree with Pre-encounter attitudes more than those who identify as Negro. Parham and Williams (1993) also reported: (1) that the higher one's education, the lower one's endorsement of Immersion attitudes; and (2) the higher one's income level, the higher one's Pre-encounter scores and the lower one's Internalization scores. They concluded that the Cross model may require further expansion, particularly with regard to the Encounter experience. They further suggested that the Encounter experience may not be restricted to issues pertaining to Whites.

In sum, researchers' efforts to understand African American identity development using the Negro-to-Black conversion model has resulted in a broad theoretical literature and a limited (Helms, 1984b) and unstable empirical literature. The Encounter construct, a key theoretical component of the Cross (1971) model was not theoretically nor statistically verified. Similar findings were reported by Helms (1984a) when conducting a multidimensional scaling analysis. Researchers have acknowledged that there are conceptual weaknesses in Cross' theory that are hopelessly confounded with the (Akbar, 1989; Helms, 1989) reliability and validity of measures used to study racial identity. Therefore, racial identity theory and research needs further attention (Smith, 1989). Beyond that, research design issues pertaining to (1) subject selection (college students); (2) situational contexts (mostly White university settings); (3) statistical reliability of results; and (4) interpretations of research findings also need improvement. One could easily argue that the study of racial identity attitudes, has been the study of the attitudes of African American college students.

An Updated View of the Negro-to-Black Model

Parham (1989) reevaluated several assumptions implicit in Cross' model and other Black identity models utilizing the stage approach in response to the weak empirical evidence. He then noted that (a) the research was conducted with mostly college students; (b) identity development in Blacks occurs during late adolescence/ early adulthood (i.e., college years); (c) Black identity issues are not resolved once a single stage cycle has been completed; and (d) the models failed to account for changes that might occur later in a person's life. Parham then extended Cross' model by describing changes occurring through the lifecycle, beginning with late adolescence. Parham redefined psychological nigrescence as the development of Black racial identity attitudes, "which begins with the late-adolescence/early-adulthood period in an individual's life" (p. 195). Parham's contributions resulted in Cross (1991) extending the Nigrescence model to reflect an individual's need to experience a resocialization of racial orientation attitudes, with regard to a Black identity. But, Cross (1991) still did not consider or explicate socialization practices that consequentially allowed Black adults to need resocialization. In fact, the model still speculated that identity challenges began in later life. This may be the case in many instances, but not in all. The current consensus in the identity development literature is that "identity development takes place throughout the life course" (Aries & Moorehead, 1989). Identification begins at age two, and racial identification begins in early childhood (Ponterotto, 1989). Documentation in the literature suggests that young children under age three lack the emotional significance of understanding race related issues (in-group/out-group preference consequences). By age seven, however, race identity has taken on emotional significance, and by age nine, same race preference is prevalent.

Also documented in the literature is the notion that identity development, including racial identity development is a continuous process, and adolescence is a time when identity concerns take on new significance or meaning. The rejuvenation of identity orientations is predicated upon the young persons' preparation for taking on the experiences of the adult world (Erickson, 1980). Ages 14-19 (Phinney, 1992) are seen as crucial to the development of adulthood identity. It is for this reason that identity, especially ethnic identity, and race relations take on a fresh meaning. The adolescent, possibly having reached a naive understanding of racial identity, has some salient event occur that disrupts his/her sense of security and understanding of race relations. For instance, disruption can result from rejection by peers due to (1) an individual's out-group orientations (integrationist); or (2) from peers perceiving the individual's neutrality to ethnic concerns (i.e., mainstream, biculturalism, or marginality). The adolescent may be compelled to examine racial issues related to identity, and possibly progress into an Immersion followed by an emission mode of behavior. Now, the individual's attitudes regarding race relation experiences are more informed. Thus, one could again reach a secure Internalization racial identity. Still, a secure Internalization racial identity can vary (bicultural competence, ethnocentrism, or neutrality) and is not perceived as a resolved endpoint. The recollections of early life experiences serve as reminders of the naive interpretations of race relations as they relate to one's identity. There maybe a feeling of vulnerability to reexperiencing life Encounters, possibly disrupting earlier beliefs. One now has a perspective for understanding race relations; the emotional destructiveness of in-group bias when accompanied by out-group devaluation (ethnocentrism); the vulnerability of racial neutrality regarding race (due to reality of racism and oppressions); and a pre-conscious sense of potential vulnerability in unguarded biculturalism. Consequently, the individual continually seeks out activities designed to move him/her toward a more secure ethnic identity resolution. The new search one engages in begins with a firm clear feeling about one's ethnic identity. It reflects a positive in-group orientation not based upon a negative devaluation of out-groups. The search also reflects an Internalization Commitment to action on behalf of group concerns. Thus immersed in the ethnic group concerns, one is constantly connected to a collective understanding of heritage, history, and knowledge base. A secure non-defensive sense of Africanness (ethnic identity) results and non-conflictual intergroup relations exist. Ethnic identity issues are compared against both within and between group preferences. As experiences accumulate, each person brings a set of ideas, notions, preferences and perspectives regarding racial identity into their adult years. Thus, race attitudes and reference group orientations are the accumulated years of socialization experiences. Support for these speculations appear in Parham (1993), who suggested "that Internalization individuals are able to negotiate relationships with persons from other ethnic groups, but they do so from a position of positive self-affirmation and cultural pride in wanting to be recognized, respected, and appreciated for their ethnicity and culture" (p. 338). It is from an in-group, not out-group, sense of security that an Internalization identity is achieved.

In summary, there is little evidence to suggest that individuals move from anti-Black attitudes to a more well-reasoned pro-Black orientation (Helms, 1989), in a stagewise progression. The majority of identity researchers agree the identity development process is lifelong and continuous. Thus, Cross' model, as applied using a stage framework, loses its persuasibility. Furthermore, the empirical research clearly suggest that cycles of psychological nigrescence should be more appropriately defined as an experiential non-linear progression model rather than a stage developmental model. Developmental stage models call forth a number of principles and assumptions which clearly are not appropriately used and therefore serve little or no explicative value in the current cycle of psychological nigrescence model. The point is verified by the limited empirical work applying Cross' framework. Racial and ethnic identity researchers point out that the only empirically tested ethnic identity model available is the Cross Model (Walters & Simoni, 1986). Therefore, a need to respond to the call for expanding research efforts in ethnic identity research is crucial. Conclusions to date indicate that current racial identity theorizing is inadequate.

References

Akbar, N. (1989). nigrescence and identity: Some limitations. *The Counseling Psychologist, 17(2),* 258-263.

Aries, E., & Moorehead, K. (1989). The importance of ethnicity in the development of identity of Black adolescents. *Psychological Reports, 65,* 75-82.

Boykin, A.W., & Toms, F.D. (1985). Black child socialization: A conceptual framework. In H. P. McAdoo & J. McAdoo (Eds.), *Black Children: Social, educational, and parental environments* (pp. 33-51). Newbury Park: Sage.

Broman, C.L., Neighbors, H.W., & Jackson, J.S. (1988). Racial group identification among Black adults. *Social Forces, 67(1),* 46-158.

Brookins, C.C. (1994). Ethnic identity intervention issues. In *Research and intervention issues in the examination of ethnic identity in African-American youth,* Unpublished monograph.

Brookins, C.C., Anyabwile, T., & Nacoste, R.B. (1992). *Racial identity attitudes and psychological feelings of closeness in African American college students.* Paper presented at the 13th Annual Conference on Empirical Research on Black Psychology. North Carolina State University, NC.

Carter, R.T. (1991). Racial identity attitudes and psychological functioning. *Journal of Multicultural Counseling and Development, 19,* 105-114.

Cross, W.E. (1991). *Shades of Black.* Philadelphia: Temple University Press.

Cross, W.E. (1985). Black identity: Rediscovering the distinction between personal identity and reference group orientation. In M.B. Spencer, G.K. Brookins, & W.R. Allen (Eds.), *Beginnings: The social and affective development of Black children,* (pp. 155-171). Hillsdale, NJ: Erlbaum.

Cross, W.E., Jr. (1971). The Negro-to-Black conversion experience. *Black World,* 13-27.

Cross, W.E., Jr. (1978). Models of psychological nigrescence: A literature review. *The Journal of Black Psychology, 5,* 81-98.

Cross, W.E., Jr. (1989). Nigrescence: A nondiaphanous phenomenon. *The Counseling Psychologist, 17(2),* 273-288.

Dansby, P.G. (1972). Black pride in the seventies: Fact or fantasy? In R.L. Jones (Ed.), *Black psychology* (pp. 145-155). New York: Harper & Row.

Derogatis, L.R., Rickels, K., & Rock, A.F. (1976). SCL-90 and the MMPI: A step in the validation of a new scale. *British Journal of Psychiatry, 128,* 280-289.

Erickson, E.H., (1980). *Identity and the life cycle.* New York: W.W. Norton & Company.

Feagan, S.R., & Feagan, C.B. (1993). *Racial and ethnic relations* (4th ed.). Prentice Hall: New Jersey.

Hall, W.S., Cross, W.E., Jr., & Freedle, R. (1970). Stages in the development of Black awareness: An exploratory investigation. In R.L. Jones (Ed.), *Black psychology,* (pp. 156-165). New York: Harper & Row.

Helms, J.E. (1984a). *Racial identity and sex-role attitudes among Black women*. Unpublished manuscript.

Helms, J.E. (1984b). Toward a theoretical explanation of the effects of race on counseling: A Black and White model. *The Counseling Psychologist, 12(4)*, 153-165.

Helms, J.E. (1989). Considering some methodological issues in racial identity counseling research. *The Counseling Psychologist, 17(2)*, 227-251.

Helms, J.E. (1990). *Black and White racial identity: Theory, research, and practice*. Westport, CT: Praeger Publishers.

Jones, R.S. (1980). Finding the Black self: A humanistic strategy. *The Journal of Black Psychology, 7*(1), 17-26.

Krate, R., Leventhal, G., & Silverstein, B. (1974). Self-perceived transformation of Negro-to-Black identity. *Psychological Reports, 35*, 1071-1075.

Looney, J. (1988). Ego development and Black identity. *Journal of Black Psychology, 15*(1), 41-56.

McAdoo, H.P. (1985). Racial attitude and self-concept of young Black children over time. In H.P. McAdoo & J.L. McAdoo (Eds.), *Black children: Social, educational, and parental environments*, (pp. 213-242). Newbury Park: Sage Publications.

Miller, P.H. (1989). *Theories of developmental psychology* (2nd ed.). New York: W.H. Freeman and Company.

Milliones, J. (1980). Construction of a Black consciousness measure: Psychotherapeutic implications. *Psychotherapy: Theory, Research and Practice, 17*(2), 175-182.

Munford, M.B. (1994). Relationship of gender, self-esteem, social class, and racial identity to depression in Blacks. *The Journal of Black Psychology, 20*(2), 157-174.

Nobles, W.W. (1989). Psychological nigrescence: An Afrocentric review. *The Counseling Psychologist, 17(2)*, 253-263.

Parham, T.A., & Helms, J.E. (1981). The influence of Black students' racial identity attitudes on preferences for counselor's race. *Journal of Counseling Psychology, 28(3)*, 250-257.

Parham, T.A. (1989). Cycles of psychological nigrescence. *The Counseling Psychologist, 17(2)*, 187-226.

Parham, T.A. (1993). Own-group preferences as a function of self-affirmation: A reaction to Penn et al. Special section: Racial identity revisited. *The Journal of Black Psychology, 19(3)*, 336-341.

Parham, T.A., & Helms, J. E. (1985). Attitudes of racial identity and self-esteem of Black students: An exploratory investigation. *Journal of College Student Personnel, 26(2)*, 143-146.

Parham, T.A., & Helms, J.E. (1985). Relation of racial identity attitudes to self-actualization and affective states of Black students. *Journal of Counseling Psychology, 32(3)*, 431-440.

Peterson-Lewis, S., & Adams, A. (1990). Television's model of the quest for African consciousness: A comparison with Cross' empirical model of psychological nigrescence. *The Journal of Black Psychology, 16(2)*, 55-72.

Phinney, J.S. (1992). The multigroup ethnic identity measure: A new scale for use with diverse groups. *Journal of Adolescent Research, 7(2)*, 156-176.

Pomales, J., Claiborn, C.D., & LaFromboise, T.D. (1986). Effects of Black students' racial identity on perceptions of White counselors varying in cultural sensitivity. *Journal of Counseling Psychology, 33(1)*, 57-61.

Ponterotto, J.G., & Wise, S.L. (1987). Construct validity study of the Racial Identity Attitude Scale. *Journal of Counseling Psychology, 34(2)*, 218-223.

Ponterotto, J.G. (1989). Expanding directions for racial identity research. *The Counseling Psychologist, 17(2)*, 264-272.

Shavelson, R.J., Hubner, J.J., & Stanton, G.C. (1976). Self-concept: Validation of construct interpretation, *Review of Educational Research, 46(3)*, 407-441.

Smith, E.M. (1989). Black racial identity development: Issues and concerns. *The Counseling Psychologist, 17(2)*, 277-288.

Stokes, J.E. (1994). *The effects of race socialization on the ethnic identity and self-esteem of African American youth*. Unpublished manuscript.

Stokes, J.E., Murray, C.B., Peacock, M.J., & Kaiser, R.T. (1994). Assessing the reliability, factor structure and validity of the African self-consciousness scale in a general population of African Americans. *Journal of Black Psychology, 20(1)*, 62-74.

Sue, D.W., & Sue, D. (1990). *Counseling the culturally different: Theory and practice*. New York: John Wiley & Sons.

Sue, D. (1991). A diversity perspective on contextualism. *Journal of Counseling & Development, 70(2)*, 300-301.

Sundland, D.M. (1962). The construction of Q-sorts: A criticism. *Psychological Review, 69(1)*, 62-64.

Thornton, M.C., Chatters, L.M., Taylor, R.J., & Allen, W.R. (1990). Sociodemographic and environmental correlates of race socialization by Black parents. *Child Development, 61*, 401-409.

Toomer, J.W. (1975). Beyond being Black: Identification alone is not enough. *Journal of Negro Education, 44*, 184-199.

Walters, K.L., & Simoni, J.M. (1993). Lesbian and gay male group identity attitudes and self-esteem: Implications for counseling. *Journal of Counseling Psychology, 40(1)*, 94-99.

Watts, R.J. (1992). Racial identity and preferences for social change strategies among African Americans. *The Journal of Black Psychology, 18(2)*, 1-18.

White, C.L. & Burke, P.J. (1987). Ethnic role identity among Black and White college students: An interactionist approach. *Sociological Perspectives, 30(3)*, 310-331.

Whittler, T.E., Calantone, R.J., & Young, M.R. (1991). Strength of ethnic affiliation: Examining Black identification with Black culture. *The Journal of Social Psychology, 13(4)*, 461-467.

Author

Carolyn Murray
Department of Psychology
University of California, Riverside
Riverside, CA 92521
Telephone: (909) 787-5293
Fax: (909) 787-3985
E-mail: carolyn.murray@ucr.edu

Nigrescence Theory: Critical Issues and Recommendations for Future Revisions

Stephanie Johnson Rowley and Robert M. Sellers

As stated in Stokes, Murray, Chavez, and Peacock's critique, the overwhelming frequency with which the Cross nigrescence model and the Racial Identity Attitudes Scale (RIAS) are cited and used to describe the racial identity development of African Americans necessitates a systematic and comprehensive critique and review (Stokes et al., 1998). Although both the conceptual model and its operationalization have been critiqued previously, these critiques have rarely examined the two distinctly in the same forum. As a result, some of the problems associated with the operationalization of nigrescence have been attributed to the theory. Likewise, the measurement of nigrescence has suffered from limitations associated with the conceptualization of nigrescence theory. The critical analysis that Stokes et al., provide makes a valuable contribution to the racial identity literature. They raise a number of important issues with respect to the limitations of nigrescence theory. There are, however, some areas of Stokes et al.'s, critique with which we disagree. There are instances in which we believe Stokes et al., overstate their argument. We believe, for example, that Cross has revised nigrescence theory in ways that address some of the issues they raised. In other instances, we believe that Stokes et al., do not go far enough in their criticism; their critique omitted some important limitations of both the conceptualization and measurement of nigrescence theory. Nonetheless, we come to the conclusion that major modifications of nigrescence theory are in order.

One problem with attempting to critically review nigrescence theory is that its manifestation in the literature is a product of more than one theorist. Although Cross is the primary author of the original the theory, other researchers, primarily Janet Helms and Thomas Parham, have expanded upon it. Much of their expansion has been as a result of their development of the RIAS—a paper and pencil measure of attitudes associated with the various stages of nigrescence (Parham & Helms, 1981). Their expansion of nigrescence theory has been informed by their empirical results and other authors' reactions to their findings (e.g., Parham, 1989). For instance, Parham's (1989) response to a special issue of *The Counseling Psychologist* devoted to nigrescence Theory, was to de-emphasize the stage properties of the original theory in favor of a perspective in which individuals are able to recycle through the various stages. Recently, Cross made substantial revisions to the nigrescence theory in his 1991 book, *Shades of Black*. Cross incorporated many of the ideas that Parham (1989) expressed. The two conceptualizations of nigrescence, however, are not identical. Similarly, Helms and other authors have written about nigrescence theory in ways that are not always synonymous with Cross' conceptualization (e.g., Carter, 1991; Helms, 1984). As a result, a critique of the evolution of nigrescence theory can become disjointed and even contradictory if one does not explicitly distinguish between the authors. Consequently, in our analysis of nigrescence theory, we will focus primarily on the evolution of William Cross' conceptualization of nigrescence. Meanwhile, our discussion of the operationalization of nigrescence will focus primarily on the pioneering contributions of Janet Helms, Thomas Parham and their colleagues in developing the Racial Identity Attitudes Scale (RIAS).

In their chapter, Stokes et al., set out to: (1) critically analyze Cross' nigrescence theory; (2) argue for the abandonment of the stage concept; and (3) suggest the adoption of an experiential rather than developmental model of racial identity. They begin their critique with a description of Cross' nigrescence theory as it was originally stated in 1971. This description of nigrescence theory becomes the primary object of their critical analysis. Although Stokes et al., acknowledge Cross' revisions, they under-appreciate the significance of these changes. As a result, some of the criticism levied against the original theory is no longer appropriate for the revised model. For instance, Cross' reconceptualization of the stages (especially Pre-encounter and Internalization) addresses Stokes et al.'s, concern that there is only one pathway towards an internalized African American identity. Cross (1991) explicitly states that not all individuals begin with a hatred or devaluing of Blacks in the Pre-Encounter stage. He, in fact, describes four attitude profiles through which the Pre-Encounter stage may be manifested—low salience, social stigma, anti-black, and miseducated. Cross' (1991) revision of the internalization stage also offers multiple manifestations of the Internalization stage.

The presumption of an optimal racial identity is another critique of nigrescence theory that is more relevant to the original conceptualization than the revised theory. Stokes et al., refer to Smith (1989) in noting that critics object to the application of nigrescence theory because there is no consensus on: (1) how to define an African American identity nor its relation to healthy adjustment; (2) how to measure it; (3) what constitutes appropriate levels of racial identity and/or its expressions. We agree that it is inappropriate for researchers to define a particular manifestation of racial identity to be optimal without considering the context in which the identity occurs and the criteria being used to define "optimal" (Sellers, Shelton, Cooke, Chavous, Johnson Rowley, & Smith, 1998). Nonetheless, Cross' revised model has backed away, somewhat, from such presumptions. Cross (1991) argues that there is no implicit relationship between reference group orientation and what he terms personality variables (for example self-esteem). In fact, he states that holding Pre-Encounter attitudes or Internalization attitudes is not directly related to individuals' mental health. Cross (1991) suggests that racial identity development may be related to mental health outcomes only during the Encounter and Immersion/Emersion stages. In these two stages, the increased anxiety is not a function of the racial identities themselves, but instead of the psychic trauma associated with the process of de-centering from an established identity and moving toward a new one. It is presumable that any identity shift may lead to the increased anxiety that Cross ascribes to the Encounter and Immersion/Emersion stages.

Not all of our points of divergence with Stokes et al., center around their focus on earlier conceptualizations of the nigrescence theory to the exclusion of the revised version. They write, "one of the most salient problems evident in Cross' approach is Cross' neglect to address the impact of socialization factors (e.g., the race orientation of immediate family) on an individual's reference group orientation." Although racial socialization by parents, peers and the media certainly influences racial identity development, the suggestion that Cross should address the impact of race socialization on racial identity in his theory is expanding the construct of racial identity too far. Although it is reasonable to expect that Cross' theory be able to incorporate agents of racial socialization in its description of the process of becoming Black, racial socialization influences must be conceptualized and operationalized independent of the conceptualization and measurement of racial identity (Sellers, Smith, Shelton, Johnson, & Chavous, 1998). Otherwise, a confounding tautology can occur in which it would be impossible to empirically investigate the actual relationship between race socialization and racial identity. Thus, Cross' failure to explicitly define the agents of racial socialization as a part of nigrescence theory is not a major limitation of the theory. It simply provides other researchers with an opportunity to test whether the theory is consistent with the research on racial socialization.

One limitation of nigrescence theory that Stokes et al., point out, and with which we concur, is that the nigrescence theory (both in its original conceptualization and its revised state) does not address adequately the fact that African Americans have multiple identities and that race is just one (Sellers et al., 1995). Cross argues that during the Pre-encounter stage, race is not a central identity component for some African Americans; other identity components are more important for these low race salient individuals. Cross implies that during the Encounter and Immersion/Emersion stages these other identity components are not relevant to the individual. These other identities, according to Cross, become more relevant once the individual reaches the internalization stage at which point the individual may integrate his/her racial identity with these other identities or remain singular in their reference group orientation. It is our contention that there is always a hierarchical ordering of different identities for all individuals at all times (Sellers et al., 1998). The extent to which a particular identity is salient (in our terminology) at a particular point in time is determined by situational factors and the centrality of identity to the person's self-concept in general. Thus, we would suspect that race should become more salient during these two stages (primarily the Immersion/Emersion stage) than other identities. Individuals, however, are still likely to utilize other identities in situations that pull for them even when they are in the Encounter or Immersion/Emersion stages.

Stokes et al., also present a number of valid concerns regarding the measurement of nigrescence via of the RIAS. Empirical work with the RIAS as a measure of nigrescence has yielded inconsistent results. We maintain that the inconsistency of these results is due in part to an incongruence between nigrescence theory and the way in which the RIAS attempts to operationalize it. Although the items of the RIAS were derived from Cross' initial Q-sort analysis, a close examination of the items suggests that they do not reflect the theoretical definitions of nigrescence offered by Cross in either its original conceptualization or his revised theory. The items represent extreme attitudes that often do not discriminate between the different stages. Some items seem as if they could belong to more than one stage (e.g., "I believe that being Black is a positive experience;" "I feel excitement and joy in Black surroundings"). Other items simply seem to represent other stages. This item on the Internalization scale, for instance, seems more appropriate as an item on the Immersion/Emersion scale: "I feel an overwhelming attachment to Black people." These inconsistencies call into question the face validity of the RIAS as a measure of nigrescence.

The psychometric performance of the RIAS has also raised several concern (Ponterotto & Wise, 1987). In particular, Stokes et al., point out the concerns regarding the poor internal consistency of the Encounter subscale, questions regarding the underlying factor structure of the RIAS, and its use primarily with college samples. There are also a number of other problems with RIAS that were not mentioned by Stokes et al. For instance, the RIAS contains a number of double-barreled questions (e.g., "I find myself reading a lot of Black literature and thinking about being Black"). Such questions make it difficult to determine the part of the question to which the individual is supposed to respond. How does a person respond to the item if she does not read a lot of Black literature, but spends a lot of time thinking about being Black? Also, some of the terminology used in the RIAS is outdated (e.g., "honkies"). Finally, the RIAS is not consistent in the phenomena that it is trying to measure. Although the title of the scale clearly implies that it is an attitude scale, the RIAS has both attitude and behavior items. Moreover, measurement of attitudes as opposed to behaviors varies systematically across subscales. Items from the Encounter subscale tend to include behaviors more so than the other subscales. The high correlation between Encounter and Immersion/Emersion may be the result of measuring the same construct using different manifest phenomena (behaviors and attitudes).

The mismatch between the conceptualization and the operationalization of nigrescence theory extends beyond the properties of the RIAS to the analytical strategies employed with the measure. As a stage theory, Cross' conceptualization of nigrescence implies that individuals either belong to a single stage or two contiguous stages when the person is in transition from one stage to another. Thus, we should expect empirical investigations of the theory to represent this aspect of the theory as much as possible. In other words, statistical techniques that place individuals within particular groups (such as cluster analysis) should be used to test both the internal validity of the measure and theory. Individuals should exhibit high scores on one or two contiguous subscales (such as Encounter and Immersion/ Emersion) and score very low on the other scales. Such a clustering approach should also be used to investigate the relationship between nigrescence and other phenomena. Unfortunately, most of the empirical work using the RIAS has used factor analytic and regression techniques which implicitly assume that each individual has racial identity attitudes and beliefs that correspond to all four stages (e.g., Carter & Helms, 1988; Parham & Helms, 1985; Parham & Williams, 1993; Watts, 1992). Such an assumption is in direct contradiction with a stage theory and the way in which the conceptual model is described by Cross (1971, 1991).

In sum, our assessment of the nigrescence literature suggests some major limitations. Although we feel that Cross' revised model addresses many of the criticisms raised, we agree with Stokes et al., that there are important issues that even Cross' revised theory of nigrescence is unable to address. Our primary concern is the constraints that the use of a developmental stage framework places on Cross' theory. As Stokes et al., point out, a developmental stage theory requires: (a) invariant sequencing; (b) hierarchical sequencing; (c) universal expression; and (d) decontextual determinism (Miller, 1989). Such requirements are quite daunting and appear to be beyond the original intent and focus of the nigrescence theory. For instance, Cross (1991) acknowledges that the conceptualization of nigrescence is both context-dependent and specific to Black people. He indicates that the social zeitgeist has had an impact on the qualitative nature of Black identity, if not the processes which drive its development. He suggests that the reference group orientation of African Americans has changed over the past half-century. Also, the use of the term nigrescence (becoming Black) strongly suggests that the theory is not attempting to explain universal racial processes, but instead is focusing on processes which may be limited to the experiences of African Americans.

Ironically, many of the refinements that Cross has made to strengthen his theory also place it further at odds with the requirements of a developmental stage model. In his revised theory, Cross (1991) allows for the possibility that not all African Americans begin in a Pre-encounter identity stage. In fact, he suggests that socialization factors, such as family, may make the process of nigrescence unnecessary for some individuals. Such a concession violates the requirement of decontextual determinism in that the ecological context in which the individual resides interferes with the unfolding of the stages in the developmental process. Similarly, Cross' attempts to broaden the theory to include a greater diversity of experiences and identity structures are in conflict with the criteria for a stage theory. For instance, the inclusion of multiple pathways with multiple outcomes in the nigrescence process makes the notion of a single, invariant and hierarchically sequenced mode of identity development implausible.

If the nigrescence theory is unduly restrained by its reliance on the utilization of the concept of developmental stages as a framework, what modifications of the theory are needed to make it a more viable framework for understanding African American racial identity? We feel that three modifications are necessary. First, consistent with Stokes et al., nigrescence must be reconceptualized as an experiential model instead of a strict developmental stage model. Such a modification would permit a discussion of developmental influences on racial identity, but not be limited by the requirements associated with the concept of developmental stages. nigrescence can still be viewed as a process that may be associated with normal development in African Americans. For example, the literature suggests that racial identity is dependent on individuals' cognitive development. Individuals need to have achieved a particular level of cognitive development in order to understand the complex meaning of racial categorization (Looney, 1988; Phinney, 1989). Thus, we should expect qualitative differences in the complexity of identity attitudes as individuals develop cognitively. African American racial identity can be viewed as developing within the context of universal human development.

The shift to a more experiential focus would not be very difficult given the current state of nigrescence theory. The underlying motivation for moving from the Pre-encounter stage towards internalization is experiential. The concept of the Encounter stage is based entirely on some experience (either positive or negative) that propels the individual to reconsider his/her attitudes and beliefs regarding the meaning of race in their self-definitions. In this regard, Cross makes no suggestion of an innate need to express a newly developing identity. Instead the theory implies that the Encounter experience makes questioning the Pre-encounter identity imperative. However, present nigrescence theory lacks an experiential stimulus to motivate the transformation from the Immersion/Emersion stage to the Internalization stage. At present, there is little discussion regarding the process (or mechanism) which characterizes this transition. Cross (1991) hints that this shift may also be the result of interactions with internalized individuals that shows the person in the Immersion/Emersion stage that there is a higher level of identity development to be achieve. As a result, there becomes an implicit assumption that there is an inevitable movement towards an internalized racial identity. Although both Cross (1991) and Parham (1989) acknowledge that some individuals may find themselves stagnated within the Immersion/Emersion stage, further explication regarding factors which result in one person moving on to the internalized stage and another person becoming stagnated is needed.

The second modification needed centers around the goal of the theory. Specifically, nigrescence theory has the potential to provide an important framework for understanding the process through which some African Americans develop an internalized racial identity. Such a modification would emphasize the process over the qualitative nature of the identities. In other words, nigrescence theory should attempt to explain how individuals' racial identity changes as opposed to developing a taxonomy of different racial identity profiles. Such an approach would be more nomothetic in nature and attempt to find patterns of development. As a result, it would rely more on longitudinal designs to examine changes in identity and the experiential predictors of these changes. It would be less interested in placing every African American on a particular continuum of racial identity.

A second aspect of this modification is the recognition that nigrescence theory is not attempting to explain a universal phenomenon among African Americans. As noted above, Cross has already acknowledged that not every African American with an internalized identity has gone through the nigrescence process. Such a reduction in focus will allow for a more definitive description of how the nigrescence process works for those individuals who go through it. The acknowledgment of the limits of the application of nigrescence would also require a more in-depth discussion of the factors that make nigrescence applicable for some individuals and not for others. This discussion would go a long way in making nigrescence theory compatible with other research that has focused on racial socialization influences. As a result, we believe that limiting the purview of the theory will help to continue its evolution toward a more context-congruent conceptual framework.

The final modification we suggest focuses on the measurement strategies used to operationalize nigrescence. Currently, the RIAS attempts to measure attitudes and behaviors that represent each stage of racial identity development (Parham & Helms, 1985). Such an approach makes testing the validity of the developmental process susceptible to potential confounds with the developmental properties of the measure (Sellers et. al., 1998). A preferable method would be to propose certain phenomena that are expected to change across the different stages and develop measures that represent them. Using the theory of nigrescence as a guide, we should be able to make predictions regarding specific profiles on these measures for individuals in different stages of development. For instance, according to nigrescence theory, we would expect that individuals who are in the Immersion/Emersion stage should have higher levels of ideological fervor regarding Black stimuli than Pre-encounter and Encounter individuals and higher levels of anxiety and emotionality regarding race than internalized individuals. This approach would provide a better test of the validity of the four stages outlined in nigrescence theory for those individuals for whom the theory is applicable. At the same time, this measurement approach would also provide an empirical tool in which to evaluate whether a person fits within the nigrescence framework. By including contextual and background information, the factors that predict for whom the nigrescence framework is applicable could be empirically identified.

In sum, we recognize the historical importance of the nigrescence theory in conceptualizing the development of African American racial identity from a pathology to a positive affirmation of oneself. Over the past 25 years, nigrescence theory has been the major stimulus of a burgeoning body of research that has examined the psyche, adaptation, and functioning of African Americans from a perspective that does not pathologize their uniqueness. However, like most pioneering work, evolution and modification is essential. Consequently, nigrescence theory has changed over the years as critics have begun to challenge the viability of many of its underlying assumptions. Although the revisions of nigrescence have gone a long way in addressing many of these critiques, there are still a number of criticisms that nigrescence theory will never be able to address in its current incarnation as a developmental stage theory. Thus, we believe that major modifications of the theory are in order. Much of the modification that we propose are consistent with the direction that Cross has outlined with his revisions and the critiques that Stoke et al., have levied. However, if nigrescence theory is to reach its full potential the modifications must be more radical than the present revisions.

References

Carter, R.T. (1991). Racial identity attitudes and psychological functioning. *Journal of Multicultural Counseling and Development, 19(3)*, 105-114.

Carter, R.T., & Helms, J.E. (1988). The relationship between racial identity attitudes and social class. *Journal of Negro Education, 57(1)*, 22-30.

Cross, W.E. (1971). Negro-to-Black conversion experience. *Black World, 20*, 13-27.

Cross, W.E. (1991). *Shades of Black: Diversity in African American identity.* Philadelphia, PA: Temple University Press.

Helms, J.E. (1984). Toward a theoretical explanation of the effects of race on counseling: A Black and White model. *The Counseling Psychologist, 12(4)*, 153-165.

Miller, P.H. (1989). *Theories of developmental psychology* (2nd ed., pp. 45-46). New York: W. H. Freeman and Company.

Parham, T.A. (1989). Cycles of psychological nigrescence. *The Counseling Psychologist, 17(2)*, 187-226.

Parham, T.A., & Helms, J.E. (1981). The influences of a Black students' racial identity attitudes on preference for counselor's race. *Journal of Counseling Psychology, 28*, 250-256.

Parham, T.A., &. Helms, J.E. (1985). Attitudes of racial identity and self-esteem in Black students: An exploratory investigation. *Journal of College Student Personnel,* 143-147.

Parham, T.A., & Williams, P.T. (1973). The relationship of demographic and background factors to racial identity attitudes. *Journal of Black Psychology, 19(1),* 7-24.

Phinney, J.S. (1989). Stages of ethnic identity development in minority group adolescents. *Journal of Early Adolescence, 9(1-2),* 34-49.

Looney, J. (1988). Ego development and Black identity. *Journal of Black Psychology, 15(1),* 41-56.

Ponterotto, J.G., &. Wise, S.L. (1987). Construct validity study of the Racial Identity Attitude Scale. *Journal of Counseling Psychology, 34(2),* 218-223.

Sellers, R.M., Shelton, J.N., Cooke, D.Y., Chavous, T.M., Johnson Rowley, S.A., & Smith, M.A. (1998). A multidimensional model of racial identity: Assumptions, findings, and future directions. In R.L. Jones (Ed.), *African American identity development* (pp. 235-262). Hampton, VA: Cobb & Henry.

Smith, E. (1989). Black racial development: Issues and concerns. *The Counseling Psychologist, 17(2),* 277-288.

Stokes, J.E., Murray, C.B., Chavez, D., & Peacock, J.P. (1998). Cross' stage model revisited: An analysis of theoretical formulations and empirical evidence. In R. L. Jones (Ed.), *African American identity development* (pp. 123-139). Hampton, VA: Cobb & Henry.

Watts, R.J. (1992). Racial identity and preferences for social change strategies among African Americans. *Journal of Black Psychology, 18(2),* 1-18.

Author

Stephanie Johnson Rowley
Department of Psychology
Dave Hall, CB #3270
University of North Carolina
Chapel Hill, N.C. 27599-3270
Telephone: (919) 962-8774
Fax: (919) 962-2537
E-mail: Stephanie_rowley@unc.edu

The Confluence of the "Both-And" in Black Racial Identity Theory: Response to Stokes, Murray, Chavez and Peacock

Howard C. Stevenson, Jr.

In their critique of the Cross model of nigrescence, Stokes, Murray, Chavez, & Peacock (1996) make a strong argument for revisions of the model by reviewing some of the racial identity measurement and attitudinal research. They conclude that the model is inadequate to capture an meaningful description of African American racial identity. The authors venture a fine effort by summarizing the concerns expressed by a variety of researchers over the last decade. Despite the authors revisionist efforts, I found there to be limited discussion of an alternative experiential perspective. I will base my comments on the importance of recognizing the changes Dr. William Cross has made in the model, maintaining the model's intuitive possibilities, and proposing adoption of multiple not singular perspectives to racial identity development and definitional research. In particular, six areas I will focus upon include the model's historical context, intuitive relevance, need for racial socialization, "both-and" dimensions of racial identity, and the imaging and stereotyping of Blackness.

To state that the nigrescence model of racial identity has been simply another theory is to state that the New Deal was just another government program. In fact, despite the faults in the New Deal, the majority of social researchers in this country still attribute it as the solitary example when America gave most of its children a chance for opportunity in the face of overwhelming poverty. As a social policy, it must be critiqued. But its dismantling is premature. The poor are still with us and the plans currently on the table portray a picture that suggests that the baby and the bath water are of no worth. The same can be said for Stokes et al., 's (1996) critique of the Cross model. The nigrescence model deserves critique based on the work of research on the reliability and validity of the Racial Identity Attitude Scale, the rigidity of the stage-centric nature of the model, and the lack of continuity between stages of racial identity. Some of these criticisms which I have proposed elsewhere (Stevenson, 1996), do not spell the end of the model, however. One issue that keeps surprising me is that the theory has been reified in ways the writings of Cross and

151

others never intended. nigrescence is the process of becoming aware of one's Blackness and that Blackness can be defined a number of ways, the specifics of which the model was never meant, in my opinion, to explain entirely. Furthermore, the book by Cross (1991), *Shades of Black*, begins to open up the discussion around the diversity of Blackness, which I believe has received too little attention in critiques to date. There are two points regarding the model's historical significance and intuitive accuracy that I believe are overlooked by the authors regarding the Cross model and stipulate why I would vote for maintaining some of its key aspects. Then there are four points I would propose as supporting Stokes et al.'s (1996) call for revision of the model and for adding to the debate about how Black racial identity ought to be engaged. These new areas include racial socialization processes, rigid imaging of Blackness, "both-and" realities, and correspondence of beliefs and action.

Many researchers forget the historical significance or political implications of the model proposed by Cross (1971) during its early years. The Cross model was a godsend in the 1970's for the simple reason that very little acknowledgment of Blackness, let alone Black identity, was possible. Still, why would one theory be expected to capture the multidimensionality of racial identity? To have available a theory that considered the racial background of individuals was a gold mine and it allowed many researchers and clinicians to raise questions in counseling (and other forms of psychology) that were previously unasked or unanswerable within a traditional psychology curricula. Despite the inconsistent research support for the model, there still remains a utility to the model that has escaped research attempts to prove its validity.

In fact, an intuitive sense still finds itself fulfilled when we look at the basic structure of the nigrescence model. It is perhaps sacrilege to suggest that we take a subjectivist perspective of the nigrescence model, a tenet very real within an African centered framework (Akbar, 1985). Nevertheless, many of us understand that our acquaintance with a society populated and controlled mostly by a "Whiteness" power structure is a weight that changes daily as to its burden. To use interactions with Whites and "Whiteness" as a barometer of how one thinks about his racial identity dos not have to mean that White people, White life, or White values constitute the center of the universe. It may simply mean that for a majority of persons of color, there are few days they can go through without interacting in a world that counts their minority status as deficient. Regardless of the degree of "Blackness" in skin color we possess, many of us identify the reality that simultaneously praises "Whiteness" as omnipotent, in word, image, and deed (e.g., White affirmation action). The skin color and other aspects of racial identity (e.g., gender and SES) were missing elements of the nigrescence model, but their absence does not dismiss our intuitive belief that many of us have moved from depreciating our racial heritage to appreciating it.

Why should the theory be criticized because our methods are limited? For example, how easy has it been to measure Encounter even though many of us admit that it is a relevant experience and that many of us can remember a few encounter experiences of our own. It is next to impossible given our current measurement technology to test that out. I believe better measurement is possible if one wishes to work withn a quantitative framework, but more finely tuned measurement development is necessary. In keeping with the intuitive accuracy of the racial identity theory, I propose an additional step to improving measurement. I suggest that qualitative investigations are necessary and must be done across time and with different SES groups.

One point I have proposed elsewhere for revising the model is resident in the belief that identity is a racially socializing experience, not an individual experience of coming to awareness (Stevenson, 1996). Identity is developed in the context of others (e.g., family, peers, society, and community) with beliefs about the world that are transmitted directly and indirectly, verbally and nonverbally to children and is sophisticatedly re-expressed by adolescents. Furthermore, there appear to be two general types of racial socialization processes—proactive and protective. Protective racial socialization beliefs in adolescents are those that reflect the importance of being aware of racial oppression where it exists and to not internalize it into one's racial or gender identity. Proactive racial socialization beliefs point more decidedly to attitudes regarding the appreciation of pride and heritage that is not oppression-derived. I have found that adolescent racial socialization beliefs (e.g., spiritual and religious coping, racism awareness teaching, cultural pride reinforcement and extended family caring) are related to mature levels of racial identity (Stevenson, 1995). In this study, I factor analyzed the RIAS (Racial Identity Attitude Scale) for an adolescent population and I did not find empirical support for the Encounter stage of the model, primarily because it represents experiences not beliefs. This raised the concern of whether it is even possible to measure racial identity processes through one tool. The need for multidimensional assessment is clear. One cannot develop a theory of racial identity, socialization, or experience without multidimensional assessment if he or she wishes to be successful within a Euro-American theoretical empiricist framework. Relevant proof within this framework requires multiple ways of measuring the various aspects of racial identity, especially if socialization processes are considered.

In addition to the racial socialization dimension of racial identity, I believe there ought to be a better appreciation of the "both-and" African psychological framework to racial identity. To say that the "both-and" concept constitutes a useful contribution to the notion of racial identity is to say that we depreciate and appreciate our "Blackness" all the time and with varying consequences. Some of my qualitative work in poor urban neighborhoods reveal that some African Americans interact with Whites little and find colorism, as Alice Walker has termed, the more frightening form of discriminating. They believe that other Black folks are the critics of their racial identity development and ought to receive greater denigration as less than human. In fact, many of these individuals do not perceive racism to be a problem or certainly not as large an issue as some might expect. Interestingly, those African Americans in our study who have to work in predominantly White contexts have strong racism struggles stories and worldviews (Stevenson & Abdul-Kabir, 1996). My point is that our revisions must keep in mind that persons of African descent can be both self-defeating and self-promoting. Interestingly enough, a "both-and" orientation implies a variety of research strategies. In fact, very few qualitative investigations have been conducted using the Cross model and one might venture the possibility that the model might be investigated further in this way.

This brings us to the next point that correspondence between attitudes and life phenomena regarding racial identity has to be established, and beyond the counseling session. Perhaps what people think in attitude about their racial identity and how they behave are different phenomena in other areas that are just as important in African American life (e.g., interacting with police oppression; domestic violence). Our revisionist thinking regarding the Cross model must consider the possibility that attitudes and actions are disparate within a racially hostile world and as long as there is support for being and acting "White," Paul Lawrence Dunbar's poem of "We Wear The Mask"— regarding the importance of hiding unique cultural struggles— will be relevant. Research on racial identity behaviors is crucial as is the link between what we believe and how we act. How this link influences our interactions with others will help to solidify the theory in many ways that overstep many criticisms. An example includes the significant positive relationship between racial socialization beliefs and kinship social support (Stevenson, Bodison, & Reed, 1995). We have also found a positive relationship between certain types of protective racial socialization experiences and anger expression. Those adolescents who report receiving high levels of protective racial socialization messages will report greater anger acting out and lower levels of anger control (Stevenson, 1996). Conversely, anger control is highest if adolescents endorse proactive forms of racial socialization (e.g., spiritual coping and pride development; Stevenson, Herrero, & Cameron, in press).

A sixth and final point involves stereotyping or the "rigid imaging of Blackness." Imaging is a term I have defined as the political phenomenon engaged in by institutions or individuals representing those societal institutions to promote the wrongful character of a subgroup of Americans. It is a process whereby stereotypes of minority groups are publicly and subtly portrayed, but are impervious to criticism since they continue to remain to influence social policy and institutional behaviors vis´-a-vis´ the stereotyped group (Stevenson & Abdul-Kabir, 1996). That is, despite our pluralism and multidimensionality, despite outrage and diversity training, all Americans and their "multi-ethnically diversified'' selves are forced to interact with (e.g., accept, reject, or some combination) these static public conceptions of Blackness. Because this country adheres to a "looking glass" racial identity interactional schema, I believe the nigrescence model is quite useful. That is, we may be bicultural, international, Caribbean, etc., but we confront stereotypical schemas from others that often care little about our multiple voices. These interactions force us into the "criminal Black male" or the "promiscuous Black woman" or the "angry Black nationalist" or the "enslaved Oreo" or the "sold-out Buppie" before we open our mouths and we often interact with these schemas by reacting first and asking questions later. The process of becoming Black still holds sway in that many of us are rigidly held to these schemas such that no process takes place fully. We are often stilted in our racial identity development because we have to stop daily in a "Whiteness" world to dodge the schemas foisted upon us as well as explain ourselves outside of the stereotypes we did not dodge. It is here that nigrescence is viewed as a process but one that is hampered by narrow-mindedness all around us and we are convinced of what Blackness means in contexts that oppress and support racial identity development. The nigrescence model helps to understand these stereotypes and how many African Americans are caught within the web of imaging and limited societal perception.

Should we challenge the nigrescence model? Yes. Throw it out? No. The context of racial stereotyping is not over despite the pluralism that invades America, and I dare say, Black racial identity development theory. The burden of representing Blackness within the academy has to be shared and broadened. The process of becoming Black is still a reality and will be as long as categorizing the image of Blackness runs central to American life.

When the authors propose their experiential model, they do not support their model with research enough to wet our taste buds. They much like the rest of us struggle with the indeterminacy of epistemology. That is, they seem to realize the worth of some Afrocentric ideas that are flexible in possibility yet still look to European research to support their critique. I rather propose a "both-and" critique of the Cross model that keeps the baby and throws out the bath water. Specifically, I propose we agree that there are elements of African-centered theoretical discourse that can co-exist with a Euro-American theoretical framework. Moreover, a developmental perspective on racial identity and socialization can co-exist with an experiential perspective. Frankly, I never thought experience was missing from the Cross model. This is why Stokes et al.,'s (1996) proposition but lack of support for an experiential model left me wanting. Nevertheless, a merging of interdisciplinary ideas is warranted and they have rightfully pushed the point. I support an African-centered framework because I believe it allows for this co-existence of the African American racial identity that is a "double-consciousness" or a "multiple consciousness" as Njeri (1993) would suggest. We are both bicultural and Black and very few theories will account for this well, in my opinion, and thus, the measurement is challenging. A longitudinal qualitative endeavor can add to our understanding of racial identity theory across the life-span. I think we need to spend our energy struggling with this "both-and" and committing our cultural, intellectual resources to it so that an applied epistemology is more attainable.

References

Cross, W.E., Jr. (1991). *Shades of Black: Diversity in African American identity*. Philadelphia: Temple University Press.

Njeri, I. (1993). Sushis and grits: Ethnic identity and conflict in a newly multicultural America. In G. Early (Ed.), *Lure and loathing: Essays on race, identity, and the ambivalence of assimilation* (pp. 13-41). New York: Penguin Books.

Stevenson, H.C. (1994). Racial socialization in African American families: Balancing intolerance and survival. *The Family Journal: Counseling and Therapy for Couples and Families, 2*, 190-198.

Stevenson, H.C. (1995). The relationship of racial socialization and racial identity in African American adolescents. *Journal of Black Psychology, 21(1)*, 49-70.

Stevenson, H.C. (1998). Theoretical considerations in measuring racial identity and socialization: Extending the self further. In R.L. Jones (Ed.), *African American identity development* (pp. 259-256). Hampton, VA: Cobb & Henry.

Stevenson, H.C., & Abdul-Kabir, S. (1996). Reflections of hope from the "Bottom": Cultural strengths and coping of low-income African American mothers. *Proceedings of the Roundtable on Cross-Cultural Psychotherapy*.Teachers College, Columbia University, New York.

Stevenson, H.C., Herrero-Taylor, T., & Cameron, R. (In press). Buffer zone: Impact of racial socialization experiences on anger expression in African American adolescents. In D. Johnson & A. Hunter (Eds.), *Racial socialization: Ecologies of child and adolescent development,* part of a series in African American Psychology (R.L. Jones, Series Editor). Hampton, VA: Cobb & Henry.

Stevenson, H.C., Reed, J., & Bodison, P. (1997). Racism stress management: Racial socializatioon beliefs and the experiences of depression and anger for African American adolescents. *Youth and Society, 29*, 197-222.

Stokes, J., Murray, C.B., Chavez, D., & Peacock, M.J. (1998). Cross' stage model revisited: An analysis of theoretical formulations and empirical evidence. In R.L. Jones (Ed.), *African American identity development* (pp. 121-140). Hampton, VA: Cobb & Henry.

Author

Howard C. Stevenson, Jr.
Associate Professor
School, Community and Clinical
Child Psychology Program
Psychology in Education Division
Graduate School of Education
University of Pennsylvannia
3700 Walnut Street
Philadelphia, PA 19104-6216
Telephone: (215) 898-5666
Fax: (215) 573-2115/9007
E-mail:HowardS@gse.upenn.edu

Commentary on The Stokes et al., Critique of Nigrescence Theory

William E. Cross, Jr.

Let me begin by stating the obvious; whether the focus is on my model or others, all nigrescence models are human inventions, and these social constructions of reality are by definition subject to contestation. Consequently, serious critiques should always be welcomed, for one cannot grow, without guidance and feedback. Circumstances (illness, family emergencies, and scheduling problems) have made it impossible for me to thoroughly engage every single point raised by Stokes et al., however, I will address their summary of the stages; the generalizability of the nigrescence paradigm to age groups other than Black adults, and in a related matter, the question of the place of nigrescence in a lifespan perspective. It is not necessary to comment on their review of the empirical literature, as that is the focus of another paper in this volume.

Stokes et al. Summary of the Stages

For what ever reason, Stokes et al., provide a jumbled summary of the model. There are only two versions of the model, the one that was produced in 1971 and the revised version that appeared in 1991. The revised version takes into account the scores of empirical studies conducted on the model between the early 1970s and the present. Most of my 1991 revisions focused on a re-write of the Pre-encounter and Internalization stages (stages 1 and 4). Stokes et al., seem comfortable summarizing the Pre-encounter stage as follows: "Initially, Black social interactions reflect an unexamined ideation of White ideas and beliefs. Cross proposed that the attitudes of Blacks at the Pre-encounter stage manifested a bias toward positive views of Whites and negative views of other Blacks." This summary, even if applied to the original model, leaves something to be desired, but as a representation of the 1991 version, it is inadequate. In fact, it is a "strawman," because, having anchored the theory with this contrite summary, they later suggest that the theory is too negative, too victim oriented, too simplistic, too dated, etc. The theory only seems that way, if you view it through the prism of their myopic and out-dated summary of Pre-encounter.

Compare their summary with the actual, 1991 version of Pre-encounter: "Persons at the Pre-encounter stage hold attitudes toward race that range from low salience to race neutrality to anti-Black. Persons who hold low-salience views do not deny being Black [but being] Black and having knowledge about the Black experience have little to do with their perceived sense of happiness and well-being . . . [they] place value in things other than their Blackness." . . . "[Pre-encounter people do] have values and do experience a meaningful existence; it is just that little emphasis is given to Blackness. As long as their Pre-encounter attitudes bring a sense of fulfillment, a meaningful existence, and an internal sense of stability, order, and harmony, such persons will probably not need an identity change, let alone a movement toward Afrocentricity."..."The extreme racial attitude pattern found in the Pre-encounter stage is anti-Blackness...[B]lackness and Black people define their internal model of what they dislike...[A]nti-Blacks loath other Blacks; they feel alienated from them and do not see Blacks or the Black community as potential or actual sources of personal support." ..."[P]re-encounter thus covers a broad range of attitudes (*Shades of Black*, pp. 190-191)"..."[I]t would be a mistake to assume that Pre-encounter is a form of mental illness. Blacks who are anti-Black may well evidence poor mental health, but the majority of Pre-encounter Blacks are probably as mentally healthy as Blacks in the more advanced stages of nigrescence. . . [What separates] Pre-encounter Blacks from those who are Afrocentric are value orienta-tion, historical perspective, and *worldview*. The complexity of the American economy means that there are all sorts of ecological niches within which Blacks are socialized, and each niche may support the growth of very particularistic *worldview*s, many of which are not framed by a racial or Afrocentric perspective. Pre-encounter Blacks are part of the diversity of the Black experience and must be understood as such." ..."[N]evertheless, whenever life's circumstances result in the social produc-tion of a Black person for whom "race" has limited personal salience or, in the case of the Black who is anti-Black, extremely negative personal salience, the scene is set for a possible identity conversion (*Shades of Black*, p. 198)."

Readers can judge for themselves whether Stokes et al., have done justice to this depiction of Pre-encounter. They claim that the theory is too negative, too simplistic, too insensitive to variations in the Black experience caused by such factors as social class. You be the judge.

The other major point of modification, which the revised theory attempts to address, is the makeup and dynamics of the Internalization stage. Here again, and for what ever reason, Stokes et al., decided to present a piecemeal summary of the advanced stages. For example, the summary of stages four (Internalization) and five (Internalization-Commitment) appear on pages 3-4 of their paper, yet some eleven pages later, they make reference to changes in the model! How is the reader to comprehend this layout of the constructs? What purpose is served by this piecemeal approach?

In any case, just as the revised model re-frames Pre-encounter to incorporate diversity issues that were missed in the original model, so does it also address diversity in Black identity that is evidenced at Internalization: "While advanced Black identity development results in giving high salience to issues of race and culture, not every person in the Internalization stage shares the same degree of salience for Blackness, as this is likely to be determined by the nature of one's ideology. Those who construct a strong nationalist framework from their Immersion-Emersion experiences may continue along this ideological path at Internalization . . . [O]ther Blacks [at Internalization may] derive a bicultural reference group orientation from their nigrescence experience ... [For them] ... Internalization is a time for working through and incorporating into [their] self-concept[s] the realities of one's Blackness as well as the enigmatic, paradoxical, advantageous, and supportive aspects of one's "Americanness." ... "[O]thers may embrace a multicultural perspective, in which case their concern for Blackness is shared with a multiplicity of cultural interests and saliencies. So we see that the cultural identity of the stage 4 person can vary from that of [a] monocultural orientation (e.g., nationalism) to the identity mosaic of [a] multiculturally oriented Black. Each ideological stance incorporates strengths and weaknesses, and there are times when the holders of one perspective may find themselves at odds with those who share another variant of Blackness (added note: recall the ideological conflicts before and after the Million Man March). This means that nigrescence may increase the salience of race and culture for everyone who successfully reaches the advanced stages of Black identity development, but Internalization does not result in ideological unity. One can look on this variability as ideological fractionation or as healthy, ideological diversity (*Shades of Black,* pp. 212-213)."

In another section that follows my discussion of Internalization, I soon return to the issue of identity diversity: "As I have tried to argue in previous sections, nigrescence does not result in a single ideological stance, and it is certainly true that not all persons in the Internalization stage gravitate toward Black nationalism or Afrocentricism. In making this observation, I am not trying to be contentious, I am simply trying to state a fact: Everyone who has a Black identity may not be Afrocentric ... and Afrocentricity does not incorporate all legitimate interpretations of what it means to be Black." ... "[We] nigrescence theorists and researchers ... have tried to offer a way of looking at, and talking about, the development of various Black identities—nationalist, biculturalist, and multicultural—including Afrocentricity. We have sought to clarify and expand the discourse on Blackness by paying attention to the variability and diversity in Blackness (*Shades of Black,* pp. 222-223)."

When one reads the actual theory, versus Stokes et al., "interpretation" of the theory, it becomes clear we are talking about observers who have an axe to grind. Where in the theory is there an exaggerated emphasis on victimization? Where does the theory lend itself to the phrase "Nigger-to-Black" conversion? Where is the "single" starting point and where is the linear, unidimensional outcome?

In a minor but related note, Stokes et al., suggest that I have flipped-flopped on whether there are four or five stages to my model. Let's see, the original model, as published in *Black World* had five stages, in *Beyond Black or White*, by Vernon Dixon and Badi Foster, we find five stages, in my 1978 *Journal of Black Psychology* on the Thomas and Cross Models, the model had five stages, in any reference for which I was the sole or first author that was published in the 1980s, five stages are referenced, and in the 1991 revision, there are five stages. Enough said.

Finally, Stokes et al., suggest that my thinking is too rooted in "traditional western psychology." This comes as close as one can get to a "Blacker-than-thou" statement. Taking this statement on its face value, let me point out the following: Almost two years before the appearance of Wade Nobles' seminal essay on African Psychology, and nearly ten years before Molefi Asante's now famous treatise on Afrocentricity, I wrote the following: "The significance of non-Western insights is dramatized when considering the problem of liberating Black scholars. The 'Negro' [Pre-encounter oriented] scholar hesitates to become involved in the Black experience because his perspective is distorted by the limitations of the philosophy and epistemology of Western science. In liberating Black scholars, we should add [the requirement of] exposure to non-Western thought (Cross, 25-26; italics added).

Let's set the record straight: I was one of the first scholars to include J. S. Mbiti's text on African Philosophies and Religions (this is the text that became the foundation for Wade Nobles' early thinking) in a class on the Black family and Black psychology; I was one of the first scholars to lecture on the ways in which Mbiti's thesis could be employed to better understand the psychology of Africans who were transported to the Americas during slavery (lectures and readings from my seminar at Princeton in the Fall of 1970; Jan Carew introduced me to Mbiti). I did not "flirt" with Afrocentricity, I explored it in depth. My life's work does not reflect a "rejection" of Afrocentricity, rather I have found it more productive to attempt a difficult fusion of Western and African perspectives. I have arrived at this position because the people I love, study, and serve tend to think, feel, and act, not as "Africans," although historically they and I are very much a part, in a historical sense, of the African Diaspora, but as African Americans. I might "wish" that we acted in a manner more consistent with Africanity, I might "prefer" that we think more in line with traditional African *worldview*s, and in the privacy of my thoughts, I might "pray" for a miracle to return us to our "roots," but as a Black scientist dedicated to understanding Black people as we are, and not as I might "wish" us to be, I have found a "purely" Afrocentric perspective to be wanting. It simply is not capable of "explaining" all that is to be explained about people of African descent who live out their lives in the United States.

Generalizability of the Model to Socialization of Children

Stokes et al., spend a great deal of time pointing out that the conversion model provides limited insight to questions pertaining to the socialization of Black children. Well, what else is new? Where have I ever written that nigrescence models should be applied to Black child development? Let's go back and read the first part of the last paragraph that ended the 1971 version of the Model, as it appeared in *Black World*: "This entire discussion has been appropriately titled, '*Towards a Psychology of Black Liberation*,' [and] for several reasons. In the first place, one person cannot capture the essence and spirit of the modern Black Revitalization Movement; thus, a definitive statement ... will result from collaboration with other Black psychologists and psychiatrists ... [F]urthermore, the conversion model is really an adult experience, while a completed psychology of Black liberation must also create socialization models and child rearing techniques that ... demonstrate to Black parents how to raise children in the image and likeness of Black heroes who [have] resisted oppression." In the concluding remarks of my 1978 *Journal of Black Psychology* article on models of psychological nigrescence, point 4 states that the models being addressed are not to be used for mapping "the evolution of [Black] identity from childhood through adult life. Conversions alter the identities that have evolved via traditional socialization experiences, and result in the production of new adult role models. As parents, [these] new role models [should] raise their children not in terms of the conversion process, but according to traditional [Black] socialization schemes." And in *Shades of Black* we find: "Nigrescence is a resocializing experience; it seeks to transform a preexisting identity (a non-Afrocentric identity) into one that is Afrocentric. The focus of the Pre-encounter stage is the preexisting identity, the identity to be changed. Of course, it is possible for a Black person to be socialized from early childhood through adolescence to have a Black identity. At adulthood, such a person is not likely to be in need of nigrescence ... [M]ore to the point, ... nigrescence is not a process for mapping the socialization of children ... (*Shades of Black*, p. 190)."

Also to be found in *Shades of Black* is the following statement which further gives credence to the fact that I have self-consciously tried to delimit where nigrescence theory comes into play and where it does not: "The Pre-encounter identity is usually the person's first identity, that is, the identity shaped by his or her early development. This socialization involves years of experiences with one's immediate family, extended family, neighborhood and community, and schools; it covers the years of childhood, adolescence, and early adulthood (*Shades of Black*, p.198)." I continue by noting that this identity is "a tried and fully tested identity that serves the person day in and day out. It helps him or her feel centered, meaningful, and in control by making life predictable. Although we can tolerate and can even come to enjoy a certain amount of change and variety in our external environment, it is almost impossible to imagine a world in which, at the beginning of each day, we [have] to reconstruct our identity. The predictability and stability functions of one's identity serve as filters against rapid and dramatic identity change. A person's identity filters incoming experiences so that the information "fits" into his or her understanding of self and the world in which she or he lives. Any fully developed identity, let alone a Pre-encounter identity, is difficult to change. Stage 2 of the nigrescence process tries to pinpoint those circumstances and events that are likely to induce identity metamorphosis in an individual (*Shades of Black,* pp. 198-199)."

Nigrescence and A Lifespan Perspective

Recently, Peony Fhagen-Smith and I co-authored (Cross & Fhagen-Smith, 1996) a conceptualization of the way Black identity develops across the lifespan, and as it turns out, our effort anticipated some of the lifespan issues raised by Stokes et al., In our work, Fhagen-Smith and I wanted to both critique and offer an alternative to Jean Phinney's Ethnic Identity Model which we believe is too linear and constrictive in its implications about Black socialization patterns. Phinney's work is designed to bring about a greater synthesis between the discourse on ethnic-racial identity development and Erik Erikson's schema on adolescent identity development. To set the stage for this discussion, we need to briefly review certain aspects of Erikson's theory. According to Erikson (1968), adolescence marks the developmental period when the healthy integration of one's personal identity, general personality, and social or group identity is achieved. Translated as stages (Marcia, 1966), Erikson's ideas state that young people enter adolescence with ideas about themselves that are unclear and negative (diffuse identity) or they may absorb uncritically the teachings of their parents (foreclose identity). To take ownership of one's self-concept, the young person must, according to Erikson, enter a period of self-reflection and self-exploration that may take on "crisis like" characteristics (identity moratorium). Under the best of conditions, the period of moratorium is followed by a state of resolution, clarity of thinking, and commitment to a well conceived notion of "who I am." The person is said to have "achieved" her or his identity, thus the label, achieved identity.

The Ethnic Identity Development Model, crafted by Jean Phinney (1989), fuses the unique identity experiences of different ethnic and racial groups with the four stages of the Erikson Model. According to Phinney, ethnic and racial minorities enter adolescents with poorly developed ethnic identities (diffuse), or with an identity "given" to them by their parents (foreclosure). They may enter into an identity crisis, during which the conflicts and challenges associated with one's minority status are sorted (moratorium), and should all go smoothly, they achieve an ethnic identity that is positive (achieved ethnicity). As should be self-evident, Phinney's model is very linear and simplistic (it assumes every Black child must make "race" and one's "racial" status the primary issues at adolescence), but less obvious are the negative implications it seems to communicate about Black socialization patterns. Phinney seems to associate both diffusion and foreclosure with psychological deficits (low self-esteem). This seems logical for parents who raise children with a diffuse identity, but in order to associate deficits with a foreclose identity, one must, by definition, view very negatively the way the average Black family raises its children. As an alternate and corrective to the flaws found in the Phinney Model, Peony Fhagen-Smith and I have designed a lifespan scenario that accounts for identity variability across the lifespan, and in addition, it shows the points at which nigrescence experiences may (or may not) enter the picture in the evolution of a Black person's identity. Our schema, reproduced below as Figure 1, builds on the ideas of Margaret Spencer, Urie Bronfenbrenner, Harold Stevenson, J. Lawrence Aber, Thomas Parham, as well as Jean Phinney. The conceptualization employs six sectors:

Sector One: The first sector seriates variables that are likely to come into play in the creation of each Black child's ecological niche. Our list in no way exhausts the possible origins of ecological variability. The point we are trying to make is that Black children don't "turn out the same," in part, because they are "molded" by influences that vary from one household to next, even when those households might be situated in the same locale, let alone different social class environments. The majority of Black children are likely to be raised in human ecologies that steer identity development toward high race salience. However, a significant number of other Black children will exist in niches for which something other than race is given preference. One should note that our thinking is heavily influenced by the work of Urie Bronfenbrenner (Western Psychology) and Margaret Spencer (An Afrocentric scholar), and reflects the type of worldview fusion that I addressed earlier in this paper.

Sector Two: During preadolescence, each Black child's identity begins to emerge, although developmental limitations associated with this period of child development, prevent these "emergent" identities from taking on adult-like qualities. This sector depicts variability in these "emergent" Black identities. This diversity is the logical outcome of the human ecology variation described in sector one. In other words, Identities A, B, C, etc., captures our way of stating that, even at the pre-adolescent period, identity variability will be evident from one Black child to another. Although our ultimate aim is to understand how various "Black" or "race" centered identities evolve, our model stresses that we don't think every Black child will be Afrocentrically "centered," because not every Black household stresses Afrocentricity (our aim is not prescriptive, as in seeking to tell Black people how they should identify, rather we are trying to capture the identity variability evidenced by a large sample of Black preadolescents, across a variety of ecological niches).

Figure 1.

Model Depicting the Relationship Between Ego Identity Development and Nigrescence

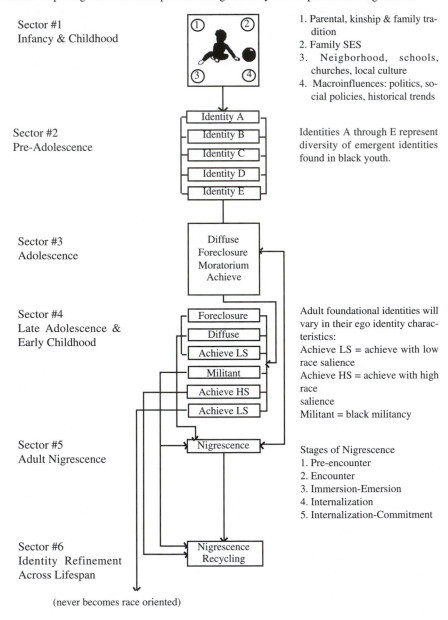

Sector #1
Infancy & Childhood

1. Parental, kinship & family tradition
2. Family SES
3. Neigborhood, schools, churches, local culture
4. Macroinfluences: politics, social policies, historical trends

Sector #2
Pre-Adolescence

Identities A through E represent diversity of emergent identities found in black youth.

Identity A
Identity B
Identity C
Identity D
Identity E

Sector #3
Adolescence

Diffuse
Foreclosure
Moratorium
Achieve

Sector #4
Late Adolescence &
Early Childhood

Foreclosure
Diffuse
Achieve LS
Militant
Achieve HS
Achieve LS

Adult foundational identities will vary in their ego identity characteristics:
Achieve LS = achieve with low race salience
Achieve HS = achieve with high race
salience
Militant = black militancy

Sector #5
Adult Nigrescence

Nigrescence

Stages of Nigrescence
1. Pre-encounter
2. Encounter
3. Immersion-Emersion
4. Internalization
5. Internalization-Commitment

Sector #6
Identity Refinement
Across Lifespan

Nigrescence
Recycling

(never becomes race oriented)

Sector Three: In our article, we described the complex events surrounding identity development during adolescence in the following way: "At adolescence, Black youth will burst into the scene with a broad spectrum of identity agendas; some will be attached to religious issues, other to sexual preference, and still others may stress their social class status or school affiliation. Because of housing segregation and the prominence of race in American society, race and culture will likely be a high priority in the self-concept struggles for many Black children. For those Black youth who make race a central organizing feature to their identities, the moratorium experience will be very nigrescence-like in dynamics. This is shown by the line that connects adolescence (sector #3) and nigrescence (sector #5). However, keeping in mind that Blacks are living and growing in a multitude of circumstances, the identity-content of Black youth will vary, from context to context. Consequently, the moratorium stage for some Black youth will focus on their religious ideas, for others it will be their gang membership, and for still others, it will center on issues that have little race content. Most Black adolescents will go through the various Eriksonian stages, yet the content of each young person's identity crisis will not always center on race (Cross & Fhagen-Smith, 1996, pp. 118-120)." That the content of each young person's identity crisis will not always center on race, is a point missed by Jean Phinney in her linear conceptualization of adolescence and ethnic identity development.

Sectors Four and Five: At late adolescence and early adulthood, each person's life will be guided by whatever identity status has taken hold. This "foundational identity" defines one's psychological foundation for adult living. Each person's adult-foundational-identity will vary in "race content and emphasis" (some will show high salience for race and Black culture, others will be grounded in things other than race) and "ego-status or general personality attributes" (diffuse, foreclose, moratorium or achieve; low self esteem or high self-worth, introversion tendencies or or extroversion proclivities, etc.). Black persons who reach this point with a foundational identity that is low in race content (Pre-encounter oriented, with low race salience), or is anti-Black in nature (Pre-encounter orientation with anti-Black themes), are prime targets for nigrescence. What makes a person vulnerable to nigrescence is not one's ego-identity status, per se (foreclosed, diffused or achieved), but one's identity content (race salience). "A Black person with a foundational identity that is "achieved," but low in Black content, may become susceptible to nigrescence, in the face of an encounter. As the [schema] shows, however, a person with low race salience may go through life and never experience nigrescence (Cross & Fhagen-Smith, 1996, p. 120)." It is possible for a person to have "positive race content" but a "foreclosed" ego-identity pattern. This results when a person has been taught to have positive ideas about being Black, but has never questioned or explored such teachings. Such persons may to go through nigrescence, not to "become Black," but as a substitute for the missed "moratorium" experience. The "diffuse" pattern is subject to nigrescence to correct for any confusions of negativity she or he may associate with being Black. Other examples might be cited but our point is that nigrescence is not a universal experience, and only Black adults who hold certain types of ideas ("race-low salience" or "anti-Black thoughts") are the most in "need" of it. Even at that, there is no guarantee in life that those Black adults who might benefit from it will ever experience nigrescence.

Sector Six: The last sector focuses on Thomas Parham's concept of nigrescence recycling (Parham, 1989). "Parham suggested that, whether one develops a Black identity at adolescence or at some later point in life, certain questions or unexpected challenges lie in waiting. As Parham explains, a youthful person's inexperience makes it impossible to anticipate all of the issues that are related to [being Black]. Consequently, as one progresses through the life cycle, certain questions and challenges take on new significance. These new "challenges" or questions are experienced by the person as [new "encounter episodes."] ... If the Encounter triggers a strong emotional response in the person, the recycling may take on the intensity of the person's first spin through Immersion-Emersion and Internalization. The response to a less striking encounter may be a cognitive "walk-through" the stages. Periodic recycling will likely lead the person to a sense of "wisdom" about the self and Black life in general (120-121; Cross & Fhagen-Smith, 1996)." That is to say, the person does not go "backwards" to an earlier stage, as misperceived by Stokes et al., Rather, the person who is operating with the Internalized identity, "encounters" a new question about her or his Blackness that requires being "worked through" to resolution. Given that all goes well, this new insight or solution is "added" to her or his already developed Black identity. Thus, one's identity is "enhanced," and an accumulation of such experiences can lead a sense of "wisdom" about one's Blackness and a philosophical perspective on the Black condition. From this perspective, the development and maintenance of a Black identity is a life long pursuit.

In summary, for each of our lifespan intervals, ... " the dual themes of identity development and identity variability are synthesized [by our schema]. In addition, the schema applies an Eriksonian perspective to map the unfolding of any Black person's identity, from one status to the next, independent of the content of that identity [emphasis added]. We account for those African Americans who make race central to their self-conceptions, as well as those who progress to the status of achieved identity, despite having a "non-ethnic" frame of reference. We show how nigrescence may enter the picture, as early as adolescence, or after the establishment of one's foundational, adult-identity. The possibility for refinement and growth into the status of "wisdom" are reflected in the sector on nigrescence recycling (121; Cross & Fhagen-Smith, 1996)." Unlike the call by Stokes et al., to "abandon" nigrescence theory, we show how the theory fills an important gap in the overall discourse on Black identity development.

References

Cross, W.E., Jr., (1971). The Negro-to-Black conversion experience. *Black World, 20,* 13-26.

Cross, W.E. Jr., (1978). The Cross and Thomas models on psychological Nigrescence: A literature review. *Journal of Black Psychology 4(1),* 13-31.

Cross, W.E., Jr., (1991). *Shades of Black: Diversity in African American identity.* Philadelphia, PA: Temple University Press.

Cross, W.E. Jr., & Fhagen-Smith, P. (1996). Nigrescence and ego identity development. In P. Pederson, J. Draguns, W. Lonner, & J. Trimble (Eds.), *Counseling across cultures* (pp. 108-123). Thousand Oaks, CA: Sage

Erikson, E.H., (1968). *Identity: Youth in crisis.* New York: W.W. Norton.

Marcia, J. (1966). Development and validation of ego identity status. *Journal of Personality and Social Psychology, 3(5),* 551-558.

Parham, T. (1989). *Nigrescence:* The transformation of Black consciousness across the life cycle. In R.L. Jones (Ed.), *Black adult development and aging.* Berkeley, CA: Cobb & Henry.

Phinney, J. (1989). stages of ethnic identity development in minority group adolescents. *Journal of Early Adolescence, 9,* 34-49.

Phinney, J., & Chavira, A. (1992). Ethnic identity and self-esteem: An exploratory longitudinal study. *Journal of Adolescence, 15,* 271-281.

Author

William E. Cross, Jr., Professor
Chair, Department of Student Development
and Pupil Personnel Services (SDPPS)
School of Education
University of Massachusetts
366 Hills South
Amherst, MA 01003-4160
Telephone: (413) 545-0543
Fax (413) 545-1523
E-mail:wecross@educ.umass.edu

The Cross Stage Model Revisited: A Rejoinder

Julie E. Stokes, Carolyn B. Murray, M. Jean Peacock and David Chavez

Introduction

Our original paper (Stokes, Murray, Chavez, & Peacock, 1998) and this rejoinder to Cross' reply were both undertaken for the purpose of critical review. In the process of scientific inquiry, psychologists construct theories containing hypothetical concepts and assumptions, and in most instances change them based upon further observation and information. Researchers constantly build on previous knowledge in order to go beyond what is currently known. Thus, theories and their findings must be presented to the scientific community in such a way that they can be replicated, criticized, or extended. Peer critique is one way that science attempts to explicate the role of agreement (or disagreement) between fact and theory in the verification process. Therefore, "serious criticism" is an important aspect of the Scientific Method of Inquiry in that ideas and experimentation undergo a honing process in which they are submitted to other critical minds for evaluation, and ideas that survive this critical process have begun to meet the criterion of public verifiability (Stanovich, 1988). In all fairness to Dr. Cross (1998), as he points out in his reply to our critique, the model has undergone revision due to "scores of empirical studies conducted on the model between the early 1970s and the present" (p. 2). However, the verifiability of the model still remains questionable and will be addressed in the present rejoinder.

The contribution of Cross' nigrescence model to understanding African American adult identity development cannot be overstated. As emphasized in the original critique, the nigrescence model is not just one theory but the only theory that has been applied to African American adult identity development. We are in agreement with Stevenson (1998), that the nigrescence model holds much historical relevance and importance. The model opened the door and paved the way for entirely new avenues of identity exploration related to African Americans. However, we also believe as Kuhn (1970) pointed out that "normal science does and must

171

continually strive to bring theory and fact into closer agreement, and that activity can easily be seen as testing or as a search for confirmation or falsification" (p. 80). Therefore, to be taken seriously a theory must operate as the theory says it does, therefore critique is necessary. Even Cross (1998) stated that without "serious critiques...one cannot grow" (p.159).

Points of Agreement

On several points Dr. Cross (1998) addressed our criticisms of the nigrescence model. Specifically, he clearly indicated that the nigrescence model was never intended to be applied to Black child development (see p. 8) as we suggested. More importantly, he noted that "nigrescence is a resocializing experience; it seeks to transform a preexisting identity (a non-Afrocentric identity) into one that is Afrocentric" (p. 10). He admitted that "it is possible for a Black person to be socialized from early childhood through adolescence to have a Black identity. At adulthood, such a person is not likely to be in need of nigrescence" (p. 10). The nigrescence model in essence, as we surmised, is applicable to only a segment of Black population, how large a segment is an empirical question that has not been addressed. Further support for this conclusion is the statement made by Dr. Cross (1998) that persons in the Pre-encounter stage, who have a low salience to race neutrality "as long as their Pre-encounter attitudes bring a sense of fulfillment, a meaningful existence, and an internal sense of stability, order, and harmony, ...will probably not need an identity change. Only those at the Pre-encounter stage who are anti-Black, purports Cross, is "the scene...set for a possible identity conversion" (p. 160).

In addition, a related issue raised in the Stokes et al., (1998) critique, the heuristic application or misapplication of the stage concept has been clarified by the point that nigrescence is applicable to only a segment of the population. Given that the nigrescence model is only applicable to a segment, "albeit a minority," [who] "do show classic signs of self-hatred" (Cross, 1995, p. 97), [who] "are transformed, by a series of circumstances and events, into persons who are more Black or Afrocentrically aligned" (p. 98), the model as proposed by Stokes et al., is more appropriately defined as an experiential progression model rather than a stage developmental model.

This conceptualization brings up a point in which we were misunderstood by both Cross (1998) and Stevenson (1998). At no time did we suggest that the nigrescence model should be discarded. We did raise theoretical and empirical criticisms concerning inadequacies inherit in the model, but only for the purpose of suggesting closer scrutiny and further refinement, not elimination. Nor did we propose an experiential model to take the place of the nigrescence model, we did, however, argue that the model is an experiential model.

The remaining issues yet to be adequately addressed in the literature or in Cross' reply to our critique are: (1) the intrinsic bias in descriptions of identifiable attitudes and behaviors considered as appropriate at the various stages; (2) the traditional Western psychological theoretical underpinnings of the model; and (3) the lack of empirical evidence for the model.

The Nigrescence Model: Inadequacies and Concerns

The nigrescence model has been purported to have four stages in some of Cross' writings, and five stages in other articles. These stages as explicated in the recent writings of Cross are the: Pre-encounter, persons who "hold attitudes toward race that range from low salience to race neutrality to anti-Black" (Cross, 1998, p. 2); Encounter, "circumstances and events that are likely to induce identity metamorphosis" (Cross, 1995, p. 104)—e.g., after being stopped and beat by a racist police officer for no apparent reason, the system refuses even to consider the complaint against the officer; Immersion-Emersion—in the beginning "White becomes evil, oppressive, inferior, and inhuman, and all things Black are declared superior..." (Cross, 1995, p. 105); by the end of this stage the person experiences "emergence from the emotionality and dead-end, either/or, racist [emphasis added], and over-simplified ideological aspects of the immersion experience" (Cross, 1995, p. 110); Internalization stage according to Cross (1998) is characterized by a "cultural identity" in which the "person can vary from that of [a] monocultural orientation (e.g., nationalism) to the identity mosaic of [a] multiculturally oriented Black" (p. 5); and Internalization-Commitment stage which Cross (1995) explicitly states that "current theory suggests there are few differences between the psychology of Blacks in the fourth and fifth stages other than the important factor of sustained interest and commitment" (p. 121).

Before the issue of intrinsic bias in the stage descriptions is discussed the issue of whether there are four or five stages needs to be reopened. In Dr. Cross' reply he claimed that he had not "flipped-flopped" on whether there are four or five stages to the model. Yet in his own words "current theory suggest there are few differences between...the fourth and fifth stages." Moreover, the only difference explicated by Cross (1995) is "sustained interest and commitment" (p. 121), in other words more of the same. Furthermore, in defense of his position that there have always been five stages and nothing has changed, he lists several of his published works which started with the original article (Cross, 1971) and ended with the 1991 revision (*Shades of Black*). It is most interesting, that he does not mention his 1991 article "The Stages of Black Identity Development: Nigrescence Models." which appeared in Reginald Jones' *Black Psychology* (Cross, Parham & Helms, 1991), or the chapter which appears in the present volume entitled *Nigrescence Revisited: Theory and Research* (Cross, Parham & Helms, 1998), both of which discuss a four stage model of nigrescence. As a matter of fact Cross, Parham and Helms (1991) stated that "nigrescence models tend to have four or five stages (we will stress four stage summary)..." (p. 322).

More importantly, Cross (1991) stated that to his "knowledge there have been no empirical studies focusing on sustained commitment that follows nigrescence" (p. 121). Consider an additional statement that "a more differentiated look at Internalization-Commitment awaits the results of future research" (*Shades of Black*, 1991, p. 220). In addition, Cross, Parham, and Helms (1998) stated in regard to the Racial Identity Attitudes Scale (RIAS) "we strongly advise that the RIAS be maintained as a four factor stage inventory" (p. 22). This issue becomes more troubling when one takes into consideration that the RIAS was developed to operationalize and test nigrescence theory, and therefore, Stokes et al., (1998), Sellers, Smith, Shelton, and Johnson (1998), and even Cross, Parham, and Helms (1991, 1998), all discuss, interpret, and apply nigrescence theory as a four stage model. Simply stating that there are five stages in the progression of Black identity does not make it so! After 25 years of nigrescence research, some empirical evidence to support the speculation of a fifth stage should have emerged. Thus, the question still remains theoretically and empirically is nigrescence a four or five stage model?

The issue of intrinsic bias in the description of the stages was not addressed adequately by Cross. One of the present authors had the pleasure of meeting Dr. Cross this summer and discussing the nigrescence model with him. She was surprised to learn that at this point his thinking is that the only truly unhealthy stage is the Immersion/Emersion Stage. The following discussion is put forth to question the logic of this thinking.

Pre-Encounter Stage

In response to comments made regarding the Pre-encounter Stage, let us begin with a direct quote "nigrescence is a re-socializing experience: it seeks to transform a pre-existing identity (a non-Afrocentric identity) into one that is Afrocentric. The focus of the Pre-encounter Stage is the pre-existing identity, the identity to be changed" (*Shades of Black*, 1991, p. 190).

The descriptions related to the Pre-encounter stage are contradictory and confusing. For example, Blacks at the Pre-encounter stage can "have values and do experience a meaningful existence; it is just that little emphasis is given to Blackness. As long as their Pre-encounter attitudes bring them a sense of fulfillment, a meaningful existence, and an internal sense of stability, order and harmony, such persons will probably not need any identity change, let alone a movement toward Afrocentricity" (*Shades of Black*, 1991, p. 191). Conversely, Cross, Parham, and Helms (1998) clearly indicated in their review of nigrescence models that "implicit in all models is the notion that Stage 1 identity (Pre-encounter) reflects some level of impaired mental health" (p. 6). So, are these statements contradictory or is it our misinterpretation? Reportedly, there are also Blacks in the Pre-encounter Stage who for them "the only meaning accorded to race is its tie to issues of social discrimination; from this perspective race is a hassle, a problem, an imposition" or "anti-Blackness" (*Shades of Black*, 1991, p. 191).

This restrictive interpretation is evidenced in that the only theoretical position captured in the Racial Attitudes Identity Scale (RAIS) is the anti-Black. This issue will be revisited later. But again, does simply trying to engage all facets of Black American discourse in a theory make it tenable?

Lets look closer at some of the statements attributed to pre-encounter individuals. Major attitudinal markers include, among other speculations, "miseducation, a Eurocentric cultural frame of reference, spotlight or race-image anxiety, a race-conflict resolution model that stresses assimilation-integration objectives, and a value system that gives preference to other than Afrocentric priorities" (*Shades of Black*, 1991, p. 192). Yet according to Cross, "Pre-encounter Blacks may be no less communalistic or individualistic than Blacks at other stages" (p. 197). "It would be a mistake to assume that Pre-encounter is a form of mental illness...the great majority of Pre-encounter Blacks are probably as mentally healthy as Blacks in the more advance stages of nigrescence" (p. 198). Moreover, if these conjectures are true, why is a theory of nigrescence "the process of becoming Black" necessary?

In summary, it does appear that attempts have been made to expand the rhetoric related to the Pre-encounter Stage. Still, given the contradictory nature of the statements made and the ideas presented, Stokes et al., responded to those substantive assumptions that remained unchanged from the original theory. That is, there are Blacks with negative anti-Black attitudes that need to be re-socialized into an Afrocentric frame of reference. Even Cross, Parham, and Helms (1998) commented that the "common point of departure is not the change process per say, but an analysis of the identity to be changed (p. 5). The person is first described as functioning in an ongoing steady-state (Stage 1), with a deracinated or "Negro identity" (p. 5). From this perspective, all the rest of the information presented in *Shades of Black* (1991) about Pre-encounter attitudes fails to make intuitive sense. Nor is there any measurement, documentation, or evidence to suggest that such speculation has been critically evaluated.

Encounter Stage

Although there was no response to any of the issues raised about Stage 2 (Encounter), we will briefly comment on remaining concerns. Cross, Parham, and Helms (1998) suggest that Stage 2 "has the effect of pulling the rug from under the feet of the person operating with the Negro identity" (p. 9). However, the "Encounter need not be negative" (*Shades of Black*, 1991, p. 200). Further stated is the notion that "a negative side to the Encounter is often introduced, for it is almost inevitable that the person will become enraged at the thought of having been previously miseducated by White racist institutions" (*Shades of Black*, 1991, p. 200). "The encounter engenders a great range of emotions: guilt, anger, and general anxiety may become energizing factors" (p. 201). "Inner-directed guilt, rage at White people, and an anxiety about becoming the right kind of Black person combine to form a psychic energy that flings the person into a frantic, determined, obsessive, extremely motivated search for Black identity" (p. 201). The language throughout the description is pejorative (e.g., frantic, obsessive). If the Encounter Stage need not be negative, why would the individual experience a sense of having the rug pulled out from under them. Is such an experience as this considered positive?

Immersion/Emersion Stage

In his reply to our critique Cross chose not to address the Immersion/Emersion Stage directly; indirectly however, many of his comments lashing out at our critique characterized our concerns with the rhetoric describing this stage. This position is particularly illuminated in his response to our criticism that nigrescence theory appears to be rooted in "traditional Western psychology." Our critique was based upon the fact that the nigrescence model assumes that Black identity is a reaction to White people or the result of societal oppression and exploitation, which is a "traditional Western psychology" approach. By characterizing Black identity from a "traditional Western psychology" approach Cross ignores the fact that African American people are culturally, philosophically, biologically and spiritually distinct from other geo-political-socio-cultural groups (Nobles, 1989). According to Dr. Cross our issue with the model's "traditional Western psychology" approach "comes as close as one can get to a 'Blacker-than-thou' statement." In his defense he gives a chronology of his life as a trail blazer in the presentation of Black thought, and ends with an expository concluding that a " 'purely' Afrocentric perspective to be wanting" (Cross, 1998, pp. 7-8). His response clearly does not address our critique that the nigrescence model is rooted in "traditional Western psychology".

Moreover, he uses the "Blacker-than-thou propensities" (Cross, 1995, p. 109) to characterize persons at the Immersion level of Stage 3. He explained that the "Blacker-than-thou propensities" are all part of the new convert's anxiety that his or her Blackness be 'pure and acceptable.' He further stated that, "We can refer to this anxiety as Weusi anxiety. Weusi is Swahili word for being or becoming Black enough" (p. 109). Further showing his annoyance with persons at this stage of identity development, Dr. Cross communicated to a group of Black psychologists, during a workshop on racial identity at the 1996 Association of Black Psychologists Annual Conference, that persons at this stage are the only ones that are suffering from poor mental illness, besides those at the Pre-encounter Stage who are anti-Black. As a matter of fact he characterized all other persons at the Pre-encounter Stage as "probably as mentally healthy as Blacks in the more advanced stages of nigrescence...[What separates] Pre-encounter Blacks from those who are Afrocentric are value, orientation, historical perspective and world view" (Cross, 1998, p. 3). We do not wish to personalize or discuss our worldviews—which are different from each other, this is neither the time nor the place—but we do believe it important to point out the fact that any theoretical model explaining the functioning of Americans of African descent that has not taken into consideration their African heritage is questionable. More importantly, what is a healthy identity for African people who live in a White racist society?

Internalization and Internalization-Commitment

During a conversation with Thomas Parham (personal communication, September 30, 1996) one of the present authors was told that Stage 4 was the internalization of a values orientation and Stage 5 was the behavioral manifestation of those values. Thus, given this information and the earlier discussion of whether the nigrescence model is a four and five stage model we have chosen to treat it as a four stage model. Clearly according to Cross (1991), the ultimate state of mental health is a person who has arrived at Stage 4, Internalization. His initial writings indicated, that this person "while still using Blacks as a primary reference group, the person moves towards a pluralistic and non-racist perspective..." (p. 11). Most recently, Dr. Cross (1998) has extended this stage to include those who maintain "a strong nationalist framework" (p. 6). So what do these two groups have in common that distinguishes them from person at Stage 3? He states that at the Internalization Stage, the defensive function becomes much more sophisticated and flexible. Instead of the iron shield of Immersion-Emersion, it becomes a translucent filter that is often "invisible" or undetectable, allowing the person to process non-threatening information and experiences without distortion. There now appears to be a blurring of the stages in which the Pre-encounter stage is distinguished from the advanced stages only in terms of salience of "Blackness," and the Immersion-Emersion stage is only distinguishable from the Internalization stage in terms of degree of "sophistication and flexibility" in regard to ones defensiveness. At least the initial version of the model presented clear distinctions between stages, which the present version of the model does not. In spite of the early model's clarity the empirical evidence for Cross' contention that a certain stage in more or less healthy than other stages has not been consistently supported. The revised version of the model can only add to this confusion. Thus, the question of what is a healthy Black identity remains an empirical question. Until this issue is answered empirically, the nigrescence model is just one man's value judgment.

Lack of Empirical Evidence

We agree with Stevenson (1998), the nigrescence model should not be expected to carry the entire responsibility for the advancement of discussion surrounding African American adult identity development. Still, after 25 years there has been a disturbing lack of consistent empirical evidence to support the theory. For instance, Cross (1995) claims that the extant depictions of the middle stages (Encounter and Immersion-Emersion) seem to hold up well. On the other hand, empirical studies call into question the validity of the original contours and dynamics of the first stage (Pre-Encounter) and advance stages (Internalization, or Stages 4 and 5) (p. 95). Cross has attempted to address this lack of empirical support for stages by revising the stages in question. However, even the reporting by Cross of the empirical evidence for the model is inconsistent. On page 20, of the Cross et al., (1998) chapter which appears in the present volume they reported that "the evanescent nature of the [Encounter] stage has led some researchers to forego any attempt to measure it." Thus, at best the empirical evidence for the model is less than adequate, at worst the empirical evidence does not support the basic tenants of the model.

In addition, there has been a piecemeal process of adding, "singly and in combination" (Kuhn, 1970, p.2) information that has led to an ever increasing stockpile of ideas that are proposed to constitute a scientific body of knowledge and technique. So while the nigrescence model should not be held solely responsible for describing African American adult identity, without consistent evidence researchers should not employ the theory as if it were the gospel.

Stevenson (1998) also suggested there still "remains a utility to the model that has escaped research attempts to prove its validity" (p. 152). There can be no argument that there is an intuitiveness about a search for identity, a tacit knowledge almost every person engages in at some point in his or her life time. For instance, college students, who to date have constituted nearly all RIAS research data supporting the model, are thrust into an environment where they are expected to experience some degree of identity confusion and conflict. In such an environment (college) cognitive shifts described within the nigrescence model are expected to take place. Moreover, there exists a reasonable probability that the increase in exposure to education, concepts, theory, and other perspectives in predominantly White college environments may create the semblance of sameness in the way the individuals express the experience of discovering who they are. One cannot entirely rule out the homogenizing effect of a college environment on student thinking and behavior. Examples of the potency of such environmental forces are most evident among athletes or members of campus clubs (sororities/fraternities). Therefore, researchers interested in African American adult identity development have no idea how generalizable the tenants of the theory are or to what segment of the African American population the theory applies, college students maybe?

The description of a subject's phenomenological experiences is an appropriate undertaking in science. To validate subjective experience, empirical testing instruments are employed, moving the focus from subjective to objective. The supposed objectivity of testing instruments allows others to critically evaluate the tenability of what was subjectively proposed. For instance, a major tenant of the model is that "Whiteness" historically and presently is the most salient issue for the development of African American racial identity. Stevenson (1998) points out "to use interactions with Whites and 'Whiteness' as a barometer of how one thinks about his racial identity does not have to mean that White people, White life, or White values constitute the 'center of the universe' " (p. 152). Today, Latino and Asian populations are presenting competing concerns for African Americans, in some cases more than Whites.

Cross (1998), unlike Stevenson (1998), only minimally considered the multiple influences one is exposed to, the effect of racially socializing experiences (other than White society), the homogenizing influence of the college environment on student thinking, perception, and behavior, or the possible multiple aspects of Black identity development relevant today. To address these multiplicities of experience Sellers, Smith, Shelton, Johnson and Chavous (1998) offered a viable way in which to explore that diversity. Their model does so by recognizing that not every issue carries the same weight for each African American. The model offers a plausible explanation for why variability may appear by introducing into the racial identity discussion the concepts of racial saliency and centrality. Also, Sellers et al., (1998) incorporate conceptualization with a potential way to measure the public and private aspects of how one experiences their racial identity.

Finally, the ranges and operationalization of racial ideologies distinctly clarifies the numerous ways African American racial identity can be framed. More importantly, Sellers et al., addressed the experience of oppression as a conceptual factor that must be considered when discussing the psychological functioning of African Americans (Akbar, 1991).

Summary and Conclusion

In the 1970's a phenomenon occurred that called for scientific recognition and investigation. Blacks were demonstrating movement from self-hatred to self-acceptance. The nigrescence theory was developed to provide a description of the process engaged in when experiencing the change. As a result, the nigrescence theory contributed greatly to the accumulation of an invaluable body of knowledge.

The theory has been widely applied and continues to make a significant impact on the thinking of researchers interested in African American adult racial identity. These important historical contributions are duly noted and acknowledged by Stokes et al., (1998). The current discussion however is long overdue.

The nigrescence theory, though once tenable, now appears to be less so. The assumptions put forth in the piecemeal effort to expand the theory are inescapably contradictory. The empirical evidence available to support some of the concepts in the theory are weak. And the defense pertaining to the utility of the theory appears to lack credence when all the evidence is carefully considered.

Sellers et al., (1998) on the other hand, offer a fresh, more contemporary, theoretically viable alternative to the nigrescence theory. The concepts are concisely articulated, with operationally defined and measurable variables. Consequently, hypotheses will be more easily generated and tested.

The research field of African American adult racial identity is on the horizon of new exploration and elaboration. The present discourse, although misunderstood at times, has served a much needed purpose, that is to once again stimulate new interest and to invite discussion of varying perspectives in this much needed area of research investigation. Simply stated, this discourse had served to reinforce the reality that only through the exchange of diverse ideas and perspectives can the field of science be propelled forward. Thank you one and all for your invaluable input.

References

Akbar, N. (1991). Paradigms of African American research. In R. L. Jones (Ed.), *Black psychology* (3rd ed.). Berkeley: Cobb & Henry.

Cross, W. E., Jr. (1991). *Shades of Black: Diversity in African-American identity*. Philadelphia: Temple University Press.

Cross, W. E., Jr. (1998). Commentary on the Stokes et al., critique of nigrescence theory. In R. L. Jones (Ed.), *African American identity development*. Hampton, VA: Cobb & Henry.

Cross, W. E., Jr. (1971). The Negro-to-Black conversion experience. *Black World*, 13-27.

Cross, W. E., Jr. Parham, T. A. & Helms, J. E. (1998). Nigrescence revisited: Theory and research. In R. L. Jones (Ed.), *African American identity development*. Hampton, VA: Cobb & Henry.

Cross, W. E., Parham, T. A. & Helms, J. E. (1991). The stages of Black identity development: nigrescence models. In R. L. Jones (Ed.), *Black psychology* (3rd ed.). Berkeley: Cobb & Henry.

Kuhn, T. S. (1962). *The structure of scientific revolutions*. Chicago: University of Chicago Press.

Nobles, W. (1989). Psychological nigrescence: An Afrocentric review. *The Counseling Psychologist, 17(2)*, 253-257.

Rowley, S. J., & Sellers, R. M. (1998). Nigrescence theory: Critical issues and recommendations for future revisions. In R. L. Jones (Ed.), *African American identity development*. Hampton, VA: Cobb & Henry.

Sellers, R. M., Shelton, N., Cooke, D., Chavous, T., Rowley, S. J., & Smith, M. (1998). A multidimensional model of racial identity: Assumptions, findings, and future directions. In R. L. Jones (Ed.), *African American identity development*. Hampton, VA: Cobb & Henry.

Stanovich, K. E. (1988). *How to think straight about psychology* (2nd ed.). Glenview, IL: Scott, Foresman & Co.

Stevenson, H. C., Jr. (1998). The confluence of "both-and" in racial identity theory. In R. L. Jones (Ed.), *African American identity development*. Hampton, VA: Cobb & Henry.

Stokes, J. E., Murray, C. B., Chavez, D., & Peacock, M. J. (1998). Cross' Stage model revisted : An analysis of theoretical formulations and empirical evidence. In R. L. Jones (Ed.), *African American identity development*. Hampton, VA: Cobb & Henry.

Author

Carolyn Murray
Department of Psychology
University of California, Riverside
Riverside, CA 92521
Telephone: (909) 787-5293
Fax: (909) 787-3985
E-mail: carolyn.murray@ucr.edu

Part 3

Other Perspectives and Models

To Be African or Not to Be: The Question of Identity or Authenticity—Some Preliminary Thoughts

Wade W. Nobles

"Where theory is founded on analogy between puzzling observations and familiar phenomena, it is generally only a limited aspect of such phenomena that is incorporated into the resulting model" (Horton, 1967).

During the 1995 Association of Black Psychologists' Annual Convention's Pre-Conference African Psychology Institute, Dr. Asa Hilliard was invited to address the issue of African Psychology. In the context of his remarks, Dr. Hilliard attempted to paraphrase Shakespeare's often quoted, phrase, "To be or not to be, that is the question." In restating Shakespeare, Dr. Hilliard's intention, I think, was to say, "To be African or not to be African, that is the question." However, in attempting to restate the phrase, I believe Dr. Hilliard's tongue was captured by the ancestral spirits of Africa and what came forward was a divinely fundamental and spiritually essential question." Asa Hilliard stated, "To be African or not to Be, that is the question. In making that simple pronouncement, the level of discourse was fundamentally clarified and simultaneously shifted.

The ancestors, through Dr. Hilliard's genius, had directed Black Psychologists to deal with "the real deal." Can we Be and not be African? While this level of question frightened many of us and made most of us uncomfortable, I think it is the only place for us, as Black Psychologists, to begin. Accordingly, I would like to address the question of African American identity development from the framework of what is fundamental to our "Be" ing.

This question *To Be African or Not to Be* becomes even more complex when one factors in the context of African people living in a non-African and/or anti-African society. Given such a context, I have suggested that the understanding of what it means to be African must be informed by what I have defined as the Triangular Law of Knowing, Being and Doing for Africans living in an anti-African reality. The three laws are (1) the law of (mis)knowing; (2) the law of (non)being;

185

and (3) the law of (un)doing. These laws note that "if you don't understand White supremacy, then everything else you think you know will simply confuse you" - law of (mis)knowing; "If you don't exist according to your cultural essence (nature/ spirit) then everything that you think you are will only be a diminishment" - law of (non)being; and "the experience of one generation becomes the history of the next generation and the history of several generations will become the tradition of the people - law of (un)doing. Several scholars (Akbar, 1984; Banks, 1992; Carruthers, 1972; Nobles, 1978) have suggested that the psychological understanding of African people, must be informed by the extent to which we understand the impact of White supremacy, the retentions, residuals, and radiance of the African nature/ spirit and the reverberating power to reinvent ourselves.

In discussing the falsification of African Consciousness as it relates to psychiatry and the politics of White supremacy, Amos N. Wilson noted specifically that, "If one doesn't understand the generalized and particular impact of White supremacy and oppression on the psycho-behavioral dynamics of the African community then everything else you think you know will simply confuse you and every treatment intervention will therefore contribute to the continual dysfunctioning and ultimate dehumanization of our community" (Wilson, 1993). Wilson went on to note that, "In the context of a racist social system, psychological diagnosis, labeling and treatment of the behavior of politically oppressed persons are political acts performed to attain political ends. For oppression begins as a psychological fact and is in good part a psychological state. If oppression is to operate with maximum efficiency, it must become and remain a psychological condition achieving self-perpetuating motion by its own internal dynamics and by its own inertial momen-tum" (Wilson, 1993). The Eurocentric mental health establishment, he rightly suggests, is a participant and beneficiary of the White domination of African peoples. Psychology and the mental health industry is a very important cog in the self-perpetuating machine of African dehumanization, mental dysfunctioning, and dehumanization.

The discipline of Western Psychology's reason for being is, to a great extent, to nurture and sanction the imperialist and racist political regime which fathered it. In this regard, Wilson concludes that the explanatory systems and treatment approaches of Western Psychology ultimately must be exposed as "political ideology and oppressive political governance parading as empirically validated principles of psychological and medical science, and 'objective' psychotherapeutic and psychiatric practices" (Wilson, 1993). This is equally true with the act of theory development.

African peoples' psychology is derived and determined by a singular unique history and cultural experience. This natural and instinctual psycho-behavioral imperative is coupled with a revolutionary drive to achieve physical, mental and spiritual liberation. Given this unique condition, Eurocentric Psychology and the mental health industrial establishment created by it as well as the Black Psychologist who knowingly or unknowingly participates in it cannot provide adequate explanations, rationales, theories and therapeutic practices.

The position taken in this discussion is that what is needed is a theoretical and therapeutic practice that is centered in our own African essence and integrity. This position is in fact consistent with our raison d'etre. The Association of Black Psychologists was formed in part to utilize our skills to benefit the African community. Specifically, the raison d'etre of the Association was to address the significant social problems affecting the African community and to positively impact upon the mental health of the national African community through planning, programs, services, training and advocacy. It was clear then as it is now that the African community's mental health depended upon our ability to (1) resist and/or inoculate ourselves from the degradation and dehumanization resulting from the effects of White supremacy and (2) to advance and/or increase our human essence and vitalism resulting from the maintenance of our cultural integrity. What emerged from these two psychological imperatives is the ultimate recognition that if our practice, including theorizing, does not respect and reflect the African essence and integrity and if we do not exist and function personally and collectively according to our own African essence (nature), then everything we do or provide (teaching, service, treatment and theorizing) will only dis-serve and de-humanize ourselves and our people.

Ofo Ase[1]: Toward a Different Discourse

"The quest for explanatory 'theory' is basically the quest for unity underlying apparent diversity; for implicity underlying apparent complexity; for order underlying apparent disorder and for regularity underlying apparent anomaly"(Horton, 1967, p. 51).[6]

If we, as Black psychologists, are to be obedient to the imperative of respecting and reflecting the human essence of our people, then our work must be guided by a discourse that is radically different from those whose intent is to verify the invalidation of our humanity (Ani, 1994). Discourse is simply a formal, honest, and intelligent discussion relative to an idea or subject. The discourse is "formal" because it is systematic and rule governed via its alignment with a particular episteme and paradigm. It is "honest" in that it is an accurate representation of the "truth" as defined and experienced by the people who are "subject" and have "agency" with the lived experience of that truth. Finally, discourse is intelligent when there is a discernible connection between thoughts, ideas and domains of functioning (i.e., it is rational).

The criteria for discourse is further clarified when it is placed in the context of the idea of "intimacy." To be "intimate" is to have "a close relationship (experience) with, detailed knowledge and deep understanding of the innermost and essential nature of a thing or another being." In terms of human beings, I would further suggest that there are at least three important realms of intimacy. First there is sexual intimacy, which at its most fundamental basis is procreation wherein humans "re-invent themselves. One could suggest that the coming together of the egg and sperm in fertilization can only occur when they have a detailed knowledge and deep understanding of each other's innermost and essential nature. Secondly, there is eating, which at its most primitive utility is nurturance whereby humans "sustain" and "replenish" themselves. The processes of ingestion, digestion and transforma-tion equally require knowledge and understanding. Finally, there is talking, which at its best expression, is "discourse" wherein humans define, perfect, educate, explain and give meaning to themselves. Not only is discourse important as human intimacy, it is important as Karenga notes because through discourse humans are able to attain authenticity, obtain historical place, and establish engagement as human subject and agent.

What should be called for in this book, is a formal, honest and intelligent discussion (discourse) of "African American Identity Development." Parentheti-cally, it should be noted that the historical shift in conceptual classification from the so-called "Negro self-concept" (i.e., Caplan, 1970; Clark and Clark, 1952; Cross, 1971; Kardiner and Ovessey, 1951) to "Black Identity" (i.e., Banks and Grambs, 1972; Cross, 1978; Helms1990; Jackson, 1975; Parham, 1989; Semaj, 1981; Thomas, 1971) to "African American Identity Development" should mean either the identification of new phenomena or the refinement of old theory. It is not clear which of these guide the contemporary discussion. Nevertheless, in terms of this discussion, when the subject of African American identity is submitted to the requirements of (1) epistemic and paradigmatic alignment (the condition of formal); (2) accuracy in its representation of our truth as human subject and agent (the condition of honesty); and (3) illustrating a discernible connection between thoughts, ideas and functioning (the condition of intelligence), then the demands of discourse (to define, perfect, explain and understand) require that we rethink the actual utility of the concept of identity.

While the constraints of this chapter limit a full explanation of this conclusion, I can briefly note that this position is driven, in part, by Dr. Hilliard's axiom, "To be African or not to Be" and the need to utilize an African epistemology and paradigm for understanding things African. A paradigm, in this regard, is simply the formalized framework which guides the assessment and evaluation of reality. As is well known, the paradigm is, in effect, the perceptual, cognitive and affective achievement representing the organizational plan for thinking, feeling, understand-ing and doing. A people's *cultural essence* (i.e., ontological, cosmological and axiological positions), *worldview* (i.e., most comprehensive ideas about order), *normative assumptions* (i.e., a priori truths) and *philosophical perspectives* (i.e., frame of reference) combine to form and inform the centrality or core of their paradigm. The episteme concerns itself with what is real (knowledge) and the study and understanding of how one knows. As such, epistemology concerns the study of (1) what is the nature of reality; (2) how truth is defined; (3) what is the relationship between the knower and the known; (4) what can be known; and (5) what should/ could be done in response to the known.

There are several features or assumptions which distinguish an "African paradigm." An African paradigm assumes that (1) the universe is cosmos; (2) the ultimate nature of reality is spirit; (3) human beings are organically related to everything in the universe; (4) knowledge comes from participation with and experience in the universe (reality); (5) human relatedness is the praxis of our humanity; and, (6) that the mode of our epistemological method is that of *Participation* (equilibrium), *Relatedness* (harmony) and Unicity (balance between rationality and intuition; analyses and synthesis; known and unknown and the visible and invisible).

In earlier works (Nobles, 1986a, 1986b), I attempted to understand the scientific treatment of Black Identity and more recently made an attempt to briefly critique one of the dominant theories of Black Identity development. However, given the requisites of an African paradigm and episteme, I am now convinced that the utility of the construct itself should be reviewed. While I will not at this time attempt to dismiss the whole notion of Black Identity, I will note that the construct of identity seems wanting when placed against the requirements of discourse and the demand for accuracy in assessing and evaluating "African" reality.

Therefore, in order to be rigorous and have scientific utility, the construct should be consistent with the above mentioned assumptions. For instance, the construct must appreciate the idea that the ultimate nature of reality is spirit. Similarly, it should illustrate the significance of participation, relatedness and unicity for the human condition and reveal the ultimate organic connection.

Ultimately the problem with Black Identity theory is that it represents only a limited (albeit damaged) aspect of what it means "to be African (or not to Be)." Black Identity theory is, for the most part, founded upon an unwarranted acceptance of the Western (aka White supremacy) notions of human functioning with African people living in an anti-African reality. And as Horton's precepts on theory suggest, these "puzzling observations" about African American identity range from the reactions to de-Africanization and the hegemonic domination of White esthetics/ existence, to creative responses to re-Africanizing and reinventing African American culture and traditions.

In order to engage a different discourse, one has to begin with a different question. The statement, To Be African or Not To Be, that is the question, requires the thinker to examine the notion of human essence and expression. Hence, I propose that our concern should be with the notion of "authenticity" rather than the idea of identity.

Atunwa[2]: Human Authenticity or Black Identity

While awesome, to address the question of human authenticity or human essence it is indeed timely, given the contemporary thrust of re-Africanization occurring in the USA. This thrust is best represented by what in some areas is called the African-centered movement. African centeredness in this context is not simply a call for Afrocentric curriculum in schools nor the inclusion of African contributions to world history and civilization. African centeredness represents a concept which categorizes a *"qualitly of thought and practice"* which is rooted in the cultural image and interest of people of African ancestry and which represents and reflects the life experiences, history and traditions of people of African ancestry as the center of analyses. It, in effect, represents the intellectual and philosophical foundations upon which people of African ancestry should create their own scientific and moral criteria for authenticating the reality of African human processes. It represents the core and fundamental quality of the *"Belonging,"* *"Being" and "Becoming"* of people of African ancestry. In essence, African centeredness represents the fact, that as human beings, people of African ancestry have the right and responsibility to "center" themselves in their own subjective possibilities and potentialities and through the recentering process reproduce and refine the best of the human essence.

This notion essentially relocates the debate. In calling for the recognition of a different quality of thought and practice and in acknowledging the responsibility for creating one's own criteria for authenticating the reality of African human processes, the African centered notion represents a radical epistemological shift and paradigmatic change wherein new questions may be raised. The real meaning and significance of African centeredness is that its logical extension directs the thinker to explore the deeper meaning of human essence and the quest for human authenticity.

The boundaries for this exploration have indeed no limitations. In fact, I would make the argument, in this regard, that African American Identity should be informed by an appreciation of our truly "pan African" definition[3]." I would further argue that a full understanding of African American identity will only be attainable when the deeper meaning of our pan African definition or constitution is fully comprehended. In order to encourage such a conceptualization, I have suggested that African (Black people) in the United States should culturally view themselves as another (no less African than the Africans left behind in Africa and made victims of European colonialism and Christian and Islamic religious conversion) African group. I have recommended, in this regard, that as Blacks in the United States of America, we call ourselves the "BUSA People." It is, in fact, the case that the BUSA People" have ancestral rights and spiritual connections to African peoples living in the *Senegambia* (Bantu, Wolof, Mandingo, Malinka, Bambara, Fulani, Papel, Limba, Bola, Balante, etc.); *The Sierra Leone Coast* (Temne, Mende, etc.); *The*

Liberian Coast (Vai, De, Gola, Kisa, Bassa, Crabo, etc.); *The Gold Coast* (Yoruba, Nupe, Benin, Fon, Ewe, Ga, Pop, Edo-Bini, Asante-Fante, etc.); *The Niger-Delta* (Efik-Ibibio, Ijan, Ibani, Igbos, etc.) and *Central Africa* (Bakongo, Malimbo, Bambo, Ndungo, Balimbe, Badongo, Luba, Loango, Ovimbundu, etc.) and, of course, the ancient Nile valley. Furthermore, the question of identity must explore the psychological residuals, retentions, and resonances of our pan African legacy from across time, space, and place.

Our ancestral rights and spiritual connections were not severed or destroyed by the circumstance of enslavement just as the ancestral rights and spiritual connections of our brothers and sisters in Africa were not destroyed or severed by colonialism. We are all African people. Those living in the United States remain an African people and should, therefore, be rightfully referred to as the BUSA Tribe or Busa People (Blacks in the United States of America).

Hence, it is correct, I believe, to seek an appreciation of the implications that ancient African thought and conceptualizations have for contemporary African conduct. Can the African discourse be informed by knowing that the scene of the "Psychostasia (Myer, 1900)" from the ancient African Hu-Nefer Papyrus depicts the Ka (human spirit) reciting from the PER-EM-HRU (Massey, 1970) (*The Book of Coming Forth from Darkness to Light*, misnamed the *Book of the Dead*) and that the Psychostasia symbolically represented the first conceptualization of human psychology (circa 1370-1333 BCE) as the "Illumination" and "Judgment" of the Human Spirit? Through its symbolism, the "Psychostasia" perceived the central and mutual interdependent roles of intellect, emotion, spirit, conduct and judgment in the process of human functioning.

In our contemporary theorizing and discourse, what is the role of illumination and judgment? Should the illumination and judgment be criteria for guaranteeing epistemic and paradigmatic alignment? Does the absence of them call into question the accuracy of the construct's or theory's ability to represent our truth as human subject and agent. Finally, will the inclusion of illumination and judgment reveal the discernible connection between thoughts, ideas, and functioning?

In classical African (Kemetic) philosophy, the significance of the human being is found in the fact of "Being, Becoming and Belonging." The human being as well as human reality were all governed by divine law and the basic divine law was simply "To Be;" and, in being, one was the "creative cause" which made humans divine. This divine law was, in turn, translated into an enduring moral mandate which stated that "To Be" was permanently guaranteed by the human instinct "To Become." The moral mandate of African Humanity was, thusly, "to become and in becoming," humans revealed their "belongingness" to God (liness) (i.e., capacity to be the creative cause).

During ancient times, the process of being and becoming was accomplished through what was later called "an alchemical process of transformation to perfect-ibility." In Africa, all life is characterized as "Being, Becoming and Belonging." In

Being, life is characterized by three basic attributes: Desire, Thought and Action. These attributes are, in themselves, also subject to transformation and thereby "perfectible." Hence, Desire when "perfected" (transformed) becomes pure love. Thought when "perfected" (transformed) becomes clear understanding, and Action when "perfected" (transformed) becomes acts of sacrifice or service to benefit the whole (all). In becoming, one's basic beingness was transformed to a more perfect being. Hence, through the experience of right living one is transformed from being a lesser material (animal) being into a greater spiritual (Godlike) being.

How should the discourse (to define, perfect, explain, and understand) on human attributes; i.e., identity, personality, esteem, etc., relate to the notion of "perfectibility"? Any theoretical model of African functioning should, at a minimum, (1) illustrate and explain how African Peoples (especially in the USA) reproduce themselves as "human beings" in a non-African and even anti African reality; (2) show how the sense of human authenticity is related to the satisfaction of "Needs" and the realization of "Power ;" (3) explain and provide an understanding of the grounding for being self-conscious of one's real "essence" in an alienating reality; and (4) illustrate and explain the relevance of African conceptualizations of human beingness for human growth and development.

Accordingly, I would like to end my preliminary thoughts on the idea of "To Be African or not to Be—the Question of Identity or Authenticity" with a brief discussion focused on (1) re-visiting the African meaning of human beingness and (2) re-examining the African meaning of the person.

Ori Ire[4]: The Quest for Authenticity

The question of human authenticity takes us directly to Dr. Hilliard's dictate, "To be African or not to Be." The term "authenticity" refers to the condition or quality of being "authentic" or "genuine". To be "authentic" is to possess the condition of actually being what one claims to be. It is to be "real." To be "authentic" is to have an undisputed origin that is directly connected to the producer or creator. It is to be "genuine, which, in turn, means to be original, unmutated or not a copy, variant or distortion. The "gen" in genuine or generate means to produce, to bring into existence. Hence, the deeper meaning of "human authenticity" is to be indisputably connected to that which brought you into existence. "To be African or not to Be" suggests, thereby, that to be human, African people must realize (have a sense of) their indisputable connection to their African origin and that which brought the African into existence. This is the quest for human authenticity. In this regard, the search for human meaning is, in fact, the search for the "authentic core" which gives one a sense of essence and drives the proper response to the demands of experiencing life.

An analysis of classical and traditional African beliefs about the "authentic core" will reveal, I believe, the importance of the construct, "human authenticity." The African "authentic core" is found in the African belief about the meaning of human beingness and the concept of the person.

The African Meaning of Human Beingness

The birth of a child is perceived by the Bantu-Kongo people as the rising of a "living sun" into the upper world (Fu-Kiau, 1991, p.8). To be human is, therefore, to be a "being" who is a "living sun" possessing a "knowing" and "knowable" spirit (energy) through which one has an enduring relationship with the total perceptible and ponderable universe. The person as energy, spirit or power is, therefore, a phenomenon of "perpetual veneration." The person is both the container and instrument of Divine energy and relationships. The human being is a "power," a phenomena of "perpetual veneration." Given this sense of human beingness, the observation regarding the spirituality of African people is somewhat of a misnomer. Spirituality pertains to having the quality of being spiritual. African people have more than the quality of being spiritual. In fact, for the African to be human is to be a spirit. Spirit is the energy, force or power that is both the inner essence and the outer envelope of human beingness. "Spiritness," rather than spirituality, pertains to the condition of being a spirit. This "Spiritness" is often misconceived as spiritual or a religious quality. As energy, spirit becomes "Spiritness"and therein serves to ignite and enliven the human state of being. Human beings experience their "Spiritness" simultaneously as a metaphysical state and an ethereal extension or connection into and between the supra world of the Deities, the inter world of other beings and the inner world of the self.

At this point, I want to explain my use of traditional African languages to represent the scientific "concepts" that emerge from the recommended African paradigm and episteme. Not only is this consistent with the dictates of the proposed new discourse, it is appropriate as an act of authenticity or authority. The use of African language terminology is critical to the reclaiming of African centered discourse. In this regard, Dr. V. Nobles (1995) points out that "concepts can be misconstrued or not fully understood or developed when they are defined, inter-preted or constructed using a language not specific to the particular culture."[2] Concepts reflect and/or represent phenomena within a particular culture. Every language reflects and represents some paerticular peoples culture. Given African peoples sensitivity to the: "power" of the word, i.e., Nommo, we more so than most people reconize that words have psychological transformative power in that they are capable of legitimizing the material manifestation of phenomena. Concepts, repre-sented by words, can and do have the ability to reinforce or reject the cultural moorings or foundations of a cultural community. African American theorist, especially should, therefore, be especially sensitive to the words used in constructing their theory.

When one uses a language that is hostile or irrelevant to the cultural system under examination, then the concepts, via the language, will severely limit the understanding of the phenomena within that culture (1995, p.7). I suspect that when the African theorists utilize non-African concepts (i.e., Latin, Greek, Roman, Anglo Saxon) to represent the social phenomena of African life, they unknowingly incorporate the psychological energy (via subliminal meanings) associated with these concepts and thereby create "false positives" in the discoveries of African American conduct. The African researcher should, therefore, at every possibility, use African concepts to describe and give meaning to African phenomena.

For the Sonay people of Mali, the word for Black is "bibi" (Maiga, 1996, p.17). "Bibi" is actually a concept used to refer to the essential goodness of things. It is never used to refer to anything negative or inferior. The full significance of this concept is found in the expression, "wayne bibi" (Black sun). Dr. Hassimi Maiga (1996, p.18) notes that the Gao people of Mali use the term "wayne bibi" to refer to the hottest part of the day when the sun is at its fullest. In effect, "wayne bibi" refers to the fullest expression of the sun. It is when the sun is the brightest, the most dazzling and the most radiant. The Black sun (wayne bibi) symbolizes "luminosity", the state of being unlimited and the condition that exists when a thing achieves its total expression. Similarly, the Sonay people use the term, "Ay moo hari bibi" (Give me Black water) to signify water that is from the deepest part of the river and the most clear and clean (1996, p.18). Bibi in this context represents the depth or essence, clarity and purity of a thing. Hence, the term, "bibi," especially "wayne bibi" connotes a state wherein a thing is pure, clean, clear, limitless luminous, radiant and exuding its totality or fullest expression.

Accordingly, I am suggesting that the Malian term "wayne bibi" be used to represent the notion of "Spiritness" in human beings. In the state of being a spirit, and in recognition of the idea that the birth of a human being symbolizes the rising of a living sun in the upper world, the Spiritness or "wayne bibi" (Black sun) of our being represents the unlimited radiance, luminosity, dazzle, and total expression of being human.

I believe that when the person and/or community experience congruity between the "supra," "inter," and "inner" realms of the "wayne bibi" (Spiritness), then the sense of human integrity is achieved. This is a critical formulation because, I believe, that for African people, particularly those who were colonized and enslaved, it is only when one has a sense of the "Black Sun," the "wayne bibi" that one has the "instinct" to resist dehumanization or oppression as well as the capability to even contemplate human liberation and potential. It is also the awakening of the "wayne bibi" that allows us to contemplate and believe in the certainty of victory and human possibility.

At the metaphysical level, the "wayne bibi," therefore, is the unlimited and total expression of energy and power that represents human possibility, probability and potential. At the physical level, the "wayne bibi" is experienced as a drive or human condition. Wayne bibi (Black sun) is experienced as an urge and desire for what is excellent, good and right. As the fullest expression of goodness, it eventuates in the ever-expanding love and feeling of "good will" for all life. It is the "wayne bibi" that makes for ethical character and proper conduct. Being the "Black Sun", the "wayne bibi." The person has an ever-present urge to kindness, goodwill and fellowship. This is often experienced as the "felt need" to love and be loved for no particular reason at all. The "wayne bibi" gives the person the desire for order and the beautiful, i.e., that which is essential, pure, clean, clear, radiant. It is the "wayne bibi" that serves as the "impetus" for concern beyond self to others and the emotional "sense of the Divine agency" and relationship in human affairs (i.e., the compelling need to understand the nature of the Divine) and thereby life itself and our meaning and purpose in life. The human being as a living sun expresses one's humanity as the magnetic pull away from mere animal/physical existence and toward that which is higher, nobler, better and more excellent (The Godness/ Goodness). It is the "wayne bibi," the Black Sun, the unlimited luminosity, the radiance, the totality or fullest expression of Divine energy that gives one the sense of inner "power" and dignity and makes one human.

The notion of being a "power" ("wayne bibi") of perpetual veneration suggests precise meanings for the concepts of "being," "becoming," and "belonging" found in the African centered discourse. "Being" is the state of "wayne bibi"; i.e., having the quality of a living sun. It is to have an essence or substance that is an attribute of the Divine and is absolutely invariant and indestructible. "Becoming" is to fulfill one's destiny. It is the continuous and constant (movement toward) achievement or realization of potential(s) to reach higher levels of actuality. "Belonging" is the condition wherein one is conscious of the state of being one with that which is whole. It is a condition wherein one is integrally and essentially infused or blended with that which is greater.

The African Meaning of the Person

Kemetic beliefs about the person are well documented and upon review, one can see that the Kemetic meaning of the person is similar to the meaning of the person reflected throughout the major cultures of Africa. In the *Book of Knowing the Evolutions of Ra*, the creator God, Neb-er-tcher, states:

"I am he who evolved himself under the form of the God Khepera. I, the evolver of the evolutions evolved myself, after many evolutions and developments which came forth from my mouth. No heavens existed, and no earth, and no terrestrial animals or reptiles had come into being. I formed them out of the inert mass of watery matter, I found no place whereupon to stand. I was alone. There existed none other who worked with me. I laid the foundations of all things by my will, and all things evolved themselves therefrom. I sent forth Shu and Tefnut out from myself. Shu and Tefnut gave birth to Nut and Seb, and Nut gave birth to Osiris, Horus-Khent-an-maa, Sut, Isis and Nephtys. At one birth, one after the other, and their many children multiply upon this earth.[5] "

These Ancient Africans believed that the Neb-er-tcher evolved himself from the primordial substance and facilitated the evolution of forms into phenomena. The "creative principle" emerged out of the primordial substance; i.e., *"Nu"* and all phenomena were, in fact, extensions of *"Nu."* The Kemites believed in the consubstantiality of all phenomena.

The key to understanding Ancient Kemetic Philosophy, is, in fact, the belief about the meaning of the person. Because the person was a manifestation or expression of *"Nu,"* the primordial substance, the ancients regarded the "form" of the human being as destined to live forever. Hence, institutions were developed to enable the person to evolve in response to the challenges of nature. The human person, like other forms, has an "unchanging value" and evolves in response to the demands of that value. The ancients regarded the primordial substance, *"Nu,"* as infinite. The infinity operated, in terms, of its law, which was its will. As a manifestation of *"Nu,"* the person represents a manifestation of "the Law."

The ancient Kemite word for the "primordial substance" is *"Nu."* The ancients believed that all phenomena emerged from *"Nu."* The person, it was believed, also evolved from *"Nu,"* the primordial substance. Ancient Kemetic mythology suggests that "Nun manifested itself as a 'person' so that it could 'appear' in 'glory' on earth."

As the antecedent form, *"Nu"* produced variant words for the person that signify a common African meaning of the person. To recognize this, one can note that different African peoples developed variant forms of *"Nu"* (e.g., Du, Nho, Ntu, Nwo, Tu, Di Ni, Ntfu, etc.), in their creation of words representing the person. For instance, the Hausa word for person is *"Mutum."* The Ibo word is *"Nmadu."* The Yoruba call the person, *"Eniya"* while the Xosha say *"Umntu."* The Zulu and the Swazi use *"Umuntu"* and *"Muntfu"* respectfully (1996, p.64).

The ancient Kemetic definition of the human being emphasized, at minimum, the consubstantiality of the primordial substance (and phenomenal expressions); the primacy of the person; perpetual evolution (perfectibility) and eternal life. The character of the person was continually challenged in response to the challenge of one's destiny. For the Kemites the challenge was, through perfecting, to live throughout the millennia, to be forever "noble", to be "the princes of eternity."

As mentioned above, the Bantu-Kongo people believe that the person is an energy, spirit or power. And as a spirit, the person is a phenomenon of "perpetual veneration." The person is both the container and instrument of Divine energy and relationships. Consistent with the Mali notion *"wayne bibi,"* to be human, for the

Bantu-Kongo, is to be a "person" who is a living (Black) sun, possessing a"knowing and knowable" spirit (energy) through which one has an enduring relationship with the total perceptible and ponderable universe.

The Zulu speaking peoples of South Africa, like almost all African people, have an ancient text, the *"Izaga,"* in which they define the meaning of what it is to be a person (Ngubane, 1979, p. 60). The text of "wise" sayings contain the Zulu interpretation of the teachings of the Sudic philosophy. Within these teachings, the Zulu say *"Umuntu Ngumuntu,"* meaning, "the person is human. In this same regard, Dr. Marimba Ani teaches that the Bantu belief about the concept of the person is crystallized in the same, *"Umuntu Ngu Muntu Nga Bantu[6]"* which means "A person is a person because there are people." In believing that the primordial substance was infinite, the Zulu believe that all phenomena were made of the primordial substance. The person was one such phenomenon. The ancient Zulu philosophers taught, in this regard, that through the *"Umunfu Ngumuntu,"* the human person was unique in that the person defined oneself and is essentially knowledgeable of one's own intrinsic value. For the Zulu to be human is to be able to say what and who one is and to be able to define oneself as a value.

Ngubane(1979, p. 62) argues that the African understanding of the person is a "protein" evaluation of the human being which flowed into Nile Valley high culture of the Ancient Kemites and subsequently created clusters of similar conceptions all over Africa. What, in fact, is recognized as African culture and civilization is the combined social conventions and inventions emerging from a common African meaning of the person.

Like the Kemites, the Zulu believed that all phenomena (*"Uluthu"*) had their origins in a "living consciousness (1976)", which they called *"UQOBU."* The person evolved from the *"UQOBU"* in response to *"Umthetho we Mvelo"* (the law of appearing); the demands of *"Isimu"* (One's nature) and *"Ukuma Njalu"* (perpetual evolution). According to Ngubane(1976, p.77) the central teachings of the Banta is that all things originated from *"UQOBU"* and evolve in response to the challenge of their nature. The person, according to the Zulu, is a self-defining value and that life's purpose for the person is perpetual evolution.

The Zulu ideal emphasized the primacy of the person and the creation of a society which equipped, enabled and ensured that the person would realize the promise of being or becoming human(1976, p. 77) (*Ukuba Ngumuntu*). As a person, the components of realizing the promise of being human are a) the person by law is human (*Umuntu Ngumuntu*); (b) the person has to evolve over the distance of being human (*Amabanga Okuba Ngumuntu*); and (c) human compassion dictates that the person can not be "thrown" away (1976, p. 93) (*Ukuba Ngumuntu*).

The Akan conception of the nature of being human also informs the concept of the person. The Akan people consider a human being to be comprised of three elements. The first element is the *"Okra"* which constitutes the innermost self, the essence of the person (Gyekye, 1987, p.9). The *"Okra"* is considered the living soul of the person and is sometimes referred to as the *"Okrateasafo."* As the living soul, the *"Okra"* is identical with life. It is also the embodiment and transmitter of the individual's *"Nkrabea"* (destiny). As the life force, the *"Okra"* is linked to "Honhom" (breath) (1987, p.95). The *"Honam,"* however, is the tangible and recognizable manifestation of the presence of the *"Okra."*

The second element of the person is the *"Sunsum."* The term *"Sunsum"* is used to refer to all unperceivable, mystical beings and forces. It is the activating principle in the person (1987, p.88). The *"Sunsum"* is what molds the child's personality and disposition. It is that which determines the character. The *Okra*, in turn, manifests itself in the world of experience through the *"Sunsum."*

The final component is simply the *"Honam "* (the body), which is made up of *Ntoro* and *Mogya* (1987). While the *Okra* and the *Sunsum* come from Onyame (God), the Ntoro and the Mogya are derived from other humans; i.e., one's parents. In their conception of the nature of the person, the Akan believe that the Ntoro is derived from the father's sperm and the Mogya is derived from the mother's blood. The *Okra and the Sunsum* constitute a spiritual unity. Hence, the person is made up of two principal components, the immaterial/spiritual (*Okra Sunsum*) and the material/physical (Honam). In terms of the relation between the soul and the body, Akan thinkers contend that not only does the body influence the soul, the soul also influences the body. The Akan believe that the relation between the soul (*Okra and Sunsum*) and the body (*Honam*) is so close that they comprise an indissoluble and indivisible unity. Hence, the person is a homogeneous entity or value.

Similarly, The Yoruba believe that the person is made up of a spirit and a body (Opoku, 1978, p.92). The body or *"Ara"* is formed by the divinity, Orisha nla. It is through the *"Ara"* that man responds to his environment. It is the part of the person which can be touched and felt. It can be damaged and disintegrates after death. The spirit component of the person is the *"Emi"* (spirit). The *"Emi"* gives life to the person. The *"Emi"* is the divine element of the person and links the person directly to God. Upon the death of the person, the *"Emi"* returns to *"Elemi"* (the owner of the spirit, God) and continues to live. In adition to the "emi", the person has an *"Okan* (1978, p.93)". The word *"Okan* means heart, but as a constituent component of the person It represents the immaterial element that is the seat of intelligence, thought and action. Hence, it is sometimes referred to as the "heart-soul" of the person. The *"Okan"* is believed to exist even before the person's birth. It is the *"Okan"* of the ancestors which is reincarnated in the newborn child. The person also has an *"Ori."* The *"Ori"* rules, controls and guides the person's life and actually activates the person. The *"Ori"* is the bearer of one's destiny and helps the person to fulfill what they came to earth to do. The *"Ori"* is simultaneously the "essence of the person" and the person's "guardian and protector" (1978, p.93). The *"Ori"* is closely associated with the *"Emi."* The Yoruba, also believe that the *"Iye"* is a component of the person. The *"Iye"* is the immaterial element that is sometimes referred to as the mind (1978, p.93). The person also has *"Ojiji"* (shadow). The

"*Ojiji*" is a constant companion throughout one's life and ceases to exist when the "*Ara*" (body) dies.

According to the Mende, the person is made up of the "*Ngafa*" (the spirit) and the "*Nduwai*" (the flesh) (1979, p.94). The "*Ngafa*" is immaterial and is provided by the mother. It leaves the body at death and goes into the land of the spirits. The "*Ngafa*" is the psychic constituent of the person. The "*Nduwai*" is the physical part of the person and is provided by the father. The "*Nduwai*" is, in part, contained in the seminal fluid. The "shadow" (Nenei) is also part of the person (Harris, 1968, p. 88) and is believed to report the death of the body to God. The Mende believe that a healthy spirit (*Ngatha*) produces a state of "*Guhun*" (total well-being). The person's name is closely associated with his "*Ngafa.*" The significance of the name is that the Mende believe that a person's "Ngafa" can travel from the person during sleep or other state of unconsciousness. However, a person can be revived or awakened when one's name is called repeatedly. The Mende, therefore, believe that the person's name may be the component that wakes up the "*Ngafa*" or the human spirit.

In their discussion of African elements of human beingness, Grills and Rowe (1996) note that the Lebou people of Senegal believe that the person is, first and foremost, comprised of the "*Fit*" (vital energy or life force) which is what makes them human. "*Fit*" is referred to as the spiritual heart of the person. The part of the person that gives one physical life is called "*Roo.*" This is the breath of life which leaves the body at death. The Lebou believe that each of us has a spiritual shadow that is always present and protects the person. This shadow is called the "*Takondeer.*" Additionally to be a person, one must possess and cultivate the qualities of "*Yel*" (intelligence) and "*Sago*" (reason). Finally to be a person is to have a "*Raab.*" "*Raabs*" are constellations of spiritual forces, like the Yoruba Orishas, that possess, guide and protect the person. They are, in fact, ancestral spirits that influence and shape the personality and behavior of the person.

With this review, it appears that the African "authentic core" is comprised of the belief that the person is human because there is an indisputable connection between the person and God. In fact, the person is really seen as an undeniable expression or manifestation of God. Included in the authentic core is also the belief that (1) the complexity (immaterial and material) of the person gives one an intrinsic human value; and (2) that the person is, in fact, a "process" characterized by the divinely governed laws of appearing, perfecting and compassion. The final common belief in the African authentic core is that harmony and balance between/within the supra, inter and intra worlds of the person are key to human well-being.

If one of the responsibilities of theory is to engage in the quest for understanding the (1) unity underlying apparent diversity; (2) implicity underlying apparent complexity; (3) order underlying apparent disorder; and (4) regularity underlying apparent anomaly, then given these preliminary thoughts, it seems that the notion of "authenticity" is a better concept to represent the unity that underlies the diversity of African people. With the idea of human essence or originality justified by an indisputable connection to one's origin, it better makes explicit the implicity underlying the complexity of contemporary African life. The sense of "authenticity, in the final analyses, gives the person, whether theorist or subject, a sense of order where disorder seems to reign, while simultaneously preventing the person, as well as the research, from experiencing the sense of alienation and anomaly."

While preliminary, my thoughts on this matter should not in any way be construed to mean that I believe that racial identity, for people living in a racist and oppressive society, is irrelevant. In fact, it is just the opposite. African American identity development is a critical concern for defining self and determining one's meaning and value. This ability is, in fact, essential to African American well-being, especially for those Africans (aka all of us) living in a society characterized by racism and other forms of human alienation and exploitation.

Sakhu Sheti[7]: Deep Thought and Theory—Some Closing Suggestions

The ideas proffered here are simply thoughts designed to suggest that our "theoretical" understanding of what it means to be African (Black) in a non-African (White supremacist) society requires "deep thought" about the psychology of African people (Carruthers, 1995, p.2). We can not, as Carruthers points out, spend a lifetime of scholarship and realize what E. Franklin Frazier (1973, p.60) identified as the "failure of the Negro intellectual." Frazier, after a lifetime career as the premier Black scholar, recognized that the Black Intellectual had "failed to study the problems of 'Negro' life in America in a manner which would place the fate of the 'Negro' in the broad framework of man's experience in this world (1973, p.60)" The 'Negro' Scholar (sic) he concludes was virtually "useless," in terms of providing "theoretical" guidance in overcoming White supremacy. Frazier (circa 1960's) believed that the sterility and irrelevance of Black intellectual activity was due to the fact that the work of the Black intellectual demonstrated that Black intellectuals had not reflected upon the fundamental problems of human knowledge and the meaning of human existence.

While this may have been the state of our intellectual tradition thirty years ago, it is not our reality now. There exists a whole army of African (Abimbola, 1976; Abraham, 1970; Armah, 1973; Ba 1981; Chinweizu, 1978; Diop, 1959, 1974, 1991; Nkrumah, 1964; Obenga, 1992; Opoku, 1978); and African American (Ani, 1991; Adams, 1979; Akbar, 1991; Ankh, Mi Ra, 1995; Asante, 1990; Ben Jochanan, 1971; Carruthers, 1995; Hilliard, 1986, 1989, 1995, 1990 ; Kambon, l992; Karenga, 1984; Myers, l988; Nobles, l972, 1985, 1986a, 1986b; Spight, 1977; T'Shaka, 1995; Van Sertima, 1985, 1989; Welsh-Asante, 1990; Wilson, 1993) intellectuals who are thinking deeply about the question of African humanity, philosophy, science, traditions and culture. It is in the tradition of "thinking deeply" about what it means to be African that I propose that the real understanding of Black identity and our resolute response to living in an anti-African society will be attainable. It is only when we first think deeply about what it means to be a human being and subsequently, therein, how that meaning shapes our responses and reactions to living, will we learn or know anything of value. Hence, I think the notion of "human authenticity" and its expression as the "person" are the constructs that could offer a new research agenda in which to explore the frontiers of "African theory development."

In thinking deeply about that small but significant moment in the history of ABPsi, when Dr. Hilliard stated, To Be African or not to Be: That is the Question, I believe the "discourse" has been forever clarified. With an African episteme and paradigm there are new questions to be asked. For instance, given the notion of *"wayne bibi"* one could ask, in what ways are the various African peoples (e.g. continental, Afro-Cuban, Afro-Mexican, Afro-Brazilian, Afro-West Indian, Afro-European, Afro-Asian, etc.) organically related? How does the *"wayne bibi"* function and/or express itself in different geo-political, socio-economic environments? Is full consciousness of the *"wayne bibi"* necessary for a complete sense of "personhood"? How does it relate to meaning of "gender" and sex-related performance? What are the physical, social, and psychological manifestations of the *"wayne bibi"*? How does the *"wayne bibi"* affect the sense of efficacy and human dignity?

In the context of "participation," are there experiences or conditions that accelerate or retard one's awareness of the *"wayne bibi"*? Are different levels of racial concentration relevant to the awareness or expression of the *"wayne bibi"*? How does an activated *"wayne bibi"* versus an inactive or dormant *"wayne bibi"* relate to various types of human conduct (e.g., intelligence, emotion, creativity, etc.)? What is the role of the *"wayne bibi"* in determining responses to different types of relationships (e.g., egalitarian, oppressive, dominating, just, harmonious, etc.)? Can one's *"wayne bibi"* be intentionally, via the mind, activated or diffused? What are the features of those "lived experiences" where African "beingness" is in a state of unlimited totality or at its fullest expression and what import does that condition have for the question of racial identity? How is *"wayne bibi"* associated with tolerance or acceptance of discrimination and dehumanization? At what point and/or under what conditions does *"wayne bibi"* cause the African, in an anti-African environment, to contemplate orthogonal possibilities and/or the certainty of self-value and collective victory?

In all of these questions, one could and should ask the additional question, how does it effect the racial identity of African populations (equally interesting would be how does an activated *"wayne bibi"* effect the racial identity of non-African peoples?). Engaging in a different "discourse" with a different paradigm obviously creates unlimited new questions and new "puzzles" to address. For this reason alone, it is worth considering.

It may even be that the requirements of our own "authenticity" dictate that we do so. Ultimately, it may be that our recognition that to be a "person" is to be human and that as humans "being," "becoming," and "belonging," we have a direct and indisputable connection to our African origin and that demands that we do no less.

Notes

1. *"Ofo Ase"* is a Yoruba term maening the word or the power of the word to evoke that which it represents. It is therefore implied that when the theories of African psychologist are guided by an African discourse, then new and more appropriate ideas, notions, etc. will become part of the scientific enterprise.

2. *"Atunwa"* is a Yoruba tern representing the idea of rebirth of character or integrity. If in psychology we are concerned with the essential and deeper meaning, then the rebirth of the essential character of an aof African people be the intent and the consequent.

3. The reader is directed to *Africanisms in American Culture* edited by Joseph E. Holloway (1991) for an excellent discussion and defense of the heritage of new world Africans.

4. *"Ore Ire"* is a Yoruba concept representing the state when one's consciousness is properly aligned with one's destiny. In this regard it clarifies and gives deeper meaning for the quest for authenticity. It is human destiny for a people to be conscious (to find and establish) of their own sense of authenticity.

5. Allen, George Thomas, translator: *The Book of the Dead*, prepared for publication by Elizabeth Blaisdell Hauser; University of Chicago Press: Chicago, 1974, Spells 63 and 64, pp. 56, 59.

6. Dr. Ani introduced this notion to W. Nobles' graduate seminar on "Theories and Concepts in Ethnic Studies" (Fall, 1994) at San Francisco State University. According to Dr. Ani, the significance of the African notion of the "person" is its equivalence to being a "human being" and that to be a "person" or "human being" requires both spiritual evolution and cultural maturation.

7. *"Sakhu Sheti"* are two terms from the Medu Netcher (Egyptian Hieroglyphs). The word *"Sakhu'"'* means " understanding, the illuminator, the eye and the soul of the being, that which inspires." *"Sheti"* means "to go deeply into a subject; to study profoundly; to search magical books; to penetrate deeply." Accordingly, I have suggested that the term, *"Sakhu Sheti"* be used to represent the deep, profound and penetrating search, study, understanding and mastery of the process of illuminating the human spirit. Hence, in closing I am suggesting that the thought and theory of African Psychologists should be governed by deep, profound and pentrating search, study, understanding and mastery of the process of "illuminating" the human spirit in its full and complete authenticity.

References

Abimbola, W. (1976). *Ifa: An exploration of the Ifa literary corpus*. Ibadan, Nigeria: Oxford University Press.

Abraham, W.E. (1970). *The mind of Africa*. Chicago: The University of Chicago Press.

Adams, H. (1979). African observers of the universe: The sirus question. *Journal of African Civilization, 1(2),* 1-20.

Akbar, N. (1990). African American consciousness and Kemet: Spirituality, symbolism and duality in reconstructing Kemetic culture: Papers, perspectives, projects. In M. Karenga (Ed.), *Reconstructing Kemetic culture: Papers, perspectives, projects* (pp. 99-114). Los Angeles: University of Sankore Press.

Allen, G.T. (1974). *Translator: The book of the dead*. Chicago: University Press,Chicago.

Ani, M. (1994). *Yurugu: An African-centered critique of European cultural thought and behavior.* New Jersey: African World Press.

Ankh, M.R. (1995). *Let the ancestors speak*. Temple Hills, MD: Jom International.

Armah, A.K. (1973). *Two thousand seasons*. Nairobi: East African Publishing House.

Asante, M.K. (1990). *Afrocentricity and knowledge*. Trenton, N.J: African World Press.

Asante, M.K., & Asante, K.W. (Eds.), (1990). *African culture: The rythyms of unity*. New Jersey: African World Press, Inc.

Ba, H.A. (1981). The living tradition. In J. Ki-Zerbo (Ed.), *General history of Africa, Vol I. Methodology and African prehistory* (pp. 166-203). Paris: UNESCO.

Banks, J. & Grambs, J. (1972). *Black self concept*. New York: McGraw-Hill.

Ben-Jochanan, Y. (1971). *Africa: Mother of western civilization*. New York: Alkebu-Lan Books.

Caplan, N. (1970). The new Negro man: A review of recent empirical studies. *Journal of Social Issues, 26,* 57-73.

Carruthers, J. (1995). *MDW NTR-Divine speech: A histiorcal reflection of African deep thought from the time of the pharaohs to the present* (p. 2). Red Sea Press.

Chinweizu (1978). *The west and the rest of us*. Ansosi: Nok Publishers.

Clarke, J.H. (1991). *Notes for an African world revolution: Africans at the crossroads*. New Jersey: African World Press.

Clark, K. & Clark, M. (1952). *Racial identification and preference in Negro children*. In T.M. Newcomb & E.L. Hartley (Eds.), *Readings in social psychology* (rev. ed.) New York: Holt.

Cross, W.E. (1971). The Negro to Black conversation experience: Toward a psychology of Black liberation. *Black World, 20(9),* 13-27.

Cross, W.E. (1978). The Cross and Thomas models of psychological nigrescence. *Journal of Black Psychology, 5(1),* 13-19.

Diop, C.A. (1959). *The cultural unity of Black Africa.* Chicago: Third World Press.

Diop, C.A. (1974). *The African origin of civilization: Myth or reality.* Westport: Lawrence Hill & Company.

Diop, C.A. (1991). *Civilization or barbarism: An authentic anthropology.* New York. Lawrence Hill Books.

Fu-Kiau, (1991). *Self healing power and therapy-old teachings from Africa.* (p. 8). New York: Vantage Press.

Frazier, E. F. (1973). The failure of the Negro intellectual. In J. Ladner (Ed.), *Death of White sociology* (p. 60). New York: Vintage Books.

Gyekye, K. (1987). *An essay on African philosophical thought: The Akan conceptual scheme* (p. 85). Cambridge University Press.

Harris W.T., & Sawyerr, H. (1968). *The springs of Mande belief and conduct* (p. 88). Freetown: Sierra Leone University Press.

Helms, J. (1990). *Black and White racial identity: Theory, research and practice.* New York: Greenwood Press.

Hilliard, A. G. (1986). *The wisdom of Kemetic governance in Kemet and the African world view.* Edited by Maulana Karenga and Jacob Carruthers. Los Angeles: University of Sankore Press.

Hilliard, A. G. (1989). Waset. The eye of Ra and the abode of Ma'at: The pinnacle of Black leadership in the ancient world of Egypt revisited. *Journal of African Civilizations,* In I. Van Sertima. New Brunswick: Transaction Publishers.

Hilliard, A.G. (1995). *The maroon within us.* Baltimore, Md: Black Classical Press.

Holloway, J.E. (Ed) (1991). *Africanisms in American culture.* Bloomington: Indiana University Press.

Horton, R. (1967). African traditional thought and western science. *Africa, 37(1),* 65.

Jackson, B. (1975) Black identity development. *Journal of Educational Diversity, 2,* 19-25.

Jackson, J.G. (1974). *Introduction to African civilization.* Senancus, NJ: Citadel Press.

James, G.M. (1954). *Stolen legacy.* New York: Philosophical Library.

Kamalu, C. (1990). *Foundations of African thought.* London: Karnak House.

Kardiner, A. & Overseey, L. (1951). *The mark of oppression.* Norton: New York.

Karenga, M. (1984). *Selections from the Husia: Sacred wisdom of ancient Egypt.* Los Angeles: Kawaida Publications.

Karenga, M. (Ed.), (1990). *Reconstructing Kemetic culture: Papers, perspectives, projects*. Los Angeles: University of Sankore Press.

Kambon, K.K.K. (1992). *The African personality in America: An African centered framework*. Tallahassee: Nubian Nation Publications.

King, L., Dixon, V.R., & Nobles, W.W. (Eds.), (1976). *African philosophy: Assumptions and paradigms for research on Black persons*. Los Angeles: J. Alfred Cannon Research Conference Series.

Maiga, H.O. (1996). *Conversational Sonay language of Mali* (p. 17). Albarka International Publishers, Inc.

Massey, G. (1970). *Ancient Egypt: The light of the world, Vol I & II*. Reprint. London: Stuart & Watkins.

Mbiti, J.S. (1969). *African religion and philosophy*. London: Heinemann Educational Books.

Myer, I.B. (1900). *Oldest book in the world: An account of the religion, wisdom, philosophy, ethics, psychology, manners, proverbs, sayings, refinements, etc., of the ancient Egyptians*. New York: Dayton Publishers.

Myers, L.J. (1988). *Understanding an Afrocentric worldview*. DuBuque: Kendall/Hall.

Ngubane, J.K. (1979). *Conflict of minds: Changing power dispositions in South Africa* (p. 60). New York: Books in Focus.

Nkrumah, K. (1964). *Consciencism*. New York: Modern Reader.

Nobles, V.L. (1995). *Emi: The concept of spirit in selected plays of August/Wilson*. Diss. UMI 6369.

Nobles, W.W. (1972). African philosophy: Foundations for Black psychology. In R.L. Jones (Ed.), *Black psychology* (pp.18-32). New York: Harper & Row.

Nobles, W.W. (1976a). Extended-self: Rethinking the so-called Negro self-concept. *Journal of Black Psychology, (2)*.

Nobles, W.W. (1976b). Psychological research and the Black self-concept: A critical review. *Journal of Social Issues, 29(1)*, 11-21.

Nobles, W.W. (1985). *Africanity and the Black family: The development of a theoretical model*. Oakland: A Black Family Institute Publication.

Nobles, W.W. (1986a). *African psychology: Toward its reclamation, reascension and revitalization*. Oakland: A Black Family Institute Publication.

Nobles, W.W. (1986b). Ancient Egyptian thought and the renaissance of African (Black) psychology in Kemet and the African worldview. In M. Karenga & J. Carruthers (Eds.)., *Kemet and the African worldwiew: Research, rescue and restoration: Selected papers of the proceeding of the First and Second Conferences of the Association for the Study of Classical African Civilizations*, 24-26 Feb. 1984 (6224-AFE), Los Angeles & 1-3 March 1985 (6225-AFE), Chicago.Los Angeles: University of Sankore Press.

Obenga, T. (1992). *Ancient Egypt and Black Africa.* London: Karnak House.

Ohaegbulam, F.U. (1960). *Toward an understanding of the African experience from historical and contemporary perspectives.* Maryland: University Press of America.

Opoku, K.A. (1978). *West African traditional religion* (p. 92). Accra, Ghana: FEP International Private Limited.

Parham, T.A. (1989). Cycles of psychological nigrescence. *The Counseling Psychologist, (2),* 187-226.

Semaj, L. (1981). The Black self: Identity and models for psychological liberation. *Western Journal of Black Studies, 5(3),* 158-171.

Spight, C. (1977). Toward a Black science and technology. *Black Books Bulletin, (3).* Chicago: Institute of Positive Education.

T'Shaka, O. (1995). *Return to the African mother principle of male and female equality, 1.* Oakland: Pan African Publishers and Distributors.

Van Sertima, I. (1985). Nile valley civilizations. *Journal of African Civilizations.* New Brunswick: Transaction Publishers.

Van Sertima, I. (1989). Egypt revisited. *Journal of African Civilisations.* New Brunswick: Transaction Publishers.

Wilson, A. (1993). *The falsification of Afrikan consciousness: Eurocentric history, psychiatry and the politics of White supremacy.* Bronx, NY: The African World Infosystems.

Author

Wade W. Nobles
175 Filbert Street, Suite 202
Oakland, CA 94607
Telephone: (510) 836-3245
Fax: (510) 836-3248

The Distinction Between African Personality Personologists and Other African Personality Scholars: Implications and an Entreatment for Reconceptualization of Racial Identity Issues

Daudi Ajani ya Azibo

Speaking of African (Black) Personality

In the African/Black personality literature, there is a great need to recognize the distinction between personologists and those whose work addresses only aspects of African personality such as Black identity development, Black consciousness and the like. When the perspective of African psychology—defined as a system of knowledge (philosophy, definitions, concepts, models, procedures and practice) concerning the nature of the social universe from the perspective of African Cosmology...[meaning] the uncovering, articulation, operationalization, and application of the principles of the African reality structure relative to psychological phenomena (Baldwin, 1991, p.131) — is invoked as a prerequisite for psychological inquiry, then African personality personologists must achieve two tasks. First, as Kambon (1992) has argued for almost two decades (Baldwin, Brown, & Hopkins, 1991), African personality has to be defined Africentrically. This task is foremost because all theory, research, and practice proceeds from a context established by definition. If the foundational definition is faulty, then all subsequent literature deriving from it will be rife with fundamental errors. For example, when African personality is not defined Africentrically there is ipso facto transubstantive error at the heart of any ensuing theory, research and practice. This error is defined

---

Many of the arguments and analysis put forth in this chapter have received thoroughgoing treatment in Dr. Azibo's forthcoming *Liberation psychology: An introduction to African personality* (Africa World Press, in press). Asante sana to Mr. Osceola Whitney for his diligent transcription of this manuscipt and his valued commentary.

207

as a mistake of meaning caused by using the framework of one racial-cultural group's experience such as the Eurasian-American to interpret and explain the experience of another, African-American for example, operating from the framework of Western psychology's pseudo cross-cultural paradigm. The result is imposition of an erroneous cultural homogeneity between the African-American and the Euro-American...that produce a basic misrepresentation of African personality and formulations about its self referents (Baldwin et al., 1991, pp.143-144).

Kambon (1992, p.43) achieved the first task of defining Africentrically with the following definition provided here as an illustration: African/Black Personality refers to the system of psychogenetic (spiritual, cognitive-emotional, biochemical) and behavioral traits that are fundamental to African people...in effect the African cultural (collective psychogenetic) reality manifesting itself in the basic psychological (spiritual, cognitive-emotional) dispositions and behaviors of African people. In general, African personality is seen to be a biogenetically grounded/based psychological Blackness/Africanity (Azibo, 1996c).

The second task to be achieved by African personality personologists is the articulation of a complete or whole theory. This is always preferable to a partial, incomplete theory that focuses on one or two aspects of African personality, especially or even more so when focusing without the benefit of grounding in an African-centered personality theory. A comprehensive theory requires, at a minimum, attention to the following five topics: (a) the structure of the personality which refers to how the personality is organized (usually, the major constructs used by the theorist will be involved here); (b) the dynamics of the personality—which refers to the energy/motivational sources on which the personality runs and the mechanisms pertaining thereto (the what and the how of the forces that move personality); (c) the development of the personality—how the personality develops which will include organismic and environmental factors involved in the development processes which impact the personality; (d) psychopathology, which describes disorder and disorganization in the African personality; and (e) treatment, which refers to both what is to be done about psychopathology and how it can be accomplished (treatment techniques).

Ideally, though not necessarily, the personologist would also want to achieve the development of assessment techniques for the measurement of the African personality and a research literature that can be used to evaluate the theory. Research can address the assessment techniques as well as any or all of the five topics just mentioned.

Theories of African personality that achieve these two tasks (Africentric definition, whole theory) yield predictions of overt and covert behavior as a function of personality, the environment, and the interaction of these two. Formulaically, this is $B=f (P,E)$. This represents the motivational-product paradigm (in contrast to the developmental-process paradigm) which emphasizes literally that which causes motion/movement or behavior (motivation) and the functional role of African personality in African's behavior (the product of African personality). Motivational-product theories are also formational (in contrast to transformational) in that they encompass a lifespan perspective from birth (actually conception) to physical death (Azibo, 1990a, 1991b, in press).

Regarding the literature which only addresses aspects of African personality as a focal point (in contrast to a complete, whole theory), much is of the developmental-process paradigm. This paradigm emphasizes how the African personality develops as a function of heredity, environment, and the interaction of these two. In formula, this is P=f (H,E). The process of the psychological metamorphosis through which a deracinated African is transformed into an African possessing psychological Blackness has been the linchpin of this literature. Accordingly, many of the theories here are also called transformational (Azibo, 1990a, 1991b; Williams, 1981).

Nonsensical Nomenclature and Incongruous Conceptual Frames

Although many of the developmental-process/transformational theories contain a pro-Black thrust, which sometimes achieves a rudimentary African-centered orientation at the level of cultural surface structure, inspection of them reveals that prevailing in their ideation and subsequent thought articulation is the *absence* of the Africentric conceptual universe. In this light, it becomes clearer that most of these transformational theories are not Africentric in location. That is, they fail to frame base conceptualization in the centered thought that characterizes African civilizations across space and time (see Azibo, [1992] for elaboration of the concept African-centered). Thus by not being Africentric many of these theories, especially the classic ones, and recent and impending formulations reacting to them, usher into African psychology discourse nomenclatures and conceptual frameworks that are (1) nonsensical in light of African-centered thought and are (2) underivable from or incongruous with African-centered thought. Some dubious examples are terms such as nigrescence and reference group orientation and notions that personal identity divorced from collective identity can constitute a legitimate conceptual platform. Is not the omission/preclusion of the African utamawazo (culturally structured thought which issues forth from the asili/cultural deep structure [Ani, 1994]) glaringly self-evident in these terms? Be that as it may, a brief discussion of each in turn should bring clarity.

First, let us consider a nomenclatorial nuance regarding the terms nigrescence vs. psychological Africanity development. Nigrescence has been defined as the process of becoming Black, psychologically (Cross, Parham, & Helms, 1998; White & Parham, 1990); Nigrescenality has been defined as the state or level or condition of the psychological Blackness (Williams, 1981). Both terms are anachronistic and incorrect to the extent that they derive from the racist-in-origin Negro, there being no such people or place called Negroland from which they might have come. And, there never will be such a people. Therefore, any such derived terms will never be appropriate. Additionally, it is inadequate to assert (as William Cross did) that these terms derive from Negritude, which refers to an intellectual-social movement of particular African ethnic groups victimized by France. The process of becoming Black psychologically and the state/level of that psychological Blackness must be described by terms that are applicable to *all* African ethnic groups because the African personality construct is applicable to all Africans. The term Negritude, then, and any derivative, is not applicable to all Africans because it relates to an ethnic-specific phenomenon. Efforts by theorists to appropriate (allegedly) derived terms like nigrescence for African-U.S. psychological phenomena are misdirected and unacceptable for the reasons noted. Therefore, I recommend these incorrect, anachronistic terms be displaced by the more generic terms psychological Africanity-development and psychological Africanity, respectively. While Africanity is used frequently in the literature with psychological implied, in no way do these terms rule out ethnic, environmental, and temporal differences in psychological Africanity or its development. Rather, they simply provide uniformity that is appropriate to the construct. Additionally, using these generic terms would not preclude using terms peculiar to a particular theory, providing they are appropriate, of course. It is also to be noted that Black and African continue to be used interchangeably (hence psychological Blackness, at present, is just as appropriate as psychological Africanity). Finally, these generic terms are bridging of adult metamorphosis and "extended identity" development in children. This is accomplished by anchoring the topic field, heretofore conceptualized erroneously as distinct, in the African personality construct. For example, Williams' (1981) and Kambon's (1992) discussions of development depict clearly the bridging of child and adult Africanity development. The term "nigrescence" is inadequate on this point as well.

Second, which term is appropriate, reference group orientation or self extension/extended self concept? Which term accurately captures the nature of identity? These two terms are neither synonymous nor interchangeable. To conflate them would lead to transubstantive error par excellence. An important part of self extension is the phenomenon of the *actual* transcendence of the personal "me, myself, and I" self component into the collective "WEUSI" self (WEUSI is a Kiswahili term used by Williams [1981] that means collective Black mind). This aspect of self extension is part and parcel of the phenomenon of the innate movement of the personal Ka to attain linkage with the divine Ka, this latter phenomena itself relying on spirituality (spiritualistic energy) and is melanin-propagated. By what justification can the ontogenetic parts of the phenomenon captured by the self extension concept be reduced to the impoverished and material-based notion that makes up the Eurocentic "reference group orientation" concept? There is none when the subject matter is approached Africentrically.

Third, whence comes terminology that brings with it the assumption that there is legitimacy in separating personal vs. collective identity? From the preceding paragraph it is evident that the reference group orientation concept cannot and does not accommodate the idea of consubstantiation in essential, base spirit and the biogenetic implications that are attendant to consubstantiation. As a consequence, the reference group orientation concept is closed to any obligations thought to be inherent in consubstantiation such as a race maintenance orientation. On the other hand the Africentric self extension concept dictates own race maintenance (Azibo, 1991a) or organismic survival maintenance propensity (Baldwin, 1984) as normalcy/appropriate/sane psychological disposition (Azibo, in press). Charles Finch's (1992) notion that biological altruism, the literal subordination and at times sacrifice of individual self for purpose of group/collective/clan maintenance, was a natural human imperative that was institutionalized in an African culture from its inception is consistent with the own-race maintenance and organismic survival maintenance propensity notions. So it is that the Africentric concept of self extension carries with it the presumably *innate* obligation to defend, develop, and sustain African life. So it is that mental health [or personality order] is then shown to be rooted in the original human's [the African's] biogenetic nature (Azibo, 1989, p. 173) of which self extension is endemic. Surely then, that personal identity divorced from collective can be a platform for construing normalcy does not enter. To wit, within the context of African cosmology, then, the individual does not draw a rigid distinction (if at all) between himself and his external world...the African thus is almost exclusively social-interpersonalistic in his basic orientation (Baldwin, 1976, pp. 10-11).

However, the reference group orientation concept is in opposition to this view and is seen to lack validity when contrasted with the self-extension concept. The reader should take the following question head on: Does the reference group orientation concept find a home with theorists unwilling to admit that race maintenance is not a matter for individual choice, but an innate dictate of the personality? This posture is consistent with the Reform School of African psychology which manifests an inordinate concern with maintaining an acceptability with Euro-American psychologists/psychology (Karenga, 1982). Well, what time is it anyway? According to Abdullah, "It's Nation Time for Black Liberation Psychology: A Reaction Paper" (1994, p. 376), if we (African psychologists) do not denounce the core philosophical non-spiritual theories (of Euro-American psychology) (by only attending to address, modify, or alter certain elements) (note this is a Reform School position), we will only serve to make the oppressive European psychology more palatable. It is time for the Reform School to be relegated to history, the underside of nascent African psychology's history to be sure.

Actually, the reference group orientation concept expressly projects an out/other-group reference orientation as entirely within the realm of normalcy/sanity. Theorists who rely on or otherwise use the reference group orientation concept wittingly or unwittingly admit this absurdity as an operating principle. It seems clear that the reference group orientation conceptual framework is neither derivable from nor congruous with African centered thought. African utamawazo-based concepts such as "WEUSI," "self extension," and "I am because we are" nowhere admit the idea of personal identity divorced from collective identity as a reference point for construing normalcy in the African self. It is the Eurasian utamawazo in which the separation of personal vs. collective self is articulated: cogito ergo sum (see Ani's [1994] analysis).

I stated elsewhere that "The reader should note that the... [self-extension] concept is not even remotely congruous with the 'reference group orientation' concept... The latter is actually a Eurocentric construct that has been injected into African psychology discourse. Consequently, it serves as a rampart for the realization of the specter of an entire, visible literature based on transubstantiation... Nothing could be potentially more regressive and arresting of African psychology's contemporary revitalization" (Azibo, 1996b, p. 52).

This discussion of the reference group orientation idea strongly supports the case for starting with Africentric conceptualizations (e.g., Azibo, 1994, in press). When the African psychologist's starting point for psychological conceptualizing is not the African worldview and its utamwazo, the *"Black researcher's* [and theoretician's] *paradox"* is being played out. This paradox is as follows:

> "Being part of the Black community and being trained in theory and research approaches which simply do not jibe with the reality of life for African persons (is dissonant and retarding where)... 'Black researchers... theorize the same theory as their White counterparts (and) continue to be part and parcel to a system (i.e., Eurocentric psychology which in Black face is seen to be the Reform School) which perpetuates the misunderstanding of Black reality and consequently contributes to our degradation" (Azibo, 1996c, p. 226).

The notion of racial identity attitudes is another perfect example of the Black researcher's paradox.

Racial identity attitudes? Some developmental-process/transformational theorists fail to acknowledge or recognize that their subject matter falls within the purview of African personality theory. That it does is shown clearly by the incorporation of P=f (H,E) by B=f (P,E). Since the motivational-product paradigm necessarily incorporates the developmental-process paradigm and since formational theories include statements of personality development, then work generated in the perspective of transformational models must be interpreted from the framework provided by the motivational-product/formational theories. In addition to providing the appropriate doorway to the conceptualization of the subject matter, grounding transformational work in formational work (Azibo, 1991b, 1996c) would benefit the African psychology field by precluding inaccurate, inadequate conceptual frameworks like racial identity attitudes.What is the meaning of this concept? Has the reader seriously thought about this? Whatever racial identity is, it cannot be conceptualized outside of the context of African personality as defined Africentically (see definition above). And, regarding attitudes, it is unlikely that the transformational work actually involves attitudes or attitude measurement in the sense of Eurocentric social psychology. So, again, and nonrhetorically, what is the meaning of racial identity attitudes? Whatever meaning the promulgators of the concept and those who come under their influence give to it will be found to contain transubstantiative error, because the work of the transformational theorists predominantly takes the ignoble Reform School position of adjusting concepts/ theories from the Eurocentric tradition so that they might be applied to African people's reality. Such a state of affairs as to use alien/non-African conceptual platforms, albeit Blacked-up variants, as the starting point for theory, research, and practice in African psychology is beyond sad, sorry, or lame. It can be maddening if for no other reason than it portends a self-inflicted death knell for the field (Azibo, 1994). African psychology can overcome this looming regression into the Eurocentric conceptual jailhouse by maintaining authentic tradition (e.g., Azibo, 1996a). However, it is apparent that too many African people who are psychologists have not overturned themselves professionally despite previous warnings/analyses like this one (e.g., Azibo, 1993, 1994; Baldwin, 1992) and sympathetic joinders (e.g., Abdullah, 1994; Edwards, 1994).

The Logical Imperative/Directive

Based on the foregoing discussion, it would appear that the foremost priority regarding the resolution of any issue-based disputes in the transformational literature is to reconceptualize all theorizing and research and to come again from the framework of the African personality personologists. This is achievable within the context of an African personality metatheory (Azibo, 1991b, in press). The reader is entreated to follow up, beginning at least with *Liberation Psychology: An Introduction to African Personality* (Azibo, in press) and *The African Personality in America* (Kambon, 1992). Having completed the follow up, I believe the reader will be poised on a threshold of theoretical enlightenment, although some may kick and scream all the way, since old ideas die hard. Nevertheless, the backwardness in African personality theorizing (i.e. models of Black psychological functioning) has lived long, but die it must.

References

Abdullah S. (1994). It's nation time for Black liberation psychology: A reaction paper. *Journal of Black Psychology, 20(3)*, 376-381.

Ani, M. (1994). *Yuruga: An African-centered critique of European cultural thought and behavior.* Trenton: Africa World Press.

Azibo, D. (1983). Perceived attractiveness and the Black personality. *Western Journal of Black Studies, 7(4)*, 229-238.

Azibo, D. (1989). African-centered theses on mental health and a nosology of Black/African personality disorder. *Journal of Black Psychology, 15(2)*, 173-214.

Azibo, D. (1990a). Advances in African/Black personality theory. *Imhotep: An Afrocentric Review, 2(1)*, 22-47.

Azibo, D. (1990b). Treatment and training implications of the advances in African personality theory. *Western Journal of Black Studies, 14(1)*, 53-65.

Azibo, D. (1991a). An empirical test of the fundamental postulates of an African personality metatheory. *Western Journal of Black Studies, 15(2)*, 183-195

Azibo, D. (1991b). Towards a metatheory of the African personality. *Journal of Black Psychology, 17(2)*, 37-45.

Azibo, D. (1992). Articulating the distinction between Black Studies and the study of Blacks: The fundamental role of culture and the African-centered worldview. *The Afrocentric Scholar, 1(1)*, 64-97.

Azibo, D. (1993, August). *Distinguished psychologists keynote lecture.* Association of Black Psychologists 25th Annual Convention, Toronto Canada, Videotape.(Available from the author)

Azibo, D. (1994). The kindred fields of Black liberation theology and liberation psychology: A critical essay on their conceptual base and destiny. *Journal of Black Psychology, 20(3)*, 334-356.

Azibo, D. (1996a). *African psychology in historical perspective and related commentary.* Trenton, NJ: Africa World Press.

Azibo, D. (1996b). Mental health defined Africentrically. In D. Azibo (Ed.), *African psychology in historical perspective and related commentary.* Trenton, N.J: Africa World Press.

Azibo, D. (1996c). Personality, clinical, and social psychological research on Blacks: Appropriate and inappropriate research frameworks. In D. Azibo (Ed.), *African psychology in historical perspective and related commentary.* Trenton, N.J: Africa World Press.

Azibo, D. (in press). *Liberation psychology: An introduction to African personality.* Trenton, NJ: Africa World Press.

Baldwin, J. (1976). Black psychology and Black personality. *Black Books Bulletin, 4(3)*, 6-11, 65.

Baldwin, J. (1984). African self-consciousness and the mental health of African Americans. *Journal of Black Studies, 15(2)*, 177-194.

Baldwin, J. (1991). African (Black) psychology: Issues and synthesis. In R. L. Jones (Ed.), *Black psychology* (3rd ed.). Hampton, VA: Cobb & Henry.

Baldwin, J. (1993). The role of Black psychologists in Black Liberation. In K. Burlew, W. Banks, H. McAdoo, & D. Azibo (Eds.), *African American psychology: Theory, research and practice.* Newbury Park, CA: Sage.

Baldwin, J., Brown, R., & Hopkins, R. (1991). The Black self-hatred paradigm revisited: An Africentric analysis. In R. Jones (Ed.), *Black psychology* (3rd ed.). Hampton, VA: Cobb & Henry.

Cross, W., Parham, T., & Helms, J. (1998). Nigrescence revisited: Theory and research. In R. L. Jones (Ed.), *African American identity development: Theory, research and intervention.* Hampton, VA: Cobb & Henry.

Edwards, K. (1994). The kindred fields of Black liberation theology and liberation psychology: A critical essay on their conceptual base and destiny: A response. *Journal of Black Psychology, 20(3)*, 360-363.

Finch, C. (1992). *Themes from the African Eden: The great mother and the origin of human culture.* Videotape of lecture given at the University of Pennsylvania.

Kambon, K. (1992). *The African personality in America: An African-centered framework.* Tallahassee, FL: Nubian Nation.

Karenga, M. (1982). *Introduction to Black studies.* Los Angeles: Kawaida.

Semaj, L. (1981). The Black self, identity, and models for a psychology of Black liberation. *Western Journal of Black Studies, 5(3)*, 158-171.

White, J., & Parham, T. (1990). *The psychology of Blacks: An African-American perspective.* Englewood Cliffs, NJ: Prentice Hall.

Williams, R. (1981). *The collective Black mind: An Afro-centric theory of Black personality.* St. Louis: Williams & Associates.

Author

Daudi Ajani ya Azibo
Department of Psychology
Florida A&M University
Tallahassee, FL 32307
Telephone: (850) 599-3014
Fax: (850) 561-2540

Theoretical Considerations in Measuring Racial Identity and Socialization: Extending the Self Further

Howard C. Stevenson, Jr.

Over the last several decades, a concerted effort to empirically assess and define the identity development processes of African American men, women, and youth has increased in intensity. Primarily, this effort has come from African American scholars, and has been promoted by different psychological disciplines including counseling, developmental, and survey research psychology (Burlew & Smith, 1991; Clark & Clark, 1947; Cross, 1991; Cross, Helms, Parham, 1992; DeVos, 1990; Jackson, McCullough, Gurin, & Broman, 1991; Phinney & Rotheram, 1987; Reynolds & Pope, 1991; Smith, 1989, 1991; Spencer, 1984, 1987; Spencer & Markstrom-Adams, 1990; Williams & Morland, 1976). The field has broadened to the point of healthy differences of opinions regarding the definition and meaningfulness of the racial identity construct. and whether it is a fixed or fluid phenomenon.

Differences between the use of the terms racial identity versus ethnic identity development have been debated (Smith, 1991), and modifications and criticisms of the theories of racial/ethnic identity development have been grounded in epistemologies ranging from logical positivism to Afrocentricity (Myers, Speight, Highlen, Cox, Reynolds, Adams, & Hanley, 1991; Reynolds & Pope, 1991). For the most part, the racial identity development process for adults has been studied as a function of racist and discriminatory experiences, the respondent's perceptions of Whites, or as an acceptance of pro-African American cultural styles and affiliation. Burlew and Smith (1991) categorized racial identity measures according to four models: developmental; Africentric; group-based; and racial stereotyping. All of the research emphasizes the importance of viewing racial identity as a multidimensional rather than a unitary construct.

Despite the increase in racial identity research, there still exist several questions regarding its' expansion. One very obvious question is "Is there any influence of family racial socialization processes to the racial identity development of youth?" How is racial identity, if it exists, shaped by and/or reflective of family systems functioning and communication? Secondly, a vision of racial identity

217

development across the life-span has yet to be formulated and integrated with the knowledge gathered from the racial attitudes research of developmental psychologists. The theory and measurement of the construct of racial identity has primarily centered around young adults (e.g., University students) and the construct of racial attitudes and awareness has been focused upon young children (Spencer, 1984). Adolescence remains a neglected area for racial identity and socialization researchers. Third, although racial identity and awareness was conceptualized from developmental, counseling, and survey research psychology, are there other knowledge domains that can be tapped to develop the conceptualization of racial identity and socialization? Ancillary disciplines like sociology, social and African American psychology, social stress theory, and family systems theory have crucial perspectives on the social construction of race, the impact of human and geographical ecologies (e.g., neighborhoods) on personal identity, and the African-centered extended self (Akbar, 1989; Jones, 1991; Kaminoff & Proshansky, 1982; Nobles, 1989; Sampson, 1992).

In this chapter I will review the theoretical underpinnings of and linkages between racial identity and racial socialization research, propose an interactional perspective for measuring racial socialization attitudes, and provide a set of assumptions that undergird a theoretical framework for the development of racial socialization for adolescents and parents. I will contrast the dichotomous and diunital worldviews and their differing influences upon racial identity theory, and then review several person-environment perspectives including cultural ecological, symbolic interactionism, African psychology and family systems concepts and relate the to the development of the racial socialization construct.

Worldview Foundations of Racial Identity and Socialization: "Either-Or" or "Both-And"?

Challenge to the unitary conceptualization of racial identity has received little empirical attention (Sanders-Thompson, 1992). The unitary conceptualization suggests that racial identification is an "all-or-none" phenomenon. That is, one either has a particular facet of racial identity or one has another. It also has meant that a measure of racial identity is expected to capture the essence of racial identity. Newer models from counseling psychology (Cross, Parham, & Helms, 1991) have modified the unitary concept by proposing aspects of cognitive development stages to racial identity theory. Helms and Parham (1990) developed a 50-item measure, the Black Racial Identity Attitude Scale (RIAS), to demonstrate the utility of the nigrescence model. Nevertheless, the racial identity stage theories hold to the notion that racial identity was developed primarily from an individual's psychological reaction to racist or discriminatory experiences. In the nigrescence model, the respondent is assessed along a continuum of pre-encounter, encounter, immersion, and internalization attitudes and is assumed to be approaching a single budding dimension of Blackness which is defined as pro-White, confused, pro-Black, and humanistic, respectively. The unitary dimension of Blackness is dichotomous in that the individual is considered to be more or less congruent or incongruent, pro-Black or pro-White in this model. The nigrescence Racial Identity Development model has been criticized for being non-Afrocentric, sporadic in reliability and validity of its constructs, representative of and reactive to race, gender, and sexual orientation relations of a past era, and overfocused on comfortable White-Black race relations (in contrast to indignancy and anger) as the epitome of psychological health for African Americans in a society that does not esteem "Blackness" in high regard (Akbar, 1989; Nobles, 1989; Ponterotto & Wise, 1987; Smith, 1989, 1991).

In my opinion, the RIAS and the nigrescence model that supports it has been unfairly criticized for not accounting for all of the variance that might constitute racial identity. The critique of the nigrescence model has in and of itself been unidimensional, however, as it assumes that the multidimensionality of racial identity can be measured by one scale (Helms, 1989). As a "developing" concept in flux and as a concept that is defined to be non-stable, multiple methods of racial identity assessment are necessary. Several authors have begun to call for a multidimensional view of racial identity that will require various measures with qualitative and quantitative dimensions (Burlew & Smith, 1991; Demo & Hughes, 1990; Sellers, et al., 1997; Stevenson, 1994).

The nigrescence model assumes that the process of "becoming Black" is a negative to positive experience. Most of the stage models of Black racial identity hold to the notion that the process of becoming Black happens primarily as a response to socially oppressive interactions (Helms, 1990; Parham & Williams, 1993). Moreover, one eventually becomes "pro-Black" after going through stages and reaches an end and there is some reasoning implicit within the model that one is not "pro-Black" until the stage process takes place. That is, one's Blackness is stage-centric. This reasoning is challenged by the idea that Black racial identity is more complex. It can be assumed in the nigrescence models that values and beliefs from different stages do not co-exist within the individual, although Helms (1989) has challenged this by stating that elements of each stage may be present simultaneously but in different degrees. Nonetheless, many who use the model assume that the stages are exclusive. They assume an individual cannot be angry from encounter experiences from majority culture persons or institutions (e.g., refused hiring on the basis one's race) and hold multicultural internalization attitudes. Also, anti-Black and anti-White attitudes within the same individual are not accounted for. It is hypothesized that elements of Blackness exist simultaneously in the individual and that based on familial, societal, and spiritual life experiences, various attitudes of racial identity (anti- and pro-White, anti- and pro-Black, anti- and pro-diversity) will be expressed— repeatedly and in different combinations over the life course. Contextual experiences will often dictate which set of racial identity attitudes one feels comfortable expressing. Racial identity attitudes are not traits, but trait-like beliefs that follow state-like conditions. They are embedded within social context and their expression are based upon the differing experiences that African Americans are likely to have (e.g., positive and negative experiences at the hands of persons of color and majority culture individuals).

Recent Advances in Racial Identity Theory

Cross, Parham, and Helms (1991) have expanded the nigrescence identity theory to be viewed as a resocializing experience and viewed less from within a dichotomous, either-or paradigm (e.g., anti-White vs anti-Black). This theory proposes a view of racial identity wherein the individual's racial attitudes transition from a pro-White and anti-Black cultural orientation toward a humanistic pro-Black cultural orientation (Helms, 1990). The following stages involve various degrees of exploration or confrontation of this comfortable existence that challenges the individual to think more directly about how his or her earlier ideas conflicted with the unfortunate social realities of race relations. It has expanded toward a view that is continuous and multidimensional with the expressed purpose to identify individuals who could experience simultaneously both pro- and anti- Black and White cultural attitudes across the stages with one theme predominating. This "both-and" understanding matches the theme of the development of racial socialization theory and measurement proposed and broadens the perception of human beings as more diverse and complex than allowed within an either-or paradigm (Stevenson, 1994). More importantly, Cross et al., (1991) have identified three dynamic functions of Black identity. They are (1) to defend and protect a person from psychological insults, and, where possible, to warn of impending psychological attacks that stem from having to live in a racist society; (2) to provide social anchorage and meaning to one's existence by establishing Black people as a primary reference group; (3) to serve as a conduit or point of departure for gaining awareness about, and completing transactions with, the broader world of which Blackness is but a part (p. 328).

The elucidation of these dynamic functions supports the assumptions of racial socialization processes as diunital and fluid. Cross (1993) notes that "a person may acquire these functions over the course of being socialized from childhood through early adulthood, given one's parents or caretakers have strong Black identities, themselves. Otherwise, the functions may unfold as part of one's re-socialization during nigrescence (pp. 214-215)."

Parham's (1989) recycling perspective has extended the nigrescence theory to include younger adolescents, thus opening up the view that the struggles of racial identity development begin much earlier than young adulthood and in fact may even recycle throughout the life-span. With this expansion comes the unenviable task of measures development that can capture the essence of adolescent racial identity development within the nigrescence model (Stevenson, 1995). Measurement, however, must rest upon some basic philosophical assumptions and before items are constructed, a rationale for their relevance must be clarified. It is precisely why the discussion of dichotomous and diunital models of identity is so crucial. Before measurement can be broached and prior to leaving the discussion of the "both-and," a brief look at competing views of ethnicity and identity is in order.

Primordialist and Optional Situational Views of Ethnic Identity. Lal (1995) makes an interesting point when clarifying the differences between primordialist and optional situational views of ethnicity. The primordialist position emphasizes the permanence of ethnic or racial identity that flows from the work of Erik Erikson and others who see identity as an "inner sameness" and defines it as rooted in similarities in physical appearance as well as in a common culture that may include a shared language, religion, and sense of common origin and history and the perception of shared life chances. Ethnic identity is seen as being of utmost importance in the organization of collective and of individual behavior (Lal, 1995, pp. 432-433).

The optional situational view of ethnic identity is more flexible and allows for multiple expressions of ethnic identity that are influenced by socio-political pressures. Lal (1995) defines the optional situational concept of ethnic identity as beginning in the "symbolic interactionist notion of the self" and is intended to suggest that the way we see ourselves on any particular occasion is influenced by the situation in which we find ourselves, the presence of real or imaginary significant others, and "altercasting" as well as the positive or negative value that we assume a particular identity will confer in a particular context (p. 432).

Lal's use of primordialist versus optional situational views tends toward a dichotomous oppositional paradigm which limits the potential that individuals are often faced by situations that warrant primordialist attitudes and experiences throughout one's lifetime. Lal (1995) argues that the optional situational view more accurately reflects the reality of ethnic identity struggles in youth and adults. I believe both models have merit. In my opinion, the view of culture implicit within Lal's distinctive either-or conceptualization is limiting. It is the history of oppression and generativity, homogeneity and heterogeneity, stress-overload and stress-management, and the fluidity and constancy of Black popular and traditional cultures that must be attended to as theories regarding ethnicity and identity of African Americans are constructed. Stuart Hall's (1992) essay on "What is this 'Black' in Black Popular Culture" confirms the problem of restrictive dichotomous identity models:

By definition, Black popular culture is a contradictory space. It is a sight of strategic contestation. But it can never be simplified or explained in terms of the simple binary oppositions that are still habitually used to map it out: high and low; resistance versus incorporation; authentic versus inauthentic; experiential versus formal; opposition versus homogenization (p. 26).

Hall continues to object to either-or views of Black popular culture:

"...though the terrain of the popular looks as if it is constructed with single binaries, it is not. I reminded you about the importance of the structuring of cultural space in terms of high and low, and the threat of the Bakhtinian carnivalesque . . . The carnivalesque is not simply an upturning of two things which remain locked within their oppositional frameworks; it is also crosscut by what Bakhtin calls the dialogic" (p. 32).

The debate over Eurocentric or Afrocentric worldviews parallels this discussion. The dialogic, the diunital, and the "both-and" propose that identity development and socialization are both static and dynamic, persistent and changing. As Hall (1992) explicates the dialogic, he complains about the essentializing moment in the definition of Black culture, that image and false rhetoric have led to weak dichotomous paradigms of Black culture. With this philosophical backdrop, the remaining portion of this chapter will investigate theoretical perspectives that reflect the importance of person-environment fit in healthy racial identity and socialization followed by the implications of these perspectives for measurement.

Racial Identity Processes Within Context: Person-Environment Fit and Misfit

Stress and coping represent relevant domains from which to understand the consequences of being an African American in America. The literature on person-environment fit has recently been integrated with the literature on the social context of stress. By viewing stress as related to how the individual responds to and is influenced by social, physical, and emotional environments, the assessment and management strategies of stress are expanded (Kaminoff & Proshansky, 1982; Pearlin, 1982). In a society that historically has fertilized a mixture of racial hatred, ambivalence, and civility, the cohesive development of racial identity for African Americans is especially tumultuous and stressful. Life in African-America is assumed to be more or less stressful depending upon one's overall person-environment fit with America's institutions (Kaminoff & Proshansky, 1982). Pearlin's (1982) social perspective on stress suggests that stress is "not the consequence of bad luck, unfortunate encounters, or unique circumstances. It is, instead, the consequence of engagement in social institutions whose very structures and functioning can engender and sustain patterns of conflict, confusion, and distress (p. 375)." Families and adolescents are required to create psychological and racial integrity and hope within emotional, physical, psychological, and spiritual contexts that reflect both poverty and wealth. As resilient coping must become the focus of African American psychological adjustment research, researchers must not neglect the mediating role of racial identity socialization.

What I find exceptionally important about the perspective of person-environment fit in understanding stress reactions and coping is the notion of perceived environment approach (Magnusson, 1982). This is remarkably relevant for the application of other theoretical positions to racial identity and socialization processes. Perception is nine-tenths of the law in psychological circles as Magnusson explains.

> Obviously, the "real world" in which we experience, feel, think, and act is the world as we perceive it and to which we give meaning. Or, as formulated by Thomas (1927) in what Merton (1957) called the Thomas theorem: "If men define situations as real, then they are real in their consequences." . . . And this view has greatly influenced research on stress and anxiety. It has changed the focus from an interest in how external stimulation per se provokes emotional, physiological, and behavioral anxiety reactions to an interest in how stress and anxiety reactions are elicited by expectations about the consequences of stressful conditions (p. 232).

Not to minimize the actual discrimination experiences of living in America, but what African Americans perceive to be oppressive or empowering in their immediate and not-so-immediate environments are often oppressive or empowering in their impact upon identity development, psychological integrity, physical health, and community survival (Guevarra & Oulette, 1994; Outlaw, 1993; Stevenson, Reed, Bodison, & Bishop, 1994). The perceived environment approach, in particular, reflects America's fanatical desire for false image and the catch-22 that some African American youth fall into as they both fight and adopt false images (e.g., gangster-like, cowboy-toting, misogynist, male images). As Jeffries (1982) aptly identifies one irony in Black urban culture, "there is nothing hipper than a 'con.' But it's ironic that the practice and execution of the con is often revered as an art form in Black popular culture because Blacks and other recent arrivals to American cities were the victims of these schemes (p. 161)." Several theoretical perspectives inherently embrace a person-environment fit ideology and they include cultural ecological systems theory, symbolic interactionism, and family systems functioning.

Cultural Ecological Influences on Racial Identity and Socialization

Cultural-ecological models pursue knowledge about how behavior is expressed in context (e.g., cultural, gender-specific, SES, and geographic contexts) (Brofenbrenner, 1979; Ogbu, 1985; Spencer, 1985). As contexts vary so do experiences and thus, we might expect there to be a diversity of identity development experiences for individuals within race or ethnicity. A discussion of ethnic or racial identity development cannot be divorced from the socio-political climate of the period. One's racial identity is partially trapped within the past, present, and hope for the future. It is developed within the surrounding socio-political conundrum which includes family, school, and peer relationships (Peters, 1985), neighborhood and community resources, safety, economy, and upkeep (Kaminoff & Proshansky, 1982; Spencer, 1987), neighborhood social capital and social disorganization (Sampson, 1991), and the political dynamics of these areas vis-à-vis local government. The interactional component to racial identity development must be considered since what others do in response to an individual's expression of racial identity will inhibit or exacerbate that expression (Reynolds & Pope, 1991; Spencer, 1992; Spencer, Swanson, & Cunningham, 1991).

This stressful experience can be psychologically uplifting or devastating—or a little of both. The environmental phenomena of social injustice, societal inconsistency, and denial of personal efficacy which Chestang (1972) has proposed is very real for African American youth and happens in school and work settings (Spencer et al., 1991). The notion of multiple identities and multiple oppressions begins to give credence to one's need to shift identities when transitioning through different contexts. For some adolescents, to shift means to adjust and survive, for others it represents a rejection of self, one's culture- and subgroup-allegiance, and thus— unthinkable. Certainly there are safer times when one can assert his or her ethnic identity and different African American groups (e.g., being poor) receive different types of oppression experiences (e.g., getting beat up by White policemen) to a greater extent than others. Moreover, the very perception of oppression or anticipated oppression is just as likely to influence decision-making and behaviors that contribute to a different phenomenological experience for a child of African descent (e.g., fearing that policeman will do him or her harm) (Parker, Onyekwuluje, & Murty, 1995). This is why a wholistic abandonment of oppression experiences as a key component of racial identity development, especially for African American adolescents, is unsupportable.

Some critics propose more global, comprehensive, and inclusive identity development models that consider the experiences of different groups of ethnic individuals (e.g., biracial persons; Lal, 1995; Myers et al., 1991; Smith, 1991). To the extent that these models broaden the understanding of identity development to include multiple oppressions, identities, and "isms," they are helpful to understanding what African American youth experience (Smith, 1991). To the extent that they attempt to be applicable to all persons everywhere, they are unhelpful if they reject the influence of context on identity development, deny the diversity of attitudes within and between racial and ethnic groups, and avoid specificity in understanding how youth come to appreciate, integrate, segregate, assimilate, accommodate, acculturate, mobilize, or reject one's racial identity— sometimes in simultaneous fashion. African American youth require a competent and tangible understanding of racial identity development that considers their unique proactive, cultural strength-producing experiences as well as their unique negative socially oppressive experiences. Our models, and the challenges to those models, must reflect this urgent need for specificity in understanding what diverse groups of African American youth struggle with, influence, and are influenced by.

Symbolic Interactionism, Extended Self and African American Psychology

The symbolic interactionism of George Herbert Mead continues to spur current theory development regarding the effect of interpersonal relations upon psychological functioning (Blumer, 1966; Lal, 1995; Mead, 1956). Mead's view of the self as a reflexive and active entity contradicted the popular view of the human being as passive and victim to intrapsychic and social forces. It is the human being who acts and influences that predominates Mead's thinking and yet this person does not act without the understandings and values of the significant others in his or her family, neighborhood, society, or world. The distinctions that Mead makes between the I, Me, and the "generalized other" constitutes a self that has internalized the community's values and chooses to abide by or not abide by these socialization values. In symbolic interactionism, the view of the other as intricately part of the self is a view that yields a reflexive and collective definition of identity reminiscent of the African psychological definition of extended self and the social interactional definition of self (Burke, 1980; Lal, 1995; Nobles, 1991).

Herbert Blumer (1969) explicates the implications of Mead's thinking and defines symbolic interactionism.

> Symbolic interaction involves *interpretation*, or ascertaining the meaning of the actions or remarks of the other person, and *definition*, or conveying indications to another person as to how he is to act. Human association consists of a process of such interpretation and definition. Through this process the participants fit their own acts to the ongoing acts of one another and guide others in doing so (p. 237).

In Mead's thinking, the "I" represents the subjective view of personality or the attitudes of the individual, while the "Me" represents the judgments of others and reflects an objective view of personality (Stewart & Glynn, 1975). Mead comments on the generalized other:

> . . . And only through the taking by individuals of the attitude or attitudes of the generalized other toward themselves is the existence of a universe of discourse, as that system of common or social meanings which thinking presupposes at its context, rendered possible . . . The self-conscious human individual, then, takes or assumes the organized social attitudes of the given social group or community (or of some one section thereof) to which he belongs, toward the social problems of various kinds which confront that group or community at any given time, and which arise in connection with correspondingly different social projects or organized co-operative enter-prises in which that group or community as such is engaged; and as an individual participant in these social projects or cooperative enterprises, he governs his own conduct accordingly (p. 230).

There is significant similarity between the generalized other concept and the extended self notion of African American psychology. A component of nigrescence models is the definition of identity as individualistic or intrapersonal. The stages are based primarily on the individual's perception of a particular attitude or construct. An alternative view of identity as extended may propose different strategies for construct design and measurement. Nobles (1973) and Semaj (1985) have proposed a different conceptualization for understanding the identity development of African Americans. Taking an African-centered view of self-identity, the extended self is the experiential reality for the individual as opposed to the traditional view of self. Semaj (1985) states that "from the Euro-American worldview the self is that which distinguishes and separates the individual from everyone else (p. 174)." By contrast, the African-centered view presupposes the maturing self-identity to include a sense of the "We" and in the words of Wade Nobles (1992), the extended self

> "is dependent upon the corporate definition of one's people. In effect, the people definition transends the individual definition of self, and the individual conception of self extends to include one's self and kind. This transcendent relationship (that between self and kind) is the 'extended self' " (p. 300).

Extended self-identity defines identity as interdependent and interpersonal. An interpersonal theoretical view of self-identity urges the investigation of key socializing institutions where interpersonal contact is likely to shape, injure and/or safeguard one's identity (See Figure 1).

A more interactive understanding of identity development is proposed (Burke, 1980). That is, one's identity development is buttressed, supported, and alienated by the messages and interactions that one experiences in the first socializing agency— the family, surrounded by other socializing agencies. Within an extended

Figure 1
Theoretical Perspectives and Research Perspectives on Racial Socialization

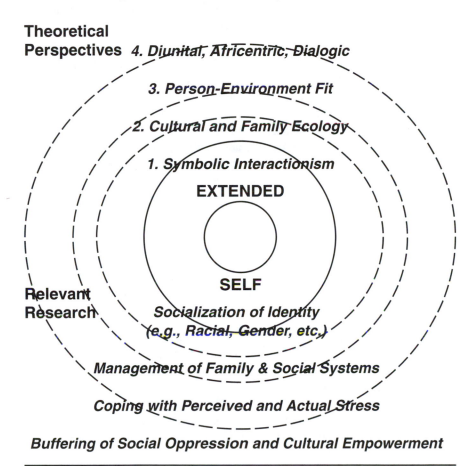

Theoretical
Perspectives *4. Diunital, Africentric, Dialogic*

3. Person-Environment Fit

2. Cultural and Family Ecology

1. Symbolic Interactionism

EXTENDED

SELF

Relevant
Research *Socialization of Identity*
(e.g., Racial, Gender, etc.)

Management of Family & Social Systems

Coping with Perceived and Actual Stress

Buffering of Social Oppression and Cultural Empowerment

view of the individual (Nobles, 1992; Semaj, 1985), it is crucial that we not only measure what the individual thinks of him- or herself, but also what he or she thinks of self in context, through the activities, experiences, and interactions that happen outside of him-or herself; experiences that represent the group, but that still relate to identity development. Again, Mead's (1969) lucid explanation of the full development of the self is helpful.

At the first of these stages, the individual's self is constituted simply by an organization of the particular attitudes of other individuals toward himself and toward one another in the specific social acts in which he participates with them. But at the second stage in the full development of the individual's self that self is constituted not only by an organization of these particular individual attitudes, but also by an organization of the social attitudes of the generalized other or the social group as a whole to which he belongs (p. 231).

Only a few researchers have considered the contextual interactions that tend to create the potential for racial identity development (Parham & Williams, 1993; Phinney & Rosenthal, 1992). As a consequence, very few measurement items relate to the respondent's perceptions of others or the interactions the individuals have experienced. That is, the items which are used to measure the construct of racial identity or identification or socialization are based upon beliefs in intra-personal phenomena, not the interpersonal. Parham (1993) points out that worldview differences between African-centered and European-centered epistemologies could account for the difference in viewing the self. To accept the interpersonal origins of identity development is to appreciate the concept of racial socialization. It is proposed that within the family the teaching of survival and cultural pride (either by its presence or absence) will have a more prolonged and healthy impact upon racial identity development (Greene, 1992; Jackson, McCullough, Gurin, & Broman, 1991). The family may be the most important institution for most individuals and especially adolescents who are struggling to find some resolution to the search for several identities (e.g., gender, sexual, racial, personal), although the link between family socialization and adolescent ethnic identity is yet to be examined (Phinney & Rosenthal, 1992).

A self that is extended is more prepared to meet the demands of a racist, homophobic, sexist, or ageist society. An extended self becomes mature when it is bolstered by various key elements, processes, and institutions that are ancillary to the family. A key related issue to assessing how attitudes and behaviors are shaped by varying contexts is to understand which contexts are likely to have the most impact. Adolescents function in primarily family, peer, community, societal contexts (Figure 2) (Phinney & Rosenthal, 1992). These are considered reality contexts because they shape the images of identity which African American youth will have to accept or reject, particularly if there is no buffering process to challenge those images and reinterpret them in a culturally empowering manner. Within these contexts are relationships with other specific subgroups and institutions (e.g., *family*—sibling and non-blood extended relationships, *peers*—gender-same and gender-different relationships, peer-individual and peer-group interactions; *community*— neighborhood, block, or local residence protection resources and deficiencies, closeness or distance of neighbors' relationships; *society*—schools, social welfare, and municipalities like police).

Figure 2 describes how the self is extended as other positive cultural and institutional experiences are available to the adolescent to access as he or she struggles to secure an identity. Both positive and negative influences (e.g., cultural empowerment and socially oppressive processes) are stressful and are available for filtering through the varying reality contexts. The role of racial socialization in ameliorating the stress of childhood and adolescence is promising. Peterson and Spiga (1982) comment on the impact of parenting in the buffering of stress that adolescents undergo.

> The availability of *social supports*, particularly parents, can moderate the effects of stress and enhance coping . . . "Better relations and frequent communication with parents may effectively prepare the adolescent for stress. Parents may provide information about what to ignore, what to attend to, and how to cope with challenges or threats. Parents may reduce the adolescent's anger and rage by allowing expression of the difficulties and providing empathy. Peers may play the same role. Social support assists the adolescent's efforts at mastering stress" (p. 522).

While Peterson and Spiga (1982) were not referring specifically to the stress of racism and discrimination, their comments correspond to the work of other researchers who view racism as a stressor (Outlaw, 1993).

It is assumed that mature racial identity development cannot occur unless sufficient buffering of negative socially oppressive messages, communications, and behaviors occurs. It is also proposed that these buffering processes are necessary in all of the reality contexts, not just the family. Furthermore, while there is serious question whether peer and community contexts are actively engaged in the filtering and promotion of social oppressive and cultural empowerment processes, there is little doubt that societal contexts often prevent, reshape, and take ownership of cultural empowerment processes and reinterpret them for African American youth to struggle more easily with. To experience less and less protection from key socializing contexts, the self will undergo more debilitating stress, be less extended, and will become more isolated and without direction to settle the identity struggle of which racial conflict resolution is only one part. One can see that racial identity is only one part of the identity development process. By investigating the influence of the African American family (and its salient functions) on the development of adolescent extended self, it is also possible to challenge (as Parham & Williams, 1993 and others have done) the notion that only negative socially oppressive phenomena (e.g., violence and racism) influence identity processes.

Family System Influences Upon Racial Identity: A Perspective of Strengths

Prior to the 1960's, Black family functioning received considerable negative attention in the research literature (Myers, 1982; Nobles & Goddard, 1985; Wilson,

1986). Today, researchers are identifying the potential destructiveness of research that assumes the behaviors of African Americans are deficient instead of different (Billingsley, 1968; Hayles, 1991; Hill, 1972). Hill (1972) is most noted for his elucidation of five key areas to which future researchers could begin to think about the strengths resident within African American family life. Those areas identified include strong kinship bonds, strong work orientation, adaptability of family roles, strong achievement orientation, and strong religious orientations. Billingsley (1968) also identified a list of goals from which a strong Black family might develop. Those goals include developing a set of values, strong religious convictions and behaviors, educational achievement aspirations, economic security, strong family ties, and community centeredness.

Royce and Turner (1980) found support for Hill's strengths by using census track data. Additional strengths uncovered by this research included the following: teaching children to respect themselves, teaching them how to be happy, disciplining them, and an emphasis on family cooperation. Christopherson (1977) found that a love for children, a general acceptance of offspring born out of wedlock, and a focus on resilience that can face negative social forces impacting upon the family were most prevalent in a rural, low income Black Oklahoma community. It is clear that prior research on Black family strengths frequently involve the domain of child-rearing.

Black family stability researchers from different disciplines have attempted to propose factors that are more likely to lead to its prevalence (Gary, Beatty, Berry, & Price, 1983; McAdoo, 1988; Scanzoni, 1971). One particular issue that has been consistently found to offset psychological identity maladjustment as evidenced through various social problems (e.g., teenage pregnancy), is religiosity or participation in religious activities (Benson & Donohue, 1989; Brown, 1985; Gary et al., 1983). Gary et al., (1983) discovered that religiosity was the most important and overwhelmingly the most identified strength by the Washington, DC Black middle income families labeled as stable in their sample. In a ten-year study of trends in at-risk behaviors among Black adolescents across the nation, Benson and Donohue (1989) found that Black high school seniors reported fewer at-risk behaviors than did their White counterparts and that religiousness along with number of "nights out" and college plans held the greatest predictive power.

Several authors have summarized the role strengths can play in the psychotherapeutic treatment of Black families, in particular the use of multisystemic, extended kinship networks, and non-blood social supports (Boyd-Franklin, 1989). It is important to identify when extended family are helpful and to be considered a strength (Wilson, 1986). Extended family may not always be helpful for a particular family and may serve to hinder instead of promote Black child development.

This research suggests that a return to the promotion of cultural values is essential to healthy African American family and adolescent identity development. Information from these areas are potentially additive to understanding the process

Figure 2
Socialization of the Extended Self in Context

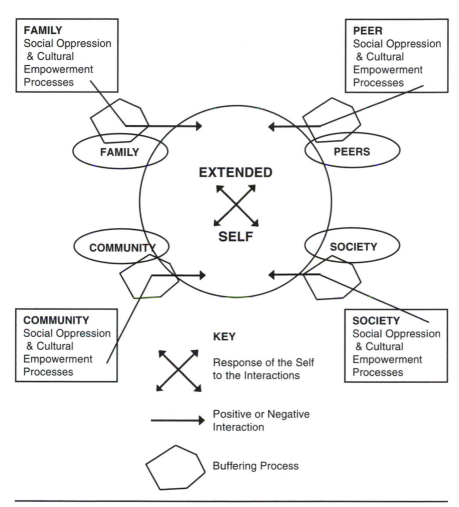

of how racial socialization takes place, who best engages in it, and how to assess it. For example, family strengths like supportive extended family kinship networks (e.g., elderly) and participation in community/church activities can significantly influence the transmission of cultural values most often defined as racial socialization.

In summary, the theoretical perspectives are discussed here to provide some foundation for understanding the construct of racial socialization. Figure 1 represents a relationship of the theories with each other as applied to the model of socialization presented in Figure 2. Also included in Figure 1 is the relevant domains of future research that are implied from these perspectives.

Racial Socialization: A Precursor or Partner to Racial Identity Development?

The process whereby children procure a sense of their unique ethnic and racial identity has been identified with several terms. Those terms include racial socialization, cultural transmission, socialization environment, race-related messages, parental values transmission, cultural parenting, ethnic socialization and others (Bowman & Howard, 1985; Jackson, McCullough, & Gurin, 1988; Peters, 1985; Rotheram & Phinney, 1987; Spencer, 1990). African American scholars have begun to acknowledge the importance of childrearing in a racially hostile world (Boykin & Toms, 1985; Hale, 1991; Harrison, 1985; Johnson, 1988; McAdoo, 1985; McAdoo, 1988; Peters, 1985; Powell-Hopson & Hopson, 1992; Spencer, 1983; Spencer, 1984; Thornton, Chatters, Taylor, & Allen, 1990). Ethnic socialization has been defined by Rotheram and Phinney (1987) as "developmental processes by which children acquire the behaviors, perceptions, values, and attitudes of an ethnic group, and come to see themselves and others as members of such groups (p. 11)." Racial socialization is defined by Peters (1985) as the "tasks Black parents share with all parents—providing for and raising children— ...but include the responsibility of raising physically and emotionally healthy children who are Black in a society in which being Black has negative connotations (p. 161)." Cultural transmission of values and beliefs has long been a factor in understanding effective African American family functioning. This socialization process is believed to be a protective buffer against societal antagonism towards people of color. It can contribute to the development of self- and community-respect.

While the definitions are varied, the concept that African American families have a special role in buffering the impact of racism and promoting a sense of cultural pride for their children has received significant attention over the last decade. Many studies have attempted to define, measure, and promote racial or ethnic socialization for African American offspring of varying ages. In the clearest example to date of the link between socialization and racial identity, Demo and Hughes (1990) found that "group identity is shaped by the content of parental socialization (p. 371)." They found that adults who had received racism preparation messages from parents while growing up were more likely to have stronger feelings of closeness to other Blacks and to hold stronger support for Black separatism. Other researchers found a clear sense of and communication about one's racial identity from family members contributed to academic, and career success (Bowman & Howard, 1985; Edwards & Polite, 1992).

Elements of Racial Socialization Among African American Families

There was considerable consensus among African Americans during the 1980's that a rediscovery of unique cultural expressions of strengths is the key to improving community and individual identity development (Barnes, 1991). As racial hostilities in America are revealed, the concern for how to raise children of color in this environment to become healthy, wise, and contributing individuals is intensified. Black families are realizing some harsh realities may never go away, but how do you address these problems with children?

Boykin and Toms (1985) developed a conceptual framework for understanding the complex socialization environment that African American families find themselves raising children in. The "triple quandary" that the authors speak of relate to the three dominant areas that African American families are challenged to respond to. They include socializing children according to mainstream societal values, socializing children with an understanding that faces the reality of oppressed persons with minority status in American society, and socializing children within a Black cultural context that is separate from outside pressures and forces (Cole, 1970). These areas are very important and seem to capture the variety of parenting strategies that are implemented. The acknowledgment of the bicultural nature of raising Black children to survive in American society is implicit within this conceptual framework. One implication of this framework is the identification of African American families which fit into either a mainstream, minority, or Black cultural socialization style. Some families include elements of two or three socialization styles in their childrearing practices and more work needs to be accomplished to investigate this possibility.

How parents prepare their children to survive in a racially hostile world has been proposed by researchers as a crucial step in the healthy psychological adjustment of African-American children (Bowman & Howard, 1985; Boykin & Toms, 1985; Franklin & Boyd-Franklin, 1985; Harrison, 1985; Nobles, 1974; Peters, 1985; Semaj, 1985; Spencer, 1983). To date, there are very few studies which have focused solely on the presence or absence of transmission of cultural values among African American families. Usually, the concept has been added to existing research programs as a curious afterthought or interesting idea whose time had not yet come. Consequently, there are several studies varying in their definition of the concept. Another concern of the restricted literature base is the varying age groups of the children studied such that limited comparison across studies on racial socialization can be made. The research literature is sparse with respect to the relationship between children's awareness and level of race identification and what parents teach their children about race conflict and history but a brief review is presented. Table 1 gives a small picture of the breadth of the research on this topic.

Table 1
Review of Racial Socialization Literature

Racial Socialization Themes	List of Themes Identified by this Author	Example of an Item that Represents a Theme	Percent of the Presence of Theme in Research Sample	Characteristics of the study
Bowman & Howard (1985)	1. Racial barriers-awareness of, blocked opportunities, sense of distrust, proactive racial orientation;	1. "Hard for Blacks to get jobs"; "Be cautious"; "Learn their ways";	13%	N=377 youth between ages of 14 and 24 without children; relationship of racial socialization to academic success and personal efficacy; Part of the National Study of Black Americans; structured interviewing
	2. Self-development - excellence in achievement, initiative, character building;	2. "You must work hard to get a good education"; "You have to be twice as good to compete equally"	14%	
	3. Ethnic pride- pride in Black history and Black unity;	3. "Taught us what happened in the past- how they coped"	23%	
	4. Egalitarianism-humanitarianism, peaceful multicultural co-existence	4. "Skin color is not a factor in one's worth"; "respect Whites";	12%	
Jeters (1994)	1. Pro-dominant Culture Socialization	1. "A White university will give better educational opportunity for my child	Not applicable since each theme represents a factor that includes several items, not just one.	N=114 dyads of African American parent and college-age child in predominantly White colleges from middle to upper class families; administered 93 item Jeter Assessment of Racial Socialization Scale for parents and for college age child
	2. Pro-ethnic Culture Socialization	2. I taught my child that Blacks were a unique and special people		
	3. Confounded Culture Socialization	3. "My child was not allowed to use race as a 'cop-out' when a situation seemed unfair"		
	4. Raceless Culture Socialization	4. "I taught my child that race was not important		

Racial Socialization Themes	List of Themes Identified by this Author	Example of an Item that Represents a Theme	Percent of the Presence of Theme in Research Sample	Characteristics of the study
Peters (1985)	1. Teaching children to survive; 2. Self-respect and pride; 3. Non-reciprocality of fair play; 4. Getting a good education; 5. Love	1. "Teach that they will get pushed around and used. 2. "Don't be ashamed to be Black" 3."Have to put up with a lot more" 4. "Get more education than others"	No percentages given	N=30; Mostly Two parent working class and middle class Black parents of 1-3 yr olds; descriptive study via monthly observations and interviews
Spencer (1983)	1. Concerns about educational success; 2. Childrearing about race, racism and discrimina-tion concerns 3. Childrearing about gender concerns 4. Knowledge of Black history for child and parent 5. Childrearing about civil rights	1. "Children will have no problems in school due to race" 2. "Greatest problem in raising a minority child is racism/ discrimination" 3. "No discussion about sex-role issues" 4. "Child knows 'a lot of' Black history 5. "No discussion of civil rights"	1. 60% agreed with this statement 2. 36% agreed with this statement 3. 36% agreed with this statement 4. 25% agreed with this statement 5. 47% agreed w/ this statement	N=45 Southern Mothers from a larger sample of 384 3, 5, 7, and 9 year old Black children; 192 middle income and 192 lower income families; parental interviews
Stevenson (1994)	1. Spiritual and Religious Coping 2. Extended Family Caring 3. Cultural Pride Reinforcement 4. Racism Awareness Teaching	1. A belief in God can help a person deal with tough life struggles 2. Having large families help Black families survive life struggles 3. Parents can teach children how to be Black without saying a word 4. A Black youth will not be harrassed because s/he is Black	Not applicable since each theme represents a factor that includes several items, not just one.	N= 236 African American urban adolescents from low-income families; reliable and valid measure, Scale of Racial Socializa-tion for Adolescents (SORS-A), 45 items.

Racial Socialization Themes	List of Themes Identified by this Author	Example of an Item that Represents a Theme	Percent of the Presence of Theme in Research Sample	Characteristics of the study
Thornton et al., (1990)	1. Same categories as Bowman and Howard (1985); 2. One additional theme is Religious principles	1. "Never be ashamed of their color"	1.6%	N=2,107; Part of the National Study of Black Americans; Adult parents' self report of racial socialization messages with focus on sociodemographic and environmental correlates

Research Review

Peters (1985) conducted a study of thirty Black children aged-3 years old to understand the impact of race discussions on child rearing. She observed child behaviors and parent-child interactions within the home environment. An acknowledgement of the need to discuss race with their children was the result of the study. Several categories of racial socialization were identified including messages about getting a good education, not expected fair play to be reciprocal, being aware of racism, expressing love, and having self-respect and pride.

In their study of 378 three generation families, Bowman and Howard (1985) asked youth to give examples of statements told by their families which helped them understand what is meant to be Black or how to get along with Whites. They found four categories of race-related socialization messages: racial barriers, self-development, ethnic pride, and egalitarianism. The theme of ethnic pride included three subcategories of race-related messages. They are one's awareness of racial barriers or blocked opportunities, a sense of distrust and defensive racial posture, and a proactive and adaptive racial orientation. The theme of self development included messages that emphasized excellence and achievement, initiative and self-reliance, and character building. The theme of racial/ethnic pride included messages of pride in one's Black identity, Black history, and sense of Black unity. The final theme of egalitarianism consisted of messages of humanitarianism, expanded opportunity, and peaceful multicultural co-existence.

The primary findings of the Bowman and Howard (1985) research is that adolescents who received race-related messages showed higher grades and a greater sense of personal efficacy than adolescents who did not receive these messages from parents. This study is important in extending the understanding of how parenting can influence directly Black adolescents' mobility within academic and interpersonal societal arenas.

Spencer (1983) found that children with some knowledge of Black history as reported by parents were more likely to obtain Afrocentric color connotations, while children who were limited in knowledge about civil rights, who had parents who did not discuss race discrimination issues or teach about civil rights were more likely to report Eurocentric racial attitudes. She also found that young children (e.g., 3-6) in general tended to hold Eurocentric racial attitudes but as they got older (e.g., 7-9), an orientation toward Afrocentric racial attitudes increased. This finding was true irrespective of geographic region. In her study, she asked parents rather than youth about their cultural values transmission.

In uncovering the various culture child-rearing strategies and messages identified by the parents in her different geographic samples, Spencer (1983) noted several themes. Those themes include parental teaching of the importance of civil rights, that integration leads to greater experiences, that the current racial climate is better than the 1950's or 1960's, and that racial discrimination exists. Parent and children's' knowledge of Black history was found to be correlated with children's pro-Black racial awareness, racial attitudes, and racial preferences. What comes out clearly for our purposes in this research is that the direct and active teaching from parents about cultural values is most crucial in instilling Afrocentric or pro-Black thought processes in children. That is, without direct intervention, Black children's pro-Black identities may be subject to confusion and instability.

Thornton et al., (1990) identified several primary categories including racial pride, Black heritage, good citizenship and moral virtues, achievement and hard work, acceptance of one's race, and the presence of blocked opportunities. Other less acknowledged themes included emphasis on religious principles, on peaceful coexistence with Whites, and on how acceptance of self (without racial overtones). Using the National Study of Black Americans (NSBA) random cross-section national sample of 2,107 Black adults, the authors investigated whether types of racial socialization could be found to exist differently depending upon various sociodemographic and environmental variables. The demographic and environmental variables included marital status, education, income, neighborhood racial composition, geographic region, locale, age, and gender. They found that older parents were more likely than younger parents to racially socialize their children. Higher educated persons were also more likely. Mothers more than fathers were more likely to engage in racial socialization. Parents who were married were more likely to socialize their children according to racial concerns. Parents, especially fathers, living in the Northeast tended to engage in racial socialization more than those in other regions of the country.

Jackson et al., (1988, 1991) investigated issues of in-group and out-group orientation according to the degree to which the respondents received direct messages about how to handle White people and what it means to be Black. This discussion is based upon the belief that racial identification may consist of out-group "dislike" as much as it consists of "in-group like." Their findings support the recently proposed notion that in-group and out-group orientations are inversely related among African Americans. That is, strong racial identification among African American adults seems to be highly related to direct messages of socialization that involves both out-group and in-group orientations. Persons who did not receive any socialization messages tended to demonstrate weaker in-group and out-group orientations. Again, like the work of Thornton et al., (1990), the work here is with adults.

Several content domains have been gathered from the literature review and they include perception of education, extended family, spirituality, racism and society, childrearing, and African American heritage and pride. These extracted content areas and the development of a scale of racial socialization based upon them are described in detail in Stevenson (1994).

The Absence of Racial Socialization among African American Families

As noted by several authors, not all African American parents prepare their children for racial hostilities (Bowman & Howard, 1985; Peters, 1985; Spencer, 1983; Thornton, et al., 1990). Given the diversity of beliefs among African Americans, several authors have noted that some parents hold that integration has significantly contributed to improved race relations—almost to the point that racism is no longer a social problem. The literature also proposes the possibility that parents and families that fail to engage in racial socialization may in fact perpetuate a retardation in the identity development of Black children. Thornton et al., (1990) state this point succinctly.

> Many of these parents, either because they accept the negative images of Blacks perpetuated by society, or because they fail to systematically address these negatives images in their socialization approaches, are ill-equipped to instill a positive racial identity in their children. As such, they can provide their children little protection from influences deleterious to the development of constructive group identity or assist them in their struggle for positive mental health (Semaj, 1985).

Varying percentages of samples have either expressed this viewpoint or have admitted to not receiving or sending direct race-related socialization messages. In Spencer's (1983) sample of parents, 50% of her sample of parents believed that teaching their children about race is unimportant. In Bowman and Howard's (1985) sample, 38% of the adolescents reported receiving no messages about their race or about Whites. Thornton et al., (1990) reported that 63.6% of the parents in their study racially socialized their children. That left a remainder of 36.4% who thought it was not necessary to do so.

Some African American parents do not care to make their children aware of issues of racism or the potential for discrimination for various reasons. Some believe it will only discourage children before they identify their potential. Some believe it only makes children angry and bitter. Some believe that the problem is too great for children to understand and that they will need to experience racism before they can truly learn. Fewer still believe racism is not as much a problem now as it was when they were growing up. They hold a strong "belief in the system" (Spencer, 1984). To teach about it will only bring up an ugly past. For whatever reason, there is a heterogeneity of views on how children should be educated about racism in the various African American communities. There needs to be more research, however, on the various effects that open or closed childrearing strategies about race have upon Black children's social and academic functioning.

There is a great need to develop compatible models, from diverse disciplines, and measures for assessing youth and adult racial identity so that new information can be added to the knowledge base on ethnic/racial identity (Ponterotto, 1989). It is understood that the endeavor to create valid and reliable measurement tools does not escape the criticism that using a Eurocentric epistemological framework may inherently lead to deficit-oriented results (Akbar, 1989; Nobles, 1989). Nonetheless, it is suggested here that a "both-and" epistemology allows one to espouse an African-centered worldview orientation and still choose from a variety of research methods with the expressed purpose that such an investigation would result in defining African American behaviors and socialization practices as functional (Boykin, 1992; Hoshmand, 1989).

How, then, does one develop measures that reflect the uniqueness of African American cultural experience (both oppressive and positive), the multidimensionality and context-based mutability of identity expression and racial socialization, and extended self-identity? Working assumptions that guide the measurement of racial socialization are proposed below.

Assumptions of Racial Socialization Processes

There are several assumptions that should be stipulated here based upon the theoretical perspectives presented.

1. *Racial discrimination is an unavoidable but fearful reality that persons from minority and majority ethnic groups resist discussing openly.* Recognizing that our fear of race dialogue and the expression of that fear through aggressive and silent rebellion is based upon long-term historical actions and inactions is the initial step toward addressing race relations problems. As long as there is little faith or fortitude in America's will to face or address its' race problem (West, 1993), there will always exist a need for socialization processes to protect children and adults of color from hostility and unresolved fear.

2. *The consequences of racial discrimination are different for some persons of color than for others.* To be minority and poor in this society is to be exposed to several types of oppression. By virtue of education and finances, wealthier persons of color cannot escape racial discrimination but can temporarily suspend the impact of racial discrimination given increased access to the resources and currency that represent success. This reality does not detract from the devastation of racial discrimination for any subgroup of African Americans, nor does it mean that only race discrimination accounts for the psychological devastation that persons of color often experience. It does suggest there is a range of racial socialization experiences among African American youth and families and this diversity must be accounted for in measurement and intervention development.

3. *Both social oppression and cultural empowerment processes contribute to extended self-identity or reference group orientation and are channeled through family, peer, community, and societal contexts.* The influence of the "both-and" worldview orientation is significant here. Social science literature that tends to deny the presence and influence of strengths in the development of racial identity of African American youth is limited in utility and will result in a primarily deficit-oriented assessment and measurement technology. Positive (and negative) experiences regarding racial identity development can be derived from blood and extended family relationships. These experiences can contribute to the shift of racial identity toward a more extended view of self.

To think that only negative experiences happen outside of one's ethnic group is to misunderstand how racial discrimination is pervasive and is perpetuated through systems with a hegemonic epistemology. To negate the real impact of Black-on-Black violence (in verbal, physical, and nonverbal psychological forms), for example, is to participate in the denial of within-ethnicity racism as a force to be reckoned with and to use faulty race-reasoning that leads to faulty solutions to within-ethnic group social problems (West, 1993). This is an issue supported by both majority culture destruction messages (e.g., "One must conquer lesser others through violence and power in order to be successful") and within-group internalization and acceptance of these negative racist views of self-identity. Conversely, it is equally myopic to downplay the potential positive influence of cultural empowerment that is derived from traditional (e.g., church, family, community) and pop culture (hip-hop music, language, and ethos) institutions (Critchlow, 1993; Dent, 1992).

4. *Extended self-identity is interpersonal, reflexive, and corporate but requires buffering and nurturance in order to mature.* As a buffer, racial socialization is not always present but necessary in multiple contexts. Without racial socialization, African American youth are more vulnerable to personal identity and reference group orientation maladjustment. While identity is always in flux, there is a need for reinterpretation of the varying social oppression and cultural empowerment messages, behaviors, and activities that African American youth face directly and

indirectly from peers, families, local relevant community, and society at large. Racial socialization is a buffering process that is traditionally defined as parents raising their children of color to survive in a racially hostile world. It is proposed that one's development of racial identity takes place as a function of the presence or absence of direct and indirect socializing messages regarding African American cultural experiences (e.g., how to survive racism and discrimination; how to use kinship support networks; the importance of appreciation or awareness of spirituality and religious activity; a promotion of success and achievement in school and the workforce, and childrearing strategy and teaching). Some cultural empowerment messages promote racial identity but may also put some youth in physical jeopardy (e.g., active defiance against perceived and actual police and authority brutality). Both socially oppressive and cultural empowerment messages require buffering and reinterpretation for the various ecological contexts that youth find themselves shifting through.

While, racial socialization is primarily found in family and peer contexts, it is not always present in African American families of color. Some families feel that buffering their children from the negative influences of racial discrimination demands not telling their children about a racially hostile world. Such a communication could lead to a sense of hopelessness, some parents feel. Moreover, it is not clear whether peer contexts give self-promoting or self-destructive forms of racial socialization given that the level of maturity regarding and knowledge of the world's manifestations of hostility are lacking in these contexts.

Racial socialization is maximally effective if it is reinforced in community and societal contexts like neighborhoods and schools, respectively. Social capital is defined as the network of resources within a residential area (local community) that contribute to the safety and promotion of the psychological and physical health of neighborhood members through communication and close relationships (Coleman, 1988, 1990; Sampson, 1992). Moreover, it is proposed that racial socialization is present (and absent) in all ethnic groups.

There are serious psychological and physical consequences to the lack of buffering, however. A general sense of hopelessness in the ability of traditional strengths and supports to be protective can increase in youth. Parents would not hesitate to protect their children from getting hit by ongoing traffic in a busy street. The analogy applies, however, to the busyness and destructiveness of direct and indirect messages that are communicated through the various socializing contexts (without reinterpretation) in which children spend most of their learning and development time. This is especially true about the school and peer contexts.

5. *Racial socialization is direct/indirect, verbal/nonverbal, proactive/protective, and creative/reactive, but it is not a promotion of race hatred.* We can only hope to capture a portion of its' expression (Boykin & Toms, 1985) since racial socialization processes are manifest by indirect frustration behaviors (e.g., a parent looking for work who comes home from another failed interview muses to herself—

but overheard by her children— "I bet if I were White, I would have gotten that job") as much as it is learned through more direct verbal means. Nevertheless, mature racial socialization is not the higher promotion of oneself or one's culture at the expense of or through the denigration of another ethnic group. Racial hatred is an extension of an "either-or," deficit-oriented, and hegemonic epistemology and is inherently self-destructive (West, 1993). To be pro-Black is not to be anti-White (Parham, 1993). The character of African American cultural experience is a diverse one. It tends to follow a "both-and" epistemology (Jones, 1991). Knowledge and experience of African American life tends toward synthesizing opposite experiences, so that it is both reactive to socially oppressive phenomena and creative apart from racism and discrimination. It has the potential to be both bi-cultural and ethnocentric in that one can hold strong pro-Black attitudes while supporting the cause of a multicultural humanity.

6. *Racial socialization processes are inclusive of behaviors and attitudes between families and youth, including adolescent perspectives on how families should raise children of African descent.* These processes may be subject to gender, economic, and environmental contexts. Measurement strategies must uniquely consider the developmental issues of adolescents and understand the parameters for understanding racial socialization for this group can be altogether different than for adults. An open research strategy will take into account multiple identities that youth must struggle with and stabilize in order to make it through adolescence.

7. *Racial socialization processes are multidimensional and precede, coincide with, and contribute to racial awareness and racial identity development across the life span.* It is a mistake to think that only children experience or require racial socialization. Regardless of age, one is always in need of buffering and teaching regarding racial identity. A major theme of this theoretical development is that racial socialization may represent a significant strength that can help to promote healthy family functioning for African American children. Future research will have to test out these assumptions as all are implicit within the current research. It is important that we review the efforts at developing ways to measure this phenomenon.

Measurement of Racial Socialization

Measuring the degree of racial socialization is difficult for several reasons. First, the definitions vary across studies and thus no single body of knowledge is comparable across studies. Second, including and excluding certain information must be informed by a theoretical base and to date, no theoretical base has existed from which to develop a consistent set of domains and subsequently construct an instrument or assessment methodology that captures the totality of those domains. It is quite possible to assess the degree of racial socialization among parents and/or adolescents, as defined by cultural heritage but not defined by the emphasis on racial barriers and still not have a better handle on which aspects of racial socialization are more likely to lead to improved personal and group-identity. Some studies have found little correlation between cultural values and personal identity (Spencer, 1983, 1984).

There is considerable variance in what constitutes a measure of racial socialization. Previous studies have used descriptive and survey interviews primarily to ascertain some of this information. I propose that there are several domains from which to assess family racial socialization processes. These domains include:

1. Parental perceptions of the importance of racial socialization
2. Adolescent or child perceptions of the importance of racial socialization
3. Parental socializing behaviors (i.e., verbal and nonverbal) to race
4. Adolescent receptivity or experience of parental socializing behaviors
5. Correspondence between family members regarding the prevalence and importance of racial socialization behaviors.

The research data on race-related messages that were gathered from the National Study of Black Americans (Bowman & Howard, 1985; Demo & Hughes, 1990; Thornton et al., 1990; Jackson et al., 1991) centers around three questions:

1. When you were a child, were there things your parents, or the people who raised you, did or told you to help you know what it is to *be Black?*(If yes to the above question, then)

2. What are the most important things they taught you? Are there any (other) things your parents or the people who raised you told you about how to *get along with White people?* (If yes, then . . .)

3. What are the most important things they taught you?

Parham & Williams (1993) asked a demographically diverse sample of African Americans one question related to racial socializing experiences. That question asked what "predominant race-specific messages" were received by the respondents from parents while they were growing up. The authors found no relationship between parental messages and racial identity attitude scales but concluded that "the question regarding messages received from parents is not sensitive enough to capture the actual differences (p. 19)."

Jeter (1994) has developed a measure called the Jeter Attitudes of Racial Socialization which has been found to have four reliable subscales, Pro-dominant Culture Socialization, Pro-ethnic Socialization, Confounded Culture Socialization, and Raceless Culture Socialization. Two forms of the measure were developed, one for parents and the other for adult children (e.g., undergraduates). All four subscales were found to have moderate to good alpha reliability for both forms (ranging from .47 to .85). Using dyads of parents and their adult child counterparts, Jeter (1994) measured the correspondence between parental and adult child ratings of racial socialization and found there to be significant and positive correlation between parents and children across all four subscales. This work shows considerable promise for broadening future measurement research in the area of family racial socialization.

To date there are few studies that measure racial socialization in a large scale manner and that take into account a multidimensional understanding of African American life experience (Stevenson, 1992). In addition, while there is considerable reference to racial socialization as an important variable in the psychological adjustment of African American children and families, there is no consensus about the definition of the concept of racial socialization or how to measure it. Third, to date no single study has attempted to develop an instrument that seeks to combine the existing literature's varied themes of cultural values transmission. Fourth, the problem of racial identification is just as crucial an issue for teenagers as young Black children and there has been no specific research agenda on racial socialization for that population. Finally, the literature on racial identity has focused almost exclusively on undergraduate college students and is limited in generalizability across the life span.

Preliminary Research

The Scale of Racial Socialization is a 45 item, five point likert measure that is designed to assess attitudes of African Americans regarding their agreement with the importance of communicating to children about race, racism, and cultural heritage. There are two forms, one for parents and one for adolescents. There are two unique aspects to the construction and administration of this measure that correspond to the basic assumptions of racial socialization processes. One is that the items are not written with an individual "I" focus but with a general focus. Second, the respondents are asked to answer the items as if they are speaking about their "community" or "my people." While data on the 45-item parent version is being gathered, some pilot and validation studies have begun with the adolescent version (Stevenson, 1993a, 1994, 1995; Stevenson et al., 1995). The adolescent version has identified four reliable factors including spiritual and religious coping, extended family caring, cultural pride reinforcement, and racism awareness teaching. The first three factors make up what Stevenson (1994) describes as proactive racial socialization and the second factor is called the protective racial socialization. These two higher order factors represent the themes of Stevenson's work for adolescent perceptions of racial socialization and reflect the "both-and" epistemology discussed earlier. All teenagers are expected to hold some degree of both types of racial socialization. More research is necessary to determine the stability of these findings, to test the assumptions mentioned earlier in this chapter, and to improve upon this multidimensional instrument for adolescents and parents.

Discussion

The theoretical perspectives in this chapter were presented to develop assumptions of racial socialization processes and implications for measurement of racial identity and socialization. The primary worldview orientation espoused is a dialogical, diunital, "both-and" epistemology that assumes opposites are synthesized. This view has implications for how identity and socialization are conceptualized and how measurement is developed. The two salient ethos differences of an African-centered experiential communality mirror this epistemology and are called "survival of the tribe" and "oneness of being." These two guiding principles are contrasted with the Euro-American principles of "survival of the fittest" and "control over nature" (Nobles, 1992). Capturing the essence of the African ethos, symbolic interactionism theory, and survey research psychology in the measurement of racial identity and socialization is difficult at best. This work is an initial step in that direction by establishing basic assumptions that undergird a theoretical framework for operationalizing racial socialization processes.

The theoretical perspectives identified all have as a guiding theme the importance of fit between person and environment in order to understand how stress is managed and mismanaged for African Americans. Racism as a stressor is an untapped area of health research and has implications for racial identity development and socialization. Racial socialization becomes a requisite process for some families to balance the sense of "misfit" by communicating to their children of color that the societal injustices they face or may face are not their doing. In this orientation, actual experiences and perceptions of injustice and empowerment play very influential roles.

Several assumptions were identified for future work on explicating the construct of racial socialization. Generally, it is hypothesized that racial socialization attitudes and behaviors figure prominently in the development of racial identity attitudes and give support to the importance of supportive family members (extended, augmented, and otherwise) in the development of a holistic sense of racial self. It is proposed that the ecological contexts of family, peer, neighborhood, and societal systems are directly and indirectly influential in the development of proactive and protective racial identity expression. The other assumptions propose that racial socialization is a major process in the survival of African American youth if it protects the youth from certain racial hostilities experienced within the different ecologies.

To that end, the measurement of racial socialization involves several thrusts. One, measurement strategies developed from earlier theoretical assumptions constitute different methods of assessing identity and socialization. One among many reasonable efforts is to merge the tools of factor analysis and test construction with a concerted commitment toward devising items that support an African American both-and, symbolic interactionistic experiential communality. Another thrust is that while the investigation of racial socialization processes has been undertaken with children as the targets and parents as the communicators of socialization messages, a research program that focuses on adolescent attitudes regarding the importance of racial socialization processes is equally worthwhile. The interpersonal and interactional nature of African American experience from the individual's point of view (e.g., applying notions of "extended self" and "interpersonal intelligence" to how items are worded and phrased in action words) but about a community concern (e.g., childrearing and identity growth) is a worthwhile method for understanding adolescent perceptions of the world.

Another thrust is an increased focus on positive messages and experiences of African American culture that also contribute to identity development as opposed to the psychological literature's narrow attention to the influence of negative messages and experiences. Moreover, this paper recognizes both positive and negative themes that influence identity development. It is acknowledged that Black personality exists "in the ways in which African cultural legacy influences the unfolding of Black culture (Jones, 1991, p. 314)." African American culture is both reactive and proactive and measurement strategies must reflect this. Finally, racial identity development and assessment is multidimensional and multiple research methods are necessary to determine which aspect of identity is to be understood.

Future research should consist of varied methods to assess racial socialization and on the other aspects of identity that coincide with ethnicity. Qualitative interviewing of parents and adolescents within the same family may also shed light on how one's attitudes about racial socialization are tied to one's experience of family racial socialization (Bowman & Howard, 1985). Additionally, future research should consider how gender (or other identities) and racial identities interconnect and how they can be conceptualized together. A merging of the available literatures from developmental, counseling, and survey research psychology with sociology and newer subfields of psychology (e.g., African American, social, and health psychology) is necessary and inevitable before this field can appreciate the multidimensionality of racial socialization. It is hoped that as this journey continues, researchers will work diligently to keep the view of the "We" deeply embedded in the varied social, environmental, and cultural contexts of the African American individual and family.

References

Akbar, N. (1989). nigrescence and identity: Some limitations. *The Counseling Psychologist, 17*, 258-263.

Baldwin, J. A. & Bell, Y. R. (1985). The African self-consciousness scale: An African personality questionnaire. *The Western Journal of Black Studies, 9(2)*, 61-68.

Barnes, E. (1991). The Black community as the source of positive self-concept for Black children: A theoretical perspective. In R. Jones (Ed.) *Black psychology,* (3rd ed.). Hampton, VA: Cobb & Henry Publishers.

Benson, P. L. & Donahue, M. J. (1989). Ten-year trends in at-risk behaviors: A national study of Black adolescents. *Journal of Adolescent Research, 4(2)*, 125-139.

Billingsley, A. (1968). *Black families in White America*. Englewood Cliffs, NJ: Prentice-Hall Inc.

Blumer, H. (1969). Sociological implications of the thought of George Herbert Mead. In W. Wallace (Ed.), *Sociological theory* (pp. 234-244). Chicago: Aldine Publishing Co.

Bowman, P., & Howard, C. (1985). Race related socialization, motivation, and academic achievement: A study of Black youths in three-generation families. *Journal of American Academy of Child Psychiatry, 24*, 134-141.

Boyd-Franklin, N. (1989). *Black families in therapy: A Multisystems approach*. New York: Guilford Press.

Boykin, A. W. & Toms, F. D. (1985). Black child socialization: A conceptual framework. In H. P. McAdoo, & J. L. McAdoo (Eds.), *Black children: Social, educational, and parental Environments*. Newbury Park: Sage.

Boykin, A. W. (1991). Black psychology and experimental psychology: A functional confluence. In R. Jones (Ed.), *Black psychology* (pp. 481-507). Hampton, VA: Cobb & Henry.

Burke, P. J. (1980). The self: Measurement requirements from an interactionist perspective. *Social Psychology Quarterly, 43*, 18-29.

Burlew, A. K, & Smith, L. R. (1991). Measures of racial identity: An overview and a proposed framework. *Journal of Black Psychology, 17,* 53-71.

Chestang, L. (1984). Racial and personal identity in the Black experience. In B. White (Ed.), *Color in a White society*. Silver Spring, Md.: NASW Publications,.

Clark, K. B., & Clark, M. P. (1947). Racial identification and preference in Negro children. In T. M. Newcomb and E. L. Hartley (Eds.) *Readings in social psychology*. New York: Holt, Rinehart & Winston.

Cole, J. (1970). Negro, Black and nigger. *Black Scholar, 1*, 40-44.

Coleman, J. S. (1988). Social capital in the creation of human capital. *American Journal of Sociology, 94*, S95-S120.

Cross, W. E. (1987). A two factor theory of Black identity: Implications for the study of identity development in minority children. In J. S. Phinney and M. J. Rotheram (Eds.), *Children's ethnic socialization: Pluralism and development.* (pp. 117-133). Newbury Park: Sage.

Cross, W. E. (1985). Black identity: Rediscovering the distinction between personal identity and reference group orientation. In M. Spencer, G. Brookins, W. Allen (Eds.), *Beginnings: The social and affective development of Black children.* Hillsdale, N.J.: Erlbaum.

Cross, W. E., Parham, T. A., & Helms, J. E. (1991). The stages of Black identity development: Nigrescence models. In R. Jones (Ed.), *Black psychology* (3rd ed., pp. 319-338). Hampton, VA: Cobb & Henry.

Demo, D. H. & Hughes, M. (1990). Socialization and racial identity among Black Americans. *Social Psychology Quarterly, 53(4),* 364-374.

Dent, G. (1992). *Black popular culture.* Seattle: Bay Press.

DeVos, G. A. (1990). Self in society: A multilevel psychocultural analysis. in G. A. DeVos & M. M. Suarez-Orozco (Eds.), *Status inequality: The self in culture* (pp. 17-74). Newbury Park, CA: Sage.

Edwards, A. & Polite, C. (1992). *Children of the dream: The psychology of Black success.* New York: Doubleday.

Franklin, A. J. & Boyd-Franklin, N. (1985). A psychoeducational perspective on Black parenting. In H. P. McAdoo & J. L. McAdoo (Eds.), *Black children: Social, educational, and parental environments.* Newbury Park: Sage.

Gary, L. E., Beatty, L. A., Berry G. L., & Price, M. D. (1983). Stable Black families: Final Report. Washington, DC: Mental Health Reserach and Development Center, Institute for Urban Affairs and Research, Howard University.

Greene, B. A., (1992). Racial socialization as a tool in psychotherapy with African American children. In L. A. Vargas & J. D. Koss-Chioino (Eds.), *Working with culture: Psychotherapeutic interventions with ethnic minority children and adolescents* (pp. 63-84).

Guevarra, J. S. & Ouellette, S. C. (1994). Assessing the experience of racism: Implications for health research. Paper presentation at the 102nd Annual Convention of the American Psychological Association, Los Angeles, CA, August 13.

Hall, S. (1992). What is this "Black" in Black popular culture. In G. Dent (Ed.), *Black popular culture* (pp. 20-33). Seattle: Bay Press.

Harrison, A. O. (1985). The Black family's socializing environment: Self-esteem and ethnic attitude among Black children. In H. P. McAdoo, & J. L. McAdoo (Eds.), *Black children: Social, educational, and parental environments.* (pp. 159-173). Newbury Park: Sage.

Hayles, V. R. (1991). African American strengths: A survey of empirical findings. In R. Jones (Ed.) *Black psychology.* Hampton, VA: Cobb & Henry.

Helms, J. (1990). *Black and White racial identity: Theory, research, and practice.* New York: Greenwood Press.

Helms, J. (1989). Considering some methodological issues in racial identity counseling research. *The Counseling Psychologist, 17(1)*, 98-101.

Hill, R. (1972). *The strengths of Black families.* New York: Emerson Hall.

Hoshmand, L. (1989). Alternate research methodologies in counseling psychology. *The Counseling Psychologist, 17(1)*, 37-98.

Jackson, J. S., McCullough, W. R., & Gurin, G. (1988). Family, socialization environment, and identity development in Black americans. In H. P. McAdoo (Ed.), *Black families*, (2nd ed., pp. 242-256). Newbury Park, CA: Sage Press.

Jackson, J. S., McCullough, W. R., & Gurin, G., Broman, C. L. (1991). *Race identity.* In J. S. Jackson (Ed.), *Life in Black America* (pp. 238-253). Newbury Park: Sage.

Jeffries, J. (1982). Toward a redefinition of the urban: The collision of culture. In G. Dent (Ed.), *Black popular culture* (pp. 143-153). Seattle: Bay Press.

Johnson, D. J. (1988). Racial socialization strategies of parents in three Black private schools. In D. T. Slaughter & D. J. Johnson (Eds.), *Visible now: Blacks in private schools* (pp. 251-267). New York: Greenwood Press.

Jones, J. (1991). The politics of personality: Being Black in America. In R. L. Jones (Ed), *Black psychology* (pp. 305-318). Hampton, VA: Cobb & Henry.

Kaminoff, R. D. & Proshansky, H. M. (1982). Stress as a consequence of the urban physical environment. In L. Goldberger & S. Breznitz (Eds.) *Handbook of stress: Theoretical and clinical aspects* (pp. 380-409). New York: Free Press.

Lal, B. B. (1995). Symbolic interaction theories. *American Behavioral Scientist, 38,* 421-441.

McAdoo, H. P. (1988). *Black families.* Newbury Park: Sage Press.

McAdoo, H. P. & McAdoo, J. L. (1985). *Black children: Social, educational, and parental environments.* Newbury Park: Sage.

McAdoo, J. L. (1988). The roles of Black fathers in the socialization of Black children. In H. P. McAdoo (Ed.), *Black families* (2nd ed., pp. 257-269). Newbury Park, CA: Sage Press.

Magnusson, D. (1982). Situational determinants of stress: An interactional perspective. In L. Goldberger & S. Breznitz (Eds.), *Handbook of stress: Theoretical and clinical aspects* (pp. 231-253). New York: Free Press.

Mead, G. H. (1969). Play, the game, and the generalized other. In W. Wallace (Ed.), *Sociological theory* (pp. 228-233). Chicago: Aldine Publishing Co.

Merton, R. K. (1957). *Social theory and social structure.*(2d ed.). New York: Free Press.

Montgomery, D. E., Fine, M. E., & James-Myers, L. (1990). The development and validation of an instrument to assess an optimal Afrocentric worldview. *Journal of Black Psychology, 17,* 37-54.

Myers, H. F. (1982). Research on the Afro-American family: A critical review. In B. A. Bass, G. E. Wyatt, & G. J. Powell (Eds.), *The Afro-American family.* New York: Grune & Stratton.

Myers, L, J. Speight, S. L., Highlen, P. S., Cox, C. I., Reynolds, A. L., Adams, E. M., & Hanley, C. P. (1991). Identity development and worldview: Toward an optimal conceptualization. *Journal of Counseling and Development*, *70*, 54-63.

Nobles, W. W. (1973). Psychological research and the Black self-concept: A critical review. *Journal of Social Issues, 29(1)*, 11-31.

Nobles, W. (1974). Africanity: Its role in Black families. *The Black Scholar, 5*, 9.

Nobles, W. (1989). Psychological nigrescence: An Afrocentric view. The *Counseling Psychologist, 17*, 253-257.

Nobles, W. (1991). African philosophy: Foundations for Black psychology. In R. L. Jones (Ed), *Black psychology* (pp. 47-63). Hampton, VA: Cobb & Henry.

Nobles, W. & Goddard, L. L. (1985). Black family life: A theoretical and policy implication literature review. In A. R. Harvey (Ed.), *The Black family: An afrocentric perspective.* New York: United Church of Christ.

Ogbu, J. U. (1985). A cultural ecology of competence among inner-city Blacks. In M. Spencer, G. Brookins, W. Allen (Eds.), *Beginnings: The social and affective development of Black children.* Hillsdale, N.J.: Erlbaum.

Outlaw, F. H. (1993). Stress and coping: The influence of racism of the cognitive appraisal processing of African Americans. *Issues in Mental Health Nursing, 14*, 399-409.

Parham, T. A. (1989). Cycles of nigrescence. *The Counseling Psychologist, 17,* 187-226.

Parham, T. A. (1993, August). Discussant in C. Markstrom-Adams (Chair) Cultural Contexts of Identity Formation—Some International Perspectives, Invited symposium at the "101st Convention of the American Psychological Association, August 22, 1993, Toronto, Ontario, Canada.

Parker, K. D., Onyekwuluje, A. B., & Murty, K. S. (1995). African Americans attitudes toward the local police: A multivariate analysis. *Journal of Black Studies, 25*, 396-409.

Pearlin, L. I. (1982). The social contexts of stress. In L. Goldberger & S. Breznitz (Eds.), *Handbook of stress: Theoretical and clinical aspects* (pp. 367-379). New York: Free Press.

Peters, M. F. (1988). Parenting in Black families with young children: A historical perspective. In H. P. McAdoo (Ed.), *Black families,* (2nd ed., pp. 228-241). Newbury Park, CA: Sage Press.

Peters, M. F. (1985). Racial socialization of young Black children. In H. P. McAdoo, & J. L. McAdoo (Eds.), *Black children: Social, educational, and parental environments* (pp. 159-173). Newbury Park: Sage.

Phinney, J. S. & Rosenthal, D. A. (1992). Ethnic identity in adolescence: Process, context, and outcome. In G. R. Adams, T. P. Gullotta, & R. Montemayor (Eds.) *Adolescent identity formation* (pp. 145-172). Newbury Park: Sage.

Phinney, J. S. & Rotheram, M. J., (1987). *Children's ethnic socialization: Pluralism and development.* Newbury Park: Sage.

Ponterotto, J. G. (1989). Expanding directions for racial identity research. *The Counseling Psychologist, 17*, 264-272.

Powell-Hopson, D. & Hopson, D. S. (1992). Implications of doll color preferences among Black preschool children and White preschool children. In A. K. Burlew, W. Curtis Banks, H. P. McAdoo, & D. A. ya Azibo (Eds.), *African American psychology: Theory, research and practice* (pp. 183-189). Newbury Park: Sage.

Ramirez III, M. (1991). *Psychotherapy and counseling with minorities: A cognitive approach to individual and cultural differences.* New York: Pergamon Press.

Ramsey, P. G. (1987). Young children's thinking about ethnic differences. In J. S. Phinney and M. J. Rotheram (Eds.), *Children's ethnic socialization: Pluralism and Development* (pp. 103-116). Newbury Park: Sage.

Reynolds, A. L. & Pope, R. L. (1991). The complexities of diversity: Exploring multiple oppressions. *Journal of Counseling and Development, 70*, 174-180.

Rotheram, M. J. & Phinney, J. S. (1987). Definitions and perspectives in the study of children's ethnic socialization. In J. S. Phinney and M. J. Rotheram (Eds.), *Children's ethnic socialization: Pluralism and development* (pp. 10-28). Newbury Park: Sage.

Royce, D. & Turner, G. (1980). Strengths of Black families: A Black community perspective. *Social Work, 25*, 407-409.

Russell, K., Wilson, M., & Hall, R. (1992). The *color complex: The politics of skin color among African Americans.* New York: Harcourt Brace Jovanovich, Publishers.

Sampson, R. J. (1992). Family management and child development: Insights from social disorganization theory. In J. McCord (Ed.), *Facts, frameworks, and forecasts, Vol.3 of advances in criminological theory.* New Brunswick, USA: Transaction Publishers.

Sanders Thompson, V. (1992). The multi-dimensional aspect of racial identification in everyday life. Paper presented at Centennial Annual Convention of the American Psychological Association at Washington, DC, August, 1992.

Scanzoni, J. *The Black family in modern society.* Boston: Allyn and Bacon.

Schofield, J. W. & Anderson, K. (1987). Combining quantitative and qualitative components of research on ethnic identity and intergroup relations. In J. S. Phinney and M. J. Rotheram (Eds.), *Children's ethnic socialization: Pluralism and development* (pp. 252-273). Newbury Park: Sage.

Sellers, R.M., Rowley, S.A.J., Chavous, T.M., Shelton, J.N., & Smith, M. (1997). Multidimensional inventory of Black identity: Preliminary investigation of reliability and construct validity. *Journal of Personality and Social Psychology, 73*, 805-815.

Semaj, L. T. (1985). Afrikanity, cognition, and extended self-identity. In M. Spencer, G. Brookins, W. Allen (Eds.), *Beginnings: The social and affective development of Black children.* Hillsdale, N.J.: Erlbaum.

Slaughter, D. T. (1988). *Perspectives on Black child development:* New directions for child development. San Francisco: Jossey-Bass.

Smith, E. J. (1991). Black racial identity development: Issues and concerns. *The Counseling Psychologist, 17,* 277-288.

Smith, E. J. (1991). Ethnic identity development: Toward the development of a theory within the context of majority/minority status. *Journal of Counseling and Development, 70,* 181-188.

Spencer, M. B. (1990). Parental values transmission: Implications for the development of African-American children. In J. B. Stewart & Cheatham (Eds.), *Interdisciplinary perspectives on Black families.* Atlanta: Transactions.

Spencer, M. B. (1988). Self concept development. In D. T. Slaughter (Ed.), *Perspectives on Black child development: New directions for child development.* San Francisco: Jossey-Bass.

Spencer, M. B. (1987). Black children's ethnic identity formation: Risk and resilience of castelike minorities. In J. S. Phinney and M. J. Rotheram (Eds.), *Children's ethnic socialization: Pluralism and development* (pp. 103-116). Newbury Park: Sage.

Spencer, M. B. (1985). Cultural cognition and social cognition as identity correlates of Black children's personal-social development. In M. Spencer, G. Brookins, W. Allen (Eds.), *Beginnings: The Social and affective development of Black children.* Hillsdale, N.J.: Erlbaum.

Spencer, M. B. (1984). Black children's race awareness, racial attitudes, and self-concept. A reinterpretation. *Journal of Child Psychology and Psychiatry, 25,* 433-441.

Spencer, M. B. (1983). Children's cultural values and parental child rearing strategies. *Developmental Review, 3,* 351-370.

Spencer, M. B., Brookins, G. K., Allen, W. R. (1985). *Beginnings: The social and affective development of Black children.* London: Lawrence Erlbaum Associates.

Spencer, M. B. & Horowitz, F. D. (1973). Racial attitudes and color concept-attitude modification in Black and caucasian preschool children. *Developmental Psychology, 9,* 246-254.

Spencer, M. B. & Markstrom-Adams, C. (1990). Identity processes among racial and ethnic minority children in America. *Child Development, 61,* 290-310.

Spencer, M. B., Swanson, D. P., & Cunningham., M. (1991). Ethnicity, ethnic idenity, and competence formation: Adolescent transition and cultural transformation. *Journal of Negro Education, 60,* 366-387.

Stevenson, H. C. (1992). Evaluation of racial socialization enrichment as a source of resilience for effective psychological functioning among African American families and their children. Unpublished manuscript: University of Pennsylvania.

Stevenson, H. C. (1993a). Validation of the scale of racial socialization for African American adolescents: A preliminary analysis. *Psych Discourse, 24,* 12.

Stevenson, H. C. (1993b). New theoretical considerations in assessing racial socialization attitudes in African American youth: Getting an eye's view of the "we." Paper presented at Invited Symposium entitled "Cultural Contexts of Identity Formation— Some International Perspectives." At the 101st Convention of the American Psychological Association, August 22, Toronto, Ontario, Canada.

Stevenson, H. C. (1994). Validation of the scale of racial socialization for African American adolescents: Steps toward multidimensionality. *Journal of Black Psychology, 20(4),* 445-468.

Stevenson, H. C. (1995). Relationship of racial socialization to racial identity for adolescents. *Journal of Black Psychology, 21,* 1.

Stevenson, H. C., Reed, J., Bodison, P, & Bishop, A. (1995). Silence is not always golden: Adolescent racial socialization attitudes and the experience of depression and anger. University of Pennsylvania: Unpublished manuscript.

Stewart, E. W. & Glynn, J. A. (1975). *Introduction to sociology.* New York: McGraw-Hill.

Tajfel, H. (1981). *Human groups and social categories: Studies in social psychology.* London: Cambridge University Press.

Taylor, R. D., Casten, R. Flickinger, S. M. (1993). Influence of kinship social support on the parenting experiences and psychosocial adjustment of African-American adolescents. *Developmental Psychology, 29,* 382-388.

Thomas, W. I. (1927). The behavior and the situation. *American Sociological Society: Papers and Proceedings, 22,* 1-13.

Thornton, M. C., Chatters, L. M., Taylor, R. J., Allen, W. R. (1990). Sociodemographic and environmental correlates of racial socialization by Black parents. *Child Development, 61,* 401-409.

West, C. (1993). *Race matters.* Boston, MA: Beacon Press.

Williams, J. E. & Morland, J. K. (1976). *Race, color, and the young child.* Chapel Hill: Univ. of North Carolina Press.

Wilson, M. N. (1986). The Black extended family: An analytical consideration. *Developmental Psychology, 22,* 246-258.

Author
Howard C. Stevenson, Jr.
Associate Professor
School, Community, and Clinical
Child Psychology Program
Psychology in Education Division
Graduate School of Education
University of Pennsylvannia
3700 Walnut Street
Philadelphia, PA 19104-6216
Telephone: (215) 898-5666
Fax: (215)573-2115 / 9007
E-mail:HowardS@gse.upenn.edu

Optimal Theory and Identity Development: Beyond the Cross Model

Linda James Myers and Kristee L. Haggins

Within psychology, there has been an increased interest in cultural diversity and multicultural perspectives in the last twenty years—from theory building to instrument development (Myers 1988; Myers, Speight, Highlen, Cox, Reynolds, Adams, & Hanley, 1991; Reynolds & Pope, 1991). Optimal theory is supporting this push to make our understanding of humanity more inclusive of non-dominant perspectives in this society. It utilizes a worldview emerging from an African American cultural reality that can be identified with a wisdom tradition centered in Africa as the historical point of generation at the beginnings of human culture and civilization, and thus is universal across cultural groups (Myers, 1988). This worldview provides an orientation more holistic and integrative than most Western psychological theory.

By applying optimal theory, we are able to achieve an approach to identity development that incorporates the multiple human diversity markers that characterize our beingness and functioning. The purpose of this chapter is to present a model of identity development that provides an integrative framework for understanding the many dynamics that configure to inform how the various aspects of beingness and functioning determine how one sees oneself and who one considers oneself to be. Cross' model will be explored in the historical context of the evolution of human consciousness in contemporary times.

Identity Development and Empirical Research

As one reviews identity development and empirical research, descriptions of and explanations about the African American's racial identity attitudes have been the focus of repeated studies (Sue & Sue, 1990). One of the most frequently cited and researched racial identity models is Cross' (1971) Black Identity Model. According to Cross' model, Black people progress through four distinct stages as they evolve from a self-perception in which Blackness is degraded to a self-perception in which they are secure in their Blackness. Questions around Cross' model have been raised on a number of counts. For some critics, definition of the concept of nigrescence is illusive; others point to the lack of empirical support for the invariant sequencing of stages; and some interrogate presuppositions regarding what a healthy racial identity is and its relationship to healthy psychological functioning (Stokes, Murray, Chavez, & Peacock, 1998). Despite the criticisms, Cross' model has been described as one of the most highly researched of the identity models proposed (Sue & Sue, 1990).

There has been a surge of research related to identity development among various other groups that follow from the Cross model. Models of identity development have been created for Asian Americans (Sue, 1981), Hispanic/Chicano/Latino Americans (Berry, 1980), European Americans or Whites (Helms, 1984, 1990; Carney & Kahn, 1984), women (Downing & Roush, 1985), and gay men and lesbians (Cass, 1979). The Multi-ethnic model by Banks (1984) and the Minority Identity Development model by Atkinson, Morten, and Sue (1983) both examine the process of identity development for oppressed groups. The former addresses it with all oppressed racial-ethnic groups, while the latter includes different types of oppression which includes gender and sexual orientation, along with race and ethnicity.

Various models have been designed to inform the identity development process for different groups, yet they seem to explain very similar processes. Cross' model has obviously resonated deeply with a number of researchers who have attempted to raise questions about and explore identity development (Brookins, Anyabwile, & Nacoste, 1992; Helms, 1984,1990; Lewis & Adams, 1990; Looney, 1988; Munford, 1994; Parham, 1989; Parham and Helms, 1981; Pomales, Claiborn, & LaFromboise, 1986; Ponterotto & Wise, 1987; Sue & Sue, 1990; Watts, 1992; Walters & Simoni, 1993).

A key factor in the Cross model of identity development is the influence of the dominant culture on individual identity, the attitudes of the dominant culture towards race, gender, ethnicity, sexual preference, and so on, are seen to affect how one sees oneself. Whatever one's personal attributes are, the response of the larger society to them is believed important. One of the criticisms of the Cross model is the assertion in the literature that racial awareness and identity are developed through social interactions related to race (Stokes et al., 1996). If, for example, one's racial group is negated, one might expect that awareness of that negation must be handled in some way. If there is no awareness, or limited awareness, development is delayed. However, there is no accounting for positive, self-determined thoughts or behaviors. Optimal theory also acknowledges that racial awareness is developed in the context of social interactions, as race is a social construct and awareness of it and its meaning comes through social relationships—from familial to societal. In societies that have constructed (assigned meaning of a magnitude significant enough to imbue perpetual salience in the minds and or actions of agents) race to the extent that one race is defined as superior and given privilege over another with hegemony, we would expect that being assigned to either the racial group of the enslavers or the racial group of the subordinated would have consequential meaning in a wide variety of ways, including having an impact on how one would see oneself and who one might believe oneself to be.

We agree that those assigned to the negated group would need to process in some way the attempts made by the dominant group to denigrate and disenfranchise them. Optimal theory teaches that any one "negative" can be understood to exist as an opportunity for growth and development and used toward that end, if one chooses to do so. As observed in nature, positive and negative are mutually interdependent constructs, so, for example, one can not apprehend "good" without first comprehending its opposite, "not good." Oppositions are seen to be essential to all life processes, including the basis for growth in consciousness in general, and in terms of positive identity development as well. Subsequently, if one is not consciously aware (denies, internalizes unconsciously, or represses) of the role of the "negation" with which one is being bombarded within a given social context in a multi-dimensional way, one's growth toward a positive identity will be delayed (as would be any other area of development). The "negation" is believed to be a primary impetus for movement toward positive, self-determined thoughts and behaviors.

Smith (1989) suggests the Cross model projects a sense of helplessness in Blacks without considering social adaptation in the context of a hostile environment. In that context, social forces are to optimal theory of a hostile nature and need not make a people helpless, but rather could be said to foster the opportunity for demonstrating indominable strength. Social adaptation in a hostile environment can take many forms. The adaptations optimal theory supports must be functionally liberating rather than disempowering and supportive of the "negation".

These issues lead to questions regarding what a positive African American ethnic identity is and the role racial identity should play in healthy psychological adjustment. Optimal theory will be used to address these questions and demonstrate a holistic and integrative perspective for understanding the interrelationships between identity as viewed from a self knowledge perspective versus identity derived from external information/validation perspective, and the implications of each for health and well being.

Optimal Theory and Identity

Optimal theory applied to identity development emerges to provide the stronger theoretical framework needed to address conceptions of racial and ethnic identity that can account for intra—as well as inter-group variability in terms of psychological health. Optimal theory provides an integrated synthesis of both cultural differences and the universal similarities that bespeak health and positive identity development.

Myers (1980, 1988) proposes a theory that places consciousness at the center of human experience on this plane. Health and well being are contingent on how one structures one's consciousness (one's conceptual system), determining how and to what one attends to create experience. This premise is the basis upon which this universal model of identity development has been derived (Myers et al., 1991). The theory which possesses an holistic integration of balance between the emic (emphasis on cultural, racial, and ethnic differences) and etic (universal similarities) approaches to identity, incorporates the common themes of self knowledge and oppression (the suppression, repression and blocking of one's good, freedom or liberation). Exploring identity development based on optimal theory, two sets of assumptions which represent different systems of structuring consciousness conceptually have to be considered—the suboptimal and optimal—when exploring identity development based on optimal theory.

The identification of an optimal conceptual system is consistent with a wisdom tradition found in ancient Africa (Obenga, 1991) dating back to the beginnings of human culture and civilization. The idea of striving for perfection or being engaged in the process of optimization is part of what Nobles characterizes as a traditionally African centered concern with perfectibility. Many cultural traditions acknowledge both the transcendent and immanent aspects of an omniscient, omnipotent, omnipresent creative force which is at the core or essence of being. The set of philosophical assumptions and principles or conceptual system we call optimal, which acknowledges the spiritual dimensions of life, the implicate order of the unseen, is also supported by modern physics, cognitive neuroscience, health psychology, Eastern philosophies, and African commonsense (Myers, 1992). Emphasis in this system of structuring consciousness is on striving for the "best" under the specified conditions of highest value placed on harmony, balance, order, reciprocity, compassion, justice and truth. Based on the ancient African dictum that self knowledge is the basis of all knowledge, optimal theory reinforces the ancient idea that our purpose in being is that of coming to know our divine (supremely good) selves more and more fully. This process of perfecting self is developmental, and requires the integration and synthesis of all aspects of how the individual manifests. An order is assumed which allows the configuration of the characteristics one needs with each incarnation to best facilitate mastery of the lessons one needs to achieve the next level of self-knowledge, wisdom and understanding necessary toward realization of one's true divine identity.

Utilizing an optimal conceptual system, the unity of the spiritual and the material, all aspects of consciousness, are assumed. The spiritual or non-material (thought/feeling, intuiting, the unconscious, etc.) is seen as primary and a most essential foundation for the material, a pattern which is consistent with the heights of knowledge across scientific disciplines such as quantum physics and neuroscience, as well as the beliefs of cultures of people of color throughout the world

(Bynum, in press). One energy is acknowledged as manifesting in an infinite variety of forms, which at its slowest levels can be appercepted by the five senses in material form.

The conceptual system which separates the material, sensory, and spiritual or non-material, extra-sensory aspects of being, and is thus fragmented in nature, is referred to as sub-optimal. This worldview emphasizes the external, more appearance-based aspects of materiality as the basis for defining reality. As the senses are used as guides, rather than acknowledged as guided and informed by pre-programmed thoughts, feelings, and other extrasensory (and by definition, spiritual) phenomenon (Myers, 1988), this view is described as less than optimal as a means of making sense of the world. And, in terms of identity, the adherent is cut-off from his/her conscious connection to the creator of experience, the influential unconscious, and a transcendent, eternal aspect of being.

While serving a valuable purpose, the external focus of this view places authority over reality's definition, and thus one's experience, outside oneself with implications for all aspects of being. Materiality, although finite and limited by nature, becomes a primary value and acquisition of objects a primary focus (Nichols, 1991). Identity and self-worth are based on external criteria and validation (e.g., how one looks, one's income, position, education, and so forth) through materialism is sought as the basis for security, well-being and worth. For example, in American society White skin and male sex characteristics are two external criteria which automatically garner privilege in terms of accessing a larger piece of the material pie and the position of being "better than" others. People who do not possess these characteristics are ascribed an inferior status, as the suboptimal conceptual system validates individuals based upon appearance versus substance. A cycle of externalized worth in flux, with fleeting satisfaction, need for acquisition of more objects or control over others, stress and anxiety, if not, greed and misdeed, is standard (Myers, 1988). However the suboptimal can serve the role in human experience of providing the opportunity for increased self knowledge, growth and stability, as one studies and gains insight into the separation created by externalized forces.

As societies and cultures at large adhere to the more fragmented worldview, practices propagated through their systems of organization and institutional structures (which at the deepest, most essential level of the reality of the individuals themselves are informed by their conceptual systems) are disjointed, supporting the breach and prompting the fragmented, superficial, materialistic orientation that drove this country to endorse the enslavement of Africans for their labor and the annihilation of Native Americans for their land. The consequences include racism, sexism, classism, tribalism, ageism, weightism, heightism, and so on, serving to place limitations on positive identity development, as well as fostering depression, violence, chemical dependency and other social ills. Optimal theory predicts that anyone who adheres to a fragmented, sub-optimal conceptual system is oppressed, to one degree or another, regardless of race or ethnicity, because the worldview is inherently oppressive due to its superficial, temporal, illusive nature.

Some may be uncomfortable with the use of the designations of optimal (the best) and suboptimal (less than the best) under the specified conditions of high value for harmony, balance, compassion, order, reciprocity, justice, and truth, processing the designations with the either/or dichotomous logic of a fragmented worldview. However, consistent with the wisdom tradition dating back to 2052 B.C., striving for the optimal or "best ways" does not imply that there is no recognition nor appreciation for the value and role of the suboptimal, simply recognition of its nature, outcomes, and consequences. Optimal theory acknowledges the law of opposites, which suggests that the nature of growth, and thus life itself is reliant on oppositions and that in order to know the optimal, one must know the suboptimal. In addition, becoming optimal is a process fully involving the unification, containment and transcension of the suboptimal, opposition or "negative." Oneness in this sense is the objective, although there is not the belief that there is only one "best way." Optimization, the process of becoming optimal, is designed to move the individual to the point of realizing that "it is all good."

Optimal Theory Applied to Identity Development (OTAID)

Applying optimal theory to identity development provides a unifying system for understanding and conceptualizing the identity development process and describes the potential effect of oppressive external forces on self-identity. Optimal theory posits that a suboptimal conceptual system is oppressive by nature in that it serves to block awareness of the intrinsic worth which comes from being one with the source of all good, and focus on and freedom of expression of the more positive non-material aspects of being such as peace, love, justice, order, reciprocity, balance, authenticity, and so on. Thus it is oppressive, having the role and function of suppressing, repressing, and depressing non-superficial, positive forces. At the same time, the optimal view allows us to see that the suboptimal orientation has a potentially positive purpose as the source of the oppositions necessary for growth. Anyone socialized within or adhering to a suboptimal conceptual system is subject to the struggles for meaning, value, security and well-being that will be fostered. The inherently oppressive suboptimal worldview is dominant in Western and westernized cultures and is at the core of their institutional structures.

Because such a worldview fosters an externalized sense of reality and worth in individuals, those utilizing the conceptual system go through a similar developmental process in which individuals progressively experience denial, devaluation, or lack of awareness of an aspect of themselves (Myers et al., 1991). And, if growth is fostered, these individuals move through to the end point where there is an integration of that part of self into a positive, whole self-identity that is grounded in more substantive, non-material issues of being such as, ethics, building good character, integrity, honesty, compassion, and so on. However everyone, regardless of race or ethnicity, suffers from varying forms of oppression in a suboptimal system, from self-alienation and externalized power to attempts at dehumanization.

The identity development model derived from optimal theory acknowledges that the various aspects of a person are not compartmentalized to be examined and experienced apart from other aspects of being and daily functioning. Experiences associated with differences (based on race, gender, age, and so forth) take on particular significance because in a sub-optimal materialist culture they may influence self and other perception.

Movement toward a more optimal worldview places importance on learning to value and appreciate all aspects of being and getting in touch with inner substance. The various human diversity markers become mechanisms for deeper self and other examination influencing positive identity development. The experience of opposition provides the increased opportunity for integration and synthesis, and thus a stronger, tempered positive identity. Issues of oppression and identity development are generally applied to "so-called" minorities, who are actually the majority outside the context of Western cultures. Myers (1988; Myers et al., 1991) asserts that people are subject to oppression when they allow their reality to be defined by others and their sense of worth to be externalized, placing power outside themselves. A positive identity is achieved and sustained by unifying, containing and transcending the oppositions to the point that what differentiates is not how we appear, but how we think, feel and behave—our character. The holistic worldview is described as optimal because of the integration and synthesis of oppositions characteristic of its logic and the consequent harmony, balance and peace it fosters (Myers, 1988). It is extant, though not commonplace, in Western cultures.

Phase Sequence

The process of identity development is described by optimal theory as occurring in a predictable sequence and it can be conceptualized as an expanding spiral. There are six phases and individuals may or may not move through all of the phases. OTAID defines a progression toward spirituality, which is described as the courage to look within and to trust a deep sense of belonging, wholeness, connectedness, and openness to the infinite (Schafranske & Gorsuch, 1984) or oneness (Myers, 1980). The concept of self grows from a narrow definition to a broad, inclusive one, with an integrated realization of self.

Phase O: The Absence of Conscious Awareness (It is) is the initial phase in which a person is an undifferentiated part of the collective unconscious, has no awareness of being and is totally innocent based on the current incarnation. All life is accepted without judgment. This phase is generally associated with transitioning from the spiritual realm into infancy.

Phase 1: Individuation (The world is the way it is) describes a phase in which the individual is manifest uniquely and specially, lacking conscious awareness of any view of self other than the one they are introduced to by their family and immediate environment. They do bring, however, the unfinished work of previous incarnations and the family unconscious. They do not assign any particular meaning to self and may lack awareness of that part of self that is valued by society.

Phase 2: Dissonance (I'm beginning to wonder who I am) is the second phase in which individuals begin to explore those aspects of self that are pointed out and may be devalued by others. This may lead to conflict between the person, the sense the person has of themselves, and the person that society sees. Feelings of awareness, anger, guilt, confusion, conflict and/or insecurity may arise.

Phase 3: Immersion (I focus my energy on people like me) is characterized by people who embrace others like themselves who may be also be misperceived or devalued. This acceptance enables people to learn about and appreciate the devalued aspects of themselves. Individuals may "immerse" themselves in the culture of the misperceived or devalued group. Feelings of excitement and pride, and a sense of belonging occur when the person identifies with the group, while negative feelings (e.g., anger, distrust) regarding the dominant group may exist.

Phase 4: Internalization (I feel good about who I know I am) is the fourth phase, in which individuals have incorporated feelings of worth associated with the part of self that was previously challenged or viewed as negative. This part is recognized as valuable and just one of many components of self identity.

Phase 5: Integration (With my deeper understanding of myself I am changing my assumptions about the world) reflects a change in the way an individual views life, others, and self — a conceptual switch is beginning to occur. People in this phase connect with more people because the criteria of acceptance go beyond appearance. One begins to understand that all people can oppress or be oppressed, depending upon one's assumptions.

Phase 6: Transformation (It is I) is the last phase of identity development, in which a person defines self multi-dimensionally as including previous and future generations, nature, and community. There has been a shift in worldview based upon the realization of intrinsic worth by virtue of oneness through the interrelatedness and interdependence of all things and the ability to reason with the unity that contains and transcends oppositions. Reality is based on a holistic and integrative (spiritual) awareness rather than external circumstances and negative experiences are understood as providing opportunities for growth.

Measurement in OTAID

Two instruments have been designed to assess the phases of development described by the OTAID model. The first instrument was developed by Sevig (1993), while the second was a revision and alteration of the first version with the intention to devise a more theoretically sound assessment of the OTAID model (Haggins, 1994). These instruments were examined in conjunction with the racial identity scales for European American and African American people. We expected that the instruments which assessed the phases described by the OTAID model would be comparable to the other developmental models based on racial identity, because, as suggested earlier, the various identity models available describe very similar processes. The research was primarily consistent with this expectation. The OTAID model differs from other one-dimensional instruments (which assess only one aspect of identity—race, gender) in that it allows the individual to identify the various aspects of self; it thus addresses multiple identities. Assuming this then, the OTAID model should be equally effective for each person, regardless of race, gender, age, or any specific group identification, due to the underlying assumption that oppression will be experienced by everyone adhering to a sub-optimal conceptual system.

Overcoming the Limitations of the Cross Model

Social Context and the Multiple Dimensions of Identity

The Cross model has been criticized because racial awareness and identity are conceived as contingent upon social interaction in terms of race. In the Cross model, Whites are always the comparative reference group against which racial attitudes are examined. The Cross model assumes that the motivational catalyst prompting developmental progression is related to racially salient social experiences. The comparison standard for optimal theory (OT) need not be Whites, although beliefs commonly held in the dominant culture often prompt the salience of the particular human diversity referent to be explored in terms of identity. The motivational catalyst for the developmental progression in optimal theory is assumed to be movement toward greater knowledge of self and the desire to become "more better" (Nobles, 1989) in the sense of improving one's alliance at all levels (from the most inward to the most outward) with the divine. The desire to feel good about oneself and secure in who one is, is believed normal for the healthy personality.

Optimal theory acknowledges the role of social interaction in terms of identity development, but emphasizes the power of conceptual system and worldview in terms of determining the nature and influence of social interactions on identity and human diversity referents. In addition, race is conceived as just one aspect of one's identity, which may change in significance and meaning over time or across generations. For example, as Black people acknowledging African descent are historically dehumanized and disenfranchised by the dominant culture, they will likely respond to the oppression process in different ways. We would expect mentacide to begin to take its toll over time (Nobles, 1989; Wright, 1987). Assimilation of the dominant culture's worldview or identification with the oppressor will create, in time among those internalizing oppression, the desire to avoid dealing with being Black or the denial of the significance of race. That is not to say that race/racism will lose significance, but that the form in which it manifests as a social condition will change. Structures (institutionalized racism) and strategies (divide and conquer/overseer) that have met with success will effect superficial changes, while maintaining the status quo. Following our example with African Americans, in earlier generations one drop of Black blood meant you were Black. Today, we have begun to acknowledge new categories of racial designations such as biracial and multiracial. Some would argue that the new categories are a function of the dwindling numbers of White offspring and the need for the reinstitution of a buffer class to whom modified privilege is given to preserve the status quo of White supremacy (Welsing, 1992). In terms of positive identity development, optimal theory posits that the more substantive issue will be the worldview of individuals as responses to meanings of race/ethnicity change or appear to change on multi levels, given experiential realities over time.

Cycles of Change and Identity

Identity does not exist in a vacuum, the zeitgeist of social conditions influence not only the identity development of those researched, but that of the researchers as well. Optimal theory posits that careful examination of the focus and formulations of research and research questions over time reflect the social consciousness evolving, and are strongly influenced by the overriding values and interests dominant in the social context, in this instance the socio-political and economic conditions of the culture. As we examine Cross' model and reactions to it, we are simply seeing the individual and collective processes of consciousness developing, based on the conceptual systems of the various social actors. Such an examination allows us to see the interdependence of popular culture (manifestations of the peoples way of life in general), the academy (educational institutions in the culture whose responsibility it is to pass on and shape societal beliefs, values, and structures), and social policy (the dominant views implemented), individually and collectively. In studying African Americans we have a particularly unique opportunity to see what happens to a people's identity (individual and collective), when their indigenous socio-cultural reality is totally disrupted and they are forced to develop over generations in an alien and hostile environment. What are the various reactions to oppression and what factors determine the salience of various coping strategies? What, if any, substantiative changes are needed to make the environment less alienating and hostile, or at least appear so?

Within each era, notions of racial identity may shift on the part of the researcher and the researched, as social attitudes shift; however, substantive change would require a shift in conceptual system. As long as members of the culture are being socialized into the suboptimal conceptual system, which pushes external validation by teaching its members to base identity and self worth on external criteria, the opinions of those outside oneself will take on special significance. Power is given up all too frequently to those without balance, harmony, order, peace, compassion, justice, integrity, honesty, authenticity and other manifestations of good character, but who by virtue of politics, position, wealth, looks, status, and so forth are deemed important. It matters not whether it is Blacks giving Whites their power of self-definition, women giving men their power, the fat giving the thin power, the poor giving the rich power, children from single parent households giving children from two parent households power, or so on. The same formula is potentially at play when the messages sent by a culture about a particular human diversity marker are negative.

In the early seventies, when Cross first developed his model, psychologists had not been focusing on the process of positive identity development among a people in a social context that sought to diminish an aspect of their being that historically had been made most central to living by the dominant culture (i.e., race determined opportunities to avoid brutality, for legal rights, education, employment, marriage, etc.). The zeitgeist of the Black Awareness Movement made racial identity and transformation from Negro to Black salient. It appears as though key elements of Cross' model were salient to a wide cross-section of researchers at particular points in time (Brookins, Anyabwile, & Nacoste, 1992; Helms, 1984,1990; Lewis & Adams, 1990; Looney, 1988; Munford, 1994; Parham, 1989; Parham & Helms, 1981; Pomales, Claiborn, & LaFromboise, 1986; Ponterotto& Wise, 1987; Sue & Sue, 1990; Watts, 1992; Walter & Simon, 1993). However, by the late 70's co-optation, assimilation, mentacide and acculturation, along with the strong conservative, reactionary mood of the country made evident the issues of double consciousness for African Americans talked about by DuBois (1902) were yet to be resolved. Akbar (1989) noted the social rewards for African Americans behaving in socially prescribed ways. Questions in the research literature regarding psychological adjustment at the upper stages of Cross' identity development model, also reflect ambivalence about the responses of the healthy individual to the dominant culture.

Cross' model does little to resolve these questions, although based on optimal theory his early thinking was on the right track, at the higher stages of development, one should feel very strong positive kinship bonds with one's own race (although not to the denigration of other races nor to their exclusion as the basis of kinship), because it is a part of oneself. In order to understand the dynamics of identity and racial identity in African Americans in particular, it is imperative that one understands the influence of one's conceptual system or worldview on perception and thinking. For example, optimal theory argues that the highest levels of positive identity development cannot be achieved without making a conceptual switch away from the dominant suboptimal belief system. Without the switch, materialist values and the faulty orientation of basing worth on external criteria, will likely inhibit one's capacity to see Black people as positive in comparison to their White counterparts, who dominant the economic scene throughout most of the world. The earlier stages of positive identity development put forth by Cross are entrenched in the suboptimal construction of reality. Parham and Williams (1993) found that the higher one's income level, the higher one's pre-encounter scores and the lower one's internalization scores. Optimal theory provides a broader conceptual framework for making sense of these patterns.

Past research has focused exclusively on models of identity which have separated people based upon obvious group membership (e.g., African Americans—Cross, 1971; Women-Downing & Roush, 1985). Optimal theory suggests that both cultural differences and other human diversity markers and universal similarities are important. Greatest value is placed on the implicate order of the spiritual dimension, which acknowledges the interconnectedness and interrelatedness of all people and is the source of a truly positive identity that is not temporal and in perpetual flux. Looking at the concept of identity development holistically, oppositions, such as oppression, become key because awareness and exploration of these unlock the door to growth and development. According to the wisdom tradition of our ancient ancestors and optimal theory, the processes of life are governed by a law of opposites. Coming to conscious awareness of the role of a particular challenge in life—including oppression, even when it is believed to be caused externally—fosters movement toward a more positive, matured sense of self which is internally formulated. Optimal theory asserts that all people, regardless of race, who have internalized a suboptimal belief system, are oppressed. Although, they may or may not have similar experiences, they will go through a similar identity development process. Sustaining a positive identity requires development to occur beyond the integration of the devalued or conflicted aspect. A conceptual switch from a fragmented, external orientation to a holistic, internal frame of reference is needed, whereby one's worth is intrinsic and appreciates based on substance of character, rather than external criteria or appearance (Myers et. al., 1991).

The available identity development theories have rarely examined the multiple identities which a person may possess (e.g., a Hispanic woman who is a lesbian; Reynolds & Pope, 1991). Optimal theory does not partition individuals into fragments of identity such as a race, gender, sexual preference, and so forth, as other models have done, but instead suggests that with self-knowledge (potentially facilitated by oppositions created by oppression). Individuals can integrate all aspects of their being (age, race gender, etc.) into a holistically, positive sense of self sustained by virtue of intrinsic worth and character. Some may have trouble seeing how White males, for example, are oppressed. The OTAID model points to the self-alienation endemic to the faulty, suboptimal worldview that fosters the need to dominate, control, and exploit others, or leaves one insecure, unfulfilled, and emotionally crippled.

A model of identity development was originally developed by Myers and other researchers at Ohio State using an emic approach and was called the Self-Identity Model of Oppressed People (SIDMOP). However, without optimal theory informing the internal nature of oppression, the concept of multiple oppression could not be meaningfully incorporated and operationalized. Myers' (1988) optimal theory was adopted as the theoretical basis for the identity development model. The current model has been identified as Optimal Theory Applied to Identity Development (OTAID; Myers et al., 1991).

The phases of development as described by optimal theory are similar to and yet different from the Cross model of racial identity development to which we have been referring. The developmental phases of the OTAID model, however, integrate all aspects of ones' being, by allowing individuals to self-identify their own salient "parts," while also incorporating spiritual development into this process (Myers et al., 1991). In addition, the higher stages of development require a conceptual switch to a more optimal system of functioning not influenced by external conditions, and is sustainable with diunital (but/and) reasoning, that allows for the unification, containment, and transcension of oppositions (Myers, 1988).

Identity and Psychological Health and Well-being

According to the Cross model there appears to be no relationship between one's racial group identity and positive self-esteem. Optimal theory (OT) predicts that there should be a positive and strong relationship between one's racial (or any other human diversity marker one possesses) group identity and self-esteem. While Cross assumes there to be a positive linear relationship between acceptance of self, as a member of an ethnic group and acceptance of racially different others, optimal theory would predict such a relationship, as well, although not necessarily assume it to be linear in nature. Preference for similar others based on gender and socioeconomic status should not be systematically related to racial attitudes according to the Cross model. OT suggests that at all stages of development preference for similar others can be predicted on the basis of the worldview of the · individual.

Cross indicates that positive expression of one's racial identity is liberating and psychologically healthy (Helms, 1990). OT affirms that positive expression of all aspects of who one is and how one is manifesting, is liberating and psychologically healthy. In addition, the Cross model purports higher stages of racial identification are reflecting better psychological functioning and result in greater interpersonal adjustment. Within the Cross Model (Cross, 1978) the last stage requires an inner security and satisfaction with self, love and compassion for all oppressed people, and commitment to improving the quality of life for the group. OT concurs, but for different reasons, providing the methods and strategies for achieving and maintaining that level of development—as previously mentioned. In the OT model, tension and defensiveness about one's identity can be utilized to achieve greater knowledge of self, yielding greater security and well-being.

The stages developed by Cross are related to levels of cognition but are apart from specific content reasoning. OT requires that the developmental progression be toward a different way of being in the world and reasoning that minimizes dichotomous logic and seeks to unify, contain and transcend oppositions (diunital logic). Parham (1994) suggests that a multistage and multidimensional structure for cycling through stages based on social demands be added to the Cross model. OT incorporates such thinking by predicting the likely response to social demands based on one's conceptual system.

Movement toward an optimal conceptual system will include reasoning, values and experiences consistent with unity consciousness. The logic characteristic of an optimal worldview informs reasoning which is diunital (the union of opposites), leading to a system of reasoning which allows one to see both two sides of an issue, and experience the "anyo kweli enyo," or two relative truths contingent on perspective comfortably without contradiction or conflict. In terms of values, highest value is in positive interpersonal relationships. Being such, the virtues of order, balance, compassion, harmony, reciprocity, justice and truth shape the ethical standard. From an optimal perspective, thinking in terms of systems, the process by which our goal of a universe governed by a standard of ethics based on the above virtues will be achieved is nutology, through human and spiritual networks (Nichols, 1976). We will through human and spiritual networks realize our true identity and realize unity consciousness. Nobles (1980) discusses the African concept of self extended in time/space to include all of the ancestors, the yet unborn, all nature, and the entire community. These are the human and spiritual networks through which we will work as we pursue the fullness of positive identity development, allowing for spiritual awareness, oneness with nature, and community healing.

These attributes also become the dimensions that must be considered as we seek to determine what a sound identity is. It becomes evident that it is problematic to determine what a sound identity is based on a fragmented, suboptimal worldview (e.g., democratic sanity, the difficulties exposed in the upper stages of Cross' model). And, racial identity, as a construct may shift as society's policies and racial attitudes cycle over time within a suboptimal framework. For example, the segregation of the 50's and earlier led to the civil rights movement of the 60's, the Black awareness and women's movements are met with a backlash in the 80's, the assimilation of the 70's led to multi-racial designations of the 90's, and so on.

Because Western psychology is for the most part based on a medical model which emphasizes the symptomatology of pathology, mental health tends to be ill-defined or defined in terms of the absence of pathology and democratic sanity (Akbar, 1984). When it comes to non-dominant groups, African Americans in particular, the situation is even more problematic, a long history of brutality, dehumanization and insensitivity make the dominant society's definitions of mental health even more suspect (e.g., draptemania was the diagnosis given a runaway enslaved African). As a consequence, consensus is lacking on the basis for determining the nature of a healthy identity and the processes for achieving one, and what aspects of identity should be explored.

Based on OT, the human purpose in being is to learn more and more about oneself as the individual and unique expression of a divine force. Bringing to awareness unconscious processes and conscious union with this divinity is an infinite process occurring simultaneously on many levels, emanating from the Black holes of inner space to the Black holes of outer space. Each incarnation brings its own special opportunities for growth and self discovery. Each human diversity marker one possesses becomes an aspect of self to be explored, learned from, and incorporated into one's identity. Those markers demeaned or devalued in one's larger social context become potentially the best catalysts for growth and knowledge of one's true self. From this perspective, our sense of separateness diminishes into infinity as our understanding and appreciation of this self becomes more and more refined.

Conclusion

Consistent with OT's premise of self knowledge, some attention should be paid to the background of the theorist. Coleman (1980) acknowledges that psychological theory is shaped by autobiography, the personal history of theoreticians directly influence their theory. That I am a woman of African and Native American descent, a Black woman, who spent most of her formative years in a rural, Midwestern, middle-class, predominantly White environment, helps to account in part for not only how I am manifesting this time around, but also contributes to who I am (what energies as information configured to become me), and how I think, define and experience reality.

The initial impetus for the development of optimal theory was the theorist's need to understand people who would be racist. How could they be thinking to judge human worth so superficially, yet with such conviction? Analysis of the mindset of the racist revealed the prototype of a mentality that held the same essential assumptions, varying only in degree and target, as that of those who would be sexist, classist, heightist, weightist, tribalist and so on. Study of my own ancestry and heritage afforded me the opportunity to see we were not simply talking about the nature of human nature, and that there truly was another way of being in the world other than that into which the dominant culture in this society would socialize us. Optimal theory would suggest that each aspect of my being was needed and contributed to what is in terms of the explicate order, but on another level of the implicate order, another coalescing of energies as information was also involved, at the deepest levels going back to the beginnings of time.

Optimal theory suggests that all people, regardless of race, gender, age, and so forth, go through a similar identity development process. Haggins (1994) explored this by examining the correlations between racial identity attitude stages and optimal theory developmental phases. The results of this research suggest that the OTAID model effectively describes the identity process for African American and European American subjects. The phases of optimal theory and the stages of racial identity (BRIAS and WRIAS) were similarly correlated and seemed to be measuring comparable attitudes. As expected, African Americans and European Americans did differ on some of the phases of development. Optimal theory assumes that people are going to vary in terms of the manner in which they progress through the phases, and that external characteristics (e.g., race, gender, weight, height, etc.) may influence this process. It is important to remember that the identity development process is a decidedly complex process. In much of past research, studies have typically only examined one aspect of a person's identity (race, gender, sexual orientation), while the instruments designed to test the OTAID model allows subjects to self-identify the "parts" of their identity and respond accordingly. This is important because it is the whole person and his or her attitudes and feelings that are key.

Optimal theory incorporates the concept of oppression as a by-product of a suboptimal worldview system and it's effects on everyone intra- and inter-individually. Understanding optimal theory in relation to identity development can assist researchers and counselors in learning how to facilitate progression through the phases (Myers, in press). Perhaps as process and outcome research done on optimal theory is developed, we can better understand the human psyche and support individuals as they move from holding a suboptimal or fragmented, disintegrative worldview to holding a more optimal or holistic worldview which can enhance well-being individually and collectively.

Exploration of the Cross and OTAID models of positive identity development accents the importance of addressing some of the pressing questions about identity development outside the context of traditional mainstream frameworks, particularly when it comes to non-dominant populations who have been historically disenfranchised and dehumanized. Understanding the multiple levels and dimensions of identity dynamics are critical to enhancing human health and well-being. It is hoped that a greater understanding of identity development will facilitate better mental health and the delivery of more effective mental health services.

References

Atkinson, D.R., Morten, G., & Sue, D.W. (1983). *Counseling American minorities: A cross-cultural perspective* (3rd ed.). Dubuque, IA: William C. Brown.

Banks, J.A. (1984). *Teaching strategies for ethnic studies* (3rd ed.). Boston: Allyn & Bacon.

Bateson, G. (1979). *Mind and nature: A necessary unit.* New York: E. P. Dutton.

Berry, J. W. (1980). Acculturation as varieties of adaption. In A. M. Padilla (Ed.), *Acculturation theory, models, and some new findings* (pp. 118-126). Boulder, CO: Westview Press, Inc.

Brookins, C.C., Anyabwile, T., & Nacoste, R.B. (1992). *Racial identity attitudes and psychological feelings of closeness in African American college students.* Paper presented at the 13th Annual Conference on Empirical Research on Black Psychology. North Carolina State University, North Carolina.

Capra, F. (1975). *The Tao of physics.* New York: Bantam Books.

Carney, C. G., & Kahn, K. B. (1984). Building competencies for effective cross-cultural counseling: A development view. *The Counseling Psychologist, 12,* 111-119.

Carruthers, J. (1995). *Mdw Ntr: Divine speech.* London: Karnak House.

Cass, V. C. (1979). Homosexual identity formation: A theoretical model. *Journal of Homosexuality, 4,* 219-235.

Coleman, D. (1980). Perspectives on psychology, reality, and the study of consciousness. In R. Walsh & F. Vaughn (Eds.), *Beyond ego: Transpersonal dimesions in psychology.* Los Angeles, CA : J.P. Tarchar.

Cross, W. E. (1971). The Negro-the-Black conversion experience. *Black World, 20(9),* 13-27

Downing, N. E., & Roush, K. L. (1985). From passive acceptance to active commitment: A model of feminist identity development of women. *The Counseling Psychologist, 13,* 59-72.

Elias, D. (1997). It's time to change our minds: An introduction to transformative learning. *ReVision, 20,* 2-5.

Fine, M. Schwebel, A., & Myers, L.J. (1988). Family stability in Black families: Values underlying three different perspectives. *Journal of Comparative Family Studies, 18(1),* 1-24.

Haggins, K. L. (1994). *An investigation of optimal theory applied to identity development.* Unpublished doctoral dissertation, The Ohio State University.

Helms, J. E. (1984). Toward a theoretical explanation of the effects of race on counseling: A Black and White model. *The Counseling Psychologist, 12,* 153-165.

Helms, J. E. (1989). Considering some methodological issues in racial identity counseling research. *The Counseling Psychologist, 17(2),* 227-252.

Helms, J. E. (Ed.). (1990). *Black and White racial identity attitudes: Theory, research, and practice.* Westport, CT: Greenwood Press, Inc.

Helms, J. E., & Carter, R. T. (1990). Development of the White racial identity attitude scale. In J. E. Helms, (Ed.), *Black and White Racial Identity Attitudes: Theory, research, and practice* (pp. 67-80). Westport, CT: Greenwood Press, Inc.

Highlen, P. S., Jecmen, D. J. & Speight, S. L. (1991). [Data from Female Identity Development study]. Unpublished raw data.

Hilliard, A. (1997). *Sba: Reawakening the African mind.* Baltimore: Kemetic Press.

Jecmen, D. J. (1989). *The development of an instrument to measure identity development in females: The female identity development scale.* Unpublished master's thesis, The Ohio State University.

Karenga, M. (1984). Selections from the Husia: Sacred wisdom of ancient Egypt. Los Angeles: Sankore Press.

Looney, J. (1988). Ego development and Black identity. *Journal of Black Psychology, 15(1),* 41-56.

Munford, M.B. (1994). Relationship of gender, self-esteem, social class, and racial identity to depression in Blacks. *Journal of Black Psychology, 20(2),* 157-174.

Myers, L. J. (1988). *Understanding an Afrocentric worldview: Introduction to an optimal psychology.* Dubuque, IA: Kendall/Hunt.

Myers, L. J., Speight, S. L., Highlen, P. S., Cox, C. I., Reynolds, A. L., Adams, E. M., & Hanley, C. P. (1991). Identity development and worldview: Toward an optimal conceptualization. *Journal of Counseling and Development, 70,* 54-63.

Myers, L.J., & Speight, S. (1994). Optimal theory and the psychology of human diversity. In E. Thickett, R. Watts, & D. Berman (Eds.), *Perspectives on people in context,* 104-114. New York: Jossey/Bass.

Myers, L.J., Stokes, D., & Speight, S. (1989). Physiological responses to anxiety and stress: Reactions to oppression, galvanic skin potential and heart rate. *Journal of Black Studies, 20(1),* 80-96.

Nobles, W.W. (1989). Psychological nigrescence: An Afrocentric review. *The Counseling Psychologist, 17(2),* 253-263.

Ornsteirn, R. & Ehrlich, P. (1989). *New world, new mind: Moving toward conscious evolution.* New York: Doubleday.

Parham, T. A. (1989). Cycles of psychological nigrescence. *The Counseling Psychologist, 17(2),* 187-226.

Parham T. A., & Helms, J. E. (1981). The influence of Black student's racial identity attitudes on preferences for counselor's race. *Journal of Counseling Psychology, 28(3)*, 250-257.

Pomales, J., Claiborn, C.D., & LaFromboise, T.D. (1986). Effects of Black students' racial identity on perceptions of White counselors varying in cultural sensitivity. *Journal of Counseling Psychology, 33(1)*, 57-61.

Ponterotto, J.G., & Wise, S.L. (1987), Construct validity study of the racial identity attitude scale. *Journal of Counseling Psychology, 34(2)*, 218-223.

Reynolds, A. L., & Pope, R. L. (1991). The complexities of diversity: Exploring multiple oppressions. *Journal of Counseling and Development, 70*, 174-180.

Schafranske, E.P., & Gorsuch, R.L. (1984). Factors associated with the perception of spirituality in psychotherapy. *Journal of Transpersonal Psychology, 16*, 231-241.

Sevig, T. (1993). The development and validation of the Self-Identity Instrument. Unpublished doctoral dissertation, The Ohio State University.

Smith, E.M. (1989). Black racial identity development: Issues and concerns. *The Counseling Psychologist, 17(2)*, 277-288.

Stokes, J.E., Murray, C.B., Chavez, D., & Peacock, M.J. (1998). Cross' stage model revisited: An analysis of theoretical formulations and empirical evidence. In R.L. Jones (Ed.), *African American identity development* (pp.123-140). Hampton, VA: Cobb & Henry Publishers.

Speight, S.L., Myers, L.J., Cox, C.I., & Highlen, P.S. (1991). A redefintion of multicultural counseling. *Journal of Counseling and Development, 70*, 29-36.

Sue, D. W. (1981). *Counseling the culturally different: Theory and practice.* New York: Wiley.

Sue, D. W., & Sue, D. (1990). *Counseling the culturally different: Theory and practice (2nd ed.).* New York: Wiley.

Sue, S., & Zane, N. (1987). The role of culture and cultural techniques in psychotherapy: A critique and reformulation. *American Psychologist, 42*, 37-45.

Terrell, F., & Terrell, S. (1984). Race of counselor, client sex, cultural mistrust level, and premature termination form counseling among Black clients. *Journal of Counseling Psychology, 31(31)*, 371-381.

Tokar, D. M., & Swanson, J. L. (1991). An investigation of the validity of Helms's (1984) model of White racial identity development. *Journal of Counseling Psychology, 38(3)*, 296-301.

Vontress, C. E. (1971). Racial differences: Impediments to rapport. *Journal of Counseling Psychology, 18(1)*, 7-13.

Walters, K.L., & Simoni, J.M. (1993). Lesbian and gay male group identity attitudes and self-esteem: Implications for counseling. *Journal of Counseling Psychology, 40(1)*, 94-99.

Watts, R.J. (1992). Racial identity and preference for social change strategies among African Americans. *Journal of Black Psychology, 18(2)*, 1-18.

Author

Linda James Myers
Department of African
American and African Studies
University Hall, Room 286
The Ohio State University
230 N. Oval Mall Drive
Columbus, OH 43210
Telephone: (614) 292-3447

A Multidimensional Model of Racial Identity: Assumptions, Findings, and Future Directions

Robert M. Sellers, J. Nicole Shelton, Deanna Y. Cooke, Tabbye M. Chavous, Stephanie A. Johnson Rowley, and Mia A. Smith

The meaning of race for people of African descent has been discussed in literary and scholarly writings since their first oppressive encounters with Europeans. The struggles associated with developing a healthy Black identity may have been best articulated by W.E. B. DuBois' (1903) discussion of the double consciousness that is ascribed to the American Negro. In *Souls of Black Folk*, DuBois suggested the only way Blacks can develop healthy self-concepts within this society is to come to "an understanding" within themselves regarding the duality of their status as African and American. The understanding that Blacks have come to is individualistic. It varies in terms of the importance that individuals place on being Black, the way individuals feel about other Blacks, and in the very definitions individuals ascribe to being Black. The way Blacks within this society negotiate the contradiction of their heritage as Africans and Americans plays a major role in shaping their individual racial identities.

Scholars should not be surprised by the fact that racial identity has been one of the most prolific areas of research in Black psychology. It should surprise no one that many of our models of African American racial identity have focused on individuals' attempts at defining themselves with respect to race within a society that devalues the intrinsic worth of their group. It should also be noted that African people (like other peoples) have consistently defined themselves as individuals within the context of the identity of their larger group (often their tribe or village) long before their interactions with Europeans. Because of these dynamics, it is important that African American racial identity be seen as a more complex phenomena than a response to centuries of oppression and stigmatization. It must also include the prosocial operations that cultural affiliations provide individuals.

This chapter presents a model of African American racial identity that attempts to provide a heuristic for understanding the ways in which African Americans define themselves in terms of race. The model is based on many of the concepts already found in both the social identity and racial identity literatures. It organizes these ideas in such a manner as to facilitate a systematic method in which we may; (1) examine the influence of race in the manner that African Americans define themselves; (2) observe the way that identity develops across the life span; (3) make predictions about the way in which racial identity influences the way that African Americans' perceive and interact with their environments.

Introduction of Terms: Black, African American, and Racial Identity

Before we introduce our model of racial identity, it is very important that we explain our usage of three terms— Black, African American, and racial identity — which play an important role in our conceptualization. First, in our distinction between the terms Black and African American, we view the term Black as being an ambiguous category that may or may not be inclusive of all persons of African descent depending upon the individual's viewpoint. Some African Americans conceptualize the Black reference group as a group that is made up of African Americans only. Other African Americans may hold a more Pan-African view of the Black reference group. These individuals may prefer to use the term Africans when referring to their racial reference group. In this chapter, we use the term African Americans to refer to those individuals of African descent who have received a significant portion of their socialization in the United States. As such, they share a heritage and set of shared values which are related to their common historical experiences in this society. Thus, we use the term *Black* when referring to the individuals' own phenomenological view of the make-up of their reference group and the term *African American* when referring to the group of people for whom our model is developed.

While the structure and the components of our model are greatly shaped and influenced by cultural and historical forces within the African American communities, we believe that the term *racial identity* most appropriately characterizes the phenomena that our model addresses. For a number of reasons, some researchers have argued that the term *ethnic* identity should be employed rather than racial identity (e.g., Smith, 1989). First, there are questions regarding the scientific validity of race as a construct. Researchers have also argued that the use of the term ethnic identity places African American group identity within a larger theoretical framework which will allow for the examination of universal processes associated with group identity (Phinney, 1990). However, we offer three reasons for our use of the term *racial* identity instead of ethnic identity.

First, the concept of race has and continues to be *the* defining construct in distinguishing African Americans from other members of this society. Unlike some models of Black identity (e.g., Kambon, 1992), our model makes no claim of any direct biogenetic influences of race on the individual's group identity. Independent of its scientific validity, race has a socially-constructed meaning which is relevant in the real world. Classification as a member of the Black race in American society carries implications for an individual's educational opportunities, health outcomes, and employment opportunities. The socially-constructed category of race is an essential feature of the African American's existence in this society; as such, the African American must address the concept of race as he or she attempts to define him or herself.

Second, although the goal of developing meta-theories of the role of ethnicity and culture in the lives of individuals is laudable (Phinney, 1990), it is imperative that we also understand the experiences of different ethnic groups which are idiosyncratic. In the case of African Americans, there are unique historical and cultural influences which impact upon the qualitative aspect of their racial identity. For instance, the form of slavery that Africans experienced in the United States did not provide many opportunities for open expression of traditional culture. The influences of traditional African culture had to be grafted on to the cultural practices of the European/American society. (For example, the worshipping activities in many African American churches display much of the verve and pageantry of many traditional African religious ceremonies.) There are common experiences among many minority groups in this society — principally oppression. A discussion of African American group identity that is derived only from experiences of oppression, however, implies that African American identity only exists in oppressive contexts. This is a premise that a number of authors emphatically reject (Akbar, 1989; Baldwin, 1981; Nobles, 1991).

Finally, we prefer the term racial identity over ethnic identity because we believe that there are subtle, but important differences in the implications of the two terms. The term ethnic identity suggest an emphasis on cultural behavior patterns, beliefs, and customs associated with being African American. Our model of racial identity focuses more on the *cognitions* and *attitudes* associated with the individuals' attempts at integrating their status as African Americans into their self-concepts. This does not mean that we do not expect behavioral consequences for these cognitions and attitudes. On the contrary, we believe that understanding the significance and meaning of race in an individual's self-concept enables us to better predict the way s/he is likely to behave in certain specific situations (Sellers, Smith, Shelton, Johnson, & Chavous, 1995).

Now that a case has been presented for the use of the term racial identity, a working definition of the term is needed. Our model defines African American racial identity as that part of one's definition of the self that is related to being an African American. This definition is consistent with that of Tajfel (1981) who defines group identity as: " that part of an individual's self-concept which derives from knowledge of his membership in a social group (or groups) together with the value and emotional significance attached to that membership," (p. 255). As such, racial identity provides a mechanism by which African Americans can define themselves in the context of other groups. It provides the means by which individuals can decide who they are as well as who they are not. Racial identity not only refers to the way that African Americans see themselves, but also has implications for how they see their world.

Multidimensional Model of Racial Identity

The Multidimensional Model of Racial Identity (MMRI) provides an integrated framework for describing the complexity of the meaning and significance that African American individuals place on race (Sellers, Smith, Shelton, Johnson, & Chavous, 1995). The model locates racial identity within the context of other components of African Americans' self-concepts. The model provides a heuristic by which specific predictions can be made regarding the relationships among different dimensions of racial identity. The MMRI is also a vehicle that facilitates the investigation of specific hypotheses regarding the way that the different dimensions of racial identity influence behavior and functioning. Finally, the model provides a taxonomy for ideographic investigations of the diversity of racial identity profiles within the African American community.

Four assumptions underlay the MMRI. First, the model assumes that racial identity, like other aspects of the self-concept, has properties that are both situationally-dynamic and stable. These properties often interact in such a way as to influence the individual's behavior in certain specific situations. Second, the MMRI embraces the assumption that individuals have a number of different identities that are ordered hierarchically (Markus & Sentis, 1982; McCrae & Costa, 1988). In other words, the MMRI acknowledges the existence of other identities within the self-concept. It also acknowledges differences in the importance of racial identity across individuals. Third, the MMRI assumes that individuals' perception of their racial identity is the most valid indicator of their identity. In other words, we take a phenomenological approach toward studying racial identity which focuses on the person's self-perceptions rather than defining the individual's self-concept in terms of objective criteria (Jones & Gerard, 1967; Weiner, 1974). A corollary to this phenomenological approach is that no value judgment is made with respect to what constitutes a healthy racial identity versus an unhealthy racial identity. Our final assumption is that racial identity is a complex component of the African American self-concept. African American racial identity is multidimensional in nature. Thus, no single dimension of the MMRI can be considered to be synonymous with African American racial identity. The dimensions represent different ways in which racial identity is manifested. Each of these dimensions of racial identity are likely to be related to different behavioral and adaptational outcomes. Researchers should choose the dimension of racial identity they study based on the goals of their research. Relatedly, racial identity should not be seen as a panacea. There are many behavioral and adaptational outcomes that are not related to racial identity.

The MMRI delineates four independent, but interrelated dimensions of racial identity in African Americans: racial *salience*; the *centrality* of the identity; the *regard* with which the person holds the group associated with the identity; and the *ideology* associated with the identity (Sellers, Smith, Shelton, Johnson, & Chavous, 1995). Of these four dimensions, three are proposed to be stable across situations, and one dimension, racial salience, is context dependent.

Salience

Racial salience refers to the extent to which one's race is a relevant part of one's self-concept during a particular moment or situation (Sellers, Smith, Shelton, Johnson, & Chavous, 1995). Racial salience is concerned with the particular event or situation as the level of analysis. Racial salience is highly sensitive to both the context of the situation and one's proclivity to define oneself in terms of race (Turner, Oakes, Haslam, & McGarty, 1994). In many ways, salience is consistent with Markus and Nurius' (1986) conceptualization of the working self-concept and spontaneous self-concept (e.g., Cota & Dion, 1986; McCrae & Costa, 1988; McGuire, McGuire, Child, & Fujioka, 1978; McGuire & Padawer-Singer, 1976). For instance, Markus and Nurius (1986) suggest that there is a working self-concept that contains a set of self-conceptions that are presently active in thought and memory. They argue that at any moment the salient identity within the working self-concept is determined by the core identity and the immediate social context. Thus, identity salience can vary across individuals and situations (Gurin & Markus, 1988).

Empirical evidence demonstrates that the social context can make various aspects of a person's identity more or less accessible at a given time (e.g., Abrams, Thomas, & Hoggs, 1990; Cota & Dion, 1986; Kite, 1992; McGuire, McGuire, Child, & Fujioka, 1978). For example, distinctiveness theory states that when confronted by a complex stimulus, one notices a given characteristic in the environment to the extent that that characteristic is distinctive from other characteristics (McGuire, McGuire, Child, & Fujioka, 1978). McGuire and colleagues have consistently found distinctiveness theory to be relevant in relation to ethnicity, gender, and a host of other factors such as age, birthplace, weight, hair color, and eye color (Kite, 1992; McGuire et al., 1978; McGuire, McGuire, & Winton, 1979; McGuire & Padawer-Singer, 1976). However, distinctiveness is not the only way in which race can be made salient for African Americans. An inspirational speech about Black History may also produce a high level of race salience in the audience.

In general, individual differences in racial salience become evident in ambiguous situations. This is a result of individual differences in the stable dimensions of

Figure 1
Schematic Representation of the Multidimensional Model of Racial Identity

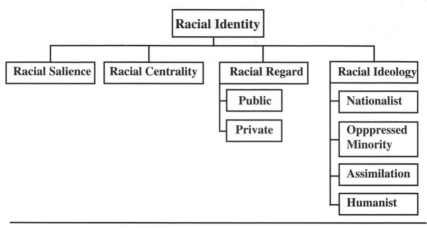

racial identity (Sellers, Smith, Shelton, Johnson, & Chavous, 1995). Specifically, racial centrality may direct individuals towards paying attention to certain cues within the social event while ignoring others. The extent to which the situation is ambiguous with respect to race interacts with the importance that race plays in the person's self-concept to determine whether race is likely to be salient to a person during a particular event. For instance, being the only African American in an all-White restaurant may make race become salient for some African Americans. Yet, in the same situation, race may not become salient for other African Americans. Some other identity may become salient to them. On the other hand, some situations are so persuasive that they make race salient for almost all African Americans; for instance, watching a Ku Klux Klan march. It is difficult to imagine many African Americans for whom race would not become salient in that situation.

Salience also serves as a mediating process between the more stable characteristics of identity and the way individuals perceive and behave in specific situations. Studies of in-group bias have consistently found that individuals behave very differently when their group identity is made salient, even when these identities are arbitrary (for review, see Messick & Mackie, 1989). For instance, in their work on stereotype vulnerability, Steele and Aronson (1995) suggest that racial salience has implications for African Americans' performance on certain cognitive tasks. They found that African American college students performed poorer on tests of reading comprehension when they were forced to identify their race on their answer sheets. A possible pathway through which racial salience may influence behavior is racial saliency's influence on individuals' perceptions of a situation. A Black person for whom race is salient may attribute poor service from a White waitress to be the result of racism, while another person for whom race is not salient at the time may be more likely to attribute the poor service to some other factor such as the waitress' unfriendly personality. These different perceptions of the same situation have very different implications in terms of the potential behavior of the two African American customers.

Unfortunately, most of the research on Black racial identity has failed to identify the process in which racial identity influences an individual's behavior in specific situations (Phinney, 1990; Sellers, 1993). Black racial identity researchers have focused exclusively on the stable aspects of racial identity as evidenced by their reliance on assessment instruments designed to measure stable personality traits (i.e., self-report questionnaires). Environmental influences on racial identity are only discussed in terms of long-term ecological influences (e.g., racial make-up of childhood environment) and global outcomes (e.g., self-esteem, anxiety) instead of predicting behavioral outcomes within specific situational contexts. The dimension of racial salience provides a conceptual framework to investigate the process through which racial identity may influence our functioning in mundane day-to-day situations.

Centrality

Racial centrality refers to the extent to which a person normatively defines his or herself in terms of race (Sellers, Smith, Shelton, Johnson, & Chavous, 1995). Centrality, along with regard and ideology, are considered to be stable across situations. The level of analysis for centrality is the individual's normative perceptions of the importance of race in defining who s/he is across different situations. Implicit in our conceptualization of centrality is the acknowledgment of individual differences in the hierarchical ranking of the importance of different identities (Banaji & Prentice, 1994; Gurin & Markus, 1988, Ingram, 1989; Phinney & Alipuira, 1990). For instance, gender is the defining characteristic in the self-definition of some African American women, whereas for other African Americans their occupation or race may be the defining characteristic.

The concept of centrality is at the core of many of the research models of group, social, racial, and ethnic identity. Personal construct theory argues that people define the world and themselves based on constructs that are idiosyncratic to themselves. The theory argues that certain constructs are more relevant (super-ordinate) and others are less relevant (sub-ordinate) to how a person views the world or themselves. In personal construct terms, central identities are analogous to super-ordinate self-constructs. Non-central identities are considered subordinate self-constructs (Ingram, 1989). The concept of centrality is also synonymous with the concept of saliency in the symbolic interactionist literature (see Stryker, 1980; White & Burke, 1987). The concept of race salience in the symbolic interactionist perspective refers to the extent to which race is meaningful in the way a person normally defines him or herself (White & Burke, 1987). We believe the term salience is more appropriately related to situationally-influenced dimensions of behavior. Consequently, we have coined the term centrality for the normative meanings individuals place on race in their self-definitions. It should be noted that our conceptualization of centrality in comparisons to the symbolic interactionist's conceptualization of salience relies less heavily on another "counter group" in determining whether a particular identity is likely to be central. We argue that viewing shared meanings as the primary determinant in the adoption of an identity is problematic. Although individuals may be aware of certain stereotypes and the stigma associated with their racial or ethnic group, there is substantial variability in the significance individuals' place on their membership in their racial or ethnic group.

A couple of existing instruments incorporate subscales that measure constructs that are consistent with our conceptualization of racial centrality. In their measure of collective self-esteem, Luhtanen and Crocker (1992) include a four-item subscale entitled, Identity, which measures the importance of an individual's membership within a specific group. At present, this aspect of their measure has been under-utilized and under-emphasized. Phinney's (1992) Multigroup Ethnic Identity Measure also includes items which tap into a person's feelings of belonging and attachment to his or her ethnic group within the Affirmation and Belonging subscale. Some of these items tap into importance of other members of their ethnic group in defining themselves and are consistent with our conceptualization of racial centrality. Unfortunately, these items are intermingled with items that measure individuals' evaluative attitudes towards their ethnic group (private regard). Thus, racial centrality can not be assessed accurately from the Affirmation and Belonging subscale.

Many existing models of Black identity assume that race is *the* central identity in a normally functioning African American (Akbar, 1981; Baldwin, 1984; Baldwin, Brown, & Rackley, 1991; Kambon, 1992). Consequently, the prominence of "being Black" in individual African Americans' self-definitions has been viewed as an indicator of both their racial identity development as well as their mental health (Baldwin, 1984). Baldwin delineates four psychological disorders that afflict people of African descent who are misoriented with respect to their racial group orientation. A central theme in this classification system is the idea that what the MMRI would refer to as a highly race central identity is optimal (Baldwin, 1984; Kambon, 1992). In contrast, some researchers argue that a de-emphasis of race in African Americans' self-definitions is developmentally adaptive (Penn, Gaines, & Phillips, 1993). Penn and his colleagues argue that "...the ability to decenter from one's own ethnic group and to appraise ethnically-related stimuli in a more objective fashion is predictive of positive psychological outcomes," (p. 310). Unfortunately, there is a dearth of systematic research that addresses the discrepancy between Baldwin and Penn's position. Few studies have investigated empirically the relationship between racial centrality in African Americans and mental health status (Sellers, 1993). Those few studies that have been conducted are limited by measures of centrality that are confounded with other aspects of racial identity (e.g., Parham & Helms, 1985).

In general, the assumption that race is *the* central aspect of the identities of all African Americans can be problematic. In fact, a number of studies have found that race is not *the* central identity for many African Americans (Ingram, 1989; Phinney & Alipuria, 1990). The assumption of the universal centrality of race in the identity of African Americans can result in inaccurate estimations of the relationship between racial identity and other outcomes (Cross, 1991). Cross (1991) discusses how many researchers ascribe a high level of racial centrality to their African American sample simply because they are classified by society as being Black. Such an approach results in a simplistic interpretation of their data and the relationship between racial identity and the other phenomena that is being studied. The overall relationship between identity and the other phenomena is overestimated for those individuals for whom race is central and under-estimated for those for whom race is highly central.

Regard

The third dimension of the MMRI is racial regard. Racial regard refers to a person's affective and evaluative judgment of his or her race (Sellers, Smith, Shelton, Johnson, & Chavous, 1995). It is the extent to which the individual feels positively about his or her race. We distinguish between two forms of regard—private and public. Private regard is defined as the extent to which individuals feel positively or negatively about Blacks as well as how positively or negatively they feel about being Black. Private regard is analogous to racial self-esteem. Much of the early work in African American racial identity focused on individuals' evaluative feelings towards their race and its impact on their feelings about themselves (e.g., Clark & Clark, 1947; Horowitz, 1936; Horowitz, 1939). In fact, much of the early work assumed that preference for Black stimuli was synonymous with a positive personal self-concept for African Americans (Clark, 1955; Clark & Clark, 1947; Kardiner & Ovesey, 1951). Although later researchers have begun to measure racial preference and/or attitudes regarding one's racial group separately from indicators of self-concept and self-esteem (e.g., Brand, Ruiz, & Padilla, 1974; Clark, 1982; McAdoo, 1970, 1977; Porter, 1967, 1971), affective and evaluative attitudes regarding one's race are still interpreted as if they were indicators of the individual's personal self-concept (Cross, 1991). Our conceptualization of private racial regard explicitly separates evaluative and affective feelings regarding African Americans from the individuals feelings about themselves. This does not mean that we do not expect a relationship between racial regard and personal self-esteem. As we discuss later in this chapter, we expect a significant relationship between the two, however we hypothesize that that relationship is more complex than the one that was so prevalent in the early research in African American racial identity.

Public regard is defined as the extent to which individuals feel that others view African Americans positively or negatively. Public regard refers to the individual's assessment of how African Americans are viewed (or valued) by the broader society. Much of the early research on racial identity was influenced by symbolic interactionist thought (Mead, 1934). This approach argued that the individual's identity development is influenced by the way in which he or she believes that other people view them. From this thesis, some researchers argue that the devaluation of African Americans by the broader society should have deleterious effects on individuals' evaluation of their own racial group (Horowitz, 1939; Kardiner & Lewin, 1936, 1941; Luhtanen & Crocker, 1992; Mead, 1934; Ovesey, 1951; Stryker, 1980; White & Burke, 1987). This implies that having a public regard which recognizes this devaluation (stigmatizing) should lead to a more negative personal evaluation of that group (private regard). Other researchers have argued that understanding and acknowledging the oppression African Americans continue to face is an important step in the development of a healthy African American racial identity (e.g., Baldwin & Bell, 1985; Parham & Helms, 1981; Terrell & Terrell, 1981). The understanding that the broader society devalues African Americans (as a result of racism) helps to keep African Americans from internalizing those negative messages regarding their worth.

Ideology

Ideology is the fourth dimension of the Multidimensional Model of Racial Identity Model. It is composed of the individual's beliefs, opinions, and attitudes with respect to the way he or she feels that the members of the race should act (Sellers, Smith, Shelton, Johnson, & Chavous, 1995). This dimension represents the person's philosophy about the ways in which African Americans should live and interact within society. The MMRI delineates four ideological philosophies that are prevalent in current models of African American racial identity. These ideologies are: (1) a nationalist philosophy; (2) an oppressed minority philosophy; (3) an assimilation philosophy; and (4) a humanist philosophy. The MMRI recognizes that individuals rarely adopt one ideology for all domains of their lives. Classifying individuals as either nationalist or humanist is overly simplistic. Most individuals hold a variety of ideologies which vary across different domains of their lives. We have attempted to take this into consideration in our operationalization of the ideology dimension by developing items representing the four ideologies across four areas of functioning. These manifest areas consist of individuals' attitudes with respect to: (a) political/economic development; (b) cultural/social activities; (c) inter-group relations; and (d) interaction with the dominant group. More precisely, a person who believes that we should treat each person as an individual with respect to social interactions (humanist) may also promote the patronage of African American-owned businesses (nationalist).

Three characteristics represent a nationalist ideology. First, a nationalist ideology emphasizes the uniqueness of the "Black experience." While nationalists are able to see similarities between African Americans and other groups, they tend to focus on the experiences that are idiosyncratic to being Black. The second characteristic of a nationalist ideology flows from this emphasis. A nationalist ideology posits that African Americans should be in control of their own destiny with minimal input from other groups. This characteristic may manifest itself in a distrust for the sincerity of other groups that want to help African Americans. Similarly, they may believe that self-help is necessary for self-determination. The third characteristic of a nationalist ideology is the belief that Blacks should work and/or socialize together in order to promote the advancement of the race. In other words, nationalists tend to believe that the destinies of all Black people are intertwined. A nationalist ideology can develop as a survival strategy against experiences of racism. It can also grow from a deep appreciation and understanding of Black culture. In many instances, a nationalist ideology arises from the combination of the two experiences. As a result, a nationalist ideology is associated with a preference for African American (or African) social environments. Many contemporary theories of Black identity have already incorporated nationalism in their models and scales, however, they differ in the significance that they place on nationalism. For instance, Baldwin's model views a nationalist ideology as being the optimal Black identity (Baldwin, 1984). Meanwhile, Cross (1991) suggest that ultra-nationalistic attitudes may be characteristic of a racial identity which has not been fully developed.

The oppressed minority ideology emphasizes the commonalties of experience between African Americans and other oppressed groups. Similar to the nationalist ideology, individuals who espouse this philosophy are acutely aware of the oppression which African Americans continue to confront. The groups that comprise the "other oppressed minority group" may vary from individual to individual. Some individuals define "other oppressed minority groups" to include women, gays, and lesbians. Other individuals may limit their definition to include only ethnic groups of color. The defining characteristic of this ideology is the belief that African Americans' experiences with oppression are similar to some other non-Black groups. As a result, individuals with an oppressed minority ideology are more likely to view coalition building as the most appropriate strategy for social change. Individuals with an oppressed minority ideology are often interested in the nature of oppression. Often, these individuals are as interested in the culture of other minority groups as they are in their own culture.

The third philosophical dimension of ideology is the assimilationist ideology. This dimension is characterized by its emphasis on the commonalties between

African Americans and the rest of American society. Such an ideology focuses on working within mainstream American structures to achieve life goals. There is an acknowledgment of one's status as an American. It should be noted, however, that an assimilationist philosophy does not imply a rejection of one's identity as an African American, nor does it imply a lack of activism with respect to racism. It simply suggests that such a person is likely to work within the existing system to change it. Interpersonally, persons with an assimilation ideology are more likely to believe that it is important to interact socially with Whites. Some of the current models of Black identity view an assimilationist ideology as being problematic. Kambon (1992) has suggested some of the ideas associated with an assimilationist ideology may be symptomatic of pathology. Early nigrescence models suggested that extreme assimilation views were associated with earlier stages of identity development (Cross, 1971; Parham & Helms, 1985). As will be discussed in greater detail later in the chapter, the MMRI makes no such assumptions.

The humanist philosophy is the fourth ideology delineated by the MMRI. The humanist ideology emphasizes the commonalties among *all* humans. Individuals who endorse a humanist ideology believe that people should be viewed as individuals as opposed to representatives of racial groups. Humanist ideologies usually evolve from larger philosophical influences that are characterized by strong beliefs in a larger force that impacts the destiny of all people. People who endorse a humanist ideology believe in kinship among all people. Religion is perhaps the most common example of such a philosophy. For example, most Christian religions preach that everyone is created by God and are God's children regardless of race, gender, or ethnicity. Other larger influences which may result in a humanist ideology include a dedication to altruistic issues such as concern for the environment, nuclear proliferation, and poverty. Oppression is seen in terms of "man's inhumanity towards man." Individuals who hold this philosophy are likely to emphasize the moral detriments of oppression for the oppressor as well as the physical and psychological detriment to the oppressed. By definition, individuals who adopt and practice a humanist ideology are less likely to define themselves in terms of race and are likely to manifest low levels of racial centrality.

In describing the diversity of the meaning of being African American, most theorists and researchers have attempted to define what constitutes *the* optimal African American racial identity. For instance, Penn and colleagues (1993) have argued that an ideology which de-emphasizes race is representative of the highest level of identity development. Unfortunately, many of these definitions of the optimal identity are based on untested and/or untestable assumptions and criteria (Sellers, 1993). In some instances, the criteria used to determine the optimal identity are so confounded with the measures of identity themselves that they constitute a tautology (e.g., Kambon, 1992). For example, Baldwin and others have suggested that to have a low level of racial centrality and what we would consider a assimilationist ideology is by definition psychopathological. This operationalization of mental health makes it impossible to empirically test the relationship between identity and mental health because the two measures are hopelessly indistinguishable.

In our conceptualization of racial ideology, we make no explicit or implicit claims with respect to which ideology is optimal. Any evaluation of the optimalness of the ideologies is dependent on the criteria one uses to define optimal. Thus, it is important that the criteria used to evaluate optimalness be explicitly stated so that it can also be analyzed for its appropriateness. In many cases the criteria used to determine optimalness is based on the researchers personal values. For example, a person who values the survival of African American culture as a unique and separate way of life may be more likely to see a nationalist ideology as being optimal. On the other hand, a person who values the acceptance of African Americans by the broader American society may view an assimilationist ideology as being optimal. Even if a consensus existed on a criterion (such as psychological well-being) to be used to determine an optimal ideology, it is likely that such a definition would have to be domain-specific. Different environments are likely to be more hospitable for different racial ideologies which may, in turn, contribute to different levels of well-being. In the end, the extent to which a particular identity is optimal is an empirical question that can only be assessed with conceptualizations and operationalizations of racial ideologies that are separate and distinct from the outcome variables they are to predict.

Relationships Among the Four Dimensions of the MMRI

The four dimensions of the MMRI are independent, but interrelated. Certain dimensions are related to each other, while others are completely orthogonal. These relationships are predictable from both intuition and previous research in related fields. For example, we predict a positive relationship between racial centrality and private regard. Consistent with both dissonance theory and self-integrity theory, we expect that most African Americans who define race as an important part of their identity are likely to have more positive feelings about African Americans (Cooper & Fazio, 1984; Steele & Spencer, 1992). Predictions can also be made regarding the relationship between centrality and different ideologies. By definition, we expect that a person with a racial ideology which emphasizes the importance and uniqueness of being African American (nationalist) is likely to view race as a central part of his/her identity and is likely to hold positive feelings and attitudes towards African Americans (private regard). On the other hand, a person who has a racial ideology which focuses on the commonalties of all people and de-emphasizes the importance of race (humanist) is not likely to have race as a central characteristic of his/her personal identity.

The four dimensions not only have simple direct relationships, but they also have more complex interactions. For instance, racial centrality is hypothesized as playing an important moderating role in the relationships between the remaining two stable dimensions (regard and ideology) and other behavioral and adaptational phenomena. In general, ideology and regard will be better predictors of race-related phenomena for persons who are more race central than for those individuals who do not normatively define themselves with respect to race. At the level of the specific event, we predict that both the situationally dynamic and the stable components of racial identity interact to influence behavior at the micro level. Such a prediction is consistent with a number of studies in the coping literature (e.g., Holahan & Moos, 1987; Lazarus & Folkman, 1984; McCrae & Costa, 1986; Vitaliano, Russo, & Maiuro, 1987). Specifically, we predict that racial salience should play an important moderating influence on the relationship between an individual's racial ideology and his/her subsequent behavior. Similarly, the MMRI predicts that in situations in which a person's racial identity is made salient, the person's attitudes regarding what that identity means (ideology) will influence the person's perceptions of the situation and his/her subsequent actions. At the same time, a person's racial ideology is less likely to influence the person's perceptions and behavior in situations in which their racial identity does not become salient.

It should be noted that the MMRI approaches racial identity from an individual differences perspective. As such, it focuses on a description of the status of the different dimensions of individuals' racial identity at a particular point in their lives. The MMRI provides a framework to conceptualize individual differences in the significance and meaning of race in African Americans beliefs about themselves. This perspective differs from developmental models (e.g., Cross, 1971, 1991; Millones, 1980; Phinney, 1992) that attempt to describe the process by which individuals' racial identity attitudes mature across the life span. Built into these models is the idea of change over the life span. The MMRI does not implicitly or explicitly propose *a* set developmental sequence for racial identity. This does not mean, however, that the MMRI is incompatible with a developmental approach to racial identity (Sellers, Chavous, Johnson, Shelton, & Smith, 1995). The three stable dimensions of the MMRI (centrality, regard, and ideology) are not invariant. Individuals may change across these dimensions as the result of some pervasive positive or negative experience. Individuals may also change aspects of their identity as a result of changes in their life circumstances. There may even be systematic changes in the three stable dimensions that occur across the life span. The MMRI provides a framework in which to investigate these propositions. By using research designs that directly measure pervasive racial experiences and/or changes in the life span separate from the measures of racial identity, we can see the influences of these factors on racial identity without the possibility of a confound between the developmental nature of the measure and the question of identity development.

Current Research Using the MMRI

The Multidimensional Inventory of Black Identity (MIBI)

The Multidimensional Inventory of Black Identity (MIBI) was constructed to measure the three stable dimensions (Centrality, Ideology, and Regard) of the Multidimensional Model of Racial Identity for African Americans (Sellers, Johnson, Chavous, Shelton, & Smith, 1995). The 65-item inventory includes items which were adapted from previous identity scales such as the Multi-Group Ethnic Identity Measure (Phinney, 1992), Collective Self-Esteem Scale (Crocker & Luhtanen, 1990), Racial Identity Attitudes Scale (Parham & Helms, 1985), African Self-Consciousness Scale (Baldwin & Bell, 1985), the Developmental Inventory of Black Consciousness (Milliones, 1980), and the Cultural Mistrust Inventory (Terrell & Terrell, 1981) as well as items generated by the authors. Subjects are asked to report the extent to which they endorse the items on a seven point Likert scale. The *Centrality* scale consists of ten items measuring the extent to which being African American is central to the respondents' definition of themselves. The *Ideology* scale consists of 44 items measuring four philosophies (Assimilation, Humanist, Nationalist, Oppressed Minority) associated with the way African Americans view political/economic issues, cultural/social issues, inter-group relations, and attitudes towards the dominant group. Each ideology scales consists of 11 items. The *Regard* scale is made up of two subscales, private and public Regard. The Private Regard subscale consists of seven items measuring the extent to which respondents possess positive feelings towards African Americans in general. The Public Regard subscale consists of four items measuring the extent to which respondents feel that others have positive feelings towards African Americans.

We investigated the psychometric properties of the MIBI within a sample of 306 African American college students. The results provide preliminary evidence that the Multidimensional Inventory of Black Identity is a reliable and construct valid measure of the Multidimensional Model of Racial Identity (see Table 1). The subscales of the MIBI, with the exception of the Public Regard subscale, display adequate levels of internal consistency. The other six subscales exhibited acceptable reliability coefficients (alphas range from .71 to .81) for the examination of both predictive and construct validation (Nunnally & Bernstein, 1994). The pattern of responses suggests that the MIBI is able to detect the diversity of experiences within the African American community that lead to an array of identities. Subjects appear to use the entire response format when responding to the MIBI items.

The inter-scale correlations suggest that the scales and subscales are associated with each other in ways that are consistent with the conceptual model (see Table 2). For instance, individuals for whom race is central were also likely to have positive Private Regard for African Americans and endorse Nationalist attitudes. Highly

Table 1
Descriptive Statistics for the Multidimensional Inventory of Black Identity
(MIBI)

	Cronbach's Alpha	Mean	Minimum	Maximum
Assimilation	.72	4.37 (.84)	1.00	6.80
Humanism	.71	4.70 (.87)	2.09	7.00
Minority	.78	4.87 (.80)	1.75	7.00
Nationalism	.81	4.39 (1.01)	1.00	6.75
Centrality	.73	4.87 (.94)	1.20	6.80
Private Regard	.73	6.31 (.70)	3.73	7.00

central individuals were also less likely to endorse Assimilation or Humanistic attitudes. The expected relationships among Private Regard, Centrality, and Nationalist subscales were evident. Expected patterns of association also emerged among the other ideology subscales. The Humanist and Assimilation subscales were positively correlated with each other. These results support the contention that each dimension of the model is independent, but conceptually related to the others. The results also support a multi-dimensional conceptualization of racial identity in African Americans.

Evidence of the MIBI's convergent validity was established in correlations with both the RIAS and MEIM. One of the most widely used developmental models of racial identity is the nigrescence model (Cross, 1971, 1991). The model describes four stages of racial identity development that African Americans experience as they develop a psychologically healthy Black identity (Cross, 1971; Helms, 1990; Parham, 1989). Recently, Cross (1991) revised the model and broadened each stage to include more diverse experiences. Briefly, in the first stage, *Pre-encounter*, individuals do not believe that race is an important component of their identity. This may include an idealization of the dominant White society or simply placing more emphasis on another identity component. Individuals in the *Encounter* stage are faced with a profound experience or a collection of events that is/are directly linked to their race that encourages them to re-examine their current identity and find or further develop their Black identity. Individuals in the third stage, *Immersion/ Emersion*, are described as being extremely pro-Black and anti-White. Externally individuals are obsessed with identifying with African American culture but internally they have not made the commitment to endorse all values and traditions associated with being Black. The *Internalization* stage is characterized by having a feeling of inner security and satisfaction about being Black. Individuals at this stage tend to have a more temperate view regarding race. Parham and Helms (1981)

Table 2
Inter-Scale Correlations for the Multidimensional Inventory of Black Identity (MIBI)

	Assimilation	Humanism	Minority	Nationalism	Centrailty	Private Regard
Assimilation	1.0					
Humanism	.58**	1.0				
Minority	.31**	-.27**	1.0			
Nationalism	-.36**	-.43**	-.20**	1.0		
Centrality	-.22**	-.30**	-.23**	.53**	1.0	
Private Regard	-.05	.01	.23**	.19**	.43**	1.0

Note: *p<.05   ** p<.01

developed the Racial Identity Attitude Scale (RIAS) to operationalize Cross's nigrescence model. They argue that the RIAS measures attitudes that represents the individual's current stage of racial identity development. As such, the RIAS produces four subscales corresponding to the four stages of the nigrescence model.

There are certain conceptual overlaps among subscales of the RIAS and the MIBI. For example, individuals who are in the Pre-encounter stage, by definition, are less likely to report high levels of centrality and private regard. In contrast, persons who are in the Immersion/Emersion and Internalization stages are more likely to be high in centrality and private regard. Because of the dynamic nature of the Encounter stage it is difficult to identify overlap between this stage and the stable dimensions of the MMRI. Some researchers have had difficulty in measuring this stage and have questioned whether it is an actual identity state or simply a precipitating event for the subsequent stages (Helms, 1990; Ponterotto & Wise, 1987).

Intercorrelations between MIBI and RIAS subscales supported the validity of MMRI subscales. Scores on the Assimilation subscale were positively related to scores on the Pre-encounter subscale and inversely related to scores on the Immersion/Emersion subscale. The Humanism subscale was negatively related to all subscales based on emphasis on African American identity (Encounter, Immersion/Emersion and Internalization). Conversely, scores on the Nationalism subscale and the Centrality scale were positively related to each of three RIAS subscales. The Centrality scale was also negatively related to the Pre-Encounter Stage. Finally, the Private Regard subscale was negatively related to Pre-Encounter and positively related to Internalization. It is interesting to note that the Minority subscale was unrelated to any of the RIAS subscales. This makes sense in that none of the items on the RIAS deal with orientation toward members of other groups besides Whites and African Americans.

Like the nigrescence model, Phinney's model of ethnic identity is also concerned with the formation of an individual's ethnic identity. However, Phinney's model emphasizes the issues common to the development of an ethnic identity for all minority groups. Phinney (1989) extrapolates Erikson's ego identity development model to the development of ethnic identity. Based on Erikson's (1968) and Marcia's (1966) work, four ethnic identity states are proposed: diffused, foreclosed, moratorium, and achieved. A diffused identity is one in which the person has not explored what it means to be a member of their ethnic group nor has he or she made a commitment about that membership. Similarly, individuals with a foreclosed identity status have not explored the area but have committed themselves based on the values to which they have been exposed. The point in which the individual actively explores his/her identity but does not make a commitment is referred to as moratorium. Finally, an individual has an achieved identity status when he/she has made the necessary exploration and has decided to commit to that status. Phinney (1992) uses the Multigroup Ethnic Identity Measure (MEIM) to assess four aspects of ethnic identity. The first component of the MEIM, self-identification of ethnicity, examines the ethnic label that an individual uses to describe her/himself. The second component, ethnic behaviors and practices subscale, examines the individual's involvement in social activities with members of his/her group as well as participation in cultural practices. The third component focuses on affirmation and belonging. It consists of both feelings of closeness with the group as well as affection for the group. The final component measures ethnic identity achievement. It combines the four identity states into a single continuous variable ranging from lack of exploration and low commitment at one end-point to evidence of both exploration and commitment at the other.

Intercorrelations between MIBI and MEIM subscales were less clear than those with the RIAS, but still sensible. With respect to the ideology scale, none of the MEIM subscales were related to either the Assimilation or the Humanist subscale. The Identity Achievement subscale of the MEIM was positively associated with the Minority subscale (p <.05). Meanwhile, scores on the Nationalism subscale was positively correlated with both the Ethnic Behaviors and Affirmation/Belonging subscales. Both the Centrality scale and Private Regard subscale were positively associated with the Affirmation/Belonging and Identity Achievement subscales. Also higher scores on the Private Regard subscale corresponded to higher scores on the Ethnic Behaviors subscale.

The significant relationships between the MIBI and the RIAS and MEIM provide further evidence that there is a meta-construct of racial identity which exists in African Americans. The fact that the correlations between the MIBI and the other two identity scales are moderate suggests that the MIBI is measuring African American racial identity in a manner that is distinct from the other measures. It should also be noted that the significant correlations with other measures do not negate the uniqueness of the MIBI.

The MIBI measures attitudes and values related to feelings about being African American without the use of behavioral references within its items. Thus, the relationships between scores on the various scales and subscales of the MIBI with various race-related behaviors were assessed in order to investigate its external validity. These race related behaviors included the amount of contact that they normally had with both Whites and Blacks, the race of their best friend, and whether or not they enrolled in Black Studies courses. MIBI subscales were found to be related to behavioral outcomes in a conceptually predictable manner. Specifically, contact with African Americans was positively related to scores on the Centrality scale (r= .32, p <.01), Nationalism subscale (r= .37, p <.001), and Private Regard (r= .27, p <.01) subscale. Thus, individuals who had greater contact with African Americans were more likely to hold nationalist attitudes, define themselves with respect to race, and feel positive about African Americans. Contact with Whites, on the other hand, was negatively related to Centrality (r=- .45, p <.001) and Nationalist scores (r= -.37, p <.001) and was positively related to Assimilation (r= .20, p <.05) and Humanist (r= .20, p <.05) scores. Contact with Whites was unrelated to either the Private Regard or the Minority subscales. Individuals who have greater contact with Whites were less likely to use race to define themselves or to endorse a nationalist ideology, but were more likely to hold both assimilation and humanist ideologies. In examining the race of the students' best friend, individuals with an African American best friend reported higher Centrality (F= 6.92, p <.01), and Nationalist scores (F= 14.95, p<.01), and lower scores on the Assimilation (F=8.6, p <.01), and Humanist (F= 10.88, p <.01) subscales. Individuals who had taken African American studies courses had scored higher on the Centrality scale (F= 6.61, p <.05), and the Nationalist subscale (F= 21.01, p <.01), and lower on the Humanist subscale (F=7.96, p <.01).

The present results suggest that racial identity attitudes and values are associated with individual behaviors. It is an open question as to the causal direction of the relationship. However, a bi-directional relationship is most likely. The racial make-up of individuals' social networks are as likely to influence their attitudes and beliefs regarding race and themselves as these attitudes and beliefs are likely to influence with whom the individual chooses to socialize. Similarly, a positive experience taking a Black Studies course can lead a person to think of him/herself more in terms of being Black. However, it is just as likely that people who are high with respect to racial centrality are more likely to take a Black Studies course in the first place. Thus, it is important that more longitudinal designs be employed to further explicate the causal relationship between racial identity and race-related behavioral outcomes.

This study was an important first step in establishing the reliability and validity of the MIBI as a unique measure of racial identity. We found support of the basic psychometric properties of the MIBI, found that it was related to the racial identity meta-construct, and also we found that its subscales are related to real life experiences and behaviors. In spite of the present investigation, further work is needed in order for the MIBI to realize its full potential. We are in the process of furthering our investigation of the internal structure of the MIBI. We are planning to use confirmatory factor analytic techniques to enhance the present findings. Additionally, further research is needed using the MIBI with more diverse samples of African Americans to examine whether the measure is generalizable to other African American populations. The use of the MIBI with other populations will allow us to answer a number of important methodological as well as conceptual questions regarding the role of social context as well as the applicability of the MIBI and the Multidimensional Model of Racial Identity. Finally, further research is needed to determine whether the MIBI can be used as a model for developing other measures of ethnic and/or racial identity with other groups based on the MMRI.

Research on the Stability and Situational Variability of the MMRI

As stated previously, a major premise of the MMRI is that racial ideology, regard, and centrality are stable dimensions of racial identity and that the salience of one's racial identity may vary according to contextual factors. In order to test this premise, a sample of 67 African American women college students were recruited to participate in a study. The study investigated situational influences and the cross-situational stability of the racial ideology, regard, and centrality dimensions (Shelton & Sellers, 1996). The participants were told that the purpose of the study was to examine the influence of violence in the media on viewers mood. In actuality, there were four conditions to the study—two experimental conditions and two ambiguous conditions. The first experimental condition was a *race salient* condition in which the participants watched a race salient video (a White man physically attacking a Black man) with three White females. The second experimental condition was a *gender salient* condition in which the participants watched a gender salient video (a White man physically attacking a White female) with three Black males. In the ambiguous conditions, the participants watched a non-race or gender salient video recording (two White men physically attacking one another) either with three African American females or with three White males. These conditions were considered ambiguous because the Black women were either identical to the other participants in terms of race and gender (i.e., Black female condition) or they were different from the other participants on both of these identity components (i.e., White male condition). In both ambiguous conditions, there was nothing specific about the contextual factors that would make race more or less salient than another identity component. Participants were randomly assigned to one of two ambiguous conditions and one of two experimental conditions. Immediately after viewing the video, participants completed the MIBI along with several other measures. The order of the conditions (experimental and ambiguous) was counterbalanced across participants.

Pearson product moment correlations were used to assess whether the racial ideology, racial regard, and racial centrality dimensions were stable constructs. Correlation coefficients suggest that scores for the four racial ideology subscales (Assimilation r= .82, p<.01; Nationalist r= .93, p<.01; Humanist r= .79, p<.01; Minority r= .73, p<.01), the two racial regard subscales (private Regard r= .64, p<.01; Public Regard r= .60, p<.01); and the racial centrality scale (r= .87, p<.01) for participants who were in the ambiguous condition second, and thus had been primed for race or gender at an earlier time, remained relatively stable across testing sessions. Similar coefficients were found for the participants in the other conditions. To investigate whether the conditions themselves influence the three stable dimensions, mean scores for each scale during the three different testing sessions were compared. Analyses were conducted to determine if there were any mean differences between the experimental group and the control group. Results indicate that there were no significant mean differences in racial ideology and racial regard scores. That is, racial priming did not change individuals' attitudes and/or beliefs regarding what Blacks should be like, nor did the racial priming effect how they felt about Blacks or how they perceived that other groups felt about Blacks.

Significant situational effects, however, were found for racial centrality. Specifically, participants who were in the racially salient condition reported that race was more important to them when they were in this condition (M = 5.11) than when they were in the ambiguous condition (M = 4.87). There was no significant difference in how important race was to the self-concept for participants when they were in the gender salient condition (M = 4.79) and when they were in the ambiguous condition (M = 4.71). Race was *significantly more* important to this sample of women when the contextual factors primed for an identity component to be salient than when the contextual factors were more ambiguous as to what identity component should be salient. The fact that these results were obtained when the Black women were placed in the ambiguous condition second suggests that being primed for race at an earlier point did not have any carry over effects with regard to how important race was to the women in the ambiguous condition. Although these findings suggest that racial identity centrality is stable across time, they also suggest that situations can influence level of centrality. In other words, individuals' level of race centrality may stay the same relative to others, but increase as a function of the situation. This situational variability in the importance of race in the individual's self-concept is, in actuality, racial salience. By definition, racial salience is the significance a person places on race in defining himself or herself at a given point in time. Thus, these data suggest that there are aspects of individuals racial identity that maintain a strong sense of interindividual consistency, while other aspects of identity are more susceptible to situational influence (Funder & Colvin, 1991).

Recommendations for Future Research

Future research must begin to examine racial identity as a more dynamic process. There are two ways in which researchers can approach changes in racial identity. The first approach is to investigate the way in which racial identity changes across the life span. A large proportion of the racial identity models that are currently in vogue are developmental models. However, we are unaware of any longitudinal studies of racial identity. The few studies that have attempted to examine differences in racial identity across the life span have employed cross-sectional designs (e.g., Parham & Williams, 1993). As a result, these studies are vulnerable to confounding cohort influences. As we noted above, our understanding of racial identity development is greatly constrained by the dearth of longitudinal data. A large longitudinal study of racial identity using the MMRI can provide a vivid description of how the different dimensions vary across the life span. Such a study can also provide clues about the normative changes in racial identity as well as an indication of how much the process varies across individuals. For instance, it would be interesting to see to what extent an individual's racial centrality changes across the life span. A large longitudinal study of racial identity could also provide valuable data on the ways that different events involving race (positive and negative) can cause changes in individuals' racial identity beliefs and attitudes.

A second approach that researchers can take to investigate the dynamic qualities of racial identity is to study the role that racial identity plays in the way that individuals construe and behave in specific situations. Generally, racial identity research has failed to address either conceptually or empirically the process by which individuals' racial identities may be influenced by situational and contextual factors (Phinney, 1990; Sellers, 1993). However, a considerable body of research outside the racial identity literature has produced evidence that contextual factors play an important role in making certain identities salient at any particular moment in time which in turn has implication for individuals' subsequent behavior (e.g., Abrams, Thomas, & Hoggs, 1990; Bochner & Ohsako, 1977; Cota & Dion, 1986; Dion, 1986; Dion & Earn, 1975; Kite, 1992; McGuire, McGuire, Child, & Fujioka, 1978; McGuire, McGuire, & Winton, 1979; McGuire & Padawer-Singer, 1976). For example, research on in-group/out-group bias has consistently demonstrated that even arbitrary criteria can be used to make group identities salient and that the salience of these identities have consequences for behavior (e.g., Oakes, Turner, & Haslam, 1991; Tajfel & Turner, 1979; Turner, Oakes, Haslam & McGarty, 1994). This research has usually limited its examination of the individuals' responses to such binary response alternatives as biased vs. unbiased rewards for in-group and/or out-group members. The use of a binary coding scheme for behavioral responses to in-group/out-group bias is in part a function of the nature of the group identities which are studied. These identities are usually experientially irrelevant to participants outside of the study. As a result, the meaning of these identities are somewhat simplistic in the meaning that the participants attach to them; and thus, it has a relatively circumscribed influence on the participants' behaviors. On the other hand, an identity that is associated with something as experientially charged as race is likely to produce ideological and behavioral alternatives that will vary across individuals.

The MMRI provides an explanation of how racial identity can uniformly influence behavior at the level of the event; and at the same time, can account for the individual variability in the way people behave in a particular situation. Individuals' regard and racial ideology beliefs offer a blueprint for interpreting the way individuals perceive and behave in a particular event. In general, individuals who endorse many nationalist attitudes are likely to perceive and behave in a particular situation in a manner that is consistent with these attitudes. However, this relationship between attitudes and behavior is moderated by racial salience. At the level of the situation, individuals' racial regard and ideological beliefs are only likely to influence the way individuals' construe and behave if race is salient to the individuals in that situation. In those situations in which some other identity is salient, individuals' attitudes and beliefs regarding that identity are likely to influence behavior. Thus, racial salience is a process through which the more stable dimensions of racial identity can influence behavior at the level of the event.

At the level of the event, individual differences in behaviors as the result of racial identity can occur from two sources. First, individual differences in regard and ideology attitudes and beliefs may result in individual differences in behavioral responses when race is salient. A second way that individual differences may occur is as the result of whether race becomes salient within a particular situation. As noted earlier, racial centrality and contextual factors interact in such a way as to determine when race becomes salient to the individual. Since individual's differ in their level of racial centrality, we expect greater variance in racial salience in more racially ambiguous situations and less variation in more racially pervasive situations. Thus, in racially ambiguous situations, race is salient for some individuals leading them to use their racial identity beliefs and attitudes in interpreting the situation, while race is not salient for other individuals who may be interpreting the same situation through some other aspect of their self-concept.

Conclusion

The MMRI provides a reconceptualization of ideas found in previous research on identity in such a way as to provide a framework for describing the variation in the importance and meaning individual African Americans place on race when they define who they are. At the same time, the MMRI provides a theoretical base from which to make predictions regarding the way individual African Americans are likely to function within different social and situational contexts. It is our hope that the MMRI will lead to the development of more sophisticated research models that are more consistent with the complex phenomena of African American racial identity. We believe the MMRI provides an initial step in describing the results of African Americans' attempts to come to "an understanding" of being a descendant of Africa and a survivor of America.

References

Abrams, D., Thomas, J., & Hoggs, M. A. (1990). Numerical distinctiveness, social identity and gender salience. *British Journal of Social Psychology, 29*, 87-92.

Akbar, N. (1979). African roots of Black personality. In W. D. Smith et al., (Eds.), *Reflections on Black psychology.* Washington, DC: University Press of America.

Akbar, N. (1981). Mental disorders among African-Americans. *Blacks Books Bulletin, 7(2),* 18-25.

Akbar, N. (1989). Nigrescence and identity: Some limitations. *The Counseling Psychologist, 17(2),* 258-263.

Baldwin, J. A. (1981). Notes on an Africentric theory of Black personality. *The Western Journal of Black Studies, 5(3),* 172-179.

Baldwin, J. A. (1984). African self-consciousness and the mental health of African Americans. *Journal of Black Studies, 15(2),* 177-194.

Baldwin, J. A., & Bell, Y. R. (1985). The African self-consciousness scale. An Africentric personality questionnaire. *The Western Journal of Black Studies, 9(2),* 61-68.

Banaji, M. R., & Prentice, D. A. (1994). The self in social contexts. *Annual Review of Psychology, 45,* 297-332.

Bochner, S., & Ohsako, T. (1977). Ethnic role salience in racially homogeneous and heterogeneous societies. *Journal of Cross-Cultural Psychology, 8(4),* 477-492.

Brand, E. S., Ruiz, R. A., & Padilla, A. M. (1974). Ethnic identification, and preference: A review. *Psychological Bulletin, 81*(11), 860-890.

Clark, K. B. (1955). *Prejudice and your child.* Boston, MA: Beacon Press.

Clark, K. B., & Clark, M . P. (1947). Racial identification and preference in Negro children. In T.M Newcomb & E. L. Hartley (Eds.), *Readings in social psychology* (pp. 169-187). New York: Holt.

Clark, M. L. (1982). Racial group concept and self-esteem in Black children. *Journal of Black Psychology, 8(2),* 75-88.

Cooper, J., & Fazio, R. H. (1984). A new look at dissonance theory. In L. Berkowitz (Ed.), *Advances in experimental social psychology* (Vol. 17, pp. 229-266). Orlando, FL: Academic.

Cota, A. A., & Dion, K. L. (1986). Salience of gender and sex composition of ad hoc groups. An experimental test of distinctiveness theory. *Journal of Personality and Social Psychology, 50(4)*, 770-776.

Crocker, J., & Luhtanen, R. (1990). Collective self-esteem and in-group bias. *Journal of Personality and Social Psychology, 58(1)*, 60-67.

Cross, W. E. (1971). Negro-to-Black conversion experience. *Black World, 20*, 13-27.

Cross, W. E. (1991). *Shades of Black: Diversity in African American identity.* Philadelphia, PA: Temple University Press.

Dion, K. L. (1986). Responses to perceived discrimination and relative deprivation. In J. M. Olson, C. P. Herman, & M. P. Zanna (Eds.), *Relative deprivation and social comparison: The Ontario symposium* (Vol. 4, pp. 150-179). New York. Wiley.

Dubois, W. E. B. (1903). *Souls of Black folk.* Chicago: A. C. McClurg.

Erikson, E. (1968). *Identity: Youth and crisis.* New York: Norton.

Funder, D. C., & Colvin, R. C. (1991). Explorations in behavioral consistency: Properties of persons, situations, and behaviors. *Journal of Personality and Social Psychology, 60(5)*, 773-794.

Holahan, C. J., & Moos, R. H. (1987). Personal and contextual determinants of coping strategies. *Journal of Personality and Social Psychology, 52(5)*, 946-955.

Horowitz, E. L. (1936). The development of attitude toward the Negro. *Archives of Psychology, 104.* Columbia University.

Horowitz, R. (1939). Racial aspects of self-identification in nursery school children. *Journal of Psychology, 7*, 91-99.

Ingram, B. J. (1989). Identity issues among African American students in three university settings (Doctoral dissertation, Miami University, 1989). *Dissertation Abstracts International.*

Jones, E. E., & Gerard, H. B. (1967). *Foundations of social psychology.* New York: Wiley.

Kambon, K. (1992). *The African personality in America. An African-centered framework.* Tallahassee: NUBIAN Nation Publications.

Kardiner, A., & Ovesey, L. (1951). *The mark of oppression.* New York: Norton.

Kite, M. E. (1992). Age and spontaneous self-concept. *Journal of Applied Social Psychology, 22*, 1828-1837.

Lazarus, R. S., & Folkman, S. (1984). *Stress, appraisal, and coping.* New York: Springer Publishing Company.

Lewin, K. (1936). *Principles of topological psychology.* New York. McGraw-Hill.

Lewin, K. (1941). Jewish self-hatred. *Contemporary Jewish Record, 4*, 219-232.

Luhtanen, R., & Crocker, J. (1992). A collective self-esteem scale. Self-evaluation of one's social identity. *Personality and Social Psychology Bulletin, 18(3)*, 302-318.

Marcia, J. E. (1966). Development and validation of ego-identity status. *Journal of Personality and Social Psychology, 3(5)*, 551-558.

Markus, H., & Nurius, P. (1986). Possible selves. *American Psychologist, 41(9)*, 954-969.

Markus, H., & Sentis, K. (1982). The self in social information processing. In J. Suls (Ed.), *Psychological perspectives on the self* (Vol. 1, pp. 41-70). Hillsdale, NJ: Erlbaum.

McAdoo, H. P. (1970). Racial attitudes and self-concepts of Black preschool children. Doctoral dissertation, University of Michigan. *Dissertation Abstracts International, 22(11)*, 4114.

McAdoo, H. P. (1977). The development of self-concept and race attitudes in Black children: A longitudinal study. In W. Cross (Ed.), *Third conference on empirical research in Black psychology* (pp. 47-64). Washington, D.C.: National Institute of Education, Department of Health, Education, and Welfare.

McCrae, R. R., & Costa, P. T. (1988). Age, personality, and spontaneous self-concept. *Journal of Gerontology, 46*, S177-185.

McGuire, W. J., McGuire, C. V., Child, P., & Fujioka, T. (1978). Salience of ethnicity in the spontaneous self-concept as a function of one's ethnic distinctiveness in the social environment. *Journal of Personality and Social Psychology, 36(5)*, 511-520.

McGuire, W. J., McGuire, C. V., & Winton, W. (1979). Effects of household sex composition on the salience of one's gender in the spontaneous self-concept. *Journal of Experimental Social Psychology, 15*, 77-90.

McGuire, W. J., & Padawer-Singer, A. (1976). Trait salience in the spontaneous self-concept. *Journal of Personality and Social Psychology, 33(6)*, 743-754.

Mead, G. H. (1934). *Mind, self, and society.* Chicago:University of Chicago Press.

Messick, D. M., & Mackie, D. M. (1989). Intergroup relations. *Annual Review of Psychology, 40*, 45-81.

Milliones, J. (1980). Construction of a Black consciousness measure: Psychotherapeutic implications. *Psychotherapy: Theory, Research, and Practice, 17(2)*, 175-182.

Nobles, W. A. (1991). African philosophy. Foundations for Black psychology. In R.L. Jones (Ed.), *Black psychology* (3rd ed.). Berkeley, CA: Cobb & Henry Publishers.

Nunnally, J. C., & Bernstein, I. H. (1994). *Psychometric theory* (3rd ed.). New York: McGraw Hill.

Oakes, P. J., Haslam, S. A., & Turner, J. C. (1994). *Stereotyping and social reality.* Oxford and Cambridge, MA: Basil Blackwell.

Parham, T. A. (1989). Cycles of psychological nigrescence. *The Counseling Psychologist, 17(2)*, 187-226.

Parham, T. A., & Helms, J. E. (1981). The influences of a Black students' racial identity attitudes on preference for counselor's race. *Journal of Counseling Psychology, 28,* 250-256.

Parham, T. A., & Helms, J. E. (1985). Relation of racial identity attitudes to self-actualization and affective states of Black students. *Journal of Counseling Psychology, 32(3)*, 431-440.

Parham, T. A., & Williams, P. T. (1993). The relationship of demographics and background factors to racial identity attitudes. *Journal of Black Psychology, 19(1)*, 7-23.

Penn, M. L., Gaines, S. O., & Phillips, L. (1993). On the desirability of own-group preference. *Journal of Black Psychology, 19(3)*, 303-321.

Phinney, J. S. (1989). Stages of ethnic identity development in minority group adolescents. *Journal of Early Adolescence, 9(1-2)*, 34-49.

Phinney, J. S. (1990). Ethnic identity in adolescence and adulthood. A review and integration. *Psychological Bulletin, 108,* 499-514.

Phinney, J. S. (1992). The Multigroup Ethnic Identity Measure. A new scale for use with diverse groups, *Journal of Adolescent Research, 7(2)*, 156-172.

Phinney, J. S., & Alipuria, L. L. (1990). Ethnic identity in college students from four ethnic groups. *Journal of Adolescence, 13,*171-183.

Ponterotto, J. G., & Wise, S. L. (1987). Construct validity study of the Racial Identity Attitude Scale. *Journal of Counseling Psychology, 34(2)*, 218-223.

Porter, J. D. R. (1967). *Racial attitude formation in pre-school age children.* Doctoral Dissertation, Harvard University.

Porter, J. D. R. (1971). *Black child, White child: The development of racial attitudes.* Cambridge: Harvard University Press.

Sellers, R. M. (1993). A call to arms for researchers studying racial identity. *Journal of Black Psychology, 19(3)*, 327-332.

Sellers, R. M., Rowley, S. A. J., Chavous, T. M., Shelton, J. N., & Smith, M. A. (1997). Multidimensional inventory of Black identity: Preliminary investigation of reliability and construct validity. *Journal of Personality and Social Psychology, 73,* 805-815.

Shelton, J. N., & Sellers, R. M. (1998). *The stable and situationally dynamic aspects of racial identity.* Unpublished Manuscript.

Smith, E. (1989). Black racial development: Issues and concerns. *The Counseling Psychologist, 17(2)*, 277-288.

Steele, C. M., & Aronson, J. (1995). Stereotype threat and the intellectual performance of African Americans. *Journal of Personality and Social Psychology, 69(5)*, 797-811.

Steele, C. M., & Spencer, S. J. (1992). The primacy of self-integrity. *Psychological Inquiry, 3(4)*, 345-346.

Stryker, S. (1980). *Symbolic interactionism: A social structural version.* Menlo Park. Benjamin Cummings.

Tajfel, H. (1981). *Human groups and social categories. Studies in social psychology.* Cambridge University Press.

Tajfel, H., & Turner, J. C. (1979). An integrative theory of social conflict. In W. Austin & S. Worchel (Eds.), *The social psychology of intergroup relations.* Monterey, CA. Brooks/Cole.

Terrell, F., & Terrell S. L. (1981). An inventory to measure cultural mistrust among Blacks. *Western Journal of Black Studies, 5(3)*, 180-184.

Turner, J. C., Oakes, P. J., Haslam, S. A., & McGarty, C. (1994). Self and collective. Cognition and social context. *Personality and Social Psychology Bulletin, 20(5)*, 454-463.

Vitaliano, P. P., Russo, J., & Maiuro, R. D. (1987). Locus of control, type of stressor, and appraisal within a cognitive-phenomenological model of stress. *Journal of Research in Personality, 21(2)*, 224-237.

Weiner, B. (Ed.). (1974). *Cognitive views of human emotion.* New York: Academic Press.

White, C. L., & Burke, P. J. (1987). Ethnic role identity among Black and White college students: An interactionist approach. *Sociological Perspectives, 30(3)*, 310-331.

Author

Robert M. Sellers
Department of Psychology
University of Michigan
525 E. University
Ann Arbor, MI 48109-1109
Telephone: (313) 647-3949
Fax: (313) 764-3520
E-mail:rsellers@umich.edu

Author Index

Author Index

Subject Index

Subject Index